Voices in the Wilderness

Six American Neo-Romantic Composers

Walter Simmons

The Scarecrow Press, Inc.
Lanham, Maryland, and Oxford
2004

SCARECROW PRESS, INC.

Published in the United States of America
by Scarecrow Press, Inc.
A wholly owned subsidary of
The Rowman & Littlefield Publishing Group, Inc.
4501 Forbes Boulevard, Suite 200, Lanham, Maryland 20706
www.scarecrowpress.com

PO Box 317
Oxford
OX2 9RU, UK

British Library Cataloguing in Publication Information Available

Library of Congress Cataloging-in-Publication Data

Simmons, Walter, 1946-
  Voices in the wilderness : six American neo-romantic composers /
Walter Simmons.
    p. cm.
  Includes bibliographical references and index.
  ISBN 0-8108-4884-8 (alk. paper)
    1. Composers–United States–Biography. 2. Music–United States–20th
century–History and criticism. 3. Neoromanticism (Music)–United
States. I. Title: Voices in the wilderness. II. Title.
ML390.S616   2004
780'.92'273–dc21   2003013955

*This book is dedicated
to the memory of my parents,
Irving and Dorothy Simmons.*

Contents

Acknowledgments

This study is the result of many years of research, listening, analysis, and reflection. Throughout this period, I have been the beneficiary of a great deal of encouragement and assistance from a wide variety of friends and colleagues: those who initially persuaded me to undertake this endeavor; those who offered valuable feedback as the work progressed; and those who provided unique insights, recollections, and factual details not generally available.

I express my appreciation to Mark Lehman, Myron Moss, and Nicholas Tawa for their initial encouragement and for their willingness to provide whatever feedback I needed as the project took shape. For valuable input on various portions of the work in progress, I am grateful to Harvey and Sybil Barten, Lawrence Diller, Elliott Litsky, Carl Margolin, Anthony Sbordoni, and Mark Zuckerman. For providing specific materials and for sharing their unique perspectives on the composers featured in this work, I am indebted to the late Suzanne Bloch, Timothy Creston, Dianne Flagello, Ezio Flagello, Gary Karr, Sita Dimitroff Milchev, and Ronald Rogers. For valuable professional advice, I thank Nancy Kramer and Isidore Silver.

I also owe a special debt of gratitude to Joseph Greco, who initially awakened my enthusiasm for twentieth-century music and who encouraged me to remain loyal to the truth of my own musical experience. Most of all, I am deeply grateful for the unwavering support of my wife, Ronnie Halperin, who provided a nurturant, stable home life, as well as consistent encouragement, and who read and pondered every word of every draft, offering invaluable editorial support.

1

Introduction

Conventional accounts of the history of American concert music throughout most of the twentieth century typically begin with Charles Ives—his rebellion against the timid Eurocentric epigones who comprised his teachers and their peers, his American Transcendentalism, and his anticipation of innovations later adopted by the European avant-garde. This is often followed by a discussion of the development of jazz and the appeal it held for European sophisticates during the 1920s, as well as for American composers like George Gershwin and others, who sought ways of incorporating its spontaneity, its rhythmic vitality, and its unmistakable "Americanness" into traditional "classical" forms. The quest for an independent national musical identity might then be juxtaposed against the "crisis of tonality" said to beset European music around the time of the First World War. Tonality refers to the tendency of conventional music to gravitate toward a particular home note, or "tonic." But more than just a musical center of gravity, tonality was developed by the Austro-Germanic classical masters into the fundamental organizing principle of large-scale works. Symphonies, sonatas, and string quartets were structured according to relationships among subordinate tonal regions to a primary tonal center, all of which were presumably audible and comprehensible to the listener. Around the turn of the twentieth century, Arnold Schoenberg and others asserted that Richard Wagner and his followers (including

Schoenberg himself) had exhausted this system upon which music had been predicated for centuries.

This alleged "crisis" led composers to explore a variety of radical new paths: Igor Stravinsky liberated dissonance from its historical role as an expression of harmonic tension requiring resolution. Instead, dissonance was exalted as a legitimate, independent class of harmonic sonority in its own right. The element of rhythm also assumed greater importance, equivalent to harmony and melody rather than subordinate to them. Some composers, like the Hungarian Bela Bartók, turned to their own indigenous folk melodies to revitalize their music and infuse it with an authentic—rather than refined and romanticized—national flavor. These new directions were part of an avant-garde movement that contributed to the development of "Modernism," an aesthetic perspective that influenced all the arts during and after World War I in reaction to the alleged extravagance of Romanticism in its later manifestations.

The Modernist position in music held that the emphasis placed on subjective experience by the Romantics—especially, the grandiose distortions and exaggerations that resulted from excessive self-absorption—had become narcissistic and self-indulgent. New areas of cultural inquiry appeared—areas that turned attention outward toward social and political issues and toward developments in science and technology that promised to take on increased importance in the years to follow. In order to reflect these trends, entirely new forms of musical expression were said to be needed.

Around 1920 Schoenberg devised an alternative to the organizing principle of tonality, proposing a means of systematizing the *absence* of tonality. His concept became known as "twelve-tone composition," later developed into a more comprehensive approach known as "serialism." The serialists argued that abandoning the system of tonality required dispensing with classical forms as well, as these were felt to be inseparable from the principle of tonality as a unifying force. Therefore, new forms were needed, specifically tailored to the premises of serial composition.

Although Schoenberg saw in twelve-tone composition a means of perpetuating the supremacy of the Austro-Germanic musical aesthetic, many of its proponents promoted their system as "international," scorning the provinciality of more nationalistic approaches. A number of American composers, such as Wallingford Riegger and Roger Sessions, were attracted to the twelve-tone approach as a means of dispelling the impression of provincialism and of distinguishing themselves from those who were embracing vernacular elements in their music.

Other innovative approaches to musical composition that arose as alternatives to traditional tonality and flourished in the United States during the middle decades of the twentieth century included indeterminacy, microtonality, and the use of electronic sound sources. The proponents of these new approaches to composition were often at odds with each other, many of their tenets being essentially mutually exclusive. But all were in fundamental agreement that tonality was no longer a viable principle in the creation of music as a serious art form. The American music-loving public, however, never accepted the music composed in the wake of the tonal system. In fact, many of those composers, roughly contemporary with Schoenberg, who did not embrace his notions of an exhausted tonal system—Ravel, Puccini, Richard Strauss, and Rachmaninoff, for example—achieved tremendous popular success. (For more elaborate discussions and analyses of these developments and those that follow, see Nicholas Tawa's *Serenading the Reluctant Eagle* [1984], *A Most Wondrous Babble* [1987], and *American Composers and Their Public* [1995].)

During the 1930s, the period of the Great Depression, another nationalist trend emerged in America, this time under the guise of populism, influenced to some extent by the Soviet aesthetic known as "socialist realism," which extolled the virtues of art for the masses and regarded avant-garde intellectual innovations as "elitist." This populist trend attracted many composers who were sympathetic to socialist ideology, as well as others who were simply unwilling to limit their work to a small esoteric audience. During this decade and the next, an American symphonic school of composition emerged. Most of the composers who participated in this movement—Aaron Copland, Roy Harris, Morton Gould, Elie Siegmeister, and others—were eager to find an appreciative audience for their work and attempted to evoke a sense of the "American character" or the "American experience" in a way that would be discernible to the untrained listener. Many incorporated explicitly American vernacular elements in their work. Other composers, among them Howard Hanson, Samuel Barber, Vittorio Giannini, and Paul Creston, were more interested in adding their voices to the traditional classical music heritage than in creating a distinctly

American "sound." These composers too enjoyed a period of attention, as well as popular and critical favor. Some—Copland and Barber, for example—developed prominent reputations that outlasted the brief period when this trend was in vogue. However, by the mid-1950s the Modernist aesthetic, led by the European serialist movement, had begun to establish influential power bases in the music departments of Princeton and other major American universities, where composers were freed from the responsibility of having to win acceptance for their creative fruits in the marketplace of music lovers. Touting its "internationalism," this approach, as articulated by provocative, outspoken European advocates like Pierre Boulez and Karlheinz Stockhausen and by Americans like Milton Babbitt, successfully preempted the American symphonic school. (Boulez had written in 1952, "I . . . assert that any musician who has not experienced . . . the necessity for the dodecaphonic [i.e., twelve-tone] language is USELESS. For his whole work is irrelevant to the needs of his epoch."[1]) With an abundance of theoretical writing to elaborate its principles and support its claim of providing a comparable alternative to the organizing power of tonality, serialism lent itself to the academic propensity for abstract rationalization, aligning itself with subjects like mathematics, linguistics, and philosophy. Conservatories, the traditional centers for musical study and less eager to embrace this point of view, were disparaged by spokesmen for the avant-garde as trade schools for the training of musical artisans. Scholars who embraced the Modernist view of musical history propagated it in their teaching and writing, and, by suppressing or discrediting alternative interpretations, succeeded in achieving intellectual hegemony. Composers like Elliott Carter and even Copland, who had embraced the nationalist-populist aesthetic during the 1940s, turned to serialism in the 1950s.

The Modernist elite defended their work against rejection by the general public by responding with an attitude of contempt, to the point where a work's success with the public became sufficient evidence of its inferiority; by extension, music that embraced the qualities valued by listeners was denounced as pandering for acceptance. Conductors and instrumentalists, intimidated by the impression of intellectual weight and authority exerted by this point of view, began to avoid repertoire that might mark them as "out of step with the times." "The dogmas of modernism," writes Tawa, "outlawed any music that entertained or proved easy for listeners to assimilate. An unforgiving breed was occupying important university positions, serving on the boards of foundations, advising the people who handed out grants and commissions and made performances possible. Those without a power base dared not cross them."[2] These attitudes filtered down to journalist-critics, who expressed them in the press, fostering a division in the public between those who prided themselves on their sophistication and disparaged new music that lacked "originality" and those who defiantly rejected "modern music" altogether. (*Time* called Copland "too popular to be a great composer."[3]) In an article in the *New York Times*, Anthony Tommasini recalled the "fractious decades after World War II," describing how university composers "seized the intellectual high ground and bullied their colleagues and students into accepting serial procedures as the only valid form of modernism. All those fusty holdouts still clinging to tonality were laughably irrelevant, the serialists argued. And if beleaguered audiences and even many critics recoiled from 12-tone music, well, . . . that was their problem."[4] Describing the critical response to new music in the 1950s and 1960s, Tawa writes:

> Anything that sported a triad or a lyric melody, that sounded beautiful in the customary sense of the word, or that evoked strong personal emotion was censured as old hat, clichéd, uninspired, unoriginal, and having nothing new to say. . . . If writers felt free to criticize prominent traditionalists . . . they had a field day with less known composers of the same persuasion. . . . Fledgling composers of such inclination were knocked down repeatedly as they took their first steps. Music lovers were discouraged from listening to their works, and performers feared to schedule anything that might win them bad publicity.[5]

The contemptuous attitude of Modernist composers was crystallized in a notorious article, published with the title "Who Cares If You Listen?" by the serial composer Milton Babbitt.[6] The result of force-feeding nontraditional musical styles to a public that became increasingly uncertain of its own reactions and insecure in its own tastes was a gradual estrangement of the audience from the music of its own time.

The piece of the truth that was suppressed during this aesthetic fiat was that there continued to be many American composers for whom the crisis of tonality never existed and who were not concerned with either the development of a distinctly American musical style or with the other issues that concerned the Modernists. Few of the conventional accounts of American musical history have included these figures, except in the lists of miscellaneous "others" typically found at the ends of chapters. Usually such composers have been dismissed as shallow, inept, unimportant hangers-on, journeymen of limited talent or intelligence, panderers to commercial interests, or guilty of some other deficiency of character or artistry. By 1979, serialist composer Charles Wuorinen conceded patronizingly, "the tonal system, in an atrophied or vestigial form, is still used today in popular and commercial music, and even occasionally in the works of backward-looking serious composers," adding, "it is no longer employed by serious composers of the mainstream," having "been replaced or succeeded by the 12-tone system."[7]

This disparagement and suppression of tonal music amounted to a *de facto* blacklisting of composers who failed to conform to the approved version of music history. The most celebrated figures, such as Aaron Copland and Samuel Barber, had admittedly enjoyed sufficient public exposure and popular success to ensure their works a foothold in the repertoire durable enough to withstand critical condescension. And others—Walter Piston, William Schuman, Vincent Persichetti, and Peter Mennin, for example—who had achieved substantial reputations as a result of their positions on college or conservatory faculties were accorded the nominal respect typically associated with such positions. But even the works of these figures, not to mention those with less prominent reputations, were simply disregarded, their contributions denigrated and relegated to the periphery of the musical arena.[8]

Twentieth-Century Traditionalists challenges the Modernist interpretation of musical history, along with many of the assumptions on which it is predicated. For example, we reject the view that the fundamental significance of tonality is its function as a macrostructural organizing principle, insisting instead that this view of tonality applies chiefly to the Austro-Germanic line of musical evolution and the aesthetics that developed alongside it, but that it does not apply to the styles of music that developed in Italy, France, England, the Slavic countries, or—to focus on the subject of this book—in the United States, except insofar as composers in these countries chose to adopt the Austro-Germanic aesthetic. We reject the assumption that the evolution of the tonal system proceeded according to a linear progression that led inevitably to the dissolution of tonality altogether. More broadly, we reject the view that music is fruitfully studied as *any* sort of linear progression, with some hypothetical goal toward which all contenders are racing, the prize going to the one who gets there first.

By the late 1970s, Modernist attitudes had begun to lose ground. Discouraged by the unwavering hostility and indifference of audiences to their works, an increasing number of composers—George Rochberg, Jacob Druckman, David Del Tredici among the most prominent—erstwhile proponents of atonality in its myriad guises, were beginning to question the linear musico-historical imperative that had served as their aesthetic premise. Many also addressed some of the consequences and hidden psychosocial agendas of the avant-garde and its public posture and began to seek ways of achieving a rapprochement with audiences by accommodating their creative work to the perceptual frameworks of the general listener. Meanwhile, composers like Philip Glass and Steve Reich had been developing a defiantly tonal, if not simplistic, approach that became known as "minimalism." A radical repudiation of the intellectual complexity of serialism, minimalism aroused an astonishingly enthusiastic response from audiences. However, most of the composers who had maintained their commitment to traditional tonality all along were now largely forgotten. While the music of a figure as prominent as Samuel Barber was soon heard widely again, he was identified more as an anachronism than as the most prominent example of a significant aesthetic alternative.

Since the late 1980s, however, a number of performers and commentators have begun to reconsider the composers who have been languishing in the footnotes of mainstream textbooks. Many dismissive judgments made decades ago are being questioned. It is this revival of interest that has made a serious survey of traditionalist composers both timely and necessary.

Twentieth-Century Traditionalists argues that the marginalization of these "alternative" figures deprived the listening public of an important and rewarding repertoire. This series asserts that the value of music lies in the myriad temperaments, personalities, perceptions, and perspectives on life-and-the-cosmos reflected in it; that the most interesting composers are those whose music reveals the most rewarding perspectives, and does so through the means that convey them most effectively and convincingly. Furthermore, it holds that the compositional languages adopted by the traditionalists of the twentieth-century allowed for a richer, subtler, more varied range of musical expression than ever before in history. That is, the renunciation of tonality as a fundamental structural principle— without its being replaced by an arbitrary system like serialism— freed tonality to function within itself as an expressive parameter of the greatest nuance, in conjunction with other parameters like melody, rhythm, tone color, and so on.

Twentieth-Century Traditionalists argues and demonstrates that the most distinguished traditionalist composers created substantial bodies of work notable for their richness, variety, accessibility, and expressive power; that their music revealed distinctive individual features, recognizable stylistic traits, consistent themes and attitudes, as did the acknowledged masterpieces of the past; that much of this music had—and still has—the ability to bridge the gap between composer and audience, to enrich a musical repertoire that has become stagnant with the endless repetition of the tried and true, and to engage the enthusiasm of those seeking the adventure of discovering new creative personalities and their masterpieces, rather than merely the reassurance and soporific comfort of the overly familiar. It is to bring the most rewarding of these voices to greater awareness by the musical public that these studies are written.

A common reaction to the courses and lectures that have led to the writing of these studies has been the bewildering question: How can music as appealing and rewarding as this have been ignored for so long? Or: How could a composer with so much creative vision and expressive breadth be so little known? Some of the reasons are discussed in this introduction; other, more individual, reasons are presented in the chapters that follow. But, ultimately, there is no *adequate* answer, just as there is no *adequate* answer to the question: If the American Declaration of Independence states, "All men are created equal," then how could the institution of slavery have flourished? It is our hope that this study and others that follow will begin to increase awareness of this repertoire among scholars and performers, as well as general listeners.

Twentieth-Century Traditionalists offers a serious examination of those composers who created significant, artistically meaningful bodies of work without abandoning traditional principles, forms, and procedures. Rather than dwelling on polemical diatribes concerning aesthetic abstractions, this series will highlight the most significant compositional figures, discussing their importance through biographical overviews and comprehensive critical assessments of their outputs, including both strengths and weaknesses, and identifying their most important and representative compositions, their distinguishing stylistic features, and their identities within the broader sociomusical context.

The term "traditionalists" is used in this work to refer to those composers for whom the dynamic force of tonality was an indispensable parameter of musical expression. Concerned more with their own individual expressive purposes than with novel compositional procedures, they preferred for the most part to work with the materials, forms, and techniques inherited from previous generations. Some continued along the stylistic lines of nineteenth-century European music; some followed the lead of Igor Stravinsky, who himself attempted to find an alternative to the grandiloquence of Late Romanticism without renouncing tonality and other traditional techniques; still others attempted in a variety of ways to "Americanize" the European musical tradition in order to give it greater meaning and relevance for the domestic public.

The first volume of *Twentieth-Century Traditionalists* is called *Voices in the Wilderness: Six American Neo-Romantic Composers*. Further studies in the series are currently in the planning stages. Projected volumes will focus on: American Neo-Classicists, American Opera Composers, American Nationalists and Populists, Three Traditionalists of the Juilliard School, and American Traditionalists—the Post-1930 Generation.

THE AMERICAN NEO-ROMANTICS

Voices in the Wilderness focuses on a group of composers born between the years 1880 and 1930 whose work is primarily concerned with the evocation of mood, the depiction of drama—either abstract or referential—and the expression of emotion—personal, subjective emotion, in particular. Embracing many of the stylistic features of late nineteenth-century music, the Neo-Romantics may be viewed as the most conservative of the traditionalists. In fact, the very term

"Neo-Romantic" is less than ideal, as the prefix "neo" implies a revival—by means of novel approach or reinterpretation—of a stylistic concept from the past. But the earlier Neo-Romantics were not reviving a style from the past—they were evolving along a continuum still very much alive. The composers who served as their chief sources of influence and points of departure were Richard Strauss, Puccini, Rachmaninoff, Sibelius, Debussy, and Ravel, most of whom are generally called "Late Romantics." It is worth noting that all of them were still alive and active when composers like Ernest Bloch and Howard Hanson began composing. And the younger Neo-Romantics viewed these same Europeans as their immediate antecedents. However, attempting to assign another, perhaps more precise, label to these composers seems unnecessarily fussy and potentially confusing; furthermore, accurately or not, the better-known figures, such as Hanson and Barber, have been identified by critics and commentators as "Neo-Romantic" for many years. So—notwithstanding all due misgivings and disclaimers—that term is used here.

The question arises as to whether there have been composers in other countries who might be characterized as "Neo-Romantic," as the term is applied here. For reasons too diverse and far afield to discuss in this study, the term has rarely been applied to composers from Europe and elsewhere whose music corresponds stylistically to that discussed here. Russians like Prokofiev, Miaskovsky, and Shostakovich; Englishmen like Vaughan Williams, Arnold Bax, Gerald Finzi, and William Walton; Honegger in Switzerland; Villa-Lobos in Brazil; Joly Braga Santos in Portugal; Henry Barraud in France; Kurt Atterberg, Gösta Nystroem, and Ture Rangström in Sweden; and the Slovak Eugen Suchon are just a few of the composers from countries other than the United States whose music displays the qualities associated with the American Neo-Romantics. Of course, the musical politics of these countries have their own histories, which influence and complicate the issue. Nevertheless it is a curiosity of musico-national stylistic nomenclature worth noting.

Perhaps more than any other group among the American Traditionalists, the Neo-Romantics have borne a stigma of disrepute. Few would dispute the claim that the general listening public is most readily drawn to music with the qualities associated with the Romantic aesthetic. However, an implied assumption underlying much critical and musicological commentary suggests that a direct appeal to the emotions represents a lower form of artistic expression, as if accessibility somehow diminished the magnitude of a work's aesthetic achievement. Such an attitude plagued the reputations of composers like Tchaikovsky, Puccini, Strauss, and Rachmaninoff for years; indeed, it is only since the last decades of the twentieth century that the critical community has acknowledged their greatness without significant reservations. Compounding the problem for the American Neo-Romantics are the additional stigmas of being Americans in a field still considered to belong chiefly to Europeans and of continuing to embrace a style whose time has allegedly passed. In 1978, when an interviewer wondered whether Howard Hanson's "Romantic" Symphony perhaps appealed to a lower order of listener, the composer commented, "That's what the intellectual would like to have you think . . . [but] I get letters to this day from those who are not morons saying that their favorites are the Fourth Brahms and [my] Romantic Symphony."[9] And as recently as 2002, *New York Times* critic Anne Midgette capped off a begrudging acknowledgment of the effectiveness of a Neo-Romantic opera by Thomas Pasatieri with the remarkably revealing statement: "'The Seagull' seems to be a solid work at the lower end of the artistic spectrum, like a piece of furniture from Ikea [a low-priced, mass-market furniture retailer]: secretly better than it's supposed to be."[10]

There may be some truth to the assertion that composers whose music appeals directly to the emotions may be less concerned with matters typically viewed as "intellectual," such as formal coherence and structural complexity. However, one may legitimately question why an appeal to the intellect necessarily represents an order of artistic experience superior to an appeal to the emotions (except insofar as it satisfies humanity's vain quest to elevate itself above the animal kingdom). But one may further question whether an appeal to the emotions *must* somehow compromise legitimate formal and structural values. This study posits a Neo-Romantic ideal, in which the expression of emotion, depiction of drama, and evocation of mood are joined with, rather than opposed to, formal coherence, developmental rigor, and structural economy. Instead of representing mutually exclusive polarities, these two aesthetic objectives can complement each other in producing a heightened, intensified artistic experience. It is this ideal toward which the greatest Neo-Romantic composers have striven, and that they have, at times, achieved.

As indicated, the stylistic antecedents of the American Neo-

Romantics were European Late Romantics with whom they felt a strong affinity, either because of a shared cultural heritage or for reasons of a more individual nature. Like them the American Neo-Romantics tended to emphasize intense, passionate emotional expression, lavishly colored instrumental sonorities, and a rich, chromatic harmonic language derived from expanded triadic harmony. The American Late Romantics on the other hand—MacDowell, Chadwick, Hadley, Strong, Beach, et al.—were more conservative than their European counterparts, modeling their styles on composers like Dvorák, Brahms, Grieg, and Liszt. Their influence on later Americans was negligible, except perhaps on Hanson, to some extent.

Though the Neo-Romantics may have been unapologetically conservative, there are some points that distinguish them as a group from their European predecessors. For one, despite the primacy of spontaneous expression over abstract formal concision associated with Romanticism, most of the American Neo-Romantics displayed a greater use—and a more economical and disciplined application—of classical forms and more modest durational proportions in general than their European models. Second, though not as obviously and flagrantly as the American composers thought of as "Nationalists," the Neo-Romantics display certain characteristics often identified as "American," chiefly a heightened importance of rhythmic drive—frequently irregular, asymmetrical, and syncopated—and associated with this—a greater and more varied use of percussion instruments. Third, especially as they approached mid-century, the Neo-Romantics expanded the harmonic language of their predecessors by raising the "dissonance quotient," so to speak, usually by emphasizing such upper tertian additions as major-sevenths, dominant-ninths, augmented-ninths, augmented-elevenths, and others. Depending on spacing, or "voicing," and instrumentation, these expansions added richness, harshness, or both, thereby expanding the expressive potential of the harmonic language.

There is a fourth point that requires a more elaborate explanation. The American Neo-Romantics approached the matter of tonality somewhat differently from most of their European predecessors. In the earlier music of the Neo-Romantics, a tonal center is usually apparent at any given moment, although such centers may shift frequently within a work or section of a work, without a primary tonic exerting a unifying or hierarchical function relative to subordinate tonal regions. In other words, rather than an overall organizing principle as in much European music, tonality functions in Neo-Romantic music as a local expressive device, its relative strength or weakness contributing to a sense of emotional stability or lack thereof in the work at hand. Furthermore, in later Neo-Romantic compositions, a subjective perception of tonality may be absent altogether for greater or lesser periods of time, allowing for the expression of more extreme emotional contrasts. But even during passages when a tonal center is largely imperceptible, subjectively experienced tensions rooted in tonal expectations serve as important expressive elements.

The term "tonal" requires further clarification, as a lack of unanimity in its usage has led to considerable confusion. The "strict constructionist" uses the term "tonal" to describe music composed according to the paradigms that developed chiefly in eighteenth-century Austria and Germany and dominated the music of those countries until the turn of the twentieth century. In this music, a primary tonal center serves as an overall organizing principle, unifying all other, subordinate aspects of a composition. The "loose constructionist" uses the term tonal to describe all music in which tension/ resolution expectations rooted in tonal harmony play a role in the expressive impact of a composition. The confusion to which this lack of unanimity has given rise has been further complicated by the advent of additional terms—atonal, nontonal, pantonal, pandiatonic, twelve-tone, serial, et al.—in efforts to provide clarification, but these have in some cases perpetuated the confusion. In adopting the loose construction of the concept of tonality, this book acknowledges the use of "atonality" as an expressive device within a tonal composition, in passages where the subjective experience of a tonal center is largely absent, even though a theoretical tonic may be adduced through elaborate objective analysis.

There is one more issue that often arises in discussions of Neo-Romantic music that should be addressed at the outset. Many listeners, hearing this music for the first time, comment that "it sounds like movie music." This is typically stated either with some bewilderment or with scornful condescension, depending on the attitude of the listener. Therefore, it is wise to examine this reaction in advance. First of all, what is meant by the generic phrase "movie music" is usually the music composed for films between the late 1930s and the mid-1960s. But even with this qualification, movie music is not one uniform style or "sound." These film scores were composed by individuals like Erich Wolfgang Korngold, Max Steiner, Miklós Rózsa, Franz Waxman, and Bernard Herrmann, along with lesser luminaries. Most received orthodox musical training and many were born and educated in Europe. Some, like Korngold, already had considerable international reputations before they began composing for film. Their music was rooted in the styles of the late nineteenth century, intensified by increased levels of harmonic dissonance. In short, they were Neo-Romantic composers, as defined in this study—indeed, the Neo-Romantic composers whose music is most widely known to the general public.

However, in composing for films these composers were producing a subordinate element in a work of another art form, for the purpose of enhancing that work. As such a film score was not created as an autonomous work of art, with its own integral structure. For this reason, heard apart from the film it accompanies, the score is rarely satisfying; without its own abstract logic, without intrinsically motivated thematic development, it is an incomplete artistic experience. This is the chief aesthetic defect of film scores—not the musical language in which they were composed; there can be nothing "wrong" with a musical language. Therefore, the observation that a particular composition "sounds like movie music" begs the question as to whether its musical vocabulary or its formal structure is being so characterized. The former—which, in my experience, is usually the case—is simply a superficial matter of overlapping melodic, harmonic, and instrumental usage, while the latter is a more serious criticism.

Although there are dozens of American composers born between the years 1880 and 1930 who might reasonably be characterized as "Neo-Romantic," six have been selected for detailed discussion in this study: Ernest Bloch (1880–1959), Howard Hanson (1896–1981), Vittorio Giannini (1903–1966), Paul Creston (1906–1985), Samuel Barber (1910–1981), and Nicolas Flagello (1928–1994). Each composer's body of work is characterized by an overall seriousness of purpose reflected in works of ambitious scope that attempt to address the fundamental existential and spiritual concerns of humanity. Each reveals an internally coherent psychoaesthetic point of view, or "vision," a relatively consistent standard of both workmanship and expressive urgency, and characteristic stylistic features that comprise a unique compositional "voice." Finally, the output of each composer is generally distributed among the standard genres of opera, symphony, choral and vocal works, chamber music, and music for keyboard.

Ultimately, the selection of featured composers is arbitrary and personal. Leo Sowerby, Randall Thompson, Douglas Moore, John Vincent, Bernard Herrmann, Norman Dello Joio, Gardner Read, David Diamond, Robert Ward, Richard Yardumian, Robert Kurka, Ned Rorem, Carlisle Floyd, Lee Hoiby, Dominick Argento, and Ray Luke are all native-born composers of the specified time period who might be characterized as Neo-Romantics, and who made distinctive contributions of their own. If one considers composers who were born elsewhere, but spent much of their creative lives in the United States, one would have to add such figures as Mario Castelnuovo-Tedesco, Erich Wolfgang Korngold, Miklós Rózsa, and Gian Carlo Menotti.

Therefore, it must be emphasized that the six featured composers are not to be viewed as a unified group, or "movement," of any kind, joined in some common purpose. Indeed, as the title of this study suggests, and as its content bears out, one trait shared by all six is a spirit of individuality, of independence, and even of isolation, to some extent. Nor does the selection of this group mean to imply that the music of these six composers represents the "best" of American Neo-Romanticism. Some of the music of the other figures noted above is arguably comparable in stature to the works of the composers featured here. Nevertheless, considering the lives and works of the six collectively does allow some relevant themes to emerge.

For example, it becomes clear that the 1930s was a brief period when American Neo-Romanticism may be said to have flourished: Many of its leading exponents were coming of age, asserting their creative voices, and beginning to attract the attention of the public—in Europe as well as in the United States. Howard Hanson's Symphony no. 2—essentially a Neo-Romantic manifesto—was introduced by Serge Koussevitzky and the Boston Symphony in 1930, and his opera *Merry Mount* enjoyed a highly publicized premiere by the Metropolitan Opera in 1934. That same year, Vittorio Giannini's *Lucedia* was mounted by the Munich National Opera, and his adaptation of *The Scarlet Letter* created a sensation at the Hamburg Staatsoper four years later. Also in 1938, Arturo Toscanini and the NBC Symphony introduced listeners to Samuel Barber's *Adagio*

for Strings and *Essay no. 1*. Barber had just returned from two years
in Europe on his Prix de Rome, during which time he had composed
his Symphony no. 1 and his String Quartet. It was also during this
decade that Paul Creston launched his career as composer and
began his meteoric rise to national attention. During this brief
period, the Neo-Romantics clearly enjoyed a central position in the
configuration of the "new music" scene in America.

Perhaps most remarkable is the realization that it was during the
period from 1955 to 1970—when the serialist movement and the
avant-garde position in general were most dominant in American
composition and when traditionalist approaches, Neo-Romanticism
in particular, were most discredited—when most of the greatest
masterpieces of American Neo-Romanticism were created. Bloch's
Piano Quintet no. 2; Hanson's Symphony no. 6; Giannini's Symphonies nos. 4 and 5, *The Medead*, and *Psalm 130*; Creston's Symphony no. 5, *Corinthians: XIII*, *Chthonic Ode*, and *Three Narratives*;
Barber's *Vanessa*, *Andromache's Farewell*, *Antony and Cleopatra*, and
The Lovers; and virtually all of Flagello's greatest works were composed during this decade and a half.

The Neo-Romantic approach did not end with the generations of
composers discussed here either. Later American Neo-Romantics
who merit consideration include Ronald LoPresti, John Corigliano,
Joseph Schwantner, Christopher Rouse, Thomas Pasatieri, Judith
Lang Zaimont, Arnold Rosner, Samuel Zyman, Robert Avalon, and
Lowell Liebermann. Indeed, some of these composers will be discussed in subsequent projected volumes to be organized around different thematic issues.

Much of the information included in this study has never been
presented in print before. My own conceptualizations of this
music—as well as access to unpublished manuscripts and recordings—have been facilitated and enriched in some cases by correspondence and direct personal contact with the composers
themselves and/or with others close to them. This contact was
sought as an outgrowth of my own interest in their music and of
my frustration with the lack of available recordings and published
information concerning their lives and work. These sources include
Suzanne Bloch (occasional correspondence and personal contact
between 1984–1990), Paul Creston (frequent correspondence and
personal contact between 1968 and his death in 1985), Nicolas Flagello (ongoing personal contact between 1972 and his death in 1994),
and Dianne Flagello (ongoing personal contact since 1986).

ORGANIZATION AND USE OF THIS BOOK

Each composer featured in this study will be discussed through a biographical overview, followed by a comprehensive survey of his compositional output. Their works will be reviewed with an eye toward identifying their distinctive stylistic features, the evolution of their creative "voices" over the course of their careers, their most important and most representative works, and their compositional strengths and weaknesses. The reactions of critics are included as well, drawn from reviews of early performances and recordings as well as from commentaries written after the passage of time and an opportunity for reflection.

An effort has been made to structure the book in such a way as to be useful to students, scholars, and performing musicians, as well as to serious music lovers and collectors of recordings, and in different ways at different times. It is not expected that everyone will read and absorb the surveys of each composer's entire output from beginning to end. The biographical portions of each chapter present narrative overviews of each composer's career, while attempting to capture something of his character, personality, and the context in which he lived. The sections addressing the composers' outputs begin with general discussions of their styles and of the natural subdivisions of their work into chronological periods or performance media, as applicable. The comprehensiveness of each chapter has been influenced not only by the varying availability of information but also by my own judgment regarding the relative importance of the totality of each composer's contribution. A list of each composer's most representative and fully realized works is provided before the works are discussed in greater detail.

The question of how much analytical detail is appropriate is difficult to answer. An effort has been made to provide descriptions that might guide and enhance listening and understanding, without indulging in excessive detail. Nevertheless, some readers may find the descriptions of individual compositions tedious and irrelevant—especially if they are not familiar with the work in question—while others may well find them superficial and insufficiently specific. A decision was made to avoid musical notation and minimize the use of specialized terminology, which will be a relief to some readers but perhaps frustrating to others.

It is hoped that this book will serve as a useful reference tool, to be revisited time and again at different stages of the reader's process of discovery and integration. While proceeding through this book, readers are encouraged to enrich their experience and understanding by gaining access to recordings of the music discussed. Without the direct aural experience of the music itself, verbal descriptions are abstract exercises in vocabulary, of limited usefulness. In order to facilitate such access, a selective discography is included at the end of each chapter. In addition, brief musical excerpts representative of each composer will be accessible on my website, www.Walter-Simmons.com.

NOTES

1. Pierre Boulez, *Notes of an Apprenticeship* (New York: Knopf, 1968), 148.
2. Nicholas Tawa, *American Composers and Their Public* (Metuchen, N.J.: Scarecrow Press, Inc., 1995), 151.
3. Aaron Copland and Vivian Perlis, *Copland Since 1943* (New York: St. Martin's, 1989), 68.
4. Anthony Tommasini, "Midcentury Serialists: The Bullies or the Besieged," *New York Times* (9 July 2000).
5. Tawa, *American Composers and Their Public*, 167–168.
6. Milton Babbitt, "Who Cares If You Listen?" *High Fidelity* (February 1958).
7. Charles Wuorinen, *Simple Composition* (New York: Longman, 1979), 3.
8. Walter Simmons, "Contemporary Music: A Weekend of Reflections," *Fanfare* (May–June 1981).
9. David Russell Williams, *Conversations with Howard Hanson* (Arkadelphia, Ark.: Delta Publications, 1988), 6.
10. Anne Midgette, Review of "The Seagull," *New York Times* (14 December 2002).

SELECTED BIBLIOGRAPHY

Babbitt, Milton. "Who Cares If You Listen?" *High Fidelity* (February 1958): 38–40, 126–127.
Simmons, Walter. "Contemporary Music: A Weekend of Reflections." *Fanfare* (May–June 1981): 22–23.
Tawa, Nicholas. *American Composers and Their Public*. Metuchen, N.J.: Scarecrow Press, 1995.

Tawa, Nicholas. *A Most Wondrous Babble.* Westport, Conn.: Greenwood Press, 1987.

Tawa, Nicholas. *Serenading the Reluctant Eagle: American Musical Life, 1925–1945.* New York: Schirmer Books, 1984.

Tommasini, Anthony. "Midcentury Serialists: The Bullies or the Besieged." *New York Times* (9 July 2000).

Ernest Bloch: Photo by Lucienne Bloch, provided courtesy of Sita Milchev.

2

Ernest Bloch

It may seem surprising to begin a study of American Neo-Romantic composers with a European-born figure who did not come to the United States until he was thirty-six years old and whose musical identity is associated chiefly with his effort to express his Jewish heritage. The decision to make Ernest Bloch the cornerstone of this study is based on the premise that his musical output embodies precisely those qualities identified in the introduction as central Neo-Romantic aesthetic values: chiefly, the primacy of emotion, spirituality, mood, and drama; that Bloch's musical language, a fusion of both French and German elements shaped through deep immersion in both musical cultures during his formative years, represents the general vocabulary of American Neo-Romanticism: a fluid, flexible continuum from diatonic modality to true atonality, from simple triadic consonance to complex chromatic dissonance, utilized according to the expressive intentions of the particular work involved or passage thereof; and that Bloch's music projects the strong sense of purpose and powerful creative personality valued in this study and shared by the others discussed herein. Additional justifications for the inclusion of Bloch—though admittedly less central—are that the overwhelming majority of his music was composed in the United States and that, as a seminal figure in the formation of two important conservatories, he contributed significantly to music education in this country as well.

Perceptions of Ernest Bloch's identity within music history have

shifted as views of the overall terrain of twentieth-century music
have undergone conceptual transformation. After immigrating to
the United States from Switzerland in 1916, Bloch enjoyed nearly
two decades of recognition as one of the most forceful creative
voices in America. His attempt to express the essential soul of the
Jewish people was viewed by Modernist commentators as a radical
assault on smugly complacent American notions of good taste, as
distilled secondhand and diluted from Western European aesthetic
values. By the 1930s, however, his lack of interest in pursuing experimental techniques and his efforts to broaden his expressive range
beyond matters of ethnicity left him open to charges of middle-brow
conservatism. As the years passed, his role in American musical life
grew increasingly peripheral. Spending his final decades in virtual
isolation, he experienced an astonishingly productive "Indian Summer," the fruits of which went largely unnoticed by the music
world. By the time of his death, a few works from early in his career
had been absorbed into the standard repertoire, but his reputation
never expanded beyond that of a "Jewish composer." However,
from the perspective of this study, Bloch's works on Jewish subjects,
though an important aspect of his output, can be seen as but one
phase of a large and varied body of music. In describing his
approach to creativity, his words capture the ethos of Neo-Romanticism: "I have no system other than to say what is in me. . . . I never
attempted to be 'new,' but to be 'true' and to be human. . . . Everything that has a soul, everything that has character, everything that
is true is beautiful" (recalled by S. Bloch).[1]

BIOGRAPHY

Ernest Bloch was born in Geneva, Switzerland, in 1880, the youngest
of three siblings. His family, whose ancestry was Swiss for several
generations, displayed no musical talent or interest of any significance. His father, who was almost fifty when Ernest was born, has
been described as a nonreligious Jew, rigid and patriarchal, with a
pessimistic outlook on life, despite his ownership of a successful
souvenir and gift shop. His mother, characterized as possessing a
sunnier, more optimistic disposition, helped manage the family
business. Having lost her second child before Ernest was born, she
doted on her youngest.

Perhaps overly indulged, young Ernest was a hypersensitive child, frequently tormented by his peers. But he was comforted by a close relationship with his sister, who was five years older than he. She took piano lessons as a child, and it was probably her playing that introduced him to music. When he was six he was given a toy flute, on which he enjoyed picking out tunes. Although his parents had no intention of fostering his interest in music, they did afford him violin lessons with a local teacher when he was nine. He made prodigious progress and began devising his own tunes as well, to the irritation of his father, who described them as "shit-music."[2] (It is notable, in view of his father's discouraging attitude, that in retrospect Bloch typically characterized his father in affectionate terms.)

It was at the age of ten that Bloch committed himself to a life as a composer. The story is recounted that in a nearby field he built an altar of stones. Writing a solemn vow on a piece of paper, he pledged his destiny to music, placing the paper on his makeshift altar and setting it aflame. Thereafter he devoted himself to musical study with a zealous fervor.

Bloch's formal academic education ended when he was fourteen, the year after he celebrated his Bar Mitzvah. He then entered the Geneva Conservatory, where he worked under the guidance of Émile Jacques-Dalcroze (1865–1950), one of the most original musical pedagogues of his time. Dalcroze offered encouragement to the talented adolescent, working with him in solfege and composition and referring him to Louis Etienne-Reyer for violin lessons. The young student thrived in this atmosphere, making rapid progress on the violin while developing his compositional skill.

In 1896, Bloch attended a recital given by the noted violinist Martin Pierre Marsick, whose concert tour had taken him to Geneva. After the performance, the sixteen-year-old went backstage to meet him and showed him a string quartet he had composed. Marsick was so impressed that he accompanied Bloch to his father's store and persuaded his parents to send the boy to Brussels to study with Eugène Ysaye (1858–1931), the eminent violinist, composer, and conductor who had been Marsick's own teacher. Ysaye, a close associate of César Franck, was one of the most influential figures in Belgian musical life, active among those who were attempting to inspire Franco-Belgian musicians toward more elevated aesthetic aspirations. Ysaye was impressed with Bloch's violin playing, but even more so with his compositions, and strongly encouraged him to concentrate his efforts in that direction. He recommended his own student François Rasse (1873–1955) as composition teacher, while referring him to Franz Schörg for violin tutelage. This was a highly formative period for young Bloch, who lived in Schörg's home and thrived under the supportive influence of Ysaye. The Belgian master exposed him to the music of such composers as Franck, Saint-Saens, Fauré, and Debussy, and imparted to him his own uncompromising aesthetic ideals, while introducing him to many of the musical luminaries of the time.

Although he gained much from his association with Ysaye's circle, Bloch did not enjoy working with Rasse and, in 1899, went on to Frankfurt to study with Ivan Knorr (1853–1916), who, upon the recommendation of Brahms, had become chief composition teacher at the Hoch Conservatory. In addition to helping to build his confidence, Knorr fostered in Bloch the development of self-discipline, an essential prerequisite to becoming a mature, self-sufficient composer. However, Knorr's contempt for the innovations of Debussy led to heated arguments with his intense young student. While at the Frankfurt Conservatory, Bloch met a young German pianist named Margarethe Schneider, who was to become his wife.

By 1901, Bloch had composed more than thirty works of all kinds, including a violin concerto and several large orchestral pieces, one of which, a symphonic poem entitled *Vivre-Aimer*, was inspired by Margarethe. This work was performed in Geneva that year and was favorably received. It was during this year that Bloch met another figure who was to exert a significant influence on his artistic life: Edmund Fleg (1874–1962), a fellow Swiss who was developing a reputation as a poet and historian. Later in 1901, Bloch went to Munich for the last phase of his apprenticeship, two years of private study with Ludwig Thuille (1861–1907), a student of Rheinberger who had come under the influence of Wagner. It was under Thuille's tutelage that Bloch composed his Symphony in C-sharp minor, generally considered to be his first mature work.

The year 1903 was something of a turning point in Bloch's development as a composer. Bidding farewell to Thuille, he traveled to Paris, where Debussy's music—most recently, his opera *Pelléas et Mélisande*—was generating considerable controversy. Bloch had become a staunch admirer and defender of the Frenchman, and the two spent some time together. (Although Bloch recalled their talks warmly, years later Debussy maligned him to third parties with

cruel disdain. Kushner quotes from Debussy's letters such contemptuous remarks as, "I was not in the least anxious to get to know
[Bloch], but he put me through a torture like King Lear's"; "His
voice sounds like that of a eunuch bursting into a harem. . . . He's
destined for higher things, like selling guaranteed rings on the
streets."[3]) While in Paris, Bloch met with Ysaye and played through
his new symphony on the piano for him. Ysaye exclaimed, "This is
beautiful, large, powerful, of immense scope!"[4] It was around this
time that Bloch discovered the music of Mahler, attending a performance in Basel of the "Resurrection" Symphony, conducted by
the composer. The experience was a transfiguring one for the
impressionable twenty-three-year-old, and he expressed his feelings
about this "titanic work, which can be reckoned among the greatest
ever born of human genius" in an article published the following
year in *Le Courrier Musical* (Paris). In reply, Mahler wrote to the
young composer, "I live in the world like a stranger. It is seldom
that the voice of a fellow-spirit reaches my ear."[5]

It was also in 1903 that Bloch became reacquainted with Edmund
Fleg, and the two began to develop an intense friendship. Their
enthusiastic conversations led to the formulation of an ambitious
project: an operatic adaptation of Shakespeare's *Macbeth*, with
libretto by Fleg and music by Bloch. Within a year, Fleg had completed his adaptation of the play into a libretto in French, and Bloch
began composing the music. He worked feverishly on the project,
although it was during this period that he and Margarethe were
married in Geneva. (A son, Ivan [1905–1980], was born the next
year; two daughters followed: Suzanne [1907–2002] and Lucienne
[1909–1999]. Suzanne became a lutenist and specialist in early
music; however, she devoted much of her later years to compiling
biographical information on her father and annotating his works.
Indeed, her documentation and recollections provided much of the
source material for the biographies by Robert Strassburg and David
Z. Kushner and, hence, for the present biography as well.)

Bloch had to fit his composing into a busy schedule, as the young
husband and father also had to devote much of his time and energy
to working in his father's store in order to support his family. Yet he
managed to complete the music for *Macbeth*, along with an orchestral piece and several song cycles, within three years. *Macbeth* was
completed in short score in 1906, at which point Bloch assumed the
responsibility for trying to engender interest in the work and, hope-

fully, to bring about a performance. Meanwhile, his friend Fleg had become "radicalized" into Jewish nationalism by the Dreyfus Affair of the 1890s and its aftermath. He was to become a leader of what was known as the "Jewish Renaissance" movement in France. Up to this point, Bloch's own exposure to Judaism and its traditions had been no more than perfunctory. However, Fleg's intense preoccupation began to awaken Bloch's own interest. Around this time he wrote to Fleg, "I have read the Bible . . . and an immense sense of pride surged in me. My entire being vibrated, it is a revelation. . . . It stirred me so much that I could not continue reading, for I felt fear . . . of discovering too much 'me' myself, to feel in a sudden blow all that had little by little agglomerated and stuck to me drop away, leaving me naked, in this past that was within me. I would find myself a Jew, raise my head proudly as a Jew."[6]

Bloch's efforts to interest opera companies in *Macbeth* had been futile until a private reading in 1907 prompted singer Lucienne Bréval and critic Pierre Lalo to bring the work to the attention of Albert Carré, director of the Paris Opéra Comique. He was sufficiently impressed that he agreed to schedule the opera for performance in 1910, casting Mlle. Bréval as Lady Macbeth. Galvanized by this promising turn of events, Bloch turned his attention to orchestrating the opera, completing the task in 1909.

In 1908, Bernard Stavenhagen led the first complete performance of Bloch's Symphony in C-sharp minor in Geneva. During this period, Bloch also fulfilled several engagements as conductor of the orchestras of Lausanne and Neuchâtel. His performances were well received, and these positions might have become more enduring had not his erstwhile student (and later advocate), then twenty-six-year-old Ernest Ansermet, successfully lobbied for those positions himself.

The premiere of *Macbeth* took place in Paris in November 1910. Although it enjoyed a successful run during that season, and drew substantial praise from critics, it disappeared from the repertoire for reasons that have been attributed to political intrigues involving several members of the cast. Although the opera was not seen again until 1938, when it was produced in Naples, the Parisian performances drew enthusiastic praise from the twenty-three-year-old Nadia Boulanger and from forty-four-year-old Romain Rolland. Rolland, a novelist, dramatist, and music critic (who was to win the Nobel Prize five years later), became a vigorous champion of Bloch's music, and the two developed a close friendship.

In 1911, Bloch's father became seriously ill, and the composer had to return to Geneva to manage the family business. But he also took advantage of the opportunity to lecture on aesthetics and related subjects at the Geneva Conservatory. Over the course of the next four years he gave a total of 115 such lectures. During this period, Bloch's absorption in his Jewish heritage was becoming an all-consuming passion, somewhat like a "conversion experience." A grand idea began to take shape in his mind: a type of music that would "express the greatness and destiny" of the Jewish people. Prophetically, he wrote to Fleg:

> I am producing nothing so far, but I feel that the hour will come and I await it with confidence, respecting this present silence imposed by all-knowing natural laws. There will be Jewish Rhapsodies for orchestra, Jewish poems, dances mainly, poems for voice for which I have no words, but I would wish them to be Hebraic. A whole musical Bible will come, and in me will sing these secular chants where the whole Jewish soul, profoundly national and profoundly human, will vibrate. New forms shall be created, free and well defined, also clear and sumptuous. I sense them without seeing them yet before me. I think one day I shall write songs to be sung at the Synagogue in part by the minister, in part by the faithful. It is really strange that all this has slowly emerged, this impulse that has chosen me, whose outer life has been a stranger to all that is Jewish.[7]

Then, in 1912, Bloch was galvanized into creative activity, producing the first work of what became known as his "Jewish Cycle": a setting of Psalm 114 (with text in French) for soprano and orchestra, dedicated to Fleg and his wife. The following year the elder Bloch died, and Ernest composed *Trois Poèmes Juifs* in his memory. This was followed by two more psalm settings—22 and 137. In 1915, Bloch conducted his Symphony in C-sharp minor in Geneva. In attendance was Romain Rolland, who wrote to the composer, "I do not know any work in which a richer, more vigorous, more passionate temperament makes itself felt."[8]

By 1916, Bloch had completed the *Israel Symphony*, which introduces solo voices into the last movement, and the work for which he is best known today, *Schelomo*, a "Hebraic Rhapsody" for cello and orchestra. Despite the intensity of his creative drive, Bloch had little success in engendering interest in his music among those in his immediate locale. Alfred Pochon, a violinist with the Flonzaley

Quartet, had urged him to consider a visit to America. Although the world was in the throes of war, an opportunity arose when Bloch learned that the English interpretive dancer Maud Allan was looking for a music director to assemble and conduct a small orchestra to accompany her on a tour of the United States. He applied for the position and was accepted. Armed with letters of introduction from his friends, he left his family in Geneva and sailed for New York, arriving in July 1916. Although the tour was aborted after two months, Bloch found himself in an exciting and novel environment.

Before he had left Switzerland, Bloch had composed three movements of a large string quartet. Now, finished with the Allan tour, he composed a finale to the quartet while pursuing some of the contacts that had been arranged for him, among them violinist, conductor, and educator David Mannes and critics Paul Rosenfeld and Olin Downes. Downes later described his first encounter with the composer:

> The experience was unique and unforgettable; the scene on an afternoon in a stuffy little bedroom with an upright piano in it, here in New York, where a maniac with blazing eyes, jet-black hair and a face lined with suffering and will and vision sat at the piano, beating it as a madman his drum, and bawling, singing, shouting, released a torrent of music which poured out of him like lava from a volcano. There was the visitor's sudden realization that he was privileged to stand in the presence of a genius—an overworked term. This however was genius, and no mistake. The piece was "Schelomo" which at that time had not been heard in America: a torrent of music, bitterly passionate, exalted, and purple and gold.[9]

The Flonzaley Quartet decided to present Bloch's newly completed work on a program in New York City on the penultimate day of 1916. The performance made a stunning impact (a critic for *Musical America* called it "one of the greatest pieces of music composed in the last twenty years"[10]), setting off a chain reaction of auspicious performances that spread Bloch's name rapidly throughout the music world. Early in 1917, Olin Downes introduced Bloch to Karl Muck, then music director of the Boston Symphony Orchestra. Bloch took the opportunity to play through his *Trois Poèmes Juifs* for the German conductor. According to the recollection of Suzanne Bloch, Muck found the music "beautiful" and expressed his inclination to present the work, adding, "But Mr. Bloch, how can one perform in Boston . . . a composition with such a title as *Three Jewish Poems*? This is a problem." Indignantly, Bloch began to leave, when Muck reconsidered and stopped him, inviting the composer to conduct the work himself the following March.[11]

Concurrently, Adolfo Betti, another member of the Flonzaley Quartet, who was also on the advisory board of the New York Society of the Friends of Music, brought Bloch and his music to the attention of Harriet Lanier, the Society's founder. Impressed by Bloch's sincerity, she arranged for the Society's conductor, Artur Bodanzky, to look at several of his scores. Upon examining them, the conductor reportedly exclaimed, "*This* man is a genius!" and immediately agreed to devote an entire program to Bloch's music. The historic concert, presented at Carnegie Hall on May 3, 1917, included the premieres of the three Psalm settings, *Schelomo*, *Trois Poèmes Juifs*, and the *Israel Symphony*, the latter conducted by Bloch himself. Herbert Peyser described the concert as "the most significant event of the year in New York."[12]

During the summer of 1917, Bloch braved the high seas during wartime to sail back to Switzerland, where he gathered together his mother, his wife, their three children, and a few possessions, and brought them back with him to New York. He returned to find an invitation from David Mannes to head the theory department of his conservatory, which he had opened the previous year. Bloch accepted the position, which brought an element of stability into what had become a very exciting life.

In January 1918, Bloch conducted the Philadelphia Orchestra in a program of his Jewish works to enthusiastic acclaim from both audience and critics. Two months later, he conducted his Symphony in C-sharp minor at Carnegie Hall. *Musical America*'s Herbert Peyser described it as "a titanic utterance, an astounding creation."[13] By now Bloch was recognized as "the" composer of Jewish music and an important exemplar of the "Jewish Constructionist" movement, which viewed Judaism as a living tradition, in continuous evolution as it adapted to developments in modern life. G. Schirmer created a logo especially for their Bloch publications, with the composer's initials engraved within the Star of David. In a 1917 interview, Bloch made what is probably his most-often-quoted statement on the meaning of his Jewish works:

> It is the Jewish soul that interests me, the complex glowing agitated soul, that I feel vibrating through the Bible; the freshness and naïveté

of the Patriarchs; the violence that is evident in the prophetic books; the Jews' savage love of justice; the sorrow and immensity of the Book of Job; the sensuality of the Song of Songs. All this is in me, and it is the better part of me. It is all this that I endeavour to hear in myself and to transcribe in my music: the venerable emotion of the race that slumbers way down in our soul.[14]

Later in 1918, Bloch became involved with a progressive summer arts academy in Peterborough, New Hampshire, where he developed and practiced his own ideas regarding arts education. He met and developed a friendship with Julius Hartt, who invited him to teach at the college of music he had recently founded in Connecticut. Bloch also formed and conducted a community chorus in New York City, for the purpose of performing the music of Josquin, Lassus, and Palestrina. At the time this music was barely known, but Bloch had great affection for it, which he attempted to convey to others around him. However, neither the music nor his advocacy was able to ignite sufficient enthusiasm, and the chorus was soon disbanded.

In 1919, Bloch's newly composed Suite for Viola and Piano won the Elizabeth Sprague Coolidge Award. By this time, he was at the forefront of modern composers, among the most controversial creative figures in America. How might Bloch's phenomenal success be explained? Charles Brotman and others have described American musical institutions during the first decades of the twentieth century as still chiefly dominated by sternly Germanic aesthetic ideals, tempered by Anglo-Saxon notions of propriety and restraint. Bloch's intensely passionate music—not to mention his uninhibited personal manner, enhanced by his unabashed assertion of his Jewishness—was experienced as a bold assault on the repressed sensibilities of these entrenched institutions, somewhat along the lines of a "noble savage." Viewed as a representative of earthy humanity, he and his music were seen as an antidote to the timid propriety of these established institutions and were embraced as a vital, revolutionary voice by the spokesmen for a radical Modernism. However, this was an early, Freudian manifestation of Modernism, represented by the unrestrained expression of primal emotional truth rather than by the display of experimental techniques, and was hence an offshoot of Romanticism. Brotman notes, "As these critics and composers mounted their assault on the Victorian cultural establishment, the utter Jewishness of Bloch, not necessarily the number of dissonances in his music, seemed for many as exotic, provocative, and groundbreaking as Stravinsky's *Le Sacre du Printemps.*"[15] This view was clearly articulated by the influential Modernist critic Paul Rosenfeld, who became one of Bloch's most fervent advocates during the late 1910s and 1920s. "Unlike the 'theatric Orientalism' of the Russians, Bloch's music [according to Rosenfeld] 'married' European form with 'the sensuousness of Asia,' and it did so . . . by fearlessly expressing 'what is racial in the Jew.' Rather than emulating the mere 'Jewish composer' who sought to color his compositions with 'Semitic pomp,' Bloch emancipated his hereditary impulses, using 'crude dissonances . . . savage and frenetic in their emphasis' when he felt necessary." Brotman quotes Rosenfeld's assertion that Bloch, along with Schoenberg, were "'the most important spirits of the new period,'" and that "Bloch created 'as Barbaric a music as any produced by a member of the occidental civilization.'"[16]

The revolutionary power of Bloch's music had reached as far as Italy, where the distinguished critic Guido Gatti wrote in 1920, "Bloch's period of fruition synchronizes almost exactly with the tremendous conflict whereby the world has been convulsed and overturned as by a terrific earthquake; can this signify that the new epoch is beginning, and that, in matters musical, Bloch is to be its leader? To affirm this seems venturesome; and yet we venture to do so, so many are the signs and tokens which present themselves to confirm us in our idea."[17]

In 1920, Bloch accepted an invitation to create and head a conservatory in Cleveland, Ohio. In the United States fewer than five years, he vigorously assumed the responsibility for hiring a faculty and shaping a curriculum according to his own ideas, which can be gleaned from the following excerpt from an essay published in 1922:

> As it is obvious that sensibility, taste and creative forces cannot be acquired, artistic education must limit itself modestly to the study of technique, and the stimulation of the latent emotional faculties of the pupils. Let me admit at once that I do not believe in the efficiency of books on music, treatises on harmony or counterpoint, and all these scholastic and lifeless rules which are used in the official schools. These things are on the border only, of true art and life. On the contrary, the deep and assiduous study of the great works of all times

seems to me indispensable to anyone who wishes a thorough knowledge of any art, music especially. To help a child acquire the means to
undertake this pilgrimage, to teach him to listen, observe and judge,
seems to me the only aim of a sensible musical education.[18]

Two years after opening its doors, the Cleveland Institute of Music
had a student body numbering more than four hundred. Bloch himself conducted the Institute chorus and orchestra and taught
advanced composition. He also wrote articles and delivered lectures
on a variety of musical subjects for the local community, often
speaking out against the emotional sterility of "technique and brain-
begotten virtuosity."

Bloch's five years in Cleveland comprise one of his most fertile
creative periods. Despite the enormous administrative responsibilities involved in running the Institute, he managed to complete two
violin sonatas, Piano Quintet no. 1 and *Concerto Grosso no. 1*, and
more than a dozen shorter pieces. In 1924, Bloch accepted an invitation to teach several courses at the Eastman School of Music in Rochester, New York. While he was away, a simmering power struggle in
Cleveland became inflamed. By the time Bloch—who was too outspoken and volatile to be an effective political manipulator—
realized what was happening, he was forced to resign. As his
student and, later, colleague Roger Sessions wrote shortly thereafter:

> Cleveland's rejection of Bloch was a rejection precisely of the best that
> he had to give. . . . His very geniality, his force of conviction, his ironic
> laughter—his richness of temperament and culture, in other words—
> stood in his way. The city which had summoned him, at first disarmed
> by his magnetism into partial capitulation, took alarm before the full
> impact of his personality. It was not, in the last analysis, an individual,
> a style, or an aesthetic that went down to defeat in Cleveland; it was
> rather just those disinterested and humane conceptions which form
> the indispensable background for artistic creation of any kind.[19]

While he was at Cleveland, Bloch had welcomed the founders of a
small music school in San Francisco, who were considering a major
expansion of their facilities. Their visit to the Cleveland Institute left
them impressed by the scope of what Bloch had been able to accomplish in just a few years. Although he left the Institute in 1925 with
much regret, before the end of the year he had accepted an invita-

tion to assume the directorship of what became known as the San Francisco Conservatory. Again he undertook the task of shaping an institution of the highest caliber, while fulfilling teaching responsibilities and continuing his own creative activity. He wrote the violin-and-piano *Abodah* for the twelve-year-old Yehudi Menuhin, who premiered it in San Francisco in 1928. A short suite for chamber orchestra called *Four Episodes* won the Carolyn Beebe Prize in 1927, while *Helvetia: The Land of Mountains and its People*, a symphonic homage to his native country, was cowinner of a substantial prize awarded by the RCA Victor Company in 1929.

But the most important development of this period—indeed, another major turning point in Bloch's career—involved a competition announced toward the end of 1925 and sponsored by *Musical America*. The magazine sought to encourage the composition of a great American symphonic work by offering a prize of $3,000 to the composer of the winning entry. The panel of judges comprised the conductors of the leading American orchestras: Walter Damrosch (New York Philharmonic), Alfred Hertz (San Francisco Symphony), Serge Koussevitzky (Boston Symphony), Frederick Stock (Chicago Symphony), and Leopold Stokowski (Philadelphia Orchestra). The prize-winning composition would also enjoy nearly simultaneous premieres by these and other major American orchestras. Bloch, who had become a U.S. citizen the previous year, began to conceive an ambitious, large-scale work in honor of his adoptive homeland. His composition would attempt to capture the spirit of America while depicting its history from the early 1600s into the twentieth century, including within its dense orchestral fabric countless folk-melodies and other national tunes. The work, entitled *America: An Epic Rhapsody*, would culminate in a simple, stirring anthem, with text in Bloch's own words. It was his hope that the audience would join in the singing of this hymn.

An examination of the sociocultural context of this competition and its implications for Bloch's reputation is recounted in a fascinating, meticulously researched article called "The Winner Loses: Ernest Bloch and His *America*," by Charles Brotman. In 1928, *Musical America* announced that Bloch's work had been selected unanimously from ninety-two entries as the winner. The award was announced with much publicity, and Bloch was heralded in the general press as a vanguard composer who had lent his genius to a work addressed with love and gratitude to the culture that had embraced him. Yet in actuality, this award precipitated a decline in Bloch's artistic reputation from which it never recovered.

Much of Bloch's stature among New York intelligentsia was based on his identity as something of an exotic alien, a savage purveyor of the raw, unvarnished truth, so to speak, to a craven society whose appreciation of art tended to be tame and secondhand. However, winning the approval of a middle-brow magazine certified him as a legitimate representative of bourgeois culture, appropriating him from the radical sidelines and reframing his identity as a beneficent, patriotic citizen. "Once regarded as an unpopular prophet struggling for truthfulness among philistines, the composer of *America* would become known more as an icon of mainstream neoromantic marketing."[20] Though *America* was not a significant musical departure for Bloch with regard to its formal and stylistic properties, its expressive content was affectionately and proudly nationalistic. Sentimental patriotism, as Bloch's undeniably was, has always been anathema to intellectuals who associate such expressions with the sort of chauvinistic jingoism that has often inspired national acts of aggression. Although the message of Bloch's music is far from jingoistic, as a recent immigrant who had been received enthusiastically by his new culture, he was naively oblivious to the extent to which the United States failed to fully live up to the democratic ideals it so proudly professed. Furthermore, the liberal or leftist political wing in America has always struggled to accommodate two largely incompatible theoretical attitudes toward the arts: an elitist position, which views conventional taste as an exaltation of the banal—of the "lowest common denominator"—as an inevitable consequence of the free-enterprise system and a populist approach, which holds that art "of the people" must be presented in a language comprehensible to the untutored layman. Bloch had been exalted by the elitists; with *America*, however, he aligned himself with the populists.

But if *America* was regarded by Modernist spokesmen as mawkish and reactionary, it was also reviled by staunch conservatives who viewed its selection as a further incursion of the avant-garde into hallowed American cultural institutions. Furthermore, xenophobes and anti-Semites were horrified that the work of a foreigner, no less a Jew, had been chosen to represent the spirit of America. Daniel Gregory Mason, a respected, Harvard-trained composer and educator who chaired Columbia University's music department for many years and a scion of one of America's oldest and most respected musical families, warned of the "insidiousness of the Jewish menace to our artistic integrity," fearing that the "violently juxtaposed extremes of passion, poignant eroticism, and pessimism" characteristic of "Hebrew art," with its "almost indecent stripping of the soul," would desensitize the public to:

> the moderation, the sense of proportion, which is the finest of Anglo-Saxon qualities. . . . The Jew and the Yankee stand, in human temperament, at polar points. . . . And our whole contemporary attitude toward instrumental music, especially in New York, is dominated by Jewish tastes and standards, with their Oriental extravagance, their sensuous brilliancy and intellectual facility and superficiality, their general tendency to exaggeration and disproportion. . . . Ernest Bloch, long the chief minister of that intoxication to our public, capped his dealings by the grim jest of presenting to us a long, brilliant, megalomaniac, and thoroughly Jewish symphony—entitled *America*.[21]

(Interestingly and significantly, as early as 1915, Romain Rolland reported having received an inquiry from Mason concerning Bloch, whom he described as "an extraordinary talent."[22])

Most of the controversy surrounding Bloch and what his music supposedly represented involved the agendas of others around him. He himself opposed both the commercialism of mainstream American culture and the sterile intellectualism of the Modernists. He wholeheartedly embraced what he viewed as deeper, more profound American ideals. The score of *America* bears a dedication "to the memory of Abraham Lincoln and Walt Whitman," and extols the virtues of "a Union, in common purpose and under willing accepted guidance, of widely diversified races, ultimately to become one race, strong and great."[23] Thus, as a result of creating the winning entry in *Musical America*'s contest with what Brotman calls "one rather ingenuous tribute to America's democratic and pluralistic ideals," Bloch with one blow alienated most of America's classical music opinion makers.[24]

True, there were exceptions to this general condemnation. Olin Downes noted, "The most individual pages, in expression and effect, are those in which Bloch the prophet curses the crassness and materialism of certain phases of present American life, as his ancestral prophets cursed of old. This music is intended as parody, as invective, and it fully justifies its purposes."[25] As Brotman points out, "Pitting the composer's spirituality against 'the crassness and materialism of American life,' Downes perceived a continuity between the 'Jewish Cycle' and *America*, between the 'Hebraic prophet' and the national sage.'"[26] And after hearing it again, ten years later, John Burk found in it "a musicianship of the highest order," adding that "it had been over-promoted in 1928, talked into a too blinding light of public attention—and at the same time talked into oblivion."[27] As musicologist John Tasker Howard summarized it, "The *intelligentsia* have lost some of their interest in Bloch since *America* was published, for he has made a straightforward declaration of idealism that has nothing of cynicism, nothing cryptic; a credo that can be taught with safety to schoolchildren. His modernism has been used for respectable purposes."[28] In the long run, "*Musical America*'s coordinated endeavor to commodify the prophetic Bloch for its mainstream readership was an especially loud and ostentatious event in the music world which rhetorically called attention to Bloch's growing musical estrangement from younger American composers."[29]

In truth, the musical avant-garde was becoming increasingly focused on experimental compositional techniques, rather than profound expressive content. Having been championed just a few years earlier as a wildly irrepressible revolutionary, Bloch now stood in staunch opposition to what he viewed as a general trend toward dehumanization. In December 1928, he wrote to Nicolas Slonimsky:

> Biblical times have not changed: "They have eyes and see not, they have ears and hear not," and I add: "They have *brains* and do not think; *hearts* and do not feel! . . . But we have obliterated Life! After demolishing God, to put man in His place, today we are destroying the *man* to substitute instead the *machine*! Machines for killing, machines for walking, machines for thinking. . . . And even music, forgetting its biological origins, the *voice* and the *larynx*, tries to turn itself into a machine for machines! . . . And all this in the name of *Progress*! Whose progress?"[30]

Then, in 1929, by a remarkable stroke of good fortune, Bloch was rescued from the changing tides of musical fashion—not to mention the economic crisis that had suddenly befallen America—when the cantor of one of San Francisco's leading synagogues raised a substantial sum of money from its wealthy patrons for the purpose of commissioning from the nation's leading Jewish composer a major work for liturgical use. This sum was augmented by an annual endowment to be provided by the Stern Foundation for the purpose of freeing Bloch to compose without financial concern for a period of ten years.

So Bloch resigned from the San Francisco Conservatory and set out for Europe. After attending a festival of his music in Holland, organized by Willem von Mengelberg, he proceeded to the Italian-Swiss Alpine region known as Ticino, where he undertook a serious study of Judaism and the Hebrew language. Because he had little substantive knowledge of these subjects, he felt that such study was necessary in preparing to compose his setting of the Sabbath morning service of the Reform Temple. There he worked intensively, finally completing the work in 1933. Despite its specific provenance, Bloch had come to view the *Sacred Service* not as a sectarian work, but as his own personal expression of universal ideals. "It far surpasses a Hebrew Service now," Suzanne Bloch recalled her father saying. "It has become a cosmic poem, a glorification of the Laws of the Universe. . . . It has become a 'private affair' between God and me."[31]

Bloch's music had been developing a considerable following in Italy. Gatti's substantial and highly laudatory article, published in 1920 in *Critica Musicale*, has already been mentioned. In 1929, Bloch had been awarded honorary membership in the Accademia di Santa Cecilia, and in 1933 the first full-length book on the composer was written (in Italian) by Maria Tibaldi Chiesa and published in Turin. As noted earlier, the second production of *Macbeth* was to take place in Naples in 1938. So it is not surprising that the first performance of the *Sacred Service* was given in Turin in January 1934, followed several weeks later by a presentation in Naples. (The American premiere took place that April in New York.) The work was presented again the following month as part of an all-Bloch program at La Scala.

Critical reaction to the *Sacred Service* was generally—though not universally—positive. Among its harshest critics was the composer's former advocate Paul Rosenfeld. After deciding that *America* and *Helvetia* were "decidedly cheap," Rosenfeld seemed to have felt that Bloch's creativity had deteriorated, finding the *Sacred Service* to be "appallingly tame, resembling work one might have expected of an English Victorian."[32] On the other hand, the consensus of critics and listeners seemed to hold the work as the culmination of Bloch's

Jewish music; indeed, many regard it today as the greatest of all Jewish liturgical works.

After completing the *Sacred Service*, Bloch turned his attention away from Jewish subject matter to some extent, though not completely. His range of interests had broadened, and he hoped that his public identity might accommodate this. However, listeners continued to hear a "Jewish accent" in everything he wrote, whether or not such reference was explicitly acknowledged by a work's title. (This matter will be discussed further in the section on Bloch's music.) Moreover, Bloch had been "adopted" by the Jewish community, which was not inclined to relinquish its sense of "ownership." But Bloch's Jewish identity had always been somewhat exaggerated by a variety of interest groups for reasons of their own, some of which have been discussed. Despite the ethnic fervor that Edmund Fleg had ignited within the composer during the 1910s, which continued to smolder throughout the 1920s and into the early 1930s, Bloch was not such a sectarian character. Not only did he not observe Jewish customs or ceremonies in his private life, but he even kept a life-size sculpture of Christ on the Cross in his study for most of his life. Members of the Jewish community often found some of his pronouncements quite perplexing. As Strassburg recounts, "To a lady who had commented upon the apparent incongruity [of his displaying a crucifix], Bloch once retorted something like this: My dear madam—yes it is true that I am a Jew. But I should be equally proud to call myself a Christian—a true Christian. For He is to me only the symbol of that Christianity which both Jew and Gentile strive to attain. Who, indeed, will have the temerity to call himself Christian?"[33] Many were surprised when he stated, "I find more authentic Jewish music in a Gregorian Chant than in what is used in the Synagogue,"[34] and that of all religious traditions, "the service which has filled me with deepest emotion has been the Catholic Church."[35] Perhaps most peculiar was Bloch's naïve obliviousness to the intense anti-Semitism that was growing around him as he composed, secluded in the Alps, during the 1930s. As late as 1934 he defended Hitler for his "sincerity."[36]

While Bloch remained in Europe, he completed four major works after the *Sacred Service*: the Piano Sonata, premiered by Guido Agosti in Geneva in 1936; *Voice in the Wilderness*, introduced by the Los Angeles Philharmonic in 1937; *Evocations*, presented by the San Francisco Symphony in 1938; and the Violin Concerto, with Joseph

Szigeti as soloist with the Cleveland Orchestra in the 1938 premiere. In 1937, an Ernest Bloch Society was formed in London, with Albert Einstein named its honorary president. Vice presidents included such notables as Walter Legge, Rolland, Arthur Bliss, Thomas Beecham, Serge Koussevitzky, John Barbirolli, Arnold Bax, Ralph Vaughan Williams, and Bruno Walter. Not until 1938, with the curtailing of the Naples performances of *Macbeth*, due to pressure from Mussolini, and other indignities, did the composer realize that he was no longer safe in Europe.

In 1939, Bloch returned to the United States, where significant changes had taken place within the world of concert music, and composers whose work reflected Neo-Romantic values were enjoying widespread attention. But Bloch no longer wanted to be in the center of this scene, with its competitive in-fighting and power struggles. Now nearly sixty, he preferred to isolate himself, perhaps feeling that his reputation was sufficiently established. So he and his wife settled in Portland, Oregon, near the home of their son. Shortly after his arrival, he was invited by Koussevitzky to conduct the Boston Symphony Orchestra in a program of his own works. His annual stipend coming to an end as per prior agreement, he took a position the following year as professor at the University of California at Berkeley.

At this point, Bloch's marriage was undergoing severe strain, owing to his frequent trips and relocations, not to mention "at least 23 mistresses" counted by his wife, according to daughter Suzanne.[37] In 1941, the Blochs moved once more, this time into a large house they had found quite by accident in Agate Beach, Oregon, overlooking the Pacific Ocean. Now, in something of a self-imposed exile, he indulged his hobbies: photography, which he had pursued avidly since his youth, collecting agates, and studying and cultivating mushrooms. He also pursued his favorite musical pastimes: studying the music of the Renaissance polyphonists and analyzing and reanalyzing the works of Bach and Beethoven. By the time war broke out in Europe, Bloch had virtually ceased composing.

Then, in 1944, Bloch entered the final and most productive period of his life: a decade and a half during which he composed more than a third of his entire output—a large piano concerto, four more string quartets, three more symphonies, and a variety of other works, large and small. These late works seemed to be of chief interest in the

United Kingdom. The *Concerto Symphonique* was introduced at the Edinburgh Festival in Scotland in 1949. Sir Malcolm Sargent conducted the BBC Orchestra in the first performances of the *Concerto Grosso no. 2* and the *Sinfonia Breve* in April 1953. The Quartets Nos. 2, 3, and 4 had their premieres in England, by the Griller String Quartet, who recorded them, along with no. 1, in 1955. The Symphony in E-flat, Bloch's final work in that form, was first played in 1956 by the BBC Scottish Orchestra, conducted by Ian White.

Though Bloch was no longer an active participant in the mainstream of contemporary music in America, he continued to receive recognition, though more for his past accomplishments than for his recent creative work. In 1942, he was awarded the Gold Medal in Music from the American Academy of Arts and Letters. In November 1947, the Juilliard School honored him with three concerts devoted entirely to his music. (In an essay published in the program booklet, former student Roger Sessions, who had gone on to become one of America's most highly regarded composers in the twelve-tone vein, called the tribute "a symbolic vindication of the career of one who has had the courage to remain always a completely individual and even a solitary figure.")

In 1950, the Chicago Federation of American Hebrew Congregations joined the Ernest Bloch Society of Chicago for a six-day festival in honor of the composer's seventieth birthday. To mark this milestone, Howard Taubman wrote an article in which he stated:

> Where other composers have sought to make revolutions in composing technique, Ernest Bloch has been content to range himself on the side of the great traditions of the past centuries. He has led no sect, formed no clique, proselytized neither for himself nor for his ideas. The result is that where the currents of discussion and controversy over contemporary music rage most strongly the name of Ernest Bloch is seldom mentioned. It is as though he occupied a place apart from and above the battle. . . . [Today] his tendency at first is to put on an air of weariness and indifference. The world, he intimates, has passed him by, and he is resigned to its judgment. But prod him just a little bit with a provocative comment about the experimentalists in composing, and the blood of the old fighter boils up. His eyes begin to blaze, his short, stocky body leans forward with concentration, and his high-pitched voice pours forth in analysis and excoriation.[38]

The following year, Bloch retired from his position at the University of California at Berkeley to concentrate on composing. In 1953,

the Italian government invited him to attend a series of performances of his works, including a revival of *Macbeth*, perhaps to atone
for their shabby treatment of him during the war. That same year
he received a double award from the New York Music Critics Circle,
for both the String Quartet no. 3 and the *Concerto Grosso no. 2*. In
1954, he was named Doctor of Humane Letters by the Jewish Theological Seminary of America, in conjunction with the Los Angeles
University of Judaism. This was followed in 1955 by an honorary
doctorate from Reed College and in 1956 by the Weil Award from
the National Jewish Welfare Board, given to those who have
advanced Jewish culture in North America. That year a series of television programs on Bloch and his music was produced by the
National Jewish Music Council.

Also in 1956, Bloch began composing a series of solo suites for
cello, violin, and viola. The following year he was diagnosed with
colon cancer, for which he underwent surgery in 1958. By this time
he had completed three suites for cello and two for violin. In the
spring of 1959, Brandeis University honored him with its Creative
Arts Award, followed by an honorary doctorate that June. On July
15, with the Suite for Viola Solo still incomplete, Bloch died in Portland, Oregon, at the Good Samaritan Hospital.

An important aspect of Bloch's influence is the legacy he left to
his students. Highly varied with regard to their own aesthetic pro-
clivities, the best known include Roger Sessions, Bernard Rogers,
Randall Thompson, Quincy Porter, and Leon Kirchner. Another
aspect of his legacy is the strong personal impact he made on those
with whom he came in contact. A memorial appreciation prepared
in 1962 by three of his colleagues at the University of California
stated:

> The creative and formal qualities of Professor Bloch's mind were
> apparent in his conversation. A warm and considerate host, a delight-
> ful guest, he was a witty and absorbing raconteur. Started on a subject,
> he would digress, seemingly farther and farther from the original
> theme as associations led him, only to draw all together in a masterly
> and often related dramatic summary that instantly demonstrated the
> relation of all the digressions and excursions to the original theme. In
> this respect, the same formal sense that controlled the musical material
> in his compositions governed the development of his ideas in other
> fields.[39]

Bloch's son, Ivan, provided a further insight into his father's personality through a revealing glimpse of his personal habits:

> He imposed integral organization on everything he did. He kept constant records of income and expenses. . . . He had a small notebook in which he entered minutiae of daily expenditures: stamps, cigars, tobacco, garden supplies. In another notebook he entered the names and circumstances when he had visitors. His files were meticulously up to date. . . . His correspondence was staggering in volume. It covered not only his business dealings but his exchanges with other composers, former students, conductors, and "plain folks" who wrote to him. Added to music communication was his equally voluminous correspondence with great writers, philosophers, geneticists, physicians. . . . Whenever he was not composing, corresponding, walking in the woods or along the beach, or polishing agates, he would rest on the living-room couch, pipe in one hand and a book in the other. He would read and reread works of an extraordinarily varied nature: Lin Yutang, Schopenhauer, Flaubert, Walt Whitman, Van Wyck Brooks, Balzac, Herman Melville, Confucius, Nietzsche, the Hindu classics. . . . He annotated each time he read with marginal expletives of admiration, agreement, cross-references, and his own observations. . . . This almost feverish but always organized logical turmoil translated itself into conversation—he was virtually tireless, unstoppable, and endless. He wore out his listeners, no matter how devoted. He was bursting with ideas, tirades on the "mismanagement of the planet," and always questions on how society was organized and disorganized, whereas nature seemed to operate within a grand scheme.[40]

Asked to identify his own set of core beliefs, Bloch responded:

> Spiritual values never die. The universal idea must prevail. This crucial idea has permeated all my life and most of my works, . . . —my ultimate faith and belief is in the unity of man, in spite of real racial values and dissimilarities. My faith is in justice . . . on earth, on the right of each man to live his life as decently and usefully and giving to the community what he has to give, according to his gifts, his forces. This is the great idea of our great prophets, and also, in many ways the ideals of other races, like Confucius, Buddha and Christ.[41]

MUSIC

Ernest Bloch was born at a most auspicious time in music history, within two or three years of such Modernist pioneers as Bela Bartók,

Igor Stravinsky, Edgard Varèse, and Anton Webern, as well as other estimable figures like Ottorino Respighi, Ildebrando Pizzetti, Gian Francesco Malipiero, Alfredo Casella, Nikolai Miaskovsky, Karol Szymanowski, Joaquín Turina, Franz Schreker, Percy Grainger, Zoltán Kodály, and Arnold Bax, and Americans like John Powell and Arthur Shepherd. Bloch shared little in common with these composers—neither the extreme Modernists nor the other, more heterogeneous group—aside from the attempt (explored by only some of these figures) to fuse national or quasi-national associations with both post-Wagnerian and Impressionistic harmonic innovations.

Rather than revealing the obvious fingerprints of particular influential elder composers, Bloch's music displays its origins in a composite of the styles that flourished in France and Germany and their environs during his years of study. Perhaps the strongest and deepest influence is the aesthetic and stylistic legacy of César Franck—itself a composite of French and German sources—which Bloch absorbed through his relationship with Eugène Ysaye, who promulgated many of the Belgian master's attitudes and values. This legacy includes a view of music as a vehicle for profound spiritual and emotional expression, a fusion of post-Wagnerian chromatic harmony with classical formal designs, the use of "cyclical" principles—the recurrence, in identical or similar shape, of a primary motif at key points throughout a large work—as a means of creating structural unity, and a pre-Impressionist use of small chamber combinations in making grand, almost symphonic statements. Added to the Franckian legacy is a post-Wagnerian use of the orchestra to create extravagantly grandiloquent gestures and sonorities. Both these sources of influence are combined with Bloch's own strongly individual voice, which began to emerge when he was in his midtwenties. The works of his "Jewish Cycle," which began in 1912, added another dimension to his musical language. This vocabulary and syntax became a rich and supple expressive vehicle that served him over the course of a creative life lasting almost six decades. Yet unlike such Neo-Romantic composers as Hanson, Giannini, and Barber, Bloch's emotionalism is not conveyed through lyrical melody, but rather through the integration of motivic development with harmonic progression, as in the music of Creston and Flagello. This may account for the limited popular appeal of so many of his major works. However, what was—and still is, to some extent—most challenging about the music of Bloch is its actual expressive content—often bitter, pessimistic, and relentless in its intensity—rather than its actual musical vocabulary. Vehemently emotional, yet abstract and speculative in character, his works seem to offer a personal perspective on life's most profound concerns.

Bloch addressed the crisis of tonality not by supplanting it with a rigid alternative system of organization, or by delving into a national folk melos, or by hiding behind a posture of sterile emotional detachment, or by exploring novel or unconventional sound sources, or by retreating into the musical practices of the past. Instead, Bloch approached tonality as a continuum, which he shaped flexibly, according to the expressive demands of the music at hand. Though anchored in traditional triadic tonality, Bloch's harmonic language embraced a complex chromaticism, with harmonic extensions that included ninths and elevenths in their various inflections, with a freedom that brought him close to atonality and even twelve-tone (though not serial) usage at times, not to mention—at the other extreme—pure diatonic and pentatonic modality. Integrating this vast harmonic vocabulary into organic coherence, he achieved an extraordinary breadth and versatility of expression. Though Bloch was not the first or the only composer to attempt such a solution to the alleged "crisis," he was perhaps the most successful in producing a body of work that maintained a high standard of quality with regard to content and workmanship, unified by a consistent, personal aesthetic vision, while achieving a broadly universal expressive perspective. With his emphasis on humanistic values, his sensitivity to mood and drama, and a taste for rich, opulent sonorities and extravagant emotions, Bloch may be viewed as the fountainhead of American Neo-Romanticism.

One might cite as confirmation a characteristically perspicacious statement by Henry Cowell: "[Bloch] has never attached himself to any one musical style; instead, his work expresses the development of a personality at once philosophical, individual, and dramatic: a romantic, in short, with so entirely romantic an approach to his world and his music that he himself has sometimes said that he was born into the wrong century."[42]

Without so labeling himself, Bloch articulated his own sense of his calling when he stated: "I have no system other than to say what is in me. I cannot engage in synthetic music making. If I had wanted to engage in mathematics, I would have become a mathematician, and if I had wanted to theorize about music I would have become a philosopher. I would rather sweep the streets than write synthetic music."[43]

Bloch's musical output, beginning with the Symphony in C-sharp minor of 1900–1901, consists of approximately seventy works, spaced unevenly throughout his long career. (Earlier works may be regarded as juvenilia.) As noted earlier, Bloch's "Jewish cycle" began in 1912, with his setting of Psalm 114. Other works associated with the Jewish heritage soon followed and continued to appear with diminishing frequency throughout his career. Despite the prominent role they played in shaping his compositional identity and reputation, works with explicit Jewish reference number only about twelve, or some 17 percent of his output. If one seeks to divide Bloch's body of work into the early-, middle-, and late-style periods that often seem helpful in gaining a grasp of a composer's output, one might postulate an "early" period comprising only the four pieces completed between 1901 and 1906. Bloch's period of "maturity" might be said to begin with the opera *Macbeth* (1909) and include all those works up through the Violin Concerto (1938). A period of "later maturity" would comprise the music Bloch composed while living in Oregon, from 1939 until his death in 1959. There is a distinct shift in aesthetic posture between these two latter periods. (One hesitates to identify the earlier of these two periods as "early maturity," as it lasted until the composer was nearly sixty years old.) An alternative schema organizes Bloch's works into six groups, according to the places where he was living and working. The resulting six periods reflect different emphases, although not necessarily distinct stylistic features. These are: 1. a "first European" period (1901–1916); 2. a "New York" period (1916–1919); 3. a "Cleveland" period (1920–1925); 4. a "San Francisco" period (1925–1929); 5. a "second European" period (1930–1939); and 6. an "Oregon" period (1939–1959). The following discussion of Bloch's works will attempt to incorporate both approaches.

Most Representative, Fully Realized Works

Macbeth (1909)
Israel Symphony (1916)
Schelomo (1916)
Sonata no. 1 for Violin and Piano (1920)
Piano Quintet no. 1 (1923)

Sacred Service (1933)
Piano Sonata (1935)
Evocations (1937)
String Quartet no. 2 (1945)
Concerto Symphonique (1948)
Concerto Grosso no. 2 (1952)
Sinfonia Breve (1952)
Piano Quintet no. 2 (1957)

Early Works: First European Period (1901–1906)

The four pieces that comprise this section, though competently crafted and ambitious with regard to expressive intent, reveal the composer still in search of a personal voice. The work with which Bloch inaugurated his professional composing career is the first of his five (unnumbered) symphonies (which ultimately appeared over the course of more than half a century): the Symphony in C-sharp minor, which he completed in Munich in 1901, while under the tutelage of Thuille.

The Symphony in C-sharp minor holds a place in Bloch's output comparable to that held by *Kossuth* in Bartók's and the Symphony in E-flat in Stravinsky's: a youthful work that suggests little of the individuality of both language and content that was soon to characterize the music of its composer's maturity. Such works reveal, with little camouflage, the formative stylistic influences and aesthetic standards operating on the composer as his identity was being formed, as well as the extent of his mastery of the technical matters required in order to meet those standards. A fervent and exuberant *Heldenleben*-type piece, Bloch's early symphony addresses with great seriousness and considerable aspiration a favorite romantic theme and one that continued to appear—though from an increasingly mature perspective—in his later work: the victory of faith and hope over life's struggles and travails. The style of the work is thoroughly representative of its time and place, following the conventional rhetoric of Central European Late Romanticism and employing a thoroughly tonal harmonic language, with little unresolved dissonance and without more than a hint of the distinctive language Bloch was to develop over the next few years.

Scored for large orchestra, the Symphony, in four classically structured but expansively proportioned movements, lasts more than three-quarters of an hour. Its spirit is made clear from the beginning of the first movement, a throbbing, portentous introduction that builds to a huge climax before the appearance of the main *Allegro agitato*. Bloch initially entitled this movement "The Tragedy of Life—Doubts, Struggles, Hopes." The music pursues a vehement drama of metaphysical conflicts, in which the sense of struggle is relieved only by a subordinate theme of ardent lyricism. The second movement is the weakest, in which a melody of Mahlerian tenderness is overdeveloped, becoming mawkish in the extreme and culminating in flat-footed grandiosity. The third movement is the most harmonically advanced: a driving *scherzo*, somewhat Brucknerian in tone, but with tritones and augmented triads featured prominently, providing the work's only hint of its composer's mature style. Contrasting material features the kind of Swiss-Alpine pastoralism later to be found in *Helvetia* and the third movement of the *Concerto Grosso no. 1*. The fourth movement is a large fugue, based on an angular, rather ungainly subject. After a diligent development, the entire symphony culminates in a reprise of the two elements of faith and hope: the second theme of the first movement and the melody of the slow movement, now inflated to a level of grandiloquence exceeding anything heard earlier in the work, followed by a long coda that leads to a tranquil conclusion.

The Symphony is remarkable for its ambitious reach, while it proclaims its immaturity through a consistent tendency toward overelaboration: that which could be suggested or implied is always spelled out completely. Yet despite this immaturity, its execution is competent in the academic sense: attention is paid at all times to matters of motivic development, harmonic richness, melodic growth, formal balance, contrapuntal interest, splendor of orchestration—nothing is overlooked. The work's chief weaknesses are its fundamental and consistent predictability and its inflation, over the course of many repetitions, of the mawkish theme of the second movement into a bombastic hymn of triumph. Perhaps the work it resembles most closely is the Symphony no. 2 of Alexandre Scriabin (composed two years later), which shares many of the same stylistic and structural traits.

The first performance of Bloch's Symphony in C-sharp minor took place in Geneva in 1908, under the direction of Bernard Stavenhagen. Bloch himself conducted the New York Philharmonic in the work's American premiere in March 1918. Although it was well received, there have been few subsequent performances. In 1984, the Symphony was presented for the first time in more than thirty years by the Saint Louis Philharmonic, a nonprofessional orchestra. A recording of this performance was made available to members of the Ernest Bloch Society the following year. The work's first commercial recording was released three years later and featured the Slovak Philharmonic, under the direction of Stephen Gunzenhauser.

The Symphony was followed in 1904 by a cycle of four songs to texts by the Symbolist poet and critic Camille Mauclair, entitled *Historiettes au Crépuscule*. Bloch's settings of these poems—naively romantic, but with rather gruesome undertones—show the striking influence of Debussy. Again, there are few hints of Bloch's own personal voice.

Bloch next turned his attention to another orchestral work, *Hiver-Printemps*, a diptych of tone poems completed in 1905 and dedicated to his wife, whom he had married the preceding year. Compared with the Symphony in C-sharp minor, *Hiver* shows a considerable advance in harmonic sophistication. Although still reflecting the influence of Debussy (who was composing *La Mer* at the same time), the piece is notable for being the first music in which Bloch's distinctive voice can be heard to emerge, albeit tentatively. *Printemps*, on the other hand, is less personal, lighter in texture and emotional content, but quite lovely, working itself up to a luscious climax. Commentator Harry Halbreich has likened its "lyrical sweep" to Mahler, but Puccini is perhaps a more apt comparison (both composers were at their productive heights at this time). The orchestration seems vastly more sophisticated than in the 1901 Symphony (although he did some retouching of it in 1934). Bloch conducted the work's premiere in New York City, in October 1916.

Bloch's young marriage came close to a sudden dissolution in 1906, when he became passionately infatuated with a poet named Béatrix Rodès. *Poèmes d'Automne* are settings of four of her poems. The music is still thoroughly French in style, with a strong affinity to the *mélodie* as practiced by composers like Chausson, as well as Debussy, although frequent use of the tritone dominant hints at one of Bloch's favorite devices. While the histrionic poems are of questionable literary merit, their character is well suited to Bloch's intense musical temperament. The settings are quite sophisticated, displaying a good deal more confidence and musical maturity than do the pair of tone poems they followed. The second of the songs in particular, the eight-minute *"L'Abri"* ("The Shelter"), is extraordinarily dramatic—perhaps even disproportionately so, relative to the poem itself. Here Bloch's own voice can be discerned, as the song reaches a towering climax of tragic eloquence. The cycle was first presented in Geneva in January 1907, by Nina Faliero-Dalcroze, accompanied by the composer. Bloch orchestrated the accompaniment in bold, lavish colors in 1917, in anticipation of a performance that was to take place in December of that year, in New York City.

Maturity: First European Period (1909–1916)

With the completion of his operatic adaptation of Shakespeare's *Macbeth* in 1909, Bloch arrived at the essentials of the mature style that was to serve him until 1938, by which time, at age fifty-eight, he had composed the music on which his general reputation is based. The foundation of this style is the Franco-Germanic language he had absorbed during his years of study, highlighted by such individual melodic and harmonic features as modal scales, open fifths in blatant parallelism, an emphasis on the tritone—used both harmonically and melodically—and tertian structures based on augmented triads; other features include an accented iambic rhythmic pattern sometimes called a "Scotch snap," as well as heavily accented and sometimes irregular rhythmic *ostinati*.

After *Macbeth*, Bloch turned his attention to the idea that had been germinating in his mind ever since it had been planted by his friend Edmund Fleg, of developing a musical expression of "the Jewish soul." The result was what has generally been termed Bloch's "Jewish cycle." Though the appellation implies reference to a specific group of pieces, it has been used with great inconsistency over the years. Some commentators have applied it to only the psalm settings, *Trois Poèmes Juifs*, *Schelomo*, and the *Israel Symphony*, all composed between 1912 and 1916; some have also included the String Quartet no. 1 of 1916, because it shares some thematic material with these works; others have included such later works as the *Baal Shem* Suite (1923) and the *Sacred Service* (1930–1933). In fact, Bloch continued to produce works with explicit Jewish reference sporadically throughout his career, up through the *Suite Hébraïque* of 1953. Therefore, the term "Jewish cycle" is misleading and is best avoided.

The musical language of Bloch's Jewish works was distinguished from that used in *Macbeth* by the use of melodic lines based on modes heavily inflected with augmented intervals (especially, augmented-seconds between 3rd and 4th and/or between 6th and 7th scale steps), suggestive of Middle Eastern music. Actual Jewish melodies appear only occasionally. However, although only twelve of Bloch's compositions are identified by explicit Jewish reference in their titles, many others of his works exhibit similar stylistic traits; furthermore, the overall style of his ostensibly nonsectarian pieces—with some exceptions that will be noted—does not differ significantly from that of the explicitly Jewish pieces. This, then, leads to the question, is there a meaningful distinction between the "Jewish Bloch" and the "secular Bloch?" The composer's own comment was: "To what extent it is Jewish, to what extent it is just Ernest Bloch, of that I know nothing."[44]

But the musical language of Bloch's mature works is more than just a matter of melodic, harmonic, and rhythmic idiosyncrasies. In most of the music he composed between 1909 and 1938, tone color and harmonic function join in conveying a broad emotional spectrum with passionate intensity and evoke mysterious, exotic moods and atmospheres. While retaining an allegiance to the formal principles inherited from the Franck tradition, Bloch attempted to imbue his works—including those that were ostensibly "abstract"—with suggestions of such notions as the dangers of the machine age, a devotion to peace and justice in opposition to the destructive forces of mankind, and a yearning to escape from the world of materialism into spiritual contemplation. As a dramatic foil to the tensions and stresses of the here-and-now, Bloch often posited musical imagery evocative of distant, exotic lands. The result was music of vehement emotional extremism, ranging from moments of ascetic spiritual rapture to passages that seem to verge on violence. It is this quality that commentators have called "rhetorical" and "rhapsodic," and gave rise to the observation that Bloch's music was implicitly programmatic, even when there were no such explicit indications, or when thematic development was closely argued and classical formal designs were clearly followed.

Although inferring extrinsic expressive content from abstract musical works is not currently in fashion, such efforts were more acceptable in some quarters at the turn of the twentieth century, as was uninhibited rhetorical and emotional display in general. Bloch, himself a fervent, passionate fellow, did not hesitate to provide verbal interpretations of his works or to sanction the attempts of others to try their hands, although as time went on, and such practices were more widely frowned upon, he became quite defensive in response to criticism of this practice.

As indicated, Bloch's period of maturity began with *Macbeth*. Although he did not complete the orchestral score until 1909, he had essentially finished the vocal score by 1906, having worked on it since 1904, when Fleg completed the libretto. The premiere was given by the Paris Opéra Comique on November 30, 1910. It enjoyed a successful run and was well received by both audience and critics, yet was dropped from the repertoire after the first season for reasons that remain unclear. It was not mounted again until March 1938, when it was presented in Naples, but again its run was terminated prematurely, this time by the Italian government, in anticipation of a visit from Adolf Hitler. Present at the Naples production was critic Raymond Hall, who wrote, "After a generation of neglect, Macbeth confirmed itself to be what critics proclaimed it at its Parisian premier in 1910: an outstanding milestone in the history of music drama."[45] Yet not until 1960, the year after the composer's death, was it performed in the United States, at the University of California at Berkeley. Subsequent productions took place at Baylor University in Texas in 1970 and at the Juilliard School in 1973. Although excerpts appeared on several obscure recordings, the complete opera was not released on disc until 2000, when a French company issued a 1997 performance broadcast from Montpellier.

In *Macbeth*, a full-length, three-act opera of two and a half hours duration, Bloch attempted to combine Wagner's system of leitmotifs with the directness and realism of Mussorgsky's *Boris Godunov*, using the French-based harmonic language he was gradually making his own. The result is a work of considerable artistic maturity and strong craftsmanship that pursues a musico-dramatic course unrelenting in its power and intensity. However, with so few performances or recordings of *Macbeth*, critical commentary throughout most of the twentieth century—usually passing references, rather than substantive discussion—has tended to reiterate received opinion based more in familiarity with its historical antecedents than in knowledge of Bloch's own body of work. Such commentary, which typically dismissed *Macbeth* as an immature work, amounting to little more than echoes of Wagner, Mussorgsky, Strauss, and Debussy, eventually hardened into a critical consensus. Some who have even witnessed productions of the work have failed to be impressed.

Reviewing the 1973 Juilliard performance, Harold Schonberg wrote, "Bloch's 'Macbeth' emerges as an eclectic opera without a really strong profile of its own. It is obviously the work of a sincere and accomplished musician, but it cannot be said that the materials are very original or, even, stimulating." However, he does add, with uncharacteristic humility, "It is altogether possible that it is a much greater work than this listener thinks it is."[46] On the other hand, many years earlier, a close study of the score led Roger Sessions to observe perceptively that although the influence of both *Boris Godunov* and *Pelléas et Mélisande* is unmistakable, "[Bloch] has molded them to his own uses, with a result that is neither Mussorgski or Debussy. One is aware of a new personality, full-blooded, uninhibited, and conscious of its own strength. The irony, the violent and uncompromising sincerity, the profound pessimism of Bloch's later works, are already here, transmitted through the impersonal medium of the Shakespearian tragedy."[47]

The claim that *Macbeth* is an immature work, lacking a strong personal profile of its own, can be readily challenged. Listeners whose notion of Bloch's stylistic identity is based on their familiarity with his Jewish-oriented works will be surprised to discover how close the musical language of *Macbeth* is to that of *Schelomo*, for example. The fundamental Bloch traits described above are evident in abundance in the opera. One might argue that all these usages are derived from Debussy in the first place. This is true up to a point. But Bloch's gestures—vigorous, dramatically impassioned, and boldly assertive—and his sense of grandeur are far removed from the ethereal textures, nebulous gestures, and rhythmic passivity of the French master, while a fluid, more attenuated sense of tonality distinguishes the opera from the world of the Symphony of 1901. No one familiar with Bloch's best-known works would have trouble identifying the composer of *Macbeth* after a few minutes' listening. Only the obviously Jewish elements have yet to make their appearance. Thus the opera may be viewed as representing Bloch's "baseline" musical language.

The chief obstacle to the popular acceptance of *Macbeth* is its primary intention as enhancement of the drama itself, with few autonomous musical episodes. The music is tightly wedded to the text and is presented through a declamation that does not permit detours for the purpose of lyrical elaboration of the emotional moment. As Gatti expressed it, "In *Macbeth* we have, first and foremost, a musical drama; all is subordinated to that; we do not find—with one or two exceptions—musical episodes, that is to say, fragments, *hors d'oeuvres* which have a life of their own and, in consequence, possess a ponderable value when detached from the scene or the act; there are no compositorial self-indulgences to cause stagnation or deviation, and to distract attention from the development of the plot."[48] Or, in Kushner's words, "The work might well be viewed as a large tone poem for orchestra, with the vocal and choral writing adding precision to the meaning of Shakespeare's words."[49] There are no serious miscalculations or lapses in taste, given the approach the composer chose to follow—and, one might add, it is an approach considered by many to be the aesthetic "high road" in operatic composition. Yet despite centuries of noble advocacy for opera as intensified drama, few works in the genre have won favor with the public without representative moments that fuse together the dramatic, emotional, and musical components of the proceedings at key points throughout the work.

But *Macbeth* is not wholly without such hors d'oeuvres, as Gatti terms them: There are two orchestral interludes, in Acts I and III, that serve just the function described above. Approximately twelve minutes in duration, they capture and distill the robust, tragic grandeur of the whole opera, while elaborating in symphonic fashion most of its key musical motifs. While the opera itself may never become a popular favorite, these two interludes have qualities that one might expect to endear them to concert audiences.

After completing *Macbeth*, Bloch delved into the works of Jewish inspiration, of which the first was a setting for soprano and orchestra of the Psalm 114, an exultant expression of awe in the face of God's almighty power. Composed in 1912, the brief setting is preceded by a three-and-a-half-minute prelude. Both luxuriant and plaintive, it serves, in a sense, as a prelude to the six works to follow. The setting of the psalm itself is proudly assertive and orchestrated in lavish colors.

Bloch's father died in 1913, and that year Bloch composed the *Trois Poèmes Juifs* in his memory. Nearly half an hour in duration, they constitute the composer's first mature, large-scale, purely instrumental effort structured without reliance on classical forms. Essentially three individual tone poems, they reveal Bloch's inexperience with such a challenge. The music is highly picturesque and richly orchestrated, but without the intense emotionalism of the major works to follow. Each movement unfolds via leisurely motivic and textural elaborations, rather than through true development, creating the effect of a loosely sprawling panorama of exotic moods and images. Nearly thirty years later, Bloch created an elaborate verbal description to serve as program notes. Though the music lacks sufficient structural focus to stand independently, the program notes provide apt imagery to guide the imagination. Though too lengthy to quote in their entirety, they describe the first movement, *"Danse,"* as conjuring a nocturnal tribal ceremony in which a half-naked woman, possessed and intoxicated, responds physically to improvised music. The second, *"Rite,"* suggests a solemn ritual sacrifice. The third, *"Cortège Funèbre,"* is evocative of the summons of Death, the anguish of the bereaved, and the eventual acceptance of the inevitable. Completed in Switzerland, the triptych was first performed by the Boston Symphony Orchestra under the composer's direction in March 1917, shortly after his arrival in the United States.

Bloch next turned his attention to two more psalm settings, both of which he completed in 1914. Psalm 137 tells of the Babylonians' demand that the captive Jews entertain them with song. In response, the Jews exalt him who shall seize the Babylonian children "and dash their brains against the stones." Bloch's setting, scored, like its predecessor, for soprano and orchestra, begins in subdued mystery, building to a bitter climax and then subsiding.

Bloch set Psalm 22 for baritone and orchestra. The singer cries out to God, "Why hast thou thus forsaken me?" This plea for deliverance from the depths of despair is transformed into a renewed sense of hope. The musical interpretation is more complex than in the two preceding settings, the prosody more declamatory and the orchestration more elaborate. Though beginning in despair, it concludes in triumph.

Along with the *Trois Poèmes Juifs*, the three psalm settings proclaim Bloch's grandiloquent rhetoric of bitter splendor, its bold gestures offset by exotic, highly perfumed harmonic textures, orchestrated with a dark brilliance. More concise than the three tone poems of 1913, the psalm settings—composed, incidentally, at about the same time as Ravel's *Two Hebraic Melodies*—are comparable in quality to the better-known works in Bloch's Hebraic style, with many powerful and beautiful moments. Of Psalms 114 and 137, Olin Downes wrote, "The music is for us one of the significant pages of the tonal art of this time, in its virility, its sweeping sincerity, in the unfamiliar and wholly original instrumental accents of barbaric triumph. It is, we believe, the work of a composer of genius—not talent, but genius."[50]

The astute French musicologist Harry Halbreich has pointed out an affinity—with regard to both spirit and character, as well as basic style—between the music of Bloch's early maturity and that of the short-lived Lili Boulanger (1893–1918), younger sister of the well-known teacher Nadia.[51] This affinity, which is most pointedly observed in the psalm settings produced by both composers at almost the same time, is especially remarkable in view of the unlikelihood that either had any awareness of the other's existence. One might almost view Boulanger's music as suggesting what Bloch might have done had he not delved into "the Jewish soul."

From 1912 throughout the period when he was composing the *Jewish Poems* and the psalm settings, Bloch was working on a more ambitious project, not completed until 1916. Originally planned as *Jewish Festivals*, it was finally entitled *Israel Symphony*, at the suggestion of Rolland. The work marks a significant further advance over Bloch's previous Jewish works, with the thorough integration of its constituent stylistic elements and influences into a rich, fully cohesive mode of expression. No longer an experiment, an attempt to create a stylistic fusion, the music had become a medium that Bloch employed with confident mastery in the service of his own individual vision, unconstrained by either psychological or technical limitations. The Symphony, a half-hour span subdivided into three connected movements, is built symbolically around two Jewish holidays of the fall season: The first two movements suggest Yom Kippur, the solemn Day of Atonement, while the third evokes the spirit of Succoth, the holiday of the harvest. The somber first movement serves as a compelling introduction, which accumulates intensity as it builds in a tightly focused expressive line. The second movement is the equivalent of a *scherzo*, a barbaric unleashing of wild energy that explodes without restraint until it achieves a subdued resolution, which leads directly into the third movement. After the tremendous concentration of the first two movements, the third is somewhat less compelling. A warm orchestral introduction builds to an exultant climax, followed by the entrance of five solo voices—two sopranos, two contraltos, and one bass—who join in a humble prayer of supplication. This section unfolds in a leisurely fashion, with melodic lines strongly marked by Semitic inflections. Perhaps the serenity of this passage seems a little too easily won after the extended brooding and turbulence that precedes it. Nevertheless, in view of the Symphony's overtly appealing qualities, it is difficult to attribute its relative neglect within Bloch's output to anything but the impracticality of requiring five vocal soloists who perform for only about eight minutes.

The last work Bloch completed before coming to America in 1916 was *Schelomo*, subtitled "A Hebraic Rhapsody." Toying with the idea of a vocal setting of portions of the Book of Ecclesiastes, the composer was unable to decide which language to use. A fortuitous meeting took place with the cellist Alexander Barjansky, who impressed Bloch with his playing and with the capacity of his instrument to capture the brooding vocal quality he was seeking. As a result of this meeting Bloch decided upon the cello as the solemn voice of King Solomon, through which to deliver an embittered commentary on the state of humanity, with the orchestra rather like a group of attentive spectators, responding with excitement and agitation. The treatment of the solo instrument serves to focus the expression, with no digressions for the purpose of virtuosic display. The work falls into three integrated sections, framed between somber introduction and coda. The second section is built around a melody Bloch recalled having heard his father sing. Dedicated to Barjansky and his wife, *Schelomo* is a work of great self-assurance and considerable mastery and is one of Bloch's most brilliantly orchestrated, pessimistic, and most passionately and overtly Jewish compositions. It shares with much of Bloch's output the sense of an idealism always threatened by disillusionment and a sense of humanism that bursts forth in blazing climaxes of unrestrained fervor. "Almost all [my] works," he wrote, "however gloomy, . . . end with an optimistic conclusion or at least with hope: [*Schelomo*] is the only one which ends . . . with an absolute negation. But the subject required it."[52]

The work's discursive structure requires that it be performed with full commitment and conviction; otherwise it can sound superficially exotic, strained, and overstated, preventing its true depth and significance from emerging. However, many performers, incapable or afraid of such grand rhetorical abandon, are guilty of half-hearted efforts. A suitable degree of conviction can be heard in a controversial 1977 recording featuring cellist Mstislav Rostropovitch and conductor Leonard Bernstein. Despite its interpretive challenges, not to mention its profound pessimism, *Schelomo* remains Bloch's most frequently played and recorded work to this day.

The overwhelming intensity of Bloch's music often elicited extravagant verbal rhetoric from early commentators. An example is Gatti's reaction to *Schelomo*:

> The orchestra palpitates in all the colors of the rainbow; from the vigorous and transparent orchestration there emerge waves of sound that seem to soar upward in stupendous vortices and fall back in a shower of myriads of iridescent drops. At times the sonorous voice of the violoncello is heard predominant amid a breathless and fateful obscurity throbbing with persistent rhythms; again, it blends in a phantasmagorical paroxysm of polychromatic tones shot through with silvery clangors and frenzies of exultation. And anon one finds oneself in the heart of a dream-world, in an Orient of fancy, where men and women of every race and tongue are holding argument or hurling maledictions; and now and again we hear the mournful accents of the prophetic seer, under the influence of which all bow down and listen reverently.[53]

Just a few years later, Olin Downes commented with a bit more American restraint, "The music of Bloch stirs us more deeply every time we hear it. It has an ancestral grandeur, an intense bitter seriousness without a parallel in any scores that come to mind. . . . The music is Hebraic in all that the word most profoundly and superbly implies."[54]

Yet as fine and moving a work as it is, *Schelomo*'s role as virtually the sole embodiment of Bloch's voice to the general public has severely limited the perceived breadth and magnitude of his achievement as a composer. Furthermore, in recent years, works like the *Israel Symphony* and *Schelomo* have been disparaged by some commentators who have likened their style to that of a Hollywood biblical epic. In light of the fact that these works long predated Hollywood and its biblical epics, such remarks are best seen as attempts to smear by association, while overlooking the significant influence Bloch's music seemed to exert on talented younger composers like Miklós Rózsa and others.

The cornerstones of Bloch's Jewish works—the three psalm settings, the *Israel Symphony*, and *Schelomo*—were all heard for the first time in one concert, which took place at New York's Carnegie Hall on May 3, 1917. (Also on the program were the *Trois Poèmes Juifs*, which had had their premiere two months earlier in Boston.) Artur

Bodanzky conducted all but one of the works—the *Israel Symphony*, which was conducted by Bloch himself. The cello soloist in *Schelomo* was Hans Kindler (who later went on to found the National Symphony Orchestra and became its first music director). This was the concert that had been described by the press as "the most significant event of the year in New York."[55]

The issue of Bloch's identity as a "Jewish composer" is unavoidable in any serious discussion of his role in the history of music. Although initially he seems to have thought of himself as the musical prophet of the Jewish people, this mantle was later to become a straitjacket, leaving him at great pains to assert his universality as a composer. For while this role certainly contributed to building his reputation, it also resulted in his being "pigeonholed" as a composer of "Jewish music," which Kushner has described as a "delimiting categorization." Noting ruefully that "it is the dominant perception of the musician and his works even to the present time," Kushner laments that the label "has clung stubbornly to Bloch like an irradicable badge and . . . has created an erroneous and delimiting assessment of his oeuvre as a whole."[56]

One must bear in mind that many years have passed since Bloch first became inflamed with his artistic raison d'être. Initially, he clearly embraced a view of Judaism as a racial, rather than purely religious, identity when he wrote, "A work of art is the soul of a race speaking through the voice of the prophet in whom it has become incarnate."[57] But such views are regarded differently today than they were during the 1910s. Kushner writes:

> So imbued was [Bloch] with this idea that he apparently did not consider the question of whether it is possible to transmit, in an art form such as music, qualities peculiar to and identifiable with a particular group of people. For Bloch, the question did not surface because he believed, with a zealous fervor, that he was offering to humankind his interpretation of Jewish music; . . . Since Bloch mixed quite freely the notions of race and religion, and as he published articles and issued statements in support of his beliefs, he was all too readily accepted at his word without the necessary conceptual component. For all intents and purposes, then, Bloch was the incarnation of the "Jewish composer" extraordinaire.[58]

Significantly, much of the musical public found Bloch quite convincing in his self-appointed role. In Gatti's impassioned prose:

When listening to Bloch's music one seems to hear old echoes from eternity, . . . Visions of majestic colonnades with statues gigantic and severe, of marble temples overladen with fine gilding and tapestries, of fabulous processions worthy of the Queen of Sheba, of all the biblical splendors; records of sacred tomes and of vanished wisdoms; heartache for times past; a rapt contemplation of elusive creatures resplendent as the sun and disdainful as the Sphynx; echoes of sacred dances, slow and voluptuous, within precincts saturated with the fumes of incense, of myrrh and cinnamon.[59]

Even a sober WASP intellectual like Sessions could write:

What [Bloch] has done is to allow his imagination to play on the embodiment of a truly Jewish spirit in music, and in so doing he has created a style which is entirely personal. . . . He is not only a Jew, but a European. The solid fruits of his musical culture are everywhere present in his work. . . . Above all, in his approach to the problems of form, he is a traditionalist in the best sense of the word. As truly as his orientalism, his classical culture is something inherent in the nature of his art. . . . Materially, this music is above all sumptuous and grandiose; rich and exuberant in color, luxuriant and full-blown in form. Its austerity, if such it can be called, is a pagan austerity of mood; intensity and concentration rather than essential restraint, a quality of his soul rather than of his art. Indeed, the overwhelming power not only of the Jewish works, but of Bloch's music as a whole, is perhaps attributable before all else to this extraordinary directness and intensity of feeling, together with the splendor of its material embodiment.[60]

In order to fully grasp the impact of Bloch's Jewish-oriented works on the public, one must consider the music written by other Jewish composers up to that time—composers as talented as Karl Goldmark, Gustav Mahler, Franz Schreker, Paul Dukas, Alexander von Zemlinsky, Erich Korngold, even Arnold Schoenberg. None of them had, by 1912, ever made as bold an assertion of their heritage in musical terms as had Bloch. Indeed, he was the first composer to attempt to capture and characterize in mainstream concert music the spirit of the Jewish people. But while some members of the American Jewish community may have initially responded to Bloch's ethnomusical message with pride, as Jews became more assimilated into American culture, many began to find the aggressiveness of his music somewhat overbearing and a bit embarrassing. And for those listeners less sympathetic to the Jewish people and their culture, Bloch's contribution could be easily minimized and dismissed—or worse (see comments of D. G. Mason quoted earlier). But not only did American cultural attitudes regarding nationalism and chauvinism change, but the attitude of Bloch himself, as he witnessed these changes during the course of his life along with the international developments related to them, changed as well. Yet without what was at the time such a daring declaration of ethnic pride and without works like *Schelomo*, which projected this declaration so vividly, would he have enjoyed anything like the fame and notoriety he did achieve? (Similarly, Aaron Copland came to find his association in the public mind with musical Americana somewhat limiting, but if he had never written *Billy the Kid*, *Appalachian Spring*, or *Rodeo*, would he have earned anything like the reputation he had and still has?)

From the standpoint of Bloch's artistic development, perhaps the most significant effect of his ethnomusical quest was its role in releasing within him the full power of his creative voice. Regardless of the actual meaning one infers from the music, Bloch's mission focused his creative energy and harnessed it confidently toward expressive goals of overwhelming power and eloquence. By the late 1910s, Bloch would arrive at a language in which the "Jewish" elements fused with the "baseline" language described earlier to form what was his own personal vehicle of expression. An essential aspect of this voice is what might be termed "exoticism," created by unusual modes and particular devices of timbre and sonority. Not only did these elements contribute to Bloch's representation of "the Jewish soul," but they also evoked images of various other "exotic" locales—Tibet, Bali, China, Tahiti, and so on—which he identified in program-note commentary, although he had no direct personal or ethnomusicological knowledge or experience of them. These places served as stimuli that kindled images and moods in his own imagination and are thoroughly misunderstood if taken literally. This was Bloch's mature language, which served him not only through the 1930s but also provided the basis for the music of his later maturity as well. Those who assert that most of Bloch's music "sounds Jewish" are simply associating what they hear with the oft-repeated references to a small number of pieces. In the final analysis, embracing Jewish subjects in a dozen works made Bloch no more a composer of "Jewish music" than composing Masses made Bach, Mozart, and Beethoven composers of "Christian music."

Maturity: New York Period (1916–1919)

Bloch's period in New York was brief, lasting only four years (1916–1920), and embraced the composition of only two major works. However, it was a period of great importance to his career, propelling him from utter anonymity to a position as one of America's most challenging new creative figures. Although this meteoric rise was largely due to the impact made by his major Jewish works, his own compositional interests had already begun to broaden beyond this somewhat circumscribed focus.

When Bloch came to the United States at the end of July 1916, he brought with him the first three movements of a string quartet-in-progress. He composed the finale toward the end of the summer, and the Flonzaley Quartet gave the premiere in New York City at the end of December. (This was some five months before the May 1917 Carnegie Hall concert devoted to Bloch's Jewish works.) His first major showcase in America, this performance launched his career in the New World.

String Quartet No. 1 is conceived on an epic scale: nearly an hour in duration, it is longer than the Symphony in C-sharp minor. Its expressive content is epic as well—uncompromisingly serious and requiring a nearly symphonic weight of sonority at times. Its structure is rhapsodic and expansive, each movement embracing a variety of affective states each of which leisurely develops its own character. One might note traces of apprenticeship absent from *Schelomo*: a lack of confidence perhaps, reflected in redundant elaborations of classical forms; as in the earlier Symphony, one senses a fear that without sufficient reiteration the listener will fail to grasp the message fully. The Quartet also clearly reveals its lineage from the Franco-Belgian tradition. Not only does its wholehearted adoption of cyclical procedures, with many intermovement cross-references, link it to the Franck group, but its approach to sonority at times suggests Debussy's contribution to the medium. But here the Frenchman's diaphanous timbral blends are wrenched and twisted to serve Bloch's very different temperamental needs. Yet despite these links to its historical sources, the work is clearly the utterance of a strong and powerful personality, revealing the same ferocious savagery and bitter despair found in the works of the previous period.

The First Quartet is also notable in inaugurating Bloch's imposing body of chamber music. Bloch was unusual among Neo-Romantic composers, including those discussed in this book, in finding the genres of chamber music to be suitable vehicles for creative efforts of grand ambition and expression. While the chamber music of most Neo-Romantic composers either reflects a sense of compromise in weight of sonority or is treated as a diversion from more serious matters, the quartets, quintets, and sonatas of Bloch—like those of Brahms—comprise some of his most full-bodied and profoundly personal statements.

Although ostensibly an abstract work, the String Quartet no. 1 displays many traits in common with the preceding Jewish works, including a prominent role for one of the central motifs used in *Schelomo*. Bloch was unequivocal about this when he wrote to Alfred Pochon of the Flonzaley Quartet that the first movement is "decidedly of Jewish inspiration—mixture of bitterness, violence, and of pain. . . . Recall those poor old fellows which you have certainly met in the streets, on the roads (around Geneva), with their long beards, sad, desperate, dirty . . . and who still have some hope . . . as they mumble their prayers in Hebrew."[61] However, the Quartet's remaining movements do not share this reference so explicitly. An expansive *sonata allegro* design, the first movement introduces a "motto theme"—a wailing, descending line—which recurs throughout the work.

The second movement introduces one of Bloch's most enduring expressive prototypes: the grotesque, bitterly sardonic *scherzo*. The example found in this quartet is ferocious, marked by slashing *ostinati* that, the composer warned Pochon, "will make you grind your teeth."[62] A central section, mysterious and ethereal, provides dramatic relief; Bloch attributed its inspiration to his notion of Tahiti, as gleaned from the paintings of Gaugin.

The third movement presents another Bloch prototype to which he was to return throughout his career: the haunted, darkly mysterious nocturne. This example is built upon a motif that toys with a haunting major-minor tonal ambiguity. The central section is a "pastorale," with "horn fifths" and other devices found in the composer's evocations of his native Switzerland.

The fourth movement is the most rhapsodic of all, reprising and reviewing most of the work's thematic ideas, with particular emphasis on the *scherzo* material. It might readily be described as episodic, although a more charitable characterization would identify it as visionary in its embracing of a vast range of expressive ideas not ordinarily pursued in such an intimate medium. The work ends in peaceful resignation.

As with many of Bloch's works, the Quartet must be performed with power and conviction in order to achieve a convincing impact. "Don't fear an excess of 'expression,'" Bloch wrote to Pochon prior to the premiere, although few groups have been able to muster the requisite stamina.[63] Perhaps the work's most fully consummated representation on recording was offered by the Pro Arte Quartet in 1982. This reading emphasizes the Quartet's dramatic intensity to the utmost, bringing to it the necessary physical power and incisiveness. Such a rendition reveals an early yet eloquent abstract embodiment of the basic Bloch *Weltanschauung*: a statement of faith in the face of overwhelming tribulations and an endless search for peace and serenity in a brutal world of strife and conflict. In the works of the 1910s, Bloch often linked these concerns to his identity as a Jew; as time went on, he was to express them in more universal terms.

Bloch next turned his attention to another work initially intended for modest forces: a Suite for Viola and Piano, which he completed in 1919, orchestrating the piano part less than a year later. As with the Quartet, Jewish references are largely disavowed, although suggestions of the "exotic" abound: much of it employs the same language as *Schelomo*. Half an hour in duration, the Suite falls into four movements: an extended, multisectional first movement, followed by three shorter movements. Bloch's ambivalence regarding extramusical "interpretations" is indicated by his initially having provided a lengthy impressionistic description, with fanciful movement titles ("In the Jungle," "Grotesques," "Nocturne," "Land of the Sun"), all of which he later withdrew. Nevertheless, commentators continued to read the most elaborate imagery into Bloch's work. One went so far as to suggest that the work deals with "the progress from the early forms of life on earth up unto the earliest of our great human civilizations."[64]

The first movement is the most eloquent portion of the work, an impassioned, freely rhetorical soliloquy suggestive of a remote time and place, which is followed by a dance-like section, highly inflected with modal melodic twists of Middle Eastern cast. The second movement is another of Bloch's grotesque *scherzi*, with some brilliant material but a little cluttered with unfocused digressions. A beautifully haunted nocturne follows, shrouded in mystery. The final movement opens with a pentatonic theme that points obviously to the Far East. However, as in the *scherzo*, an excessive number of shifts in tempo and mood produce an episodic effect before the work comes to an uncharacteristically jubilant conclusion.

Relative to the works of Bloch that surround it, the Viola Suite is weakened by episodic and digressive tendencies that tend to blunt its effect, especially in the later movements. In fact, the argument can be made that the twelve-minute first movement might have been more effective as a work in itself. Nevertheless, the Suite enjoyed a successful premiere in September 1919, at the Berkshire Music Festival in Pittsfield, Massachusetts, where it was presented by violist Louis Bailly accompanied by pianist Harold Bauer. Herbert Peyser found it to be "a colossal, a staggering work, but so new, so unusual, so overwhelmingly original that the listener, to gain an adequate idea of its profundity, its vast significance, its incredible store of genial material, must revisit it again and again."[65] The orchestral version was also introduced by Bailly the following year, this time with the National Symphony Orchestra, conducted by Artur Bodanzky.

Entered (anonymously) in the Elizabeth Sprague Coolidge Competition, Bloch's Suite tied for First Prize, until Ms. Coolidge herself cast the tie-breaking vote in Bloch's favor. (What is especially remarkable about this anecdote is that the tying work was the Viola Sonata by the notable English American composer Rebecca Clarke [1886–1979]. The obvious debt to Bloch clearly discernible in this and other works by Clarke testifies to the compelling dominance of his musical style at that point in time.)

One other important point raised by Bloch's Viola Suite involves its dual versions with either piano or orchestra. The brilliance of Bloch's orchestral palette is often overlooked in discussions of his music. Early on he revealed a remarkable gift for employing a wide range of instrumental color to evoke vividly the brilliant, mysterious, dream-like, and other-worldly realms that were so important to the core of his expression. Conversely, Bloch's writing for the piano was often awkward and ineffective—more so than that of most major composers. As Gatti expressed it, "When he composes for the pianoforte . . . one feels the orchestra; the pianoforte, that most perfect medium for the creation of an atmosphere of intimacy and delicate coloring, does not suffice him for portraying the vast complex of his visions."[66] Indeed, virtually all of Bloch's keyboard writing sounds like orchestral music reduced for simulation on the piano:

Tremolo effects, tightly voiced dissonances, mysterious murmurs all beg the imagination to translate them into more fully realized instrumental garb. Nowhere is this revealed more clearly than in a comparison between the two versions of the Viola Suite. Because so much of its appeal lies in the richly perfumed atmosphere of its subjective orientalism, the version with orchestral accompaniment is far preferable to that with piano, revealing an implicit aesthetic dimension that remains dormant in the piano writing.

Shortly after the premiere of the Viola Suite in orchestral garb, Oscar Sonneck wrote, "In either version Ernest Bloch has given us the greatest work for viola in musical literature, and what is more important, one of the most significant and powerful works of our time."[67] The Viola Suite—in both versions—has continued to be one of Bloch's more frequently performed works.

Maturity: Cleveland Period (1920–1925)

Bloch had been in America only four years and was still new to its ways when he arrived in Cleveland in 1920 with the task of creating a new conservatory before him. Yet despite the enormous responsibilities he faced in planning, structuring, and administrating such an institution, his five years in Cleveland proved to be one of his most prolific periods, during which he produced some twenty new works. Although many of them are of relatively modest dimensions, others are among his most powerful, ambitious, and fully realized personal statements. These are some of the earliest masterpieces of the Neo-Romantic aesthetic.

One such masterpiece—indeed one of Bloch's three or four greatest works—is the Sonata no. 1 for Violin and Piano. Early in 1920 the composer had written to a friend that he was "haunted by a music; new, strange, clear and mysterious . . . primitive and refined, yet a music of savage nature—exotic—a music wherein the elemental forces play, a music which goes further back than Palestine, a music of the 'origins' which goes beyond Judaism."[68] A significant advance in the consolidation of his musical style, the First Violin Sonata concentrates on the sustained elaboration of an abstract expressive scenario through the development of purely musical ideas. Digression is curtailed, as are Hebraicisms or other modal suggestions of alien locales. As in the greatest works, all musical elements are focused toward enhancing and fulfilling a coherent expressive vision.

A three-movement work of thirty minutes duration, the Sonata builds on the superficial stylistic features of comparable sonatas by Franck, Lekeu, and Fauré, with plenty of soaring melodies in the violin accompanied by billowing piano *arpeggios*. But its actual musical content and the vision thereby evoked is far away from those models and is, indeed, more extreme than anything Bloch had penned so far. In fact, few works in the literature display so vividly such a brutal and bitterly pessimistic vision of humanity. All the thematic material is constructed from distinctive motifs, several of which appear within more than one thematic idea. Thus intermovement cross-referencing of motifs is far more integrated, the result of organic development rather than simply literal quotation. The harmonic language is also much more dissonant than anything Bloch had hitherto composed, while tonality is often attenuated or ambiguous for extended passages.

The first movement opens in a state of agitation. The opening thematic material is fierce and harsh, rhythmically irregular but highly accented and is followed by a succession of ideas of great intensity—resolute, searing, and doleful—all developed at the highest emotional pitch and with unflagging urgency. The only notable structural weakness is an overreadiness to resort to sequences in ascending minor-thirds. The second movement is reflective, haunted, and mysterious, as if invoking visions of another world. An eerily ethereal *pizzicato* idea first heard in the *scherzo* of the Quartet no. 1 reappears here. Gradually, this movement too builds to an enormous climax almost operatic in its externalization of extreme emotion. The third movement begins with a purposefulness almost martial in effect, based largely on ideas introduced in the first movement, now transformed in character—one even taking on a triumphant quality. A central section returns to the ethereal mood of the second movement. This is followed by an altered recapitulation of the first section, as the triumphant material seems to prevail. After further reminiscences of earlier material, a quiescent epilogue brings the Sonata to a close.

Once again the eloquent emotionalism of the music—poured forth without apparent restraint, yet musically coherent—seemed to make extravagant verbal interpretation irresistible. Paul Rosenfeld, dedicatee of the Sonata and one of Bloch's early advocates, felt that the work depicted "the titanic, virulent, and incommensurable forces upon whose breast man lies tiny and impotent."[69] It was most likely this work that moved Gatti to write, "Bloch's music grips you and shakes you; it seizes you like a savage and sways you at will. His music makes you suffer; . . . [It] reveals to us the tragic meaning of life; it unrolls before us the eternal panorama of the world, where warring passions clash and on the horizon hovers the dazzling red of a conflagration continually renewed, that fitfully illumines the fatal struggle of humankind."[70] Perhaps most apt, despite their presumptuousness, are the words of English critic Alex Cohen, who felt that the first movement "projects into sound the nightmare feeling that man is not only at the mercy of the eternal cosmic machine that he himself created; but also that by some ruthless freak of an inexorable determinism he is fated to be its creator and destroyer." Cohen felt that the third movement was like a "terrible march . . . a barbaric procession with mounted elephants trampling to death a crowd of prostrate bodies—scapegoats doomed to die in a mass atonement, to lay the ghost of an obsession and propitiate some imagined spirit, in order that life might be safe for the survivors."[71]

While the twenty-first-century reader may look with scornful condescension on such subjective "interpretations," music this vivid in its expressive extremism seems to evoke commensurate imagery almost unavoidably. It is partly a testament to the unequivocal content of Bloch's music, and to his eloquence in realizing it, that such commentaries strike the listener as largely accurate, florid though their verbiage may be. Part of their purpose was to help listeners penetrate the surface of music whose brutal ferocity was largely unlike anything that had been heard at the time. Nevertheless the music must ultimately succeed or fail by dint of its own intrinsic merits.

Bloch's Sonata no. 1 was first performed in New York City in February 1921 by violinist Paul Kochanski, accompanied by the thirty-four-year-old Arthur Rubinstein. Today the work is recognized by many as one of the masterpieces of the violin repertoire. Although it is heard fairly often, it is rarely played well, as its demands on both technique and endurance—psychological, emotional, and physical—tax all but the mightiest virtuosos. The chief impediment to its successful realization lies in the inadequacy of the piano part to fully project the aural images and gestures indicated in the score with the richness and power that is clearly intended, although some

of the most recent recordings (e.g., those by Alexis Galperine and
Frédéric Aguessy [ADDA 581044, 1988] and by Donald and Vivian
Weilerstein [Arabesque Z6605, 1989]) have accomplished this. Truly
symphonic in scope and weight, the work might easily have been
something on the order of a *"concerto symphonique"* had it been
orchestrated. (In view of the number of piano pieces and piano
accompaniments that Bloch orchestrated himself, the notion of such
a transcription should not be regarded as a sacrilege.)

The next major work from Bloch's Cleveland years was his Piano
Quintet no. 1, dating from 1923. It stands alongside the First Violin
Sonata as one of the composer's greatest achievements. Once again
Bloch transforms the general approach of Franck and his disciples
into a grim, angry, yet ultimately redemptive vision that seems to
address the important spiritual and metaphysical issues of mankind. In so doing, Bloch further expanded the texturally and harmonically rich language that served as his point of departure to
include a much more harsh level of dissonance, aggressively slashing rhythms, unusual string techniques, and plaintive motifs whose
wailing character is enhanced by the use of microtonal melodic
inflections. (Although much was made of this avant-garde technique
at the time, it was used essentially as an expressive device.)

Describing the transition from Bloch's Jewish works into these
abstract chamber works of the early 1920s, Sessions astutely noted:

[In works like the First Violin Sonata and the First Piano Quintet,
Bloch] gradually divests his style of its Jewish garments. . . . If, in the
Jewish Cycle, he gave voice to a positive belief in the value, the grandeur, of human suffering, in the greatness of the human spirit, in these
later works his dominant moods are those of pessimism, irony, and
nostalgia, felt with the utmost intensity and embodied in works whose
emotional or even philosophical tendencies are defined with unmistakable clearness. . . . Bloch no longer writes as a Jew, but rather as a
solitary individual. His language becomes, in fact, at once more individual and more detached. In abandoning the expression of a collective faith, he grows increasingly aware of the menace of superhuman
forces over which he has only a limited control. The violence of his
later music is ruthless and mechanical; it is no longer the voice of
human suffering and revolt. It externalizes itself more often in brusque
and vehement rhythms, insistent sometimes almost beyond endurance, than in the sharp and broken pathetic accents of his earlier style.
Irony, of which there is hardly a trace in the Jewish works, becomes

one of his characteristic moods, manifesting itself above all in a fondness for the grotesque, for caricature; . . . A serenity akin to that of the
end of *Israel* returns, deeper and richer in true eloquence in the wonderful last pages of this *Violin Sonata*; but whereas in the earlier work
this serenity arises from faith and ultimate confidence, it is in the later
one imbued with profound sadness. The nostalgia at which we have
already hinted grows out of this disillusion. A longing for distant
lands, softer climates, simpler conditions of life, shows itself in the
guise of an increasing fondness of the exotic, quite different in essence
from the orientalism of the *Jewish Cycle*.[72]

Similar in expressive cast to the Violin Sonata, with an equally
arresting opening, the Quintet begins with a driving undercurrent
of turbulence quite striking in its gruffness, as the work's "motto
theme" is introduced, a grimly resolute motif built from two
fourths: one ascending and the other descending, but in dissonant
relationship to each other. Although the opening tonality is more
strongly established here than at the opening of the Violin Sonata,
the motif soon gives rise to other, less tonally stable thematic ideas.
Falling generally into the shape of a *sonata allegro*, the first movement is perhaps less tightly focused than the corresponding portion
of the Violin Sonata, but its thematic material is more deeply integrated into the fabric of the music. While the overall tone of the
movement is unremittingly grim, material of a more mysterious,
reflective cast provides some contrast.

The haunting second movement opens with a transformation of
the "motto theme." Mournful and full of woe, the movement builds
to a huge climax on that theme before receding into the distance.

The third movement is fierce in its sense of abandon and looser
and more rhapsodic in form. It opens brusquely, with a driving,
aggressive sense of kinetic energy, its use of dissonance deliberately
harsh. This relentless energy is offset by passages of reflection, suggesting some sort of profound abstract dialectic on the state of mankind. A climax of tremendous angst is achieved, after which the
music seems to slip gently into a serene resolution, ending with a
surprisingly straightforward perfect cadence.

Piano Quintet no. 1 was first performed by Harold Bauer and the
Lenox String Quartet, in November 1923. Olin Downes described it
as the "greatest work in its form since the piano quintets of Brahms
and Cesar Franck,"[73] while the English pedagogue Tobias Matthay

called it the greatest achievement in chamber music since the death of Beethoven.[74] Ernest Newman wrote, "No other piece of chamber music produced in any country during that period can be placed in the same class with [Bloch's First Quintet]," bestowing upon it the ultimate compliment, that it "combines the maximum of passionate expression with the maximum of logical construction."[75] Bloch never again returned to the spirit and style of the First Piano Quintet. Many other works were to address the tragedies and mysteries of life, but never with quite such wild, extravagant abandon.

Bloch composed a second violin sonata in 1924, while on a sojourn to Santa Fe, New Mexico, as a spiritual antidote to the brutal pessimism of its predecessor, and it is different from that work in most every way. Subtitled *Poème Mystique*, it comprises a single movement that seems to convey a sense of faith and hope. If the First Sonata is tightly structured, the Second is freely rhapsodic, rhetorical, and episodic. Its chief idea is a simple motif of descending, then ascending, fourths and fifths, while parallel fifths are significant elements in a piano part in which tremolos abound, along with rolling and swirling *arpeggios*. The opening section displays more obvious Hebraic elements than are found in the preceding works. However, what is perhaps most striking is a central section that introduces Gregorian melodies associated with the *Credo* and *Gloria* of the Roman Catholic Mass. These melodies are set against achingly beautiful modal *arpeggios* that lend a slightly plaintive, Semitic cast. The work seems to be a fervent, heartfelt statement of Judeo-Christian unity, although the subsequent return of the initial thematic idea, with many repetitions, begins to take on a hectoring quality. The first performance of the *Poème Mystique* was given in January 1925 by its dedicatees, violinist André de Ribeaupierre and Beryl Rubinstein, both members of the Cleveland Institute faculty.

During the same visit to Santa Fe, Bloch also composed his *Concerto Grosso no. 1*. In one of those ironic twists that dot musical history, this piece—perhaps, after *Schelomo*, his most popular and frequently performed composition—was actually conceived as an exercise, to demonstrate to his skeptical students the continuing viability of supposedly outmoded formal designs and techniques. However, despite its didactic intentions, it is an affectionate work in which Baroque devices are used in the service of warmly romantic expressive content. In this work, Bloch did not adopt the *concertino* versus *ripieno* opposition most commonly associated with the *con-*

certo grosso style, but rather treated the piano as a pseudo-*continuo*— really more an *obbligato*—along the lines set by Bach in the *Brandenburg Concerto no. 5*, but with a romantic fullness and weight. Although some portions—notably the concluding "Fugue"—apply historical practices with some rigor, for the most part the Baroque elements amount to little more than regular rhythmic patterning and symmetrically balanced phrases.

The "Prelude" begins the work with a brusque vigor, although secondary material is gentler in character. The "Dirge" that follows deviates considerably from Baroque practice, with a romantic density of texture, rich, chromatic harmony, and even some Hebraic melodic turns. The third movement, "Pastorale and Rustic Dances," is one of the most fully developed examples of Bloch's "Swiss Alps" vein, to which he returned frequently for his lightest, sunniest diversions. Sprightly dance tunes and "horn fifths" characterize this hearty, exuberant music. Despite its contrapuntal rigor, the Fugue—like much of the work as a whole—displays a light touch and brings the work to a vigorous and decisive conclusion. The premiere of the *Concerto Grosso no. 1* took place in May 1925, just a few months after it was completed, with the composer conducting the orchestra of the Cleveland Institute, soon after his departure from the school had been announced.

Many commentators have characterized the *Concerto Grosso no. 1* as a precursor of Bloch's alleged "Neo-Classical" phase, relating it to contemporaneous works of Stravinsky and others. This represents a serious misunderstanding both of Neo-Classicism and of Bloch's aesthetics and the evolution of his style. While a thorough explication of the meaning of Neo-Classicism is beyond the subject of this study and will be treated in a subsequent volume, suffice it to say that Bloch's *Concerto Grosso* is a diverting Neo-Baroque exercise, not a work of Neo-Classicism. Fundamental to the spirit of Neo-Classicism is a rejection of both the sentimental indulgence and the expressive weight of Romanticism in its various phases and manifestations. Bloch never participated in this rejection and was never a Neo-Classicist. Even in his later works, when he hemmed in his own expansive, sentimental, and excessively rhetorical tendencies, he never renounced his view of music as a vehicle for serious spiritual and emotional content, and never embraced the Neo-Classical view of music as the abstract manipulation of sounds devoid of expressive meaning.

During his years in Cleveland, in addition to the four major works just discussed, Bloch also composed quite a few shorter pieces. For the most part these are sketches—brief character pieces of three or four minutes' duration, evocative of a particular mood. Some stand alone, others are collected into small groups, and, for the most part, they explore the same expressive realms that he favored in his larger works. Despite their brevity, they generally fulfill their aesthetic objectives with unerring taste, judgment, and craftsmanship. It is unfortunate that, with some exceptions to be noted, most of these pieces have been relegated to the periphery and are rarely performed. Only recently have many of them come to light through recordings: Not only do these evocative miniatures fill out the composer's creative profile, but they are also well suited to meet a variety of programming needs.

The type of character piece that Bloch produced most copiously during this period is the nocturne—a genre of "night music" that he made his own, much as did Bela Bartók. However, rooted in his own personal adaptation of Impressionism, these pieces resemble—in effect more than in actual language—the late works of Scriabin more than the music of his Hungarian contemporary. Suffused with Bloch's characteristically perfumed aura of exotic mystery, this genre achieved its apotheosis in the second movement of the Violin Sonata no. 1. However, a shorter, self-contained example is the piano solo *In the Night* (1922), cryptically (in light of its dark character) subtitled "A Love Poem." Haunted by a sense of yearning, the piece builds to a torrid climax before drifting away into silence. But as effective as it is, an alternate version for orchestra completed later that year indicates just how much Bloch's keyboard music is enhanced by the rich coloration such a transcription provides.

Perhaps the most elaborate and involved of Bloch's autonomous nocturnal compositions is the eight-minute *Nuit Exotique* (1924) for violin and piano, dedicated to Joseph Szigeti. *Five Sketches in Sepia* (1923) are ruminative, improvisatory piano pieces notable for their fragmentary figurations and attenuated tonality. At about two minutes apiece, they are among Bloch's most dissonant and sparsely textured efforts in this vein. *Nirvana* (1923) is perhaps the piano solo that would most benefit from orchestral transcription. Deeply introspective, the piece contains intimations of strange, unearthly images that can only be suggested or implied on the piano.

Atmospheric, epigrammatic, and plaintive, only the first of the

Three Nocturnes (1923) for piano trio is truly nocturnal in character. The second exemplifies Bloch's "Swiss pastoral" vein, while the third begins in turbulence and ends in triumph. All three miniatures display true musical substance despite their brevity. Similarly, two of the three short pieces for string quartet Bloch grouped under the title *In the Mountains* (1925) display the character of nocturnes: the first, "Dusk," and the third, "Night," the latter said to be inspired by the film *Nanook of the North*. The second, "Rustic Dance," is hearty and exuberant, with a Swiss accent. The same year Bloch produced another trio of sketches for string quartet, entitled *Paysages*, which might be described as "travelogues of the mind." The first of these, "North," was also prompted by the Flaherty film and falls into the category of nocturne, as used here. The second, "Alpestre," deviates from the composer's familiar exuberant and rustic approach to the "Swiss dance," exploring instead a more rarefied, abstracted manner. The concluding "Tongataboo" is one of the composer's anthropomusical evocations of primitive, savage humanity.

Despite its subdued, reflective character, *Prelude* (1925) for string quartet does not belong among the nocturnes. It is a heartfelt elegy, unfolding through modal polyphony, composed one evening shortly after his separation from the Cleveland Institute was announced.

Also during the Cleveland period, Bloch composed several groups of pieces on Jewish subjects. As Kushner pointedly observes, the Jewish pieces of the Cleveland years differ from those of the mid-1910s in that they represent a "Yiddish" style rooted in Eastern European *shtetl* (ghetto) life, while the earlier works suggest images of the ancient Hebrews of the Old Testament.[76] Of the "Yiddish" pieces, the best known is *Baal Shem* (1923), named for a leader of the Hassidic movement. Originally composed for violin and piano (an effective orchestral version was made in 1939), the impassioned three-movement suite is direct in its appeal, speaking in broad, expansive gestures and straightforward contrasts, intensified by the conventional expressive devices of virtuoso violin music. The music is overtly Jewish in its melodic character and even includes hints of Yiddish song. In the first movement, *"Vidui"* (Contrition), a passionate lyrical outburst is framed between commentaries in cantorial style. *"Nigun"* (Improvisation) is even more intensely passionate, as well as more overtly violinistic. *"Simchas Torah"* (Rejoicing in the Holy Scriptures) is lively, friendly, and engaging. Along with *Schel-*

omo and the *Concerto Grosso no. 1*, *Baal Shem* is one of the works of Bloch that are known to the general, music-loving public. Its style, scope, and treatment of the solo instrument have won it—"*Nigun*" especially—an enduring place in the repertoire of most major violinists.

Similar to *Baal Shem* but more subdued and reflective in character are the *Méditation Hébraïque* and the short, three-movement suite, *From Jewish Life*. Both were composed in 1924 and are scored for cello and piano.

Other, less easily classifiable short pieces and groups of pieces came from Bloch's pen as well during his years in Cleveland. Among the least characteristic and least well known are the broadly comical *Four Circus Pieces* for piano solo, composed within the space of a few days in 1922. While exhibiting a decidedly Debussyan flavor with suggestions of *Petrushka*, these impish burlesques are nevertheless skillful, tasteful, and quite sophisticated, with touches of polytonality.

Somewhat better known are the *Poems of the Sea*, written the same year and said to be inspired by the composer's visit to Canada's Gaspé Peninsula. Preceded in the published score by a quotation from Walt Whitman's *Leaves of Grass*, the three short piano pieces are less personal, more "objectively" Impressionistic, and relatively conventional in their manner of effect. Nevertheless they are attractively evocative, with some uncharacteristically folk-like melodic touches in the second movement. Once again, Bloch's writing for the piano is rather limited in its deployment of the instrument's sonorous resources, his distinctive *misterioso* atmospheres usually created by figurations more naturally suited to string instruments. Two years after completing the *Poems*, Bloch made an orchestral arrangement that is rarely played. In this version the work becomes an imposing fifteen-minute suite of vividly picturesque tone poems flavored with the composer's characteristic exotic tinge. Although it makes a much more dramatic impact in this guise, the final movement, "At Sea," becomes a five-minute tempest whose explosive climax is perhaps disproportionate to the scope of the work as a whole.

Disappointed in the quality of most piano music intended for children, Bloch decided to compose a set of his own in 1923. Despite the evident influence of Debussy once again, the ten *Enfantines* are tastefully conceived, well suited to the young pianist, and surprisingly lovely, with a sweet, delicate warmth quite uncharacteristic of the composer's more familiar persona as an impassioned prophet of doom.

Also from 1923 is *Danse Sacrée*, a slow, exotic piece of quasi-Oriental Impressionism, a bit more symmetrical and predictable than Bloch's best efforts in this vein. Its chief point of interest is its provenance as one of the only surviving fragments from the aborted opera *Jézabel*.

Maturity: San Francisco Period (1925–1929)

Bloch's five years in San Francisco were much less fruitful compositionally than the previous five years had been. While twenty new works appeared during the Cleveland years, only four were to appear during the subsequent five-year period. Moreover, two of them were to prove controversial: Both won important prizes, while arousing considerable criticism; their stature remains questionable to this day. One was a homage to his adopted homeland: *America: An Epic Rhapsody* (1927); the other, to the land of his birth: *Helvetia: The Land of Mountains and Its People* (1929).

However, the first work completed in San Francisco was a fifteen-minute piece for chamber orchestra called *Four Episodes*. As a group of four character pieces, each elaborating one particular idea, it resembles the groups of short pieces written the previous year (e.g., *In the Mountains, Paysages*). However, it is remarkable in being Bloch's first orchestral work to content itself with relatively modest aesthetic aspirations. Its scoring for an ensemble of woodwind quintet, string quintet, and piano produces lighter sonorities, while it is shorter and less complex both technically and emotionally than his prior orchestral works. Although such pieces are generally easier to program than larger, more demanding efforts, *Four Episodes* has not enjoyed the success of Bloch's best-known works. However, it is a nicely balanced group of sketches, orchestrated with great imagination despite the small ensemble and would likely prove successful with more frequent exposure.

The first movement, "Humoresque Macabre," is based on a snickering major-minor motif and creates a remarkably colorful effect as it limps along grotesquely. It has a more obsessive quality than the second movement, entitled "Obsession." Although it too is based on a single motif, its jig-like character lends it a fresh, exhilarating quality almost reminiscent of Percy Grainger. "Pastorale" is warm, contemplative, and lyrical, while "Chinese Theatre" is a typically Blochian evocation of exotic and primitive imagery, in which elements from the previous movements reappear. Shortly after its completion in 1926, *Four Episodes* was awarded the Carolyn Beebe Prize of $1,000 from the New York Chamber Music Society.

A work of far greater ambition is *America: An Epic Rhapsody*, Bloch's expression of affection and gratitude for his new homeland, of which he had become a citizen just two years earlier. Long in gestation, the work attempted to embrace the nation's entire history within its three movements: I) 1620; II) 1861–1865; III) 1926. A more detailed program for each movement is indicated in the score. Just under an hour in duration, *America* is like a musical pageant, beginning with the simple, peaceful, natural lives of the Native Americans, which are interrupted by the arrival of the Europeans, then following with the painful tragedy of the Civil War, and leading up through the "Roaring Twenties," which represented, of course, "the Present." The piece culminates in a simple, heartfelt anthem in which the audience is invited to participate, set to the composer's own words extolling the virtues of "Freedom, Justice, and Peace." The rhapsody is unified by a single simple motif, characteristically structured of fourths and fifths, which, first heard at the outset of the work, sows the seeds of the concluding hymn (which was actually composed before the rhapsody itself). Elements of the hymn are woven throughout the work, while each of the first two movements ends with a more elaborate anticipation. The rhapsody unfolds through a seamless fabric, Neo-Romantic in its richness, of familiar folk melodies, patriotic songs, and motifs of presumably Native American character, including almost Gershwin-like fragments of jazz in the third movement, not to mention the cacophony of Bloch's despised "Machine Age."

America is a grand conception indeed. Many composers have pursued similar notions (e.g., Roy Harris's *Folksong Symphony*, Earl Robinson's *Ballad for Americans*) more modest in dimension and aspiration, but few have attempted anything so ambitious in scope. Like a gigantic quodlibet created in the service of a great, noble vision, the work is masterful both in the ingenuity of its overall structure and in the seamlessness of its polyphony. Kitsch it may be, but kitsch of a very high order. One can well imagine how it towered over the ninety other entries in a contest sponsored by *Musical America*. On the panel of judges who selected the work unanimously was Serge Koussevitzky, who stated, "although I found a number of capable scores in this contest, when I reached this man's score I considered its qualities so outstanding, the whole work was so superbly conceived and developed that there was not a moment's doubt in my mind that this work above all should receive the prize."[77] After its first performance in New York, Lawrence Gilman wrote, "*America* is a breath-taking, a truly great conception . . . the Symphony as a whole is nothing less than an implicit hymn of the noblest ideals that can sway the artist with a sense of human destiny—that ideal of brotherhood which has included Beethoven and Schiller, Mahler and Whitman in its capacious far-flung net."[78]

The controversy that followed the selection of *America* as prize-winner was discussed at some length in the biographical portion of this chapter. As suggested there, the negative responses of some critics are best understood as sociopolitical responses in the guise of musical judgments. Bloch's chief sins were not truly compositional, but rather lapses of taste, largely attributable to his naivete, such as the incorporation of tunes of questionable significance (e.g., "Pop Goes the Weasel"). Hardest to defend is the concluding anthem, so elaborately anticipated and prepared throughout the work that its arrival is almost inevitably a let-down. Even Bloch's professed intention that the hymn be simple and direct enough for audience participation seems inadequate to justify its utter banality. To this day, *America* remains tainted by a general aura of unseemliness.

America was followed by another prize-winning failure: *Helvetia: The Land of Mountains and Its People.* Similarly patriotic in conception, this homage to Bloch's native land is more modest in scope, less than half the duration of its predecessor. After completing the work in 1929, Bloch entered it in a competition sponsored by RCA Victor. A $25,000 prize was divided among four winners: Bloch, Robert Russell Bennett, Louis Gruenberg, and Aaron Copland. (Three of the five judges were also on the panel that had selected *America* two years earlier.) As suggested by its subtitle, the central idea of *Helvetia* involves symbolic connections that have united the Alps and their inhabitants throughout the centuries, with much of the music evoking Switzerland's medieval roots. It is structured in five connected sections, or "frescoes," and, like *America*, makes much use of national tunes, following a rather elaborate program about which the composer displayed considerable ambivalence. While freely disclosing in interviews and program notes the images and scenes that guided him, he defended the structural autonomy of both works when challenged with writing "program music"—deemed by some to be an

inferior genre. However, *Helvetia* is a considerably looser, more episodic structure than *America*. Much of its music is quite beautiful,
reflecting the warm, humanistic side of Bloch's creative personality,
although it too culminates in a fervent hymn whose banal, diatonic
simplicity undermines the stature of the work.

Helvetia was first performed by the Chicago Symphony Orchestra
in February 1932. Several months later it was played in Geneva by
l'Orchestre de la Suisse Romande. It remains perhaps the least-often
performed of all Bloch's orchestral works, although, not surprisingly, it has generally been received well in Switzerland.

Between *America* and *Helvetia* Bloch composed a short work for
violin and piano called *Abodah*, or "God's Worship." He wrote the
piece, a soulful incantation in an overtly Jewish style that falls somewhere between *Poème Mystique* and *Baal Shem*, after having heard "a
little boy who played as if God has spoken through him."[79] *Abodah*
was dedicated to that boy, the twelve-year-old Yehudi Menuhin,
who gave the premiere in San Francisco in December 1928.

Maturity: Second European Period (1930–1939)

After resigning from the San Francisco Conservatory, Bloch
returned to Europe during the summer of 1930, to prepare for the
challenge of devising a musical setting of the Sabbath Service. He
was to remain in Europe until the spring of 1939, spending most of
his time in the Italian-Swiss Alpine region known as Ticino. During
this decade, he completed only five compositions, although all were
works of significance and substance.

Living in a chalet overlooking Lake Lugano, Bloch was deeply
immersed in the creation of the *Sacred Service* from 1930 until 1933,
preceding the actual process of composition with a thorough study
of the Hebrew language, of which he had been largely ignorant up
to that time. He chose for his setting the Sabbath Service as it
appears (with minor modifications) in the Union Prayerbook, consisting of a variety of Old Testament texts, grouped into five sections
(suggesting an unavoidable analogy with the Roman Catholic
Mass). He based the work on a six-note motif in the Mixolydian
mode, which is subtly interwoven throughout its largely contrapuntal fabric, and deliberately designed the music to be relatively simple to perform, so that it might be adopted by amateur groups, as

well as by professionals. To this end, he also authorized an organ accompaniment in the absence of a symphony orchestra.

By the time he completed the work, Bloch had come to see the *Sacred Service* as an expression of universal values. "Though intensely Jewish in its roots, this message seems to me above all a gift of Israel to the whole of mankind." (In order to emphasize its universality Bloch had hoped to have the celebrated black bass-baritone Paul Robeson in the role of cantor, but his inability to read music prevented him from accepting.)[80] The work is the apotheosis of Bloch's deepest spiritual and humanitarian ideals—the ideals whose betrayal and disregard gave rise to so many works of pessimism and bitterness. If *America* and *Helvetia* displayed certain lapses in taste and judgment, no such charges can be made with regard to the *Sacred Service* and the way in which it balances the spiritual realm and the emotional, the sectarian and the universal. Generally held to be the greatest work of Jewish liturgical music, it is certainly one of Bloch's most fully realized achievements.

The music for the *Sacred Service* is generally solemn and reverent in character, though not without its moments of agitation, affectionate warmth, mournfulness, and vigor. The solo contributions of the cantor are offset by extended choral passages. The soloist's musical role flows smoothly between a somewhat generic *arioso* in a dignified *bel canto* style and a more specifically cantorial style with exotic melismata and Semitic modal features. There are a number of passages where cantor and choir alternate in a "call and response" fashion, although most of the extended choral portions display a highly expressive, yet largely diatonic modal polyphony that reflects Bloch's deep admiration for the works of Josquin, Lassus, and Palestrina, as well as his appreciation of the choral style of Handel. These comprise some of the most glorious and deeply moving passages ever composed by Bloch (although their more generic or "universal" approach may be what so incensed Paul Rosenfeld when he derided the work as "appallingly tame" and "Victorian"). Much of the orchestra's role is supportive of the soloist and chorus, but there are notable outbursts with the blazing harmonic richness of *Schelomo* and the *Israel Symphony* that emerge naturally and with emotional appropriateness.

A problematic situation has arisen with regard to the proper manner of performing the fifth section—the Epilogue. In several portions of this section, a "minister" is directed to deliver the text in what Bloch called "spoken voice," using the local language, against the orchestral backdrop. It is apparent that Bloch was calling for a recitative-like delivery, as both pitch and rhythm are fully notated for these passages. However, shortly after the composer's death, the work was performed and recorded under the direction of Leonard Bernstein, with Robert Merrill as cantor. For this performance Bernstein persuaded Suzanne Bloch to approve the participation of a rabbi, who would offer a *spoken* reading of the texts in question. As she later recounted the incident, Bernstein felt that a true recitative "would overshadow the 'marvelous orchestral part,' and was 'too theatrical,'" adding that Merrill "would have refused to sing the very difficult part. At the time I had not the 'guts' to make a scene, which I now regret. This 'Lenny' interpretation set a tradition by which the work is now regularly desecrated."[81] Indeed, at this writing, more than four decades after the Bernstein rendition, performances in which these passages are recited outnumber those that follow the composer's score. With no legitimate justification, this practice considerably reduces the work's aesthetic universality.

The first performance of the *Sacred Service* took place in Turin, Italy, in January 1934, and was repeated several weeks later in Naples. The American premiere was given that April, in New York's Carnegie Hall, under the direction of the composer, followed by a performance in Milan the following month. Aside from some critical carping noted earlier, the general consensus seemed to be that this was "Bloch at his best."[82]

In 1935, Bloch and his wife moved on to the Haute-Savoie region of the French Alps. There he composed his Piano Sonata, which he dedicated to the Italian pianist Guido Agosti, who had become a friend and active advocate of Bloch's music. Agosti delivered the first performance of the Sonata in Geneva, in April 1936.

Another of Bloch's most fully realized works, the Piano Sonata marks a return to the aggressively harsh, bitter emotionality of the Violin Sonata no. 1 and Piano Quintet no. 1, but it is tighter and less discursive in form. No overt or obvious Hebraic references are suggested. Despite the awkwardness of Bloch's writing for the piano, already discussed, its pervasive intensity of conviction and its tightly integrated formal structure overcome the limitations of its pianism *per se*, so that a statement of considerable power and eloquence can be achieved by a pianist who can both meet its technical demands and match its emotional fervor. On the other hand, it is another excellent candidate for orchestration by a knowing, sympathetic hand.

The work opens with a series of flourishes within a context pervaded by stern dotted rhythms—an introduction that suggests a rather ferocious French Overture in the Phrygian mode. Outlined within the flourishes is a three-note motif—an ascending fourth followed by an ascending major-second—that becomes the source of most of the thematic material for the Sonata. This section is followed by an *Animato* section, also Phrygian, based chiefly on the opening motif, in what feels like an approximation of a *sonata allegro* design. As the movement unfolds, the motif is gradually expanded and reshaped in a restless, turbulent development marked by some of Bloch's most dissonant music, before a varied recapitulation. Although key signatures are used, tonality is often obscure for extended passages. This movement elides directly into the second movement, *Pastorale*, a typically Blochian evocation of a mysterious tropical paradise haunted by dark portents. Joining the main motifs from the first movement, which weave among the misty textures, is a new one with major-minor features. This motif builds to a towering climax before the movement subsides, leading directly into the third movement. Quite similar to the finale of the Violin Sonata no. 1, the third movement of the Piano Sonata suggests a blatantly polytonal, foot-stamping march. Amidst its savage shrieking and pounding, the motifs heard earlier in the Sonata all make their appearances, transformed in character, until the movement slowly dies away, the martial motif receding into the distance, like a ferocious bear in retreat.

Bloch turned next to another work for cello and orchestra. Although he averred no Jewish implication, his publisher suggested a title with reference to the Old Testament, *Voice in the Wilderness*. The work, completed in 1936, is often viewed as a sequel to *Schelomo*, from the vantage point of two decades later. It comprises six orchestral episodes—less theatrical and more concentrated rhetorically, but more diffuse formally, though no less passionately expressive than the earlier work. Somber in character, each episode is followed by a commentary from the cello that ruminates and expands upon the ideas presented by the orchestra. The *tutti* episodes are exquisitely sensuous and exotic psychoemotional *tableaux* in Bloch's mature secular language, displaying his remarkable subtlety of harmonic nuance and almost alchemical mastery of orchestration. However, the commentaries by the cello are somewhat redundant in their elaboration of what has already been clearly and concisely stated. The first performance took place in Los Angeles in January 1937, with Otto Klemperer conducting the Los Angeles Philharmonic.

In 1940, under the title *Visions and Prophecies*, Bloch transcribed for piano solo five of the orchestral episodes from *Voice in the Wilderness*, minus the cello commentaries. The result is a concise and effective group of highly perfumed mood-pieces, alternately truculent and reflective, exemplifying Bloch's personal adaptation of Impressionist devices into his own distinctive brand of Neo-Romanticism. However, what might be the most propitious adaptation of this material seems not to have been undertaken as yet: an orchestral version of *Visions and Prophecies*. The task involved is purely editorial, rather than creative, as the orchestrations may simply be taken as they are from *Voice in the Wilderness* and brought to the conclusions that appear in the piano versions. The result would be a twelve-minute suite of great appeal.

Among the most fully realized purely orchestral works of Bloch's maturity are the *Evocations*, composed in 1937, although they have been performed infrequently and never appeared on recording until 1994. Composed between *Voice in the Wilderness* and the Violin Concerto, the *Evocations* comprise a much stronger work than either of them. Here all the elements of mood, atmosphere, emotion, and gesture typical of Bloch's music are realized with a tight sense of direction and a concise sense of structure. Inspired by Chinese artwork Bloch had found in a book on the subject, the movements are entitled "Contemplation," "Houang Ti (God of War)," and "Renouveau (Springtime)." Their orientalism is wholly a fruit of the composer's imagination, evoked along somewhat the same lines as found in works of Ravel. Yet this music is as representative of Bloch as anything he wrote. The second movement, a demonic *scherzo*, is one of his most vivid and brutally exciting creations, while the Impressionistic atmosphere of the outer movements is enriched by a warm lyricism. The entire work is lavishly orchestrated so that barely a measure fails to enhance the exotic mood and atmosphere that prevail throughout. Pierre Monteux conducted the San Francisco Symphony in the premiere in February 1938.

Throughout the 1930s Bloch had been working on a violin concerto, which he did not finish until 1938. Though beloved to many of the composer's admirers, and championed by such distinguished soloists as Joseph Szigeti and Yehudi Menuhin, it is an uneven work and a curious one. Though Bloch adamantly denied any Jewish reference within the substance of the Concerto, insisting that, if anything, he was inspired by Native American sources, it is the most explicitly Hebraic-sounding music he had composed since the *Sacred Service*. Semitic modal inflections abound throughout the work, especially its first two movements. As Arthur Berger wrote in the *New York Herald Tribune* shortly after the premiere, "There is scarcely a work in the whole category of art music in which Jewish associations are stronger."[83] By this time, Bloch had probably grown so weary of the incessant references to presumed Hebraic influences in his work and of the superficial and circumscribed perspective conveyed by these references that perhaps he overreacted to such suggestions a bit perversely.

The Violin Concerto is a loose, discursive work built around an almost-pentatonic motto theme whose proclamation has a stubbornly dogmatic quality, the result of hewing too tightly to the tonic. The first movement is marked *Allegro deciso*—an indication that Bloch used with increasing frequency to characterize his music throughout the remainder of his career. However, here the movement seems diffuse, strained, and rhetorical, drawing one's attention to mannerisms and devices used more effectively elsewhere in the composer's output. The gently nocturnal second movement is more successful, projecting an ethereal aura strongly tinged with Middle Eastern exoticism. After a stentorian and rather obvious cyclical treatment of the motto theme, the finale introduces sunnier thematic material in Bloch's Swiss-Alpine mode. This more optimistic disposition eventually triumphs, after a reconciliation with the turbulent material of the first movement. Overall, the Concerto suffers from a repetitious, heavy-handed treatment of the motto theme, an overuse of sequences, a lack of rhythmic drive, and a great deal of empty virtuoso noodling. Its premiere took place in December 1938. The soloist was Joseph Szigeti, and the Cleveland Orchestra was conducted by Dmitri Mitropoulos.

Later Maturity: Oregon Period (1939–1959)

Bloch and his wife returned to the United States in 1939, settling in Portland, Oregon, near the home of their son. In 1941, they bought a house overlooking the Pacific Ocean in the small town of Agate Beach, Oregon. There the composer would remain for the rest of his life.

Bloch had not completed a new work since the Violin Concerto of 1938. This creative hiatus has generally been attributed to a sense of despair engendered by the horrors of World War II. Other contributing factors may have been the disruptive effects of relocation and the tensions that were surfacing in his marital relationship. However, one also wonders whether the composer might have arrived at some sense of creative impasse, a feeling that he had reached a point where a change in direction was needed; perhaps he was aware of the weakness of the Violin Concerto and the danger of possibly having succumbed to mannerisms, or for some other reason felt the need to take stock, to impose a greater degree of discipline on his mode of expression.

In any case, when he finally completed the *Suite Symphonique* in 1944, he indicated some awareness of having entered a new phase, describing the piece as "quite different from any classical work and possibly from any work I have written so far."[84] The *Suite* heralded what was to be the most fruitful period of Bloch's creative life: During the next fifteen years he was to compose some twenty-eight works—more than a third of his entire output. Among them are three symphonies, four string quartets, and a variety of other works, many of substantial import. Yet the fruits of this period represent the least-known and least-understood portion of his *oeuvre*.

Bloch's late music is notable for both its differences from and its consistencies with his earlier work. These later works continue to reveal a Neo-Romantic outlook in their strong emphasis on emotional and spiritual expression, but their emotionalism is more contained, with less rhetorical underlining: Long passages of rising sequences signaling major climaxes are less frequent; there is less reaching for emotional extremes, less indulgence in luxuriant orchestral textures or in exotic musical imagery. The emotional cast continues to be largely one of disconsolate soul-searching, but instead of hand-wringing pathos there is a grim, sometimes resigned or ironic—but relatively detached—perspective on the human condition. In addition to its affect, the structure of the music is more controlled—more regular in phraseology, and more concise formally, often with self-generated rather than classical designs. Formal logic and concentration dominate the expression of emotion, rather than the reverse. Most notable of all, with some few exceptions, there is considerably less suggestion of Hebraic melos or other extrinsic reference. There is no question but that many of these later works are less vivid, less immediate, and less arresting than many of his earlier masterpieces, but they reveal the evolution and maturation of an eloquent artistic voice as it achieved a masterful balance between expressive power and formal integration.

As noted earlier, some commentators have characterized Bloch's later work misleadingly as Neo-Classical. This misunderstanding has given rise to lukewarm performances that flatten out the music's considerable expressive impact and thereby diminish its effectiveness, contributing to the impression that Bloch's later work is in some way inferior to his earlier output. The direction in which the composer was moving is perhaps more aptly identified as a sort of "Expressionism"—a correlate of Neo-Romanticism, usually associated with the pre-twelve-tone compositions of the "Second Viennese School" (e.g., Schoenberg's *Five Pieces*, op. 16), in which abstract musical forms are imbued with a subjective emotionalism of heightened intensity. Bloch's elaboration of this approach, which he pursued with utter independence from his Viennese contemporaries, proved to be far more fruitful than theirs and is one of his greatest, but as yet unrecognized, artistic contributions.

However, this new direction is only hinted at in the *Suite Symphonique*, a romantic treatment of Baroque stylistic elements, along lines also pursued by other Neo-Romantic composers: Giannini in his *Prelude, Chorale, and Fugue* (1939), *Concerto Grosso* (1946), and *Frescobaldiana* (1948); Creston in his *Partita* (1937) and *Pre-Classic Suite* (1957); and Bloch himself in his *Concerto Grosso no. 1* and *Concerto Grosso no. 2* (yet to come). However, unlike the latter two works, the *Suite Symphonique* utilizes the resources of the full symphony orchestra, although its treatment here is more subdued than the composer's earlier norm. The first movement, "Overture," suggests a "French Overture," with its stately, majestic opening in modal harmonization, recalling moments from the *Sacred Service*, followed by an *Allegro giocoso*—a colorful and dramatic *fugato* in the composer's familiar "grotesque" manner. A brief return of the opening material brings the section to a close. The largely diatonic lines and regular rhythmic patterning join with a predominantly contrapuntal treatment in creating a Baroque "feeling."

The second movement, "*Passacaglia*," continues in a similar fashion—romantic in its richness and fullness of texture, but quite formalized and strophic in its development. (By comparison, the *passacaglia* that concludes Samuel Barber's Symphony no. 1 [1936], for example, is far more fluid in its phraseology though no less tonal in its harmonic stability.) After what is perhaps an overextended series of variations, the diatonic modality gradually gives way to a more conventionally romantic tonality, as the section builds to a grandly triumphant conclusion.

After this, the *Allegro molto* "Finale" seems almost anticlimactic, as it returns to the grotesque-*scherzo* manner of the *Allegro* from the "Overture." It pursues a vigorous course, during which the *Dies Irae* motif appears, for which Bloch gave no explanation. The premiere of *Suite Symphonique* was given by the Philadelphia Orchestra, conducted by Pierre Monteux, in October 1945.

Throughout the early 1940s Bloch had been working on a new string quartet, finally completing it in 1945, nearly thirty years after its predecessor in the genre. The Quartet no. 2 joins the Violin Sonata no. 1 and the Piano Quintet no. 1 as Bloch's most important pieces of chamber music. However, in comparison with the two earlier works, this quartet—though nearly forty minutes in duration—is far more concentrated in expression and tighter in structure and far more dissonant and less tonally stable than anything he had composed previously, yet with no sacrifice of emotional intensity.

The Quartet no. 2 begins with a mysterious, highly chromatic contemplation for solo violin, unstable both rhythmically and tonally. Not only does this soliloquy begin with one of the work's chief motifs, with an apparent tonal center of A, but it also introduces intervalic cells that will grow into two other significant motifs. These three motifs serve as the thematic material of the entire quartet. Motif 1, often called the work's "motto theme," constitutes the first measure and consists of a held E, followed by an ornamental figure that drops a fifth to A, returns to E, then moves to upper- and lower-neighbors F and D-sharp, then returns to E. In addition to being one of the central elements of the work, this motif also emphasizes the minor-seconds E-F and D-sharp-E. Elaborating this idea, the measure that follows consists of three more sets of minor-seconds, two descending and one ascending. In the sixth and seventh measures, two pairs of descending seconds appear: C-B and E-flat-D. This is the birth of Motif 2, which will recur throughout the work, assuming a dominant role in the final movement. The following measures then present a series of thirds—some falling, some rising. These thirds will become Motif 3, heard in ascending form when the viola enters in the eighth measure and in descending form when the second violin enters in the thirteenth measure. Thus, within the work's first seven measures, lasting some thirty seconds, its three main thematic elements have gradually come to life.

As this violin soliloquy is answered contrapuntally by the remaining voices, a rather austere, yet reflective mood prevails, suggesting the exploration of some unknown spiritual region (a mood, one might add, reminiscent of that evoked in *Flos Campi* by Ralph Vaughan Williams, a composer whose place in twentieth-century music is analogous in many ways to that of Bloch). Toward the middle of the movement, a more homophonic passage adds an ominous sense of foreboding before the earlier texture returns. This movement, the work's shortest and most chromatic, serves an introductory function, while conveying a sense of restless uncertainty.

The second movement begins with Motif 2, which heralds an energetic *scherzo*-like movement, propelled by driving triplet figures that project a grim vigor, recalling the sardonic character of the corresponding movement of the Quartet no. 1 of 1916. As this section proceeds, Motif 3 is brought into play as well, and both are developed and transformed. In addition, subordinate rhythmic and textural material is also oriented around the intervals of the fifth and the second, the bases of Motifs 1 and 2 respectively. A slower second section suddenly introduces a subdued, reflective interlude, with a contrapuntal development focused primarily on Motif 3. Then the *scherzo* material returns but now subjected to a somewhat different—though no less driving or contrapuntal—developmental treatment. Again passages that may seem like no more than accompanimental motoric patterning prove to be clearly derived from the primary motifs. A second interlude follows, introduced by a "twelve-tone row" created by an interlocking, descending sequence of tritones. Against this a subdued contrapuntal development, chiefly of Motif 3, takes place. Then the *scherzo* material returns and undergoes still further development, chiefly concentrating on Motif 2.

The third movement is the most clearly and consistently tonal of the quartet, opening in C-sharp minor. A sad, haunting melody, based chiefly on Motif 2 but with traces of Motif 1, is played by the viola over a pulsating triadic accompaniment. As it develops, a beautifully poignant counterpoint unfolds, picking up and pursuing threads from the first movement, including a distinctive dotted-rhythm variant of Motif 3. The movement ends in F-sharp minor.

The fourth movement is the true culmination of the quartet, both formally and expressively. It opens with a clear tonal center of D, as an *Allego molto* brings all three motifs into play, *molto ritmico*, suggesting a ferocious, almost savage war-dance that recalls the finale of the First Piano Quintet. This sets the stage for the *passacaglia* that follows. This *passacaglia* is far more chromatic in substance and stringent in character than the one that appeared in the *Suite Symphonique*. Its theme comprises Motif 2, with Motif 3 tagged on, followed by three pairs of tritones. The fourteen variations proceed continuously, rather than strophically. The theme undergoes some variation in rhythm, but generally is clearly recognizable, as most recurrences remain in the original key and are stated within one voice. There is some canonic treatment, as the section builds tremendous cumulative power, until the savage, driving rhythms heard at the beginning of the movement return, almost as if the increasing contrapuntal complexity required a release into a more primal form of expression. However, there is no loss of momentum as emphatic unison statements of Motif 2 build toward the unleashing of a fugue whose subject is the *passacaglia* theme, stated in even half notes, against a more rhythmically active countersubject. The intensity continues to mount as the subject is developed rigorously according to traditional fugal procedures, while the active countersubject material contributes to the densely woven contrapuntal texture. The complex counterpoint gives way once again, as the driving rhythmic patterns heard earlier in the movement come to the fore, then become backdrop to further treatments of Motifs 1 and 2. Finally, as the complex textural activity begins to congeal, Motif 3 appears, pressing forward to a cathartic, almost ecstatic climax in D major. For the first time in this thirteen-minute movement, the energy gradually diminishes, as Motif 3 is heard in counterpoint with Motif 2 in an increasingly serene epilogue, against a stable harmonic background. The energy continues to subside gradually until the end, as the first violin presents Motif 1 once more as valediction.

Dedicated to his passionate advocate Alex Cohen, the Quartet no. 2 was first performed in London by the Griller Quartet in October 1946, and the following year it was awarded the New York Music Critics Circle Award. At the time, Olin Downes found the quartet to be "in the deepest meaning of the word, the most personal music that [Bloch] has produced; for in these pages he has followed only his inner vision, with no thought of preestablished ideas or concepts of form."[85] The esteemed English critic Ernest Newman called it "the finest work of our time in this genre, one that is worthy to stand beside the last quartets of Beethoven."[86] A number of commentators have identified it as Bloch's greatest work, and it is perhaps the greatest Neo-Romantic string quartet composed in America, capturing both the grim harshness and noble idealism of the composer's spiritual vision at its most eloquent, while representing his compositional mastery at full maturity. A performance of the work by the Pro Arte Quartet, originally released in 1984 (Laurel LR-826CD), is perhaps its most persuasive recorded representation to date.

A work given far less attention than its quality warrants is the Piano Concerto that Bloch completed in 1948. The most expansive work of his Oregon years, it is a moody, dramatic example of mature Neo-Romanticism. As its title suggests, the *Concerto Symphonique* features the piano in the role of shrewd commentator, rather than heroic protagonist, as in the conventional Romantic virtuoso vehicle. Active contributions from the orchestra successfully offset Bloch's limitations in writing for the piano, though the instrument's role is unquestionably central to the work. Although the generally astute commentator Hewell Tircuit describes it as "heroic classicism,"[87] the Concerto is thoroughly romantic in most every way, from its portentous, Rachmaninoffian opening to its extroverted finale. It is classical only in the Brahmsian sense, with a motivically disciplined formal articulation that belies the loose, rhapsodic impression it creates (although the composer does indulge his weakness for sequences in rising minor-thirds as a means of increasing tension). It is also Brahmsian in its expansive scope (with a duration just under forty minutes) and its consistently serious—even grim—attitude.

The opening *Pesante* introduces two important motifs that reappear in various transformations throughout the work. In the first movement, they are associated with two emotional states: the first, brash and resolute, the second, wailing and pleading. The second movement is structured along the lines of a large *scherzo* and trio, in which the trio serves the function of slow movement. The *scherzo* is characteristically grotesque, while the slow trio is predominantly gloomy, with some respite of sweetness. In this movement just a hint of Semitic melodic inflection can be detected. The third movement is a further exploration of the work's main motifs in a free development, grim and emphatic in tone, with little resemblance to classical prototypes. Its most notable feature is a curiously memorable march-like tune—a composite of both of the work's main motifs—sardonic and defiant in character. Though considerably less well known than the Violin Concerto, the *Concerto Symphonique* is a far more interesting and substantive work.

The premiere of the Concerto took place in September 1949 at the
Edinburgh Festival. Bloch conducted the BBC Scottish Orchestra,
with Corinne Lacomblé as piano soloist. Shortly after the performance, D. Hugh Ottaway wrote:

> Blunt in expression, rigorous in structure, this severe and strenuous
> music is a logical late product for a composer of Bloch's qualities. Far
> from being unrepresentative, as some have said, it is an important cul-
> mination of previous trends: like Sibelius's "Tapiola," or the sixth
> symphony of Vaughan Williams, it has the sort of plainness and con-
> centration that comes only with the experience of years. . . . It is the
> music of a man who is clearly to be ranked among the mere handful
> of securely rooted contemporary composers.[88]

Shortly after completing the *Concerto Symphonique*, Bloch produced another work for piano and orchestra. Entitled *Scherzo Fantas-
que*, it may represent the fulfillment of an alternative direction the
composer had considered, then rejected, for the Concerto, but may
have felt was too promising to dismiss altogether. Relative to the
majority of Bloch's output the nine-minute movement might be considered rather lightweight, but this exciting, power-packed little
piece is hardly a frivolous romp. The opening and closing portions
of its straightforward ternary design pursue rapid triplet material in
a driving, percussive *moto perpetuo*, while the central section is somber and brooding, with a distinctly Semitic flavor. Although the relative directness of its impact may be uncharacteristic of Bloch, the
character of the material makes its source easily identifiable. Tersely
articulated, the *Scherzo* is a thoroughly consummated work in which
form, substance, and scope are optimally matched. One can attribute its neglect only to the unwillingness of concert planners to
regard short, one-movement works for solo and orchestra as viable
program options. Its first performance took place in November 1950
as part of a six-day seventieth-birthday tribute to the composer held
in Chicago. Ida Krehm was piano soloist with the Chicago Symphony Orchestra, under the composer's direction.
    Bloch next turned his attention to several smaller pieces, some of
which were more practical, less ambitious, or just simply entertaining. *Six Preludes* (1948) for organ were followed by *Four Wedding
Marches* (1950) and then by *Two Pieces* for string quartet. Of the latter
pieces, the first was actually composed in 1938; its partner appeared

in 1950. In truth neither practical nor entertaining, they are, however, brief—some four minutes apiece. Relative to the short pieces
for string quartet from the 1920s, they are quite stern and severe in
tone, displaying a considerable degree of gritty harmonic dissonance. Terse and concise, they function effectively together as a sort
of prelude and *scherzo*.

That same year (1950), Bloch also composed a *Concertino* for flute,
viola, and strings, on commission from the Juilliard Music Foundation. In three short movements, it is one of the few purely diverting
works in Bloch's entire canon. The first movement is very congenial in
tone, with a sweetly gentle, diatonic modality that anticipates the *Suite
Modale* yet to come. In a similar vein but perhaps a touch more serious,
the second movement maintains a gentle warmth, while offering hints
of ideas that were to be developed more fully in the *Concerto Grosso
no. 2*. The most peculiar third movement starts as a rather ungainly
fugue that, before concluding, breaks into an obviously incongruous
polka. An even broader burlesque is afforded via an alternate ending
entailing the sudden entrance of a full symphony orchestra!

Early in 1951, Bloch composed a group of five short pieces for viola
and piano. Having second thoughts, he separated them into two
smaller subdivisions: *Suite Hébraïque* comprises three of the pieces—
"Rhapsody," "Processional," and "Affirmation"—while the remaining two were presented as *Meditation and Processional*. "Rhapsody" is
the longest movement, occupying more than half the duration of the
Suite Hébraïque. With an explicitly Jewish melos, it represents something of a return to the impassioned language of *Baal Shem*. However,
the four other movements are shorter and more subdued—warmly
melodic and engaging without probing too deeply, their diatonic
modality elaborated through simple polyphony. Bloch arranged the
Suite alternately for violin and piano. Two years later, he orchestrated
the accompaniment as an additional option.

After spending several years on such less ambitious projects,
Bloch then experienced a final burst of creative energy. Between
1952 and his death in 1959 he would complete eight new major
works along with several shorter pieces. None of these compositions
(with the exception perhaps of one of the shorter pieces) has ever
made a significant impact on the public—even the more sophisticated musical public. This is partly because by the 1950s Bloch had
in a sense outlived—and transcended—the pigeonhole to which his
contribution had been consigned. He now found himself an active

participant in America's midcentury traditionalist mainstream in which the leading figures were younger men like Barber, Copland, Hanson, Piston, Creston, Schuman, Persichetti, and Mennin—at a time when most of his own contemporaries had either died or ceased composing. And not only was Bloch still creatively active, but he was still developing artistically, thereby requiring the critical fraternity to continue absorbing and reassessing the nature of his contribution. Rather than do this, they simply disregarded these later works. There were other reasons as well, some of which were specific to individual works and will be noted in the pages that follow. But there are further stylistic factors that make these works difficult to absorb: Consistently serious in tone, they lack ingratiating features—for example, distinctive melodic ideas—that might prove endearing to listeners or at least help to focus their attention; consistently abstract or "absolute" in meaning, they offer nothing picturesque, symbolic, or metaphorical to fix their identity in the listener's mind. Furthermore, Bloch avoided the familiar formal prototypes, with their reassuring symmetries and clear divisions among movements, replacing them with autogenetic multisectional designs and movements often linked together without pauses. The listener is thus left with the experience of a sequence of contrasting episodes connected according to an abstract developmental progression that requires several attentive listenings to grasp. This factor, combined with the remarkable structural concision of these works, largely free of repetition or redundancy, could be expected to leave many listeners quite bewildered.

Bloch produced three compositions of major import in 1952 alone, the year he turned seventy-two. In his String Quartet no. 3, Bloch delved into the drier, abstract approach described above, along the lines of the masterful quartet that preceded it—an approach governed largely by the development and transformation of a few short motifs. At twenty-six minutes, the shortest of his quartets, no. 3 begins vigorously, even aggressively, as it introduces the work's main motifs—especially a sequence of falling fifths, which plays a significant role in each movement. The slow second movement builds inexorably to an impassioned climax before receding. The third movement is a sardonic *scherzo*, with a middle section highlighted by icy harmonics. Based on a twelve-tone theme, the finale recalls the corresponding movement of the Second Quartet—severe in tone and highly contrapuntal, with elements suggesting both *pas-*

sacaglia and fugue—while also anticipating some ideas to be developed more fully in the *Concerto Grosso no. 2*. Despite its complex structure and somewhat forbidding surface impression, the Third Quartet is not purely a product of the intellect: The inner psycho-emotional dynamics that vitalized the composer's previous works remain present but are built into the substance of every phrase instead of being conveyed through broad, theatrical gestures. The result is a rather austere distillation of Bloch's metaphysical essence, as all the abstract elements join in articulating a personal expression focused on the human condition. While the casual listener may find such music harsh, grim, and undifferentiated, greater familiarity enables the work to become increasingly clear and coherent, reflecting an ongoing evolution of the expressive and structural principles that concerned Bloch throughout his career. The Quartet no. 3 was first performed in England by the Griller Quartet, who had also given the premiere of the Quartet no. 2.

Within several months of completing the Quartet no. 3, Bloch composed a second *Concerto Grosso*. This work differs from its predecessor of twenty-seven years earlier in a number of ways beyond simply the absence of a piano. Most significantly, in addition to the didactic intention that engendered it, the *Concerto Grosso no. 1* was largely a diverting work in which superficial characteristics suggestive of the Baroque lent a warmly affectionate "period" flavor to an essentially romantic conception. The later work, however, is a true Neo-Baroque hybrid: a new composition created through an extended application of Baroque principles to materials generally consistent with the norms of the period. The extensions chiefly involve greater—yet still restrained—tolerance and freedom with regard to chromatic modulation and unresolved harmonic dissonance. The finished work is the result of a thoroughly integrated language, rather than merely an application of practices from one era overlaid onto materials characteristic of another. For these reasons, it is one of the most ambitious, substantial, and artistically significant of the many Neo-Baroque efforts pursued during the middle decades of the twentieth century. Other Baroque features of the second *Concerto Grosso* include a strong sense of tonality; largely diatonic melodic lines; regular, motoric note patterns; the use of a string quartet as *concertino* against the full string ensemble as *ripieno*; and an active propensity for tonal and modal counterpoint. Yet at the same time, one of the chief thematic elements, hidden within subordinate lines throughout much of the work, is a motif based on the chromatic scale.

The *Concerto Grosso no. 2* is also remarkable for its healthy affect-ive balance and overall tone of affirmation. It comprises four move-ments: The first opens with a stern majesty, then breaks into a rapid, though equally stern, *fugato* before returning to the stately character of the opening. The slow second movement, based on the opening idea from the first movement, highlights the Dorian mode in a polyphonic treatment of a bittersweet, folk-like melody. The third movement is vigorously contrapuntal and peppered with some sur-prising dissonance. The fourth is suggestive of a chaconne, based on the descending chromatic line. What is notably absent from the work is the "grotesque" element, perhaps the most enduring—indeed ubiquitous—feature of Bloch's style.

Immediately upon completion of the previous work Bloch turned his attention to what he planned as a third *Concerto Grosso*. How-ever, within a few days he changed his conception to a work for full orchestra. Entitled *Sinfonia Breve*, it became his third composition identified with the symphonic genre; not since the *Israel Symphony*, completed thirty-six years earlier, had he used such a title. Compris-ing four movements, with a duration under twenty minutes, the work has the proportions of a classical or Neo-Classical symphony. Yet despite its structural concision, the symphony's titanic emo-tional content, with its progression of rapidly shifting moods, its still-opulent harmonic language notable for a subtly calibrated treat-ment of dissonance, and the richly colored presentation of its musi-cal ideas all qualify it as a work of Neo-Romanticism—indeed, as one of the greatest of Neo-Romantic symphonies—a masterpiece of expressive power distilled into a purely musical discourse con-ducted largely through contrapuntal motivic development.

As the work begins, the opening motifs are embodied in a gesture that seems to be snarling fiercely at the heavens. Henry Cowell com-pared the "unforgettable majesty and purposefulness" of this open-ing to such "glimpses of the infinite" as "the beginning of the Brahms First or the St. Matthew Passion."[89] The symphony's main idea, a five-note motif comprising a conjunct ascent followed by a descent, infuses each movement of the work. After this powerful opening sub-sides into solemn reflection, the tempo suddenly quickens for an energetic contrapuntal development of the main thematic ideas. A cli-max is reached, then the activity subsides once again into an eloquent passage of subdued contemplation, followed by a brief recapitulation of the opening. The slow movement pursues a somber, profoundly searching polyphony, coincidentally (and perhaps coyly), based on a twelve-tone row. Although it does not follow Schoenbergian processes, the tonality is tenuous and the counterpoint often quite dissonant. But as theoretically atonal as the music may be, it never renounces tonal harmonic tendencies as important mechanisms within its dynamic emotional vocabulary. The third movement revives the familiar sardonic *scherzo*—this one especially mocking in character. The trio section evokes primitive, exotic imagery reminiscent of Bloch's music from the 1920s. The finale returns to the vigor and forcefulness of the opening movement for further development of the main motifs, then subsides into a reminiscence of the second movement, followed by a subdued return to the closing of the first movement, bringing the work full circle to a quiescent resolution.

Both the *Concerto Grosso no. 2* and the *Sinfonia Breve* were introduced at the same concert in London in April 1953. Sir Malcolm Sargent conducted the BBC Orchestra. Discussing the two works, Cowell wrote:

> [Bloch] has broadened his resources to include more free dissonance, more chromaticism, and an extension of the use of old modes to include rapid modulation and transposition. The highly charged emotional utterance of his earlier music is still there, but it is framed in clearer form, and the improvisatory quality of his passionate outbursts has given way to a calmer level of musical intensity and compassion. It bears little relation to present-day musical fashion but it is music that by its humanity, its honesty, and its technical mastery is fit to stand beside the great music Bloch himself has most admired.[90]

Sinfonia Breve was introduced to American audiences in November 1953 by the Cleveland Orchestra, conducted by George Szell.

During the closing days of 1952, Bloch managed to complete one more orchestral piece: an elegy in memory of Ada Clement, one of the founders of the San Francisco Conservatory. Less than five minutes long, *In Memoriam* is a solemn processional displaying an almost Elgarian nobility and beauty.

The following year, Bloch composed a fourth string quartet, which he dedicated to the English critic Ernest Chapman. It reveals a considerable step in the direction of further abstraction, relative to its predecessor of the previous year. Indeed, a number of factors make it perhaps the most difficult of all Bloch's works to grasp and appreciate: It is harmonically harsh and dissonant, largely atonal, tightly focused on the development of motifs identifiable more as abstract combinations of intervals than as characterizable entities, with frequent shifts of mood and tempo, its forms developed organically, rather than through classical expectations and symmetries. In fact, considered apart from the rest of the composer's output, its emphasis on abstract process over expressive content makes the quartet hard to justify as an example of Neo-Romanticism.

The first movement of the Quartet no. 4 opens in a mood of repose, as wisp-like ideas gradually germinate, focusing on the expansion of a minor-third to major and on the tritone as central motivic units. The austere opening leads to a more vigorous developmental passage. This alternation between repose and activity is repeated until the movement ends similarly as it began. The second movement has a more tangible lyrical focus, introducing a modal melody of Dorian cast. The movement gradually builds to a climax of considerable intensity. The *scherzo* is built upon two ideas: The first is introduced against a *pizzicato* background, the second is a simple motif characterized by a breathless urgency. The trio section presents this same, rather peculiar melody—almost like a child's whining—*sul ponticello*, in an eerie polytonal context. Bloch identified this tune, which found its way into several of his later works, as Eskimo in origin. The fourth movement is similar to the first in character, beginning and ending slowly, with frequent reminders of the Eskimo tune and with a vigorous central section devoted to the contrapuntal development of a twelve-tone theme. The Quartet no. 4, like its two predecessors, was introduced by the Griller Quartet in London in January 1954.

Having completed his Fourth String Quartet, Bloch next turned his attention to a fourth symphony—this one highlighting the solo trombone. The idea for such a work was prompted by the trombonist Davis Shuman, who actively commissioned works featuring his instrument from a number of leading composers. Why Bloch decided to conceptualize the work as a "symphony," rather than a "concerto," is unclear. Although his Violin Concerto might be characterized as a virtuoso vehicle, while not without deeper aspirations as well, the *"Symphonique"* identification of the Piano Concerto makes its disavowal of the "showpiece" approach more explicit. Perhaps calling the new work *Symphony for Trombone and Orchestra* simply took the point one step further. In any case, the Trombone Symphony is far from a virtuoso vehicle. Its musical language hearkens back to the richly colored Hebraic evocations of *Schelomo* and the *Israel Symphony*, although its mode of expression avoids the rhetorical abandon found in those works, maintaining the greater sense of composure heard in his more recent compositions. Although commentators have often related the use of the trombone to the *shofar*, the instrument made from a ram's horn described in the Old Testament and still used in Jewish religious services, this is only partially warranted; much of the instrument's role suggests that of a wise and eloquent cantor, delivering an extended commentary on the parade of life. Shorter in duration than the *Sinfonia Breve*, the Trombone Symphony places an extended *scherzo*-type movement with long cantorial episodes between a short introductory incantation and a ferociously energetic peroration highlighted by grand gestures but ending in tranquil resignation. More so than in Bloch's other recent works, some of the thematic material draws upon archaic associations, and the fundamentally triadic basis of the symphony's harmonic language and its strong sense of tonal rootedness are clearly apparent. But much of the writing is so consistently chromatic that there is little actual tonal stability. Completed in June 1954, the first performance of the Trombone Symphony did not take place until April 1956 when Davis Shuman introduced it with the Houston Symphony, under the direction of Leopold Stokowski.

Upon finishing the Trombone Symphony, Bloch turned his attention once more to what he envisioned as another *concerto grosso*. But again the ideas that began to germinate required the full orchestra, giving rise to one more essay in the symphonic genre—his fifth and last, the Symphony in E-flat. The work may be readily characterized as Bloch's most "classical" symphony: Not only does it return to the traditional four-movement format, but it is also less turbulent in expressive content, its emotionalism kept well in check, contained within the inherent stresses of motivic development. However, more consistent with Bloch's recent approach to form than with classical practice, the first movement follows an autogenetic, rather than *sonata allegro*, design, beginning slowly and mysteriously and introducing a four-note motif that will be the symphony's essential germ. This motif—consisting of a descending minor-second, an ascending diminished-fourth, and another descending minor-second—is aptly compared by commentators to the familiar B-A-C-H motif (although it resembles Shostakovich's perhaps less well-known autobiographical motif—D-Es-C-H—just as much). The potential of this motif is explored through a somber polyphony until a passage marked with the increasingly common *Allegro deciso* follows with a vigorous, rhythmically syncopated, less contrapuntal treatment of the material. This alternation of tempos is repeated until the movement ends in the sober manner with which it began. The character of the *scherzo* that follows suggests the composer's familiar sardonic manner, but its execution is more abstract and reserved, less obvious or visceral in its impact. The use of a twelve-tone theme creates an atonal effect, although there is enough stability among other elements—rhythm, especially—that it is barely noticeable. The trio section offers only a slight change in character. The slow movement that follows is darkly introspective, developing its long melodic line with considerable eloquence but toward a climax that is again more conceptual than visceral. There is a curious, though unmistakable, reference to a motif that figured significantly in the last movement of the Piano Quintet no. 1. The finale—*Allegro deciso* again—recalls the grim, rhythmically accented character and actual material of the fast portions of the first movement before returning to the somber eloquence of the slower passages. The work ends quietly, but somewhat quizzically, without the sense of comfort and resolution one has come to expect from Bloch's endings.

Bloch completed the Symphony in E-flat in March 1955. Ian White conducted the BBC Scottish Orchestra in the work's first performance in September 1956. The American premiere took place two months later, with Thor Johnson conducting the Cincinnati Symphony Orchestra. However, no recording of the symphony appeared until 1997; a second recording followed five years later.

Within a couple of months of completing the Symphony in E-flat, Bloch wrote a short *Proclamation* for trumpet and orchestra, dedicating it to Samuel Laderman, a vigorous advocate of the composer's music in Chicago. The five-minute *Proclamation* is conceived along similar lines to the Trombone Symphony, gently evoking the Jewish context familiar from Bloch's works of forty years earlier, while using the solo instrument to trigger associations with both the *shofar* and the cantorial voice in delivering a commentary of rather dour eloquence.

Although his health had begun to deteriorate, Bloch spent the rest of 1955 on his fifth and last string quartet, completing the work in early 1956. A little more than half an hour in duration, the Quartet no. 5 follows the approach pursued by the composer in most of his recent abstract works. Rather difficult to grasp and appreciate, it is consistently severe in tone, with the slight exception of the *scherzo*, whose discrete sections and contrasting material make it somewhat easier to follow. On the other hand, although the work comprises four movements, the first two and the last two are connected, further complicating the task of following it aurally. Again, there is a strong overall awareness of tonal dynamic tendencies, although much of the thematic material is in itself atonal. The first movement, which introduces some seven different motifs, is subdivided into three sections—two *Grave* sections flanking a central *Allegro*. However, the *Allegro* itself comprises three sections, of which the central one is slow and similar to the large outer sections of the movement. The overall character of the movement, during which the main motifs are developed, chiefly through counterpoint, is austere, somber, and introspective. The subdued ending of the first movement elides with the slow second movement. Also quite severe, following on the heels of the opening, it makes a rather drab, colorless impression, with little expressive contour. The *scherzo* that follows is marked *Presto*, offering the quartet's strongest point of contrast. As in others of Bloch's recent works, the "grotesque" element is considerably softened to the point where the music is best characterized as simply grim. The trio section introduces an ironic note with an oddly banal tune fragment. The final movement opens with a sequence of triads—an unusual effect for Bloch that calls Messiaen to mind. Though it is marked *Allegro deciso*, the vigor of the opening soon abates, as motifs heard earlier in the work are reviewed, leading to a quiescent ending. Bloch's daughter Suzanne, to whom the quartet is dedicated, commented that not until she watched her father die three years later did she realize that the ending of the Fifth Quartet was a musical anticipation of that moment.[91]

In April 1956, Bloch embarked on a project clearly in homage to his beloved Johann Sebastian Bach: a series of six suites for unaccompanied string instruments. There were three for cello, two for violin, and one for viola, the latter of which remained incomplete at the time of his death. He finished the three for cello in January 1957, dedicating the first two to Zara Nelsova, the Canadian cellist whose frequent performances of both *Schelomo* and *Voice in the Wilderness* were highly favored by the composer. The three Cello Suites differ somewhat in concept. Nos. 1 and 3 follow Baroque precedent fairly closely. No. 1 comprises four movements according to the pattern of a *sonata da chiesa*, while the five movements of no. 3 suggest a conventional Baroque suite. The Baroque style is also suggested by regular note patterns, symmetrical phrase sequences, and strong tonal centers, despite some Blochian flights of chromaticism. Suite no. 2 is longer than the other two, however, and quite different in style. Although again comprising a sequence of four movements in contrasting tempos, the Baroque notion functions here more as a theoretical abstraction, the basis of a modern treatment. The movements are linked together, rather than discrete. The music itself bears little similarity with eighteenth-century practice: deeply personal, introspective, and searching, the Suite no. 2 is quite austere, with irregular phrases and tenuous tonal centers.

The one work from Bloch's final years that has made some inroads into the active repertoire is the *Suite Modale*, a twelve-minute piece for flute and strings completed in 1957, although it is played often in an arrangement for flute and piano as well. Its relative popularity is easily explained by its warm and gracious accessibility, as well as by the fact that it was recorded by Murray Panitz and the Philadelphia Orchestra during the late 1960s. One of Bloch's few works of diverting intent, the *Suite* comprises four linked movements in a style that recalls such compositions as the *Concertino* of 1950, the *Meditation and Processional*, and portions of *Suite Hébraïque*. The overall mood is slightly plaintive, but sweet and gentle, with little significant contrast. The melodic lines are largely diatonic, with occasional chromatic interjections that proclaim Bloch's identity. The modes featured are primarily the Phrygian, Aeolian, and Dorian, but modulations and modal mixtures occur freely.

The first performance of *Suite Modale* took place in March 1957 when it was presented in the version with piano by flutist John Wummer, accompanied by Leonid Hambro. The orchestral version was not performed until April 1965 when Elaine Shaffer, to whom the *Suite* was dedicated, performed it at the College of Marin, in Kentfield, California.

Bloch's last major work was the Piano Quintet no. 2, composed during the first half of 1957. If the Quintet no. 1 is one of the masterpieces of the 1920s, then the Second, composed thirty-four years after its predecessor, occupies a similar place among the works of the 1950s. Although similar gaps separate the First and Second *Concerti Grossi* (twenty-seven years) and the First and Second String Quartets (twenty-nine years), a comparison of the two Piano Quintets reveals—more clearly than any other works—the differences and consistencies in style, form, expression, and technique between the music of Bloch's early maturity and that of his later maturity. If the major chamber works of the 1920s seem like extravagant emotional outbursts, ablaze with nightmarish visions of impending doom, by the time he had reached the last decade of his life, Bloch had achieved a significant condensation of his musical language, without really diminishing its intensity or otherwise moderating its expressive content. The rhetoric is simply less extravagant, the form less rhapsodic, the rhythm more regular, and the gestures less expansive. There is also a reduced emphasis on texture or on evoking exotic atmospheres.

The Second Piano Quintet is an astonishing work for a man of seventy-seven, already afflicted with terminal cancer: outer movements bold and forceful, with a driving, heavily accented rhythmic vigor and a slow movement of grave, contemplative eloquence. Like his other late chamber works, the Second Quintet, a little more than half the length of its predecessor, can be described as concise and contained. It is also the fullest realization of Bloch's unique mode of Expressionism: powerful emotional and spiritual content conveyed through the concentrated development of abstract musical ideas within a harmonic language with allegiance to neither tonality nor the enforced absence of tonality, but, rather, based on the expressive power of subtly graded dissonances and inherent tonal tendencies within an atonal context. Along with the *Sinfonia Breve*, the Second Piano Quintet may be regarded as the masterpiece of Bloch's final decade. It was not performed until December 1959, several months after the composer's death, when it was introduced in New York City by the Juilliard String Quartet, with pianist Leonid Hambro.

Moved by the flute playing of Elaine Shaffer, who had sent him a tape of the *Suite Modale*, Bloch decided to feature the instrument in one more work, which he entitled *Two Last Poems*, scoring the accompaniment for full orchestra. He composed the piece during the autumn of 1957, completing it in January of the following year. There is no mistaking the concerns on Bloch's mind while working on these pieces: The first, called "Funeral Music," leads directly into the second, "Life Again?" Here the flute plays a role not unlike that assigned to the trombone and the trumpet, in the Symphony of 1954 and the *Proclamation* of 1955 respectively (i.e., as the voice of a spontaneous and rather rhapsodic discourse on the weighty issues of life). As in those works, although there is no explicit reference to the effect, the musical style displays Semitic modal inflections and other features familiar from the composer's overtly Jewish pieces. Despite its title, there is no anguish or morbidity to the "Funeral Music," which is subdued, reflective, even tranquil in character. "Life Again?" offers little contrast, maintaining much the same tone as the first piece, although it develops into the semblance of a slow, Middle Eastern dance, the flute's role evoking an almost serpentine image. Picturesque and colorful, the music builds, through romantic gestures, to quite a climax before subsiding into calm, benign acceptance. It is remarkable that after forty-five years of stylistic evolution, development, and maturation, Bloch produced a work at the end of his life that strongly harks back to the style and tone of the *Trois Poèmes Juifs*, which he had composed in 1913 in memory of his father, who had just passed away.

On the front of the manuscript of the *Two Last Poems*, Bloch had appended a parenthetical "Maybe," and this word has generally been taken to be part of the title, although it may actually have been a marginal comment of a more personal nature, stemming from a superstitious fear. In any case, the word proved prophetic, because Bloch had still more to say in music. In the spring of 1958, the composer had been delighted by a visit from Yehudi Menuhin and his wife. After looking at the unaccompanied Cello Suite Bloch had recently completed, Menuhin asked for a piece of this kind for violin. Soon afterward, Bloch complied with his request, sending off a Suite for Violin Solo with a dedication to Menuhin. The violinist promptly sent off a rather large check in gratitude to the surprised composer, who responded by writing a sequel to the Suite as a gift. Menuhin was deeply moved by this gesture from a man who had honored him similarly thirty years earlier, when he was a boy of twelve, with *Abodah*. The violinist described the two Suites as "heart-searching, profoundly moving and noble expressions of a human soul and a human mind, which remained incredibly constant throughout his life."[92]

Both Suites are approximately eleven minutes long. No. 1 comprises three movements, of which the last is subdivided into three sections, while no. 2 is composed of four connected movements. The respective first movements of each Suite combine dramatic, even romantic, gestures with an angular, acerbic tonal language, and are quite searching in character. The subsequent movements settle a bit more comfortably into Neo-Baroque figurations and a more clearly tonal syntax. The rapid last movement of Suite no. 2 is especially virtuosic, but both Suites are extremely challenging to the violinist throughout. Although the music is readily comprehensible at all times, its appeal is understandably limited in light of its fundamental restrictions with regard to harmony, texture, and tone color. Although a number of commentators, perhaps influenced by a "less is more" aesthetic that equates distillation and condensation with mastery, have proclaimed Bloch's solo suites as "the ultimate expression of the composer's genius,"[93] it is difficult to consider music so rarefied to be the ultimate expression of such an expansive, robust, and carnal creative personality.

As the summer of 1958 approached, Bloch undertook another unaccompanied suite, this one for viola. However, his energy was rapidly waning, and in late summer he underwent major surgery. Although he was to live another ten months, he composed no more. The vigorous fourth and final movement of the Suite for Viola Solo remained incomplete. As in the Violin Suites, the first movement is speculative and searching. The second movement suggests a gigue, while the slow third is quite chromatic, yet tonal; the fourth, appropriately enough, carries what had become the composer's favored tempo indication: *Allegro deciso.*

CONCLUSION

When Ernest Bloch died in July 1959, the obituary in the *New York Times*—a representative measure of public stature at a given time—stated:

> Mr. Bloch, one of the most important composers of the present century, neither founded a school nor had active disciples, as has been the case with many of his contemporary colleagues. His music was much too original to be imitated; and, while Mr. Bloch himself was a noted pedagogue, he never foisted his own theories upon his pupils, . . . Yet by force of his musical personality and the uncompromising honesty of his ideas, he was recognized even by those who did not agree with his principles as one of the masters of contemporary music.[94]

But Bloch's reputation among the musical public was still based primarily on the works associated with his Jewish heritage, chiefly *Schelomo*, the *Sacred Service*, and *Baal Shem* (the *"Nigun"* movement, in particular)—all composed before the mid-1930s. The *Concerto*

Grosso no. 1 (1925) had found a niche in the repertoire as well. A number of other works, for example, *America: An Epic Rhapsody*, were well known by name but were infrequently performed.

During the 1960s, as contemporary musical fashion became increasingly polarized between the fashionable serialists and the outmoded traditionalists, Bloch's reputation as a composer of rhapsodic, passionately emotional, richly scored orchestral canvases relegated him to the periphery of the contemporary scene. Less and less frequently was his name linked with other moderate Modernists still held to be "important," like Stravinsky, Bartók, and Prokofiev.

Some have attributed Bloch's marginalization to the overpopularity of *Schelomo*. It has happened more than once that music initially responsible for drawing widespread attention to a composer later proves to circumscribe his identity. In fact, the Ernest Bloch Society, which was revived in the United States in 1967 by daughters Suzanne and Lucienne, urged (with tongue somewhat in cheek) a moratorium on performances of *Schelomo* to enable some of his other works to gain a hearing.

During the 1970s, a new schism within the world of classical music began to develop. Although a thorough examination of the phenomenon is beyond the purview of this study, suffice it to say that this division entailed the world of "live performance" on the one hand and the world of recordings on the other. The world of live performance (i.e. touring celebrity soloists, municipal orchestras, their jet-set music directors, and their subscription series) increasingly concentrated on a narrow repertoire of established classics. While the largest and most venerable classical record companies continued to concentrate on this narrow repertoire, as performed by the most celebrated conductors, soloists, and ensembles, smaller independent companies began to explore an ever-broadening range of repertoire, featuring lesser-known works by major composers as well as major works of lesser-known composers, performed by less-familiar artists and orchestras located in more peripheral countries. During the 1980s the gap continued to widen, as ever-increasing recording costs faced by the major companies further reduced the number of new releases they could afford to issue, while improvements in recording technology and the advent of the compact disc revitalized the independent classical recording industry, which now offered a competitive alternative— rather than supplementary—medium through which to discover and appreciate classical music, tailored to an individual's personal tastes and interests. Of particular significance was the fact that this recording-driven market for classical music was less subject to the influence of "recognized" authorities and their "official" aesthetic doctrines. As a result, many composers known to concertgoers through only a handful of works were gradually represented on recordings that documented their entire outputs.

Ernest Bloch was one of the composers whose reputations benefited from this new and growing constituency. With the occurrence of his 100th birthday in 1980, independent record companies began to undertake major projects to document previously unexplored areas of his output. Among the most notable were a project begun in 1982 by Laurel Records to record all of Bloch's chamber music, the first recording of all five string quartets by the Portland String Quartet in 1983, the first commercial recording of the Symphony in C-sharp minor in 1988 and the first recording of the complete piano music in 1989—both by Marco Polo, first recordings of the *Evocations* in 1994, of the Symphony in E-flat in 1997, and of *Macbeth* in 2000 (followed by another in 2001). By 2002, virtually all of Bloch's music was available on recordings, most in performances of the highest quality. However, although journals catering to this constituency have heralded these recordings with enthusiasm, there has been little corresponding recognition from the academic mainstream. As Brotman wrote in 1998:

> Ernest Bloch is rarely described as a major composer in general surveys of "twentieth-century music" in America. Mostly remembered today as a talented "late-romantic" eclectic who used Jewish themes in his best scores before turning to a neoclassical style later in life, he has been relegated to a position on the sidelines of modern music history, depicted as a relatively insignificant composer in comparison with such aural experimentalists as Edgard Varèse and Charles Ives.[95]

On the other hand, during the mid-1980s, the French scholar Joseph Lewinski began an exhaustive, four-volume account of Bloch's life. Published in Geneva by Editions Slatkine, the first volume appeared in 1998, the second in 2001, the third in 2003, with the fourth scheduled for 2005. An English-language edition is currently in progress. And, at the other extreme, in 2002 Greenwood Press published David Z. Kushner's concise 198-page *Ernest Bloch Companion*.

Although Bloch might not have spawned a school of disciples, a number of commentators, including this writer, have pointed to his work as a model of artistic integrity. During a period when competition for the limelight among the sterile, the fraudulent, and the meretricious left the field in a state of aesthetic anarchy, Bloch held steadfastly to a view of art as a vehicle for the expression of a personal perspective on life's most serious issues, while emphasizing the equivalent importance of sound compositional craftsmanship in making such expression coherent and meaningful. As George Jellinek wrote, Bloch was "a great composer without any narrowing qualifications whatever, and the forerunner of a world of music which has superseded dodecaphony and returned to counterpoint and modal juxtaposition."[96] As an eloquent exponent of traditional romantic musical values during a period when such values were held in disrepute, Bloch earns a place as the first great American Neo-Romantic.

On the other hand, the Neo-Romantic aesthetic, as represented by Bloch, is not to everyone's taste. As Tim Page wrote with remarkable candor, "Bloch attracts a partisan audience; generally speaking, a listener takes to his work strongly or not at all. As one who is temperamentally uncomfortable with displays of angst, this listener has often found Bloch's expressionism difficult to take. It's all so emotive, so deadly serious; even the composer's occasional humor seems clenched in grimace. One occasionally wishes that Bloch had learned to bear his lot with greater resignation."[97]

Robert Strassburg concluded his monograph *Ernest Bloch: Voice in the Wilderness* with a statement that eloquently captures the quality of this composer's symbolic greatness and links him aesthetically with the other composers selected for this study:

> Bloch regarded composing as an act of faith, a means of making man more human. His music possesses an ethos and spirituality associated with the music of Bach and Beethoven, and he shares in large measure their unshakable faith in an eternal God, and their humanistic concerns with mankind's problems. Whatever may be the final judgment regarding the enduring quality of his works, there can be little doubt that he fulfilled his destiny as a composer in such a way that at the close of his life he could truthfully say, "My sole desire and single effort has been to remain faithful to my Vision, to be True."[98]

NOTES

1. Quoted by Robert Strassburg, *Ernest Bloch: Voice in the Wilderness* (Los Angeles: Trident Shop, 1977), 58.

2. Strassburg, *Ernest Bloch*, 5.

3. Quoted by David Z. Kushner, *The Ernest Bloch Companion* (Westport, Conn.: Greenwood Press, 2002), 44–45.

4. Quoted by Kushner, *Ernest Bloch Companion*, 20.

5. Ernest Bloch, "Gustav Mahler and the Second Symphony," trans. David Sills, reprinted in *Ernest Bloch Society Bulletin* (1984).

6. Quoted by Strassburg, *Ernest Bloch*, 20.

7. Quoted by Kushner, *Ernest Bloch Companion*, 31.

8. Quoted by Strassburg, *Ernest Bloch*, 15.

9. Olin Downes, "Ernest Bloch at Sixty," *New York Times* (27 October 1940).

10. Unsigned review, *Musical America* (12 April 1919): 9.

11. John Rockwell, "Critic's Notebook," *New York Times* (23 August 1984), reprinted in *Ernest Bloch Society Bulletin* (1985).

12. Herbert Peyser, "Unique Music by Ernest Bloch Receives Notable Exposition," *Musical America* (12 May 1917): 10.

13. Peyser, Review, *Musical America* (19 March 1918), quoted in Ernest Bloch, *Biography and Comment* (San Francisco: Margaret Mary Morgan Co., 1925), 11.

14. Peyser, "Unique Music," 9.

15. Charles Brotman, "The Winner Loses: Ernest Bloch and His *America*," *American Music* (Winter 1998): 420.

16. Brotman, "The Winner Loses," 427–428.

17. Guido Gatti, "Ernest Bloch," *La Critica Musicale* (April–May 1920), trans. Theodore Baker, reprinted in *Musical Quarterly* (January 1921): 35.

18. Quoted by Strassburg, *Ernest Bloch*, 51–52.

19. Roger Sessions, "Ernest Bloch," *Modern Music* (Nov–Dec 1927): 10.

20. Brotman, "The Winner Loses," 429.

21. Daniel Gregory Mason, *Tune In, America* (New York: Knopf, 1931), 160–161.

22. Kushner, *Ernest Bloch Companion*, 43.

23. Ernest Bloch, *America: An Epic Rhapsody* (Boston: C. C. Birchard, 1928), i.

24. Brotman, "The Winner Loses," 440.

25. Olin Downes, Review, *Musical America* (29 December 1928): 7.

26. Brotman, "The Winner Loses," 434–435.

27. John Burk, Review, *Modern Music* (May–June 1939): 256.

28. John Tasker Howard, *Our American Music: Three Hundred Years of It* (New York: Thomas Y. Crowell, 1931), 517–518.

29. Brotman, "The Winner Loses," 440.

30. Quoted by Kushner, *Ernest Bloch Companion*, 88.

31. Quoted by Strassburg, *Ernest Bloch*, 70.

32. Kushner, *Ernest Bloch Companion*, 152.

33. Quoted by Strassburg, *Ernest Bloch*, 49.

34. *Ernest Bloch Society Bulletin* (1982), 2.

35. Quoted by Strassburg, *Ernest Bloch*, 138.

36. Quoted by Kushner, *Ernest Bloch Companion*, 94.

37. Kushner, *Ernest Bloch Companion*, 111.

38. Howard Taubman, "Ernest Bloch at 70—A Musician Apart," *New York Times Magazine* (18 July 1950): 17.

39. Quoted by Strassburg, *Ernest Bloch*, 88.

40. Ivan Bloch, "Pater Familias," in *The Spiritual and Artistic Odyssey of Ernest Bloch: A Centenary Retrospective* (Charleston, SC: Piccolo Spoleto, 1980), 35–36.

41. David Ewen, "Ernest Bloch, The Composer Speaks," in *The Book of Modern Composers* (New York: Alfred A. Knopf, 1950), 252.

42. Henry Cowell, "Current Chronicle," *Musical Quarterly* (April 1954): 235.

43. Alfred Meyer, "What Music Means to Ernest Bloch," *Christian Science Monitor* (16 March 1939).

44. John Erling, Record Liner Notes, Laurel LR-120, 1982.

45. Raymond Hall, Review, *New York Times* (27 March 1938).

46. Harold Schonberg, Review, *New York Times* (11 May 1973).

47. Sessions, "Ernest Bloch," 4.

48. Gatti, "Ernest Bloch," 24.

49. Kushner, *Ernest Bloch Companion*, 27.

50. Olin Downes, Review, *New York Times* (11 February 1924).

51. Harry Halbreich, Record Liner Notes, Timpani 1C1052, 1999.

52. Quoted by Strassburg, *Ernest Bloch*, 38.

53. Gatti, "Ernest Bloch," 31.

54. Olin Downes, Review, *New York Times* (6 February 1924).

55. Herbert Peyser, Review, *Musical America* (12 May 1917).

56. Kushner, *Ernest Bloch Companion*, 5.

57. Ernest Bloch, "Man and Music," *The Seven Arts* (March 1917): 498.

58. Kushner, *Ernest Bloch Companion*, 5.

59. Gatti, "Ernest Bloch," 20–21.

60. Sessions, "Ernest Bloch," 5–6.

61. Bloch was unequivocal about this when he wrote to Alfred Pochon. Suzanne Bloch and Irene Heskes, *Ernest Bloch: Creative Spirit* (New York: Jewish Music Council of the National Jewish Welfare Board, 1976), 52.

62. The composer warned Pochon, "will make you grind your teeth." Suzanne Bloch and Heskes, *Ernest Bloch*, 53.

63. Quoted by Kushner, *Ernest Bloch Companion*, 37.

64. A. Veinus, Record liner notes, RCA Victor M-575, 1939.

65. Herbert Peyser, Review, *Musical America* (4 October 1919).

66. Gatti, "Ernest Bloch," 29.

67. Oscar Sonneck, Footnote to Gatti Article, *Musical Quarterly* (January 1921): 34.

68. Suzanne Bloch, Record Liner Notes, Arabesque Z6605, 1989.

69. Paul Rosenfeld, "The Bloch *Violin Sonata*," in *Musical Chronicle (1917–1923)* (New York: Harcourt, Brace, and Co., 1923), 131.

70. Gatti, "Ernest Bloch," 34–35.

71. Alex Cohen, Program Notes, Ernest Bloch Society (London), 1937.

72. Sessions, "Ernest Bloch," 6–8.

73. Olin Downes, "Bloch Festival," *New York Times* (10 December 1950).

74. David Z. Kushner, Record Liner Notes, Arabesque Z6618, 1991.

75. Ernest Newman, "The Bloch *Quintet*," in *More Essays from the World of Music* (London: John Calder, 1958), 46.

76. Kushner, *Ernest Bloch Companion*, 56.

77. "Bloch's Rhapsody Wins Award," *Musical America* (9 June 1928).

78. Lawrence Gilman, Review, *New York Herald Tribune* (21 December 1928).

79. S. Bloch, Record Liner Note, Arabesque Z6605. 1989.

80. Program Notes, *The Spiritual and Artistic Odyssey of Ernest Bloch* (Charleston, SC: Piccolo Spoleto, 1980), 6.

81. Quoted by Kushner, *Ernest Bloch Companion*, 93.

82. Quoted by Strassburg, *Ernest Bloch*, 71.

83. Quoted by Strassburg, *Ernest Bloch*, 74.

84. Ernest Bloch, Letter to Henry Minsky, 17 September 1944.

85. Olin Downes, Review, *New York Times* (27 February 1947).

86. Ernest Newman, Review, *London Sunday Times* (13 October 1946).

87. Hewell Tircuit, Record Liner Notes, Vanguard VCD-72031, 1988.

88. D. Hugh Ottaway, "Looking Again at Ernest Bloch," *Musical Times* (June, 1950): 235.

89. Cowell, "Current Chronicle," 237.

90. Cowell, "Current Chronicle," 242.

91. Suzanne Bloch, Record Liner Notes, Arabesque 6511-3, 1983.

92. Suzanne Bloch, Record Liner Notes, Arabesque Z6606, 1989.

93. Quoted by Strassburg, *Ernest Bloch*, 97.

94. Unsigned Obituary, *New York Times* (16 July 1959).

95. Brotman, "The Winner Loses," 419.

96. George Jellinek, "Ernest Bloch Begins a Modest Comeback," *New York Times* (18 September 1988).

97. Tim Page, Review, *New York Times* (4 November 1984).

98. Strassburg, *Ernest Bloch*, 98.

Howard Hanson: Photo provided courtesy of Carl Fischer Music

3

Howard Hanson

There is probably no composer more closely identified with Neo-Romanticism as an ideology than Howard Hanson. A man of enormous energy, ambition, and intelligence, driven by fervently held ideals, he devoted his long and immensely productive career to realizing his vision of music in America. Musicologist Joseph Machlis wrote of Hanson, "It may safely be said that in the second quarter of the twentieth century, no individual in the United States did more for the cause of American music than he."[1] As a composer, Hanson is known chiefly for one work, a symphony to which he defiantly added the subtitle "Romantic." Achieving nationwide acclaim while still in his twenties, he lived to see himself marginalized during the last two decades of his life, because of his consistent adherence to values and ideals, rooted in the piety of small-town life in "middle America," that increasingly seemed "old-fashioned" and authoritarian when seen against the hard-edged intellectualism, anarchic radicalism, and sneering cynicism of the 1960s and 1970s.

BIOGRAPHY

Howard Hanson was born in 1896 to Swedish parents in the town of Wahoo, Nebraska, which boasted a large Swedish American community. His father Hans owned a local hardware store, and his mother Hilma was an enthusiastic amateur musician; Howard was

111

their only surviving offspring. "My mother was very musical," he told an interviewer in 1978:

> She had a good voice and was a good singer. She studied very seri-ously, she played the piano, and even . . . studied strict counterpoint. I think I got a great deal of my musical interest from her. My father liked music and was always very interested in what I was writing, and he listened to it and got me to play it for him when I was very young and making my beginning efforts in composition, but he had had no study of music at all; he just happened to appreciate it.[2]

His mother began giving Howard music lessons at a young age, and he made rapid progress, studying both piano and cello while still a schoolboy.

Deeply infused with the Lutheran values that pervaded his family and his community, the young Hanson grew up with a sense of moral obligation to use his talent and intellect for noble purposes and to use the means at his disposal to share the joys of musical expression as widely as possible.

> I was very much interested in religion, I think too much so, really. I worried too much about religion. I remember that as a young boy, when the minister would say when he gave you the bread, "Eat ye all of it" and I'd think, "Suppose a crumb should get caught in my teeth—would that lead to everlasting damnation?" The Lutherans were very strict, at least in those days. I wasn't exactly fundamental, but it was very much the Old Testament—a very stern religion. The music of the chorales is pretty serious material, and this impressed me very greatly.[3]

In high school, Hanson played in the school orchestra (conducting it occasionally as well) and sang in the choir; he graduated as vale-dictorian at the age of fifteen, while taking courses in theory and composition and conducting at Wahoo's Luther College. "Basically, . . . I was (probably without knowing it) very ambi-tious—I didn't want to be second or third in the class—I wanted to be first in the class, and I always was. I wanted to be the best pianist around there, not the next best. That was a kind of an ambition that probably helped me in professional life later on—that I was driving myself a little bit, probably, all my life."[4]

In 1913, Hanson traveled to New York City to study at the Institute of Musical Art (later the Juilliard School). There he worked intensively with the conservative theorist Percy Goetschius, who granted him a diploma after one year. "I learned a lot about counterpoint from him, but very little attention was paid to original composition," he later recollected. "They were mostly exercises that you did. You wrote canons and fugues and different forms. . . . He wrote me after my fourth symphony won the Pulitzer Prize; . . . By that time, he was in his eighties, and he said that he had heard it on the radio, and that he liked it very much . . . but he wanted to warn me against using modern devices."[5]

While in New York, Hanson had the experience of hearing one of his orchestral works conducted by Frank Damrosch and made the decision to concentrate his efforts on composing. However, realizing that he would need to find a way of supporting himself, he decided upon teaching and entered the liberal arts program at Northwestern University, with a major in music. There he continued his studies in piano, cello, and composition, receiving his bachelor's degree after two years. While he was studying at Northwestern, Frederick Stock led the Chicago Symphony in another of his orchestral works.

In 1916, Hanson was offered a position as full professor of theory and composition at the College of the Pacific, in San Jose, California. Three years later, he accepted an appointment as Dean of the College's Conservatory of Fine Arts, thus beginning his career as an arts administrator at the age of twenty-three. During his years at San Jose, Hanson composed quite actively as well, producing a number of substantial works, including the *Concerto da Camera,* a Piano Sonata, *Scandinavian Suite,* and the *Symphonic Rhapsody.*

In 1921, Hanson won the Prix de Rome, the first such prize to be awarded by the American Academy in Rome. In addition to giving the precocious but provincial young man firsthand exposure to the Old World, the award enabled him to enjoy three years with no other responsibilities than to study and compose. While in Italy, he arranged to take lessons from Ottorino Respighi, who deepened Hanson's understanding of orchestration. He also became acquainted with the English conductor Albert Coates. During this period, he composed his Symphony no. 1, "Nordic," the String Quartet, and the tone poem *Lux Aeterna.*

While he was in Italy, Hanson's reputation was growing in the United States. He even interrupted his European sojourn to conduct his "Nordic" Symphony with the Rochester Philharmonic, at the invitation of Coates, then the orchestra's music director. While he was in Rochester, Coates introduced him to George Eastman, a wealthy entrepreneur who had used part of the fortune he had made in the photography business to establish a music school within the University of Rochester. Seeking to propel the school to national prominence, he solicited Hanson's thoughts on the matter. Realizing the opportunity that lay before him, Hanson presented Eastman with his vision for a truly "American" music school. Then, in 1924, having completed his three years in Rome, he accepted Eastman's invitation to become the new director of the Eastman School of Music. At age twenty-eight he moved to Rochester, bringing his parents to live with him. Committed to caring for them, he remained unmarried until he was nearly fifty.

Hanson's vision for the Eastman School centered around two basic principles. One was to integrate instrumental study with the scholarly aspects of music—theory and musicology—together within one institution, unlike the European approach, in which the academic disciplines were restricted to universities, while the practical or "applied" skills were taught in separate music training schools. He instituted the Doctor of Musical Arts as terminal degree for his new form of conservatory, a practice later adopted in music schools throughout the country. Hanson's second principle involved the encouragement of American music in particular—by drawing the most talented young composers, by attracting the most distinguished faculty members, by raising performance standards of student ensembles to professional levels, and by using their performances as opportunities to showcase American music. Almost immediately, Hanson instituted an annual festival of American music that continued until 1971. He also took Eastman's student ensembles on national and international tours, not only as a means of promoting the school and its performing groups, but also as an opportunity to present American music in many areas that had little previous exposure to this young repertoire. By the time he retired, Hanson had led the premieres of hundreds of new American works.

One of Hanson's most far-reaching programs was a series of recordings that featured both the Eastman symphony orchestra and its wind ensemble, largely in American repertoire. These recordings, distributed widely through standard retail outlets, introduced a number of American works that have since entered the active repertoire. Many of these recordings—now on compact disc—are still on the market today—and compare favorably as interpretations with some more recent efforts featuring professional orchestras and world-renowned conductors. Hanson also presided over a group of recordings called "The Composer and his Orchestra," in which he discussed such matters as form and orchestration, illustrating his points with excerpts from his own music, performed by the Eastman orchestra. In 1955 Hanson also undertook a series of thirteen television programs in which he attempted to illuminate the process of musical composition through commentary and musical examples.

During his years at Eastman, Hanson took a leadership role in American music education. Through position papers and lectures throughout the country he advocated for greater emphasis on music in the educational curriculum, for the formation of a national organization for music education, and for greater exposure of music by American composers. In frequent newspaper and magazine articles he expressed his opinions forcefully and outspokenly on a variety of subjects, from the need for greater government funding of the arts and the proper way to sing the national anthem to the dangers of rock music and the guitar as a poor choice with which to begin instrumental study. He supported the growth of summer music camps and frequently accepted invitations to conduct student orchestras. He was an active member of the U.S. Commission for UNESCO, and in 1960 his theoretical text *Harmonic Materials of Modern Music* was published. In it Hanson developed an approach, long in gestation, that he applied to the composition, as well as the analysis, of musical works. This approach posited the interval itself, rather than the manipulation of tonality—traditionally viewed as the fundamental organizing principle—as the chief structural element in the development of both harmony and melody. Hanson's approach has proven useful in understanding music far afield both stylistically and structurally from his own, while anticipating the application of "set theory" to musical analysis, which became a dominant theoretical approach years later.[6]

During the early 1940s Hanson met a young singer by the name of Margaret Nelson. "We had a very interesting contact: I was conducting in Chautauqua, and her parents had a big house on the lake. She, of course, was much younger—twenty years younger than I. When I would be rehearsing the symphony there, I would always see this young gal there at the rehearsals, and I considered her as

being a cute youngster. But it finally developed into more than just
a casual friendship with an older man."[7] In 1946, he and Margaret
were married, spending the rest of their lives together in Rochester,
where they became two of the city's best-known citizens, veritable
symbols of its artistic life.

Hanson's efforts on behalf of the Eastman School and on behalf of
music education in general did not prevent him from pursuing his
own career as a composer and conductor. Indeed, some accused him
of using the school to promote his own music to an excessive degree.
There were also complaints that he favored those student composers
whose music conformed to his own aesthetic predilections
(although this charge can be leveled at composition professors of all
stripes). Certainly his recording series gave special prominence to
his own music, as did his many guest appearances as conductor. But
unlike most other composer-conductors, whom one typically
expects to showcase their own music, Hanson also featured the
music of his peers. Ernest Bloch was one of the composers whose
music Hanson championed on recordings. "I think [Ernest Bloch]
had tremendous talent," he commented in 1978. "He had so many
fine works in addition to *Schelomo*. He became kind of a one-compo-
sition composer in a way, but the two *Concerti Grossi* . . . are tremendous pieces."[8] Samuel Barber was another whose works benefited
from Hanson's advocacy. "I think Barber is probably the most gifted
American composer (beside myself); this man has a real gift for melody, a real gift for orchestration, a real gift for emotional expression.
I think his First Symphony is a great piece."[9]

Throughout his Eastman years, Hanson continued to compose,
and many of his works attracted substantial attention. His Symphony no. 2, "Romantic," was commissioned by Serge Koussevitzky—along with Stravinsky's *Symphony of Psalms*—to commemorate
the fiftieth anniversary of the Boston Symphony Orchestra in 1930.
At the time of its premiere, the composer made some remarks—
quoted often during the ensuing years—that reveal Hanson's own
view of his identity as a composer:

> The symphony represents for me my escape from the rather bitter type
> of modern musical realism which occupies so large a place in contem-
> porary thought. Much contemporary music seems to me to be showing
> a tendency to become entirely too cerebral. I do not believe that music
> is primarily a matter of the intellect, but rather a manifestation of the

emotions. I have, therefore, aimed in this symphony to create a work that was young in spirit, lyrical and romantic in temperament, and simple and direct in expression.[10]

Looking back at the work nearly fifty years later, he commented, "It was a genuine expression of romanticism and a protest against the growing Schoenbergism of the time—the cold music—and I wanted to write something that was warm and young, vigorous and youthful."[11] The "Romantic" Symphony made a tremendous impact, and was performed widely by youth orchestras as well as by Toscanini and the NBC Symphony, becoming Hanson's "signature piece"; indeed, the main theme became something of a Howard Hanson "logo," and appeared in a variety of arrangements, from dance band to a choral version to which words were added. Hanson himself quoted the theme in more than a few of his subsequent works. To this day, the "Romantic" Symphony is Hanson's best-known and most consistently performed work. Indeed, this consistent and nearly exclusive association has to some extent—not unlike the case of Bloch and *Schelomo*—worked to the composer's disadvantage. Though its virtues have become indelibly identified with Hanson's general compositional identity, so have its undeniable weaknesses, to the point where his stature as a composer is based largely on that one work alone.

Three years after the "Romantic" Symphony came Hanson's major contribution to the world of opera. *Merry Mount*, with an American setting and a libretto based on a story by Nathaniel Hawthorne, was presented by the Metropolitan Opera Company, with baritone Lawrence Tibbett in the leading role. The work was a tremendous success with audiences, prompting fifty curtain calls at the premiere. Its subsequent disappearance is hard to explain and is usually attributed to extramusical politics.

Hanson's Third Symphony proved quite successful at the time and was performed—and even recorded—by the Boston Symphony under the direction of Koussevitzky, who championed a number of the composer's other works as well. Hanson's Fourth Symphony was awarded the 1944 Pulitzer Prize and to this day is perhaps the work of his most admired by critics.

Hanson retired as Director of the Eastman School in 1964. At that time, the school founded an Institute for American Music and named Hanson as Director. There he devoted the rest of his life to developing an archive documenting the school's contributions to American music. He also continued to compose, although the values represented by his music were now so alien to the mainstream of American composition at the time that his work made little impact and was often met with scornful derision. An exception was his Sixth Symphony, written in 1967 for the 125th anniversary of the New York Philharmonic. Invited by Leonard Bernstein to conduct the work, he arrived at Lincoln Center like a visitor from another era. Yet *New York Times* critic Harold Schonberg called it "a well-made, expert piece of music," adding that "it has dignity, strongly marked melodies, a bit of rhetoric and a ground plan that uses a motto theme to link together the six short movements."[12]

The strong role played by religion during Hanson's formative years lent an intense moral fervor to his lifelong dedication to music:

> I've never been much wedded to any dogma—I've never been particularly concerned with whether someone is a Lutheran or Catholic or Hindu or whatever, as long as they have what seems to be the basic tenet of all religions, which is the good, the true, and the beautiful—that, I think, is true of Hinduism, Shintoism, everything. . . . With me, it's more of a basic conviction that the arts were put in the world for a purpose, and that that purpose was to do good rather than harm, so that the artist has a responsibility to his fellow man . . . to use that [gift] for what he thinks would be the benefit of his fellow man, which to me means giving up things that are salacious and cheap and demeaning.[13]

Despite his professed ecumenism, Hanson's enduring constituency was found chiefly among the youth orchestras and choruses of the Midwest, where clean-cut Christian values continued to earn respect. Hanson further marginalized himself by aligning himself with some extreme aspects of right-wing culture. Perhaps not surprisingly, his most ambitious late works featured the chorus: a cantata called *Lumen in Christo* (1974), a large-scale work written for the American Bicentennial, *New Land, New Covenant*, and "*A Sea Symphony*" (1977), his no. 7, based on Whitman texts. Awarded thirty-six honorary doctorates and other honors too numerous to list, he spent his final years enjoying the respect and admiration of those who shared his values and whose lives he had touched. He died in Rochester in 1981, at the age of eighty-four.

MUSIC

Howard Hanson was a bold and outspoken advocate of music as a euphonious vehicle for untrammeled emotional expression during a period when the new-music community had become hostile to such a point of view. "Music should come from the heart more than from the head," Hanson commented toward the end of his life:

> I think there is a basic difference in the approach of the scientific mind and the creative mind. . . . I don't feel that knowledge is necessarily dangerous, but I think that as soon as your major interest becomes the diagram of the work or the mathematical relations within the work, you are missing your calling. You should be doing something else. . . . Composition must involve a certain free flow of fantasy that has nothing to do with a preconceived system or even preconceived knowledge.[14]

The central works of Howard Hanson's compositional output are his symphonies and his 1933 operatic masterpiece, *Merry Mount*. His many other pieces pursue expressive tributaries that are distilled in these compositions. Born within a few years of such figures as Walter Piston, Roger Sessions, Roy Harris, Virgil Thomson, and Aaron Copland, Hanson is probably the most immediately appealing of the group; his music offers little to bewilder or alienate the most conservative listener. And compared with the earnest, self-effacing, emotionally constrained efforts of so many of his American predecessors, his work displays a much stronger personal profile, with far more flair and style.

Hanson identified the music of Grieg as his earliest influence. "That was because my teachers urged it on me, as they were Scandinavians, and they felt I should develop myself in the tradition of the music of the North."[15] However, the composer's mature compositional language was shaped by the simple chorale style of Lutheran hymns, the stark, somber spaciousness of Sibelius, the modal harmony and brilliant orchestration of Rimsky-Korsakov, and the sumptuous textures of Debussy and Ravel. "Once Respighi told me I was a student of Rimsky-Korsakov because he had studied with Rimsky, and that made me a pupil. . . . I think that my love for big luxurious orchestral sonorities undoubtedly was influenced by Respighi, but of course, by a lot of other people too."[16] Hanson also cited Palestrina as a significant influence. "I learned an awful lot from Palestrina about letting the lines flow through the harmonies. It was probably the biggest single influence in my life, because when I went to Rome in 1921, I was fascinated by St. Peter's, and Gregorian chant, and the Sistine choir, . . . I once orchestrated the *Pope Marcellus Mass* for chorus and orchestra—it was on the official banned list of the Roman Catholic Church! . . . I learned a tremendous amount about voice leading by doing that, and we actually performed it down at the Eastman School."[17] To these background influences Hanson added his own warm, ardent lyricism, which is his most distinctive contribution.

During his long creative career Hanson produced some music of endearing appeal, although many works suffer from uneven inspiration and questionable craftsmanship. Although some achieve the dual ideal of instant accessibility and enduring artistic value, many others fail to develop promising thematic material and ingratiating sonorities into strong, coherent structures. Nevertheless, Hanson's music is immediately identifiable as his own, while offering the sort of emotional immediacy and visceral excitement that are engaging to audiences. For these reasons, his better works provide the general listener with an ideal point of entry into the world of twentieth-century American symphonic music.

Howard Hanson's body of creative work comprises approximately seventy works, which can be divided into three general periods of development: 1. an early period, which extends roughly through his tenure at the College of the Pacific; 2. early maturity, extending from the time of the Prix de Rome (1921) roughly to the late 1940s; and 3. later maturity, comprising the last three decades of his life.

Most Representative, Fully Realized Works

Symphony no. 1, "Nordic" (1922)
Pan and the Priest (1926)
Merry Mount (1933)
Symphony no. 3 (1938)
Symphony no. 4, "Requiem" (1943)
Cherubic Hymn (1949)
Symphony no. 5, "Sinfonia Sacra" (1954)
Mosaics (1957)
Symphony no. 6 (1967)

Early Period (until 1920)

The music of Hanson's early period speaks through the language of generic European Late Romanticism. The composer's personal voice, though hinted at occasionally, has yet to achieve strong characterization. A substantial example is the *Concerto da Camera* for piano and string quartet, written in 1917, when the composer was twenty-one, during his first year in San Jose. It is a fifteen-minute, single-movement work that reflects a French-flavored hyperchromaticism, highlighted by a certain Grieg-like melodic simplicity. Lush, passionate, and dark-hued, it shares many of the qualities found in the chamber music of such contemporaries as Amy Beach or Edward MacDowell, with hardly a suggestion of the mature Hanson style, aside from a characteristic richness of sonority, transparency of texture, and looseness of structure. A key motivic element is the "theme of youth" upon which Hanson built his *Fantasy Variations* some thirty-five years later.

The following year saw the appearance of an ambitious large-scale piano sonata in one movement, which distinguishes itself from comparable works of Beach and MacDowell by a surging lyricism that seems to strive toward a sort of ecstatic delirium, not unlike what Erich Korngold was producing at about the same time. However, less deeply probing or tightly focused than the sonata composed by Charles Tomlinson Griffes (twelve years Hanson's senior), also in 1918, Hanson's Piano Sonata is weakened by the use of shallow rhetorical devices, for example, long sequential build-ups over sustained dominant-pedals, to inflate and extend its expressive and formal dimensions beyond the confines of its genre. More successful are several shorter piano works composed during the next couple of years: *Three Miniatures* (1918–1919), the "Impromptu in E minor" from the *Yuletide Pieces* (1920), and—especially—the *Three Etudes* (1920). These fervent, ultraromantic character pieces, though relatively easy to play, reveal the first unmistakable suggestions of the distinctive Hanson voice.

Early Maturity (1921–1946)

The style of Hanson's early maturity—the style with which his name is most widely identified—seemed to blossom with the first work he completed during his stay in Italy: the Symphony no. 1,

"Nordic," op. 21. To the four sources of influence noted earlier—Lutheran chorales, the somber starkness of Sibelius, Russian modality, and Impressionist harmony and texture—Hanson contributed characteristic features of his own: especially, a distinctive rich, throbbing melody, often emerging from the tenor or baritone register or—when introduced in higher registers—presented in thirds. There is a hedonistic exultation in the way these melodies, couched in sumptuous yet lucid textures, and accompanied by pulsating timpani pedals, soar with unabashed gusto toward extravagant, lavishly orchestrated climaxes, often reinforced by brass flourishes. Tension and poignancy are intensified by frequent use of *appoggiaturas* and other types of contrapuntal dissonance. A distinctive aspect of Hanson's scoring is his sectional treatment of the orchestra: brass and woodwinds and—later—percussion are often heard independently of the strings, in contrast to conventional nineteenth-century usage, in which the strings serve as a constant foundation, with winds and percussion added for reinforcement or color. These stylistic elements contribute to the musical representation of a psychological dynamic that seems to underlie much of Hanson's music—especially those works dating from this period—and contributes to its interest and appeal: a sense of inner conflict between the spirit and the flesh—or, more precisely, between the sternly righteous and the hedonistically sensual. This is the central theme of the opera *Merry Mount* and is explicitly indicated by a title like *Pan and the Priest*, while it can be readily apprehended in the musical content of many other works, most notably the Third and Fourth Symphonies.

The "Nordic" Symphony, one of Hanson's most satisfying works, is also one of his most artistically successful efforts in symphonic form. It reveals an ease and a seamlessness of construction that proved difficult for the composer to recapture in subsequent works. It is also one of the most distinctive, fully realized American symphonies of the first quarter of the twentieth century. Written when he was twenty-six, it exudes the fresh, youthful spirit characteristic of much of Hanson's music, as he seems to yield unself-consciously to his natural propensities, producing a work that pours forth a ceaseless flow of melody, generously and without inhibition. Looking back at the work some fifty years later, he regarded it with a certain embarrassment. "The Nordic was too early—I was too young for a first Symphony, though it holds up astonishingly well for such a young piece, but it has too many climaxes, one right after another, a real pile-up."[18] Though there is some truth to this charge, the symphony's formal coherence is remarkable. There are no dry spots, no static or extraneous passages, and no stopping points, aside from movement divisions. Something "expressive" is happening at all times, as each phrase flows smoothly into the next. Though both the form of the work and its thematic materials are basically simple and straightforward, its structure is solidly unified and well integrated, while the treatment of the orchestra is masterful. (Listeners quick to associate its ingratiating gestures and sonorities with Hollywood are reminded that in 1922 the Neo-Romantic film score had yet to be born.) Though its subtitle and some of its themes draw attention to the composer's Scandinavian heritage, the flavor of the work is more personally expressive than descriptively nationalistic. The first performance of the "Nordic" Symphony took place in Rome in May 1923, with the composer conducting the Augusteo Symphony Orchestra.

In three movements, the symphony opens solemnly with a statement of the main theme, a Dorian melody in 5/4 meter. This melody serves as the source of all the work's thematic material, contributing to its tremendous sense of integration and flow. The second theme is simply a variant of the main theme, as is the main theme of the work's tender slow movement. The third movement comprises two parts—a *scherzo* followed by the finale. The *scherzo* is based on a tiny figure (in dotted rhythm) that served as a transitional motif in the first movement and as a gentle accompanying pattern (in the high woodwinds) in the second movement. This leads directly into the finale, a lugubrious "march" in 3/4, which, though supposedly based on an authentic Swedish folk tune, bears a strong resemblance to the symphony's opening theme. Not only is the "Nordic" Symphony unified thematically, but it is also truly developmental—not elaborately so, perhaps, but unmistakably.

Unfortunately, and rather inexplicably, Hanson was not able to maintain the easy formal fluency he achieved in the "Nordic" Symphony. Most of his subsequent works reveal structural weaknesses that he attempted to overcome with a number of compositional devices, with varying degrees of success. Hanson's musical ideas tend to be rather short-breathed and static, yet he clearly aimed for long-breathed statements and highly charged musical activity. So he developed a formal approach based on the juxtaposition of a series of tableaux, each suggesting a distinctive emotion or attitude, formed around a particular motif. Instead of progressing coherently and fluidly through organic growth and development, these episodes unfold via melodic/harmonic sequences and/or by the repetition of driving, brilliantly orchestrated rhythmic *ostinati* (i.e., repeated patterns), which build in intensity through increasing dynamics and textural density—admittedly, techniques often used by film composers. Also like them he displayed a tendency to overstate, overextend, or overelaborate moments to a degree unwarranted by their intrinsic significance. Thus, overall, one's appetite for Hanson's music depends on one's willingness to tolerate such structural weaknesses and lapses in taste in the interests of enjoying the hedonistic sensory delights of driving rhythm, melodic warmth, and richness and brilliance of sonority and texture.

Shortly after completing his first symphony, Hanson composed what he termed a "symbolic poem" for large orchestra with wordless chorus called *North and West*. It was introduced by the New York Symphony Orchestra, under the composer's direction, in 1924. However, shortly thereafter, Hanson transformed the work into a Concerto for Organ, Harp, and Strings. In one movement, the result is a rhapsodic, sixteen-minute *tour de force* of warm, exuberant emotions and simple, modal melodies embedded within a sumptuous texture of expanded triadic harmonies, all sewn into a loose, episodic structure. Tender, lyrical moods predominate, rather than virtuosic elements, except for a challenging cadenza for pedals.

The concerto was followed by a rather unconventional String Quartet—like the concerto, a loosely structured work in one movement. Drawing upon textural and rhetorical devices more commonly (and more effectively) utilized with massed sonorities, the quartet seems to aim toward the sort of extravagant emotional expression found in the composer's larger orchestral works. Here, however, the result often sounds thin and obvious, although there are convincing moments of tenderness and passion.

The last work Hanson completed in Italy was *Lux Aeterna* (1923). This seventeen-minute orchestral tone poem does not reveal the distinctive Hanson voice as clearly as does the "Nordic" Symphony, nor does it share that work's coherence of phraseology. Featuring viola *obbligato*, the work consists of a sequence of lush, fervent, and colorful episodes juxtaposed with no concession to classical formalities.

Returning to the United States in 1924, Hanson assumed his new position at the helm of the Eastman School of Music. The first composition he completed in his new role was a work for chorus and orchestra entitled *Lament for Beowulf* (1925). The text describes a solemn funeral ceremony for the brave and heroic Beowulf, who gave his life in the process of slaying a terrible monster. Hanson's choral writing is typically homophonic, while the orchestral accompaniment effectively evokes the stark, ancient setting. Also notable for illustrating the composer's use of driving *ostinati* to achieve stirring climaxes, the *Lament*—like many of his choral works—is a favorite of both performers and audiences and is heard with some frequency.

Both the thematic material and its elaboration in Hanson's next orchestral work, the tone poem *Pan and the Priest* (1926), represent something of an advance beyond *Lux Aeterna*. Similar to the *Lament for Beowulf* in its evocation of an ancient Nordic tribal scene, the work suggests a confrontation between pagan and Christian elements. Although it is typically episodic in structure, the first half boasts some of the composer's most infectious material, while the second half seems to disintegrate into a frantic succession of overstated gestures. Nevertheless, in a sympathetic but carefully disciplined performance, the work proves to be one of Hanson's most effective early tone poems.

Hanson's next major work was the one that is most closely associated with his name, the Symphony no. 2, "Romantic," op. 30, completed in 1930 on commission from the Boston Symphony Orchestra and its conductor, Serge Koussevitzky, who gave the premiere later that same year. As noted earlier, the subtitle clearly indicates that the work was a deliberate—indeed, defiant—statement on behalf of music as a vehicle for emotional expression, at a time when new music was expected to reject techniques of the past and sensibilities of "the heart," in a bold and uncompromising search for a musical style that "reflects our time." Though its language is essentially the same as that heard in the "Nordic," the "Romantic" Symphony differs structurally from its predecessor in many ways.

The work opens with a motto-theme—a stepwise three-note rising figure—which immediately builds in sequence to an expansive climax, and then subsides—all without intrinsic musical motivation. The mood suddenly becomes more turbulent, as a descending figure, "protesting" in character, is heard in the horns. After a dramatic elaboration, the mood suddenly shifts, as a tender, ardent motif is introduced by the oboe, then picked up by the lower strings, who extend it toward another climax. Finally, after hushed preparation, the "big tune" is heard, a lush, quintessentially Hansonian melody shared by the solo horn and the strings. This melody enjoys a leisurely, throbbing elaboration, before bringing what seems to be an exposition to an end.

This opening portion of the first movement is worth a closer examination. Although it has the "feel" of an exposition, it is far from a classical presentation of two contrasting "themes." True, all the thematic ideas share a family resemblance and are largely derived from the motto-theme, their motifs interwoven among each other. Yet one has the sense of a sequence of emotional states, juxtaposed with no apparent sense of progression, either psychological or purely musical.

The "exposition" is followed by a section that has the "feel" of a development. But instead of a true exploration of the inner potential of the ideas for growth and transformation, the various motifs tumble among each other, occasionally emerging as if to say "peekaboo," before returning to the unstable texture. It is this aspect of Hanson's compositional technique—not merely the materials he uses—that gives so many of his works, and the "Romantic" symphony in particular, its "movie music" character.

The second movement—an interlude of warmth and languor—introduces a "new" theme, although it too is related to the previous ideas, which continue to reappear throughout the movement. The finale provides an abrupt contrast, beginning with freshness and dynamism, as a new theme—bright, eager, and fanfare-like—is heard. Further contributing to a superficial sense of unity in both the second and third movements is the use of little fragments of the main motifs in rhythmic diminution as the substance of *ostinati* whose rapid repetitions form accompanimental textures. After some elaboration of the fanfare-like theme, further new material is heard, interspersed with reminiscences of the motif from the second movement. Finally, the "protest" theme from the first movement reappears, leading the way for a grand reprise of the "big tune." This is followed by final reminiscences of the work's various motifs, propelled forward by flourishes of rhetoric, eventually bringing the symphony to an emphatic conclusion.

It is reasonable to examine the "Romantic" Symphony in such detail because not only is it Hanson's best-known work, but it is also the work upon which his reputation most decisively rests and the one by which his stature as a composer is usually assessed. As this discussion makes abundantly clear, the "Romantic" flagrantly displays the hedonistic qualities that make Hanson's music so appealing to less sophisticated listeners, while also displaying the structural weaknesses that have made his music so appalling to less indulgent, more critical commentators. These qualities are somewhat more disturbing in works designated as "symphonies," as the symphonic genre—unlike the symphonic poem, for example—entails expectations of a coherent progression of autonomous musical ideas that unfold according to their own intrinsic logic by means of organic development. Hanson was not incapable of reaching this ideal, but, as with Tchaikovsky, such an approach seems not to have come naturally to him. In truth, the "Romantic" Symphony is not one of Hanson's stronger works, although it certainly is a representative one. The "Nordic" Symphony, as well as many later works, illustrate his craftsmanship at a higher level of mastery.

Before completing the "Romantic" Symphony, the thirty-three-year-old composer had already begun work on a commission from the Metropolitan Opera. The result was to be *Merry Mount*, a grand opera with libretto by Richard L. Stokes, who used as his point of departure a short story by Nathaniel Hawthorne called "The May-Pole of Merry Mount." Stokes's libretto is set in 1625, in a Puritan settlement in Massachusetts where worldly Cavaliers have recently arrived from England. The story involves Wrestling Bradford, a feverishly repressed Puritan minister, who becomes irresistibly infatuated with Lady Marigold Sandys, a Cavalier maiden who is already engaged to a Cavalier knight. Bradford's tortured psyche is revealed through grotesque dreams haunted by lascivious psychological projections of his own desires and fears. In one of these dreams he is persuaded by Lucifer to renounce God in order to possess Lady Marigold. In the final scene, a group of Indians—offended earlier by one of the Puritan leaders—sets fire to the settlement, and Bradford, with Marigold in his arms, leaps into the flames.

In devising music for this story, set 300 years in the past, Hanson made no alteration of his usual compositional style, doling out generous helpings of his most appealing and effective devices. The stern, punitive Puritans are depicted through modal chorales, while Bradford's carnal yearnings are represented by some of the composer's ripest lyrical effusions, floating on lush cushions of expanded triadic harmony. There is very little of the recitative and declamation that comprise so much twentieth-century opera. A few basic motifs unify the entire work, which originally required several hundred participants, including the orchestra, chorus, dancers, and a large cast of soloists. Rhythmically driven *ostinato* build-ups occur frequently in the orchestra during extended ballet episodes (such as the Maypole dances, where one can also hear some of the clearest examples of Hanson's generally unacknowledged debt to Rimsky-Korsakov) and also underlie choral episodes to suggest the emotional frenzy unleashed among the various hostile factions. The chorus is featured so prominently throughout that the opera often has the feel of an oratorio.

The first performance of *Merry Mount* was a concert presentation in Ann Arbor, Michigan, in 1933. The "official" staged premiere took place the following February at the Metropolitan Opera, with Lawrence Tibbett as Bradford and Gladys Swarthout as Marigold. The audience was ecstatic, responding with fifty curtain calls. The Met production ran for nine performances and was considered to be the most successful American opera of major proportions yet produced at the time. Critical comment was mixed, however.

Lawrence Gilman wrote, "There is a sumptuous provision of spectacle, which reaches its climax in an infernal ballet irradiated with red fire and made perilously alluring by a corps of satanic and beauteous damsels, whose charms were so liberally disclosed at yesterday's premiere that one could almost hear the commiserating gasps of a sympathetic audience shivering in its protective mink." Gilman found "Mr. Hanson's score impressive in its security and ease of workmanship, its resourcefulness and maturity of technique," adding that "at its best, . . . it is moving and individual and expressive." On the other hand, Gilman found the musical depiction of Wrestling Bradford "not savage enough."[19] While acknowledging that the audience response gave "every indication of a triumph," Olin Downes also criticized the characterization of Bradford, finding him "a figure of melodrama, set up to be knocked down."[20] W. J. Henderson reserved his praise for the choral sections, which he found "admirably composed. They have breadth and depth and they are distinctly that part of Mr. Hanson's score which most nearly makes itself at home in the theater."[21]

Henderson's colleagues shared similar feelings about the choral portions. Gilman found them to be "of stunning effectiveness," and believed that they would "in all likelihood, [prove] to be [*Merry Mount's*] most memorable artistic achievement."[22] Downes too agreed that "its strongest point is the choral writing," astutely observing that "these are essentially concert choruses—cantata choruses, oratorio choruses, which happen to be sandwiched in the scene of an opera. As such they have moments of sonority and climax, and in some places there is strong contrast between this hymnology and the sensuous music of Bradford's passion for Marigold."[23]

Hanson later acknowledged that the major influence on *Merry Mount*:

> undoubtedly was *Boris Godunov*, for two reasons: 1) because it's a choral opera, and 2) because it's oriented to a male character as the principal protagonist. Bradford carries the show in much the same way that Boris does. It relies very heavily on the juxtaposition of the chorus with the solo voice, and some of the scenes are actually choral scenes with all of the problems that entails from the standpoint of dramatic action—there's really no dramatic action! The example that was held up to me by Giulio Gatti-Casazza, who was general manager of the Metropolitan at that time, was Verdi's *Aida*, because what he wanted was a big opera. He didn't want a chamber opera, nor did he want an opera for five voices and chamber orchestra; he wanted a ballet, a chorus, a big orchestra, everything, so he kept saying, "Think of *Aida*." I like it very much, but I don't think there is any influence of Verdi in there, or if there is, I don't know where it is.[24]

After the Met production, Hanson made a number of revisions in the work. Yet despite its popularity with listeners, *Merry Mount* was not mounted again until 1955, with roughly one production per decade since then. In 1996, in commemoration of the centenary of Hanson's birth, the Seattle Symphony Orchestra presented a semistaged concert performance of the work, under the direction of Gerard Schwarz. (Throughout the 1990s, Schwarz spearheaded a comprehensive revival and reassessment of Hanson's music through both concerts and recordings.)

It is interesting to compare the critical reaction to the work more than sixty years later. Reviewer R. M. Campbell observed, "Some of Hanson's most original and piquant music is contained in the opera, which is both remarkably cogent in its harmonic force and predictably expansive in its melodic lines."[25] Melinda Bargreen praised its "arch-romantic tunes and orchestration and its great choral writing."[26] Echoing the New York critics, Cary Smith wrote that "the performance was dominated by the ubiquitous chorus, which turned every possible opportunity into a choral production number." He added, "which is not to say that there were not inspired moments. Hanson's prodigious musical technique allowed him to write passages of impressive power and breadth. Both the orchestral and choral writing were unashamedly symphonic and the opera progressed not so much as drama, but as a series of sonorous movements, tied together by broadly romantic themes."[27]

Perhaps the best mode of presentation for *Merry Mount* is a semistaged or unstaged concert performance in which the dominance of the chorus is less jarring to audience expectations than it is in operatic drama and where its association with oratorio is perceived as less of a liability. On the other hand, the orchestral suite that Hanson created from the opera in 1936 has become one of his most widely performed works. Its four movements include the Overture, the Children's Dance, the Love Duet, and the Maypole Dances. More than the "Romantic" Symphony, *Merry Mount* is a compendium of the most essential features of Hanson's musical style in their most ecstatic and fully elaborated representations, and the orchestral suite presents them in a relatively concise format.

Walt Whitman has been a favorite poet of many American and British composers, including Howard Hanson, who set many of his poems in works for chorus. In *Songs from "Drum Taps"* (1935), three of Whitman's reflections on war are interpreted with the freshness and youthful innocence that so often mark the composer's persona in his choral works. The youthful perspective on war is often naively idealistic, however, with the result that some of Whitman's irony seems missing from Hanson's settings. The first, "Beat! beat! drums!", is martial and stirring. The second, "By the Bivouac's Fitful Flame," is a baritone solo of plaintive cast. In the third movement, "To Thee Old Cause!," the martial spirit returns, culminating in a fervent peroration of optimism. A quotation from *Merry Mount*'s "love" music is heard in both the second and third movements, for no apparent reason.

Howard Hanson came of age at a time when the music of Jan Sibelius was very much in fashion, so it is no surprise that, what with Hanson's Nordic heritage, his music was frequently compared with that of the elder Finnish master, with similarities often noted. However, familiarity with Hanson's output as a whole indicates that such similarities are often overstated. Not until the appearance of the Symphony no. 3 in 1938 was the influence of Sibelius truly evident. "There is much Sibelius influence there," Hanson readily acknowledged, "because I was steeped in Sibelius at that time."[28] This can be heard clearly in the darkly austere solemnity of the work's opening moments, as well as in portions of the *scherzo*. Written to commemorate the 300th anniversary of the first Swedish American settlement, the work honors those pioneers who immigrated to the United States from Sweden. Commissioned by the Columbia Broadcasting System, the work was dedicated to Serge Koussevitzky, who became its ardent champion. The premiere, however, was a broadcast performance in March 1938, featuring the NBC Symphony Orchestra under the composer's direction.

In this symphony, his most extended essay in the form, Hanson is heard at the height of his creative power. The first of its four movements introduces a solemn, darkly brooding theme based on an ascending scale pattern. This theme sprouts other motifs, including a hard-bitten, three-note descending figure that recurs throughout the work. The second main idea is a chorale theme, a simple expression of hope, which becomes the motto-theme of the entire symphony. A leisurely development of these ideas comprises the remainder of the movement. The main theme of the slow movement is a warm, tender melody that bears a loose family resemblance to both themes of the first movement. The third movement is a vigorous and dynamic *scherzo* with a sweetly poignant middle section. The fourth movement, which was completed some time afterward, recalls both themes from the first movement before introducing a new idea of its own. After some development of this material, the chorale motto returns, followed by the heartfelt melody from the second movement, which reaches an ecstatic apotheosis. The juxtaposition of these two ideas, one simple and humble, the other passionate and yearning, points to the "spirit versus flesh" conflict noted earlier.

The interrelationships among the work's thematic ideas are conveyed with subtlety, and if the listener's requirements for tightly focused formal development are relaxed somewhat, the Third can be seen as one of Hanson's most fully consummated symphonies. All his familiar earmarks are abundantly evident: the flowing modal counterpoint, throbbing melodies surging through the baritone and tenor registers of the orchestra, radiant chorales, lively rhythmic *ostinati,* all orchestrated to brilliantly colorful effect. Overall the symphony seems to be a statement about courage and fortitude in the face of adversity, supported by a simple, straightforward reliance on faith, hope, and trust. Such wholesome sentiments could easily result in music of banal, mawkish optimism. However, as is the case with other works of Hanson's early maturity, the symphony's power lies in the unabashed hyperbole of its gestures, the unstinting lavishness of its orchestration, and, most of all, in its youthful fervor and sincere conviction. Dedicatee Koussevitzky hailed it as the finest American symphony to date, and "the equal of any of the great symphonies."[29] Perhaps even more remarkable is the comment of 32-year-old Elliott Carter, later revered as one of America's foremost serial composers. He felt that the work "proved once again how skillful, fine and ambitious a composer [Hanson] is." While noting its resemblance to Sibelius, he added, "To me this work compares more than favorably with the best works of the Finnish composer. . . . [I]t has many more interesting musical events and more meaty material."[30]

Hanson worked for several years on his next work—another symphony. Not completed until 1943, the Symphony no. 4 bears the subtitle "Requiem" and is inscribed, "In memory of my beloved father." Like its predecessor, it is divided into four movements, each of which is identified by a section of the Requiem Mass: Kyrie, Requiescat, Dies Irae, and Lux Aeterna. Yet despite its four movements, the work conforms to classical structural models even less than do his previous symphonies, moving closer to the sheer sequence of moods and emotional states that seemed to be the composer's natural inclination.

The symphony is based chiefly on two ideas: an upward octave leap, which serves largely as a frame for each movement, and a conjunct ascending and descending pattern, from which most of the thematic material of the work is derived. The opening movement presents a sequence of attractive ideas, the first somber and lugubrious, the second playful and dance-like, and the third warm and reverent. These ideas are elaborated, rather than developed, chiefly by varying orchestration and texture. The second movement treats a typically warm and heartfelt Hansonian melody based on the conjunct ascending-descending pattern. It unfolds with particular richness and poignancy. The brief third movement is a driving *scherzo* clearly based on the main theme of the first movement. Like the first, the fourth movement is sectional and is also based on the conjunct pattern. The character of the movement is hymn-like, and, despite some turbulence, ends with a calm serenity.

Hanson himself conducted the Boston Symphony Orchestra in the first performance of his Fourth Symphony, in December 1943. The work was awarded the Pulitzer Prize the following year, and for many years the composer himself cited it as his own favorite among his works in the genre. It has been admired consistently by critics as well, perhaps because of the dignity of its thematic material, its avoidance of lapses in taste, and the fact that it accomplishes its expressive ends with greater concision than its predecessors.

Later Maturity (after 1947)

Although Howard Hanson's stylistic development never made the abrupt shifts in materials and technique typical of many composers, something of a change in emphasis can be detected in the works written after the mid-1940s. One notes less reliance on the rich melodies and lush harmonic textures that so strongly characterized his earlier work. Whether this is attributable to a feeling on Hanson's part that his music was becoming increasingly anachronistic, as the compositional mainstream moved further away from anything that might be construed as sentimental, or whether the change represented the composer's own sense of having outgrown such emotional directness, or whether that aspect of his creativity had simply run dry is a matter of speculation. One also notes an increased interest in irregular meters, such as five-beat and seven-beat patterns, along with a willingness to experiment with other forms of musical expression than the purely emotional. Perhaps as a direct outgrowth of the process of developing the ideas articulated in his theory text *Harmonic Materials of Modern Music,* his later works reveal a greater emphasis on abstract structural concepts and, in some cases, new musical resources were introduced into the Hanson vocabulary. In a retrospective interview conducted in 1978, Hanson said, ''In a sense, all the later works of mine were influenced by my study of harmonic materials. You can't be working as intensively as I was for forty years on a theory without being automatically influenced. I have always been fascinated by how much logic there is in musical progression.''[31]

Perhaps the first example of this new emphasis is Hanson's Piano Concerto, composed in 1948 and introduced by Rudolf Firkusny and the Boston Symphony Orchestra, under the composer's direction, on the last day of that year. Although Hanson was a pianist himself, his compositions reveal little interest in the instrument as it is conventionally featured. His works for piano solo are few in number and quite limited in scope (aside from the ambitious sonata discussed earlier), while his accompanied works treat the instrument rather idiosyncratically. For example, in the concerto at hand, the piano is used primarily in single-line figurations, doubled at the octave—a usage that places the instrument in a subordinate role within the orchestra, similar to that of a xylophone (a favorite Hanson sound), rather than as a powerful protagonist rivaling the orchestra—the conventional *concertante* approach.

The work comprises four short, loosely structured movements, with its share of flashy, exciting moments and pretty, leisurely melodies. Although the slow movement does have some darker aspects, the character of the concerto is generally light and breezy throughout, with thin, transparent textures rather atypical of Hanson's norm. The first movement opens with a three-note motto that recurs throughout the work, while concentrating primarily on two larger thematic ideas, one lively and vigorous, the other warmly affectionate. A brief, driving *scherzo* follows, not unlike the character of such movements in Hanson's symphonies. The third movement is a nostalgic lyrical effusion typical of the composer. Commentators have often noted the influence of jazz in this piece, but this amounts to little more than the occasional "blue-note" and added-sixth chord—what might be described as dilute Gershwin. This element is heard chiefly in the finale, although touches occur in the first two movements as well.

One of the most deeply moving and fully realized of Hanson's many works for chorus and orchestra is the *Cherubic Hymn*, a twelve-minute setting of a portion of the Liturgy of St. John Chrysostom, composed in 1949 and introduced the following year at the Eastman School. The text is an important element in the worship services of the Eastern Orthodox Church. The work opens with a dark solemnity; toward the middle a seven-beat *ostinato* builds to an almost orgiastic climax of spiritual ecstasy before receding to a quiet conclusion.

Hanson turned to the piano again in 1951 for his *Fantasy Variations on a Theme of Youth.* As has been mentioned, Hanson's creative gifts were inclined more toward the *elaboration* of themes than toward their *development*, in the strict sense of the word. This predilection made the theme-and-variations format an especially suitable medium for his musical thinking. Yet not until the *Fantasy Variations* had he turned his attention to this form in a significant way. However, it proved to be one to which he would return frequently during his later years.

Fantasy Variations is a retrospective work in which the composer stepped back to consider with some detachment the wistful poignancy of the motif from his 1917 *Concerto da Camera* that serves as the theme in the title. Here the piano plays something of an *obbligato* role, lending a crisp, dry quality to the string orchestra timbre. Each of the four variations is freely developed into a substantial and consistently engaging little character piece. Modestly proportioned and tastefully sequenced, they form a satisfying whole, whose vigor and clarity of texture and sonority recall Ernest Bloch's *Concerto Grosso no. 1*, as does its warm, romantic core.

During this period Hanson composed a number of short pieces of lesser importance. The *Serenade* (1945) for flute, harp, and strings and the *Pastorale* (1949) for oboe, harp, and strings are short, rather subdued mood-pieces, fairly similar in effect, though the latter is somewhat cooler and drier in tone. Both were written as gifts for his wife. *Centennial Ode* (1950) commemorated the University of Rochester's hundredth commencement. *How Excellent Thy Name* (1952) is a rather bland setting for women's voices of a portion of Psalm 8.

During the two decades following the end of World War II, the aggregation of woodwinds, brass, and percussion known as the *symphonic band* leaped rather suddenly into prominence as a medium for serious musical expression. The reasons for this are beyond the scope of this study, but one very relevant factor was Hanson's appointment in 1939 of a brilliant young graduate named Frederick Fennell to the Eastman School faculty. Fennell conducted a number of the school's ensembles and in 1952 brought to fruition a concept he had developed, which he called a "symphonic wind ensemble." Unlike the typical college concert band, an often unwieldy group of nearly a hundred players of varying abilities, with massed doublings of parts, and a repertoire that included everything from military marches and Broadway medleys to awkward transcriptions of classic symphonic works, the wind ensemble as Fennell envisioned it was a small group of select expert players, with minimal doubling of parts, capable of the precision and flexibility necessary to master the most difficult repertoire. Such a group would concentrate on music of high aesthetic intent originally conceived for band, and many important American composers had already begun to build a repertoire of such works. The Eastman Symphonic Wind Ensemble (ESWE) was soon included in the recording project that Hanson had developed in conjunction with Mercury Records and quickly achieved nationwide acclaim as one of the few ensembles of its kind to reach the highest levels of musicianship. Many of the ESWE recordings are still among the most highly prized items in the Eastman series.

But at the time when Fennell was developing his wind ensemble concept, Howard Hanson had not yet addressed the medium as a composer. Finally, in 1954, in response to a commission from the American Bandmasters Association, Hanson composed his *Chorale and Alleluia*. Though only five minutes in duration, and shaped by some of the composer's most familiar devices—a hymn-like opening, followed by a more rousing section based on a motif from the Chorale, presented in diminution as a repeated background *ostinato*, until the chorale returns, bringing the work to a jubilant conclusion—*Chorale and Alleluia* was an instant success. In an article that appeared the following year, Fennell wrote, "This impassioned score was the most awaited piece of music to be written for the wind band in my twenty years as a conductor in this field."[32] The work was promptly recorded by the ESWE and has since become a classic of its genre.

Later in 1954, Hanson turned his attention to another symphony, his fifth. Drawing its inspiration from the story of Christ's Resurrection, the work was alternately titled *Sinfonia Sacra*. The Fifth is remarkable in that the composer appears finally to have abandoned any effort to force his symphonic concept into the sort of classical template that had seemed increasingly alien to the substance of each successive symphony. What resulted is a single-movement work, barely fifteen minutes in duration, divided into three sections. Thus it is more akin to a "tone poem," in which sections reflective of emotional, spiritual, or poetic states are linked together to form a psychological or emotional progression of some kind. An examination of Hanson's work back to the 1910s suggests that this form is more compatible with his musical thinking than the classical notion of an abstract progression driven forward by thematic development.

Sinfonia Sacra was first performed in 1955 by the Philadelphia Orchestra, under the direction of Eugene Ormandy. The work opens with stern, portentous utterances reminiscent of Sibelius, which are elaborated in somber polyphony by the lower strings. A declamatory section follows, leading to another passage of mournful string polyphony. (This section contains some of Hanson's most successful and deeply moving contrapuntal writing.) The second major section presents a lighter, more pastoral melody, introduced by the English horn. Soon picked up by the strings, this lyrical melody begins surging and becoming more animated until a state of considerable agitation is reached. The build-up continues as an exciting series of episodes based on irregular *ostinato* patterns accelerates in intensity to a tremendous climax, which seems then to collapse into banal gestures. The third major section returns to the portentous mood with which the work began. A reverent chorale suggesting a spirit of hope follows, leading the symphony to a quizzical, unresolved conclusion.

Hanson's next work was *Elegy*, subtitled "To the memory of my friend, Serge Koussevitsky," and was written in 1955 to mark the seventy-fifth anniversary of the Boston Symphony Orchestra. Almost fifteen minutes in duration, it is rather short on substance, though long on richness of sonority, with much empty extender material. Nevertheless, it is one of the composer's more frequently performed pieces.

Hanson returned to the poetry of Walt Whitman for his *Song of Democracy*, composed in 1957 to mark the hundredth anniversary of the National Education Association and the fiftieth anniversary of the Music Educator's National Conference. In it Hanson fused Whitman's grand and hearty optimism with his own sincere musical idealism, producing an ardent paean to youthful creativity. During the orchestral prelude, an unmistakable reminder of the "Romantic" Symphony appears, as a sort of signature motto, and is heard again during a subsequent interlude—a practice that Hanson applied in a number of his later works. The largely homophonic setting for chorus culminates in a fervent hymn, making this an especially suitable work for occasions celebrating the boundless possibilities of American youth. Hanson conducted the National Symphony Orchestra in the premiere in Washington, D.C., before an audience of 23,000. Twelve years later, *The Song of Democracy* was performed in Washington again, this time for the inauguration of President Richard Nixon.

Although elements previously foreign to Hanson's musical language were heard as early as 1948 in the Piano Concerto, the first work to offer a strikingly different surface sound was *Mosaics*, composed in 1957 for George Szell and the Cleveland Orchestra. Hanson explained that he chose the title to suggest "the way mosaics seem to change color and even form as lights and shadows play upon the composition."[33] He constructed this work—a kind of variation form—in an analogous way, using the melodic intervals of the opening theme as the basis of the variations. This was clearly an outgrowth of the ideas he had been developing concurrently in his theory text, which was to be published three years later. Using the variations to illuminate the expressive potential of intervals, rather than of a theme per se, results in a less melody-based tonal foundation and a somewhat more dissonant harmonic language than is the composer's norm.

With a duration of twelve minutes, *Mosaics* is remarkably concise and concentrated in effect, with a more objective emotional tone than that found in Hanson's earlier work. But perhaps its most salient features are its great transparency of texture and its concentration on crisp, dry, brilliantly colored sonorities, created by an emphasis on high woodwinds and sharp percussion timbres. The strings, though featured in the lyrical second variation, for example, are less dominant throughout much of the work. This distinctive orchestral sound became an enduring characteristic of Hanson's later works.

Hanson's next work of major proportions was another commission from the Cleveland Orchestra. Entitled *Bold Island Suite*, it was named for the island retreat off the coast of Maine that Hanson had inherited from a relative. The second of its three movements was originally completed in 1959 as an independent composition called *Summer Seascape*. The two outer movements were added in 1961. The suite is lightweight and picturesque in character, with simulated bird sounds and frequent use of irregular rhythmic *ostinati*. The first movement, "Birds at the Sea," has moments reminiscent of *Mosaics*, while the third, "God in Nature," is built around a hymn-like chorale that seems to recall *Merry Mount*. The work was well received by audiences, if not by critics.

Similarly lightweight is the orchestral suite Hanson composed in 1962, called *For the First Time*, as an attempt to suggest a young child's impressions of a day filled with new experiences. Despite the simplicity of its musical substance and expressive content, Hanson set himself a technical challenge: "The suite is an experiment in telling a very simple and unsophisticated story in music through a series of movements, each written in a different technical medium and using a limited and diverse tonal vocabulary." Its twelve tiny movements also serve the didactic purpose of further illustrating the ideas Hanson developed in *Harmonic Materials of Modern Music*. "For each episode I have chosen a specific tonal relationship, a 'chemical mixture' of tones, which seemed to me to suit the particular episode."[34] Hanson generates both melodic and harmonic materials from the sequencing and overlapping of basic pitch intervals, rather than proceeding from a conventional thematic and tonal framework. Each brief movement attempts to suggest its chosen programmatic image through the exploitation of a particular intervalic structure.

Despite these background concerns, *For the First Time*, first performed at the Eastman School in April 1963, is of unusually trifling aesthetic import. Its chief significance lies in the array of new harmonic and melodic combinations (and concomitant expressive possibilities) introduced into Hanson's vocabulary as a result of the generative techniques he was exploring. Its sparse textures and paucity of substance also call attention to the richness, vividness, and abundance of his timbral imagination.

As Hanson proceeded through his seventh decade, he was increasingly called upon to supply music whose chief purpose was to celebrate important occasions. In 1963, he responded to a commission from UNESCO to produce a work to mark the fiftieth anniversary of the Universal Declaration of Human Rights with the *Song of Human Rights*. The text of this composition for chorus and orchestra included portions of John F. Kennedy's Inaugural Address. Its premiere took place before an audience of 5,000 at Constitution Hall in Washington, D.C., less than three weeks after President Kennedy's assassination. Needless to say, the audience response was overwhelming.

During the 1960s, Hanson composed a number of settings of the Psalms. Perhaps the most ambitious and most artistically successful is the combined group of settings he wrote in 1964, *Four Psalms* for baritone, cello solo, and string quartet. First performed later that year at the Library of Congress, the four settings (Psalm 46: God is our refuge and strength; Psalm 6: O Lord, rebuke me not in thine anger; Psalm 47: O clap your hands; Psalm 8: O Lord our Lord, how

excellent thy name) are joined together within one movement, separated by instrumental interludes. Displaying a tempered, more
inward emotionality, the settings are remarkable for their dignity
and depth of expression, as well as for the subtlety, polish, and integrated flow of the instrumental component. In the second section
(Psalm 6), a motif is introduced, accompanying the lines, "O Lord,
heal me for my bones are vexed," which figures prominently in a
number of Hanson's subsequent works. The only lapse of taste
involves the brief third section, "O clap your hands," which receives
a syncopated, "gospel-style" treatment somewhat out of character
with the rest of the work. Reminiscences of Ernest Bloch (who also
set several of the Psalms), which seem to dart fleetingly under the
surface of a number of Hanson's later compositions, are clearly felt
throughout these psalm settings.

The year 1968 marked the hundredth anniversary of Hanson's
native state of Nebraska, and he was asked to provide a composition
for the occasion. The result was *Dies Natalis*, a fifteen-minute orchestral work based on a Lutheran Christmas chorale, which serves as
the theme for a series of seven lively variations, framed by an introduction and finale. A series of steady drumbeats leads into the
theme of the introduction, a typically Hansonian melody, ardently
throbbing upward. The chorale melody itself also has a characteristic contour, a major-key version of the Dorian chorale that opens the
opera *Merry Mount* (and even makes a brief appearance in the early
tone poem *Lux Aeterna*). As in the case of Hanson's other later works
utilizing the variation principle, such as the *Fantasy Variations* and
Mosaics, each variation has its own distinctive character, creating a
richly imaginative array of moods. After the variations, the introductory material returns, providing a moving sense of summation,
somewhat reminiscent in spirit of the finale of the Symphony no. 3.
In 1972 Hanson created an arrangement of the work for symphonic
band, which he called *Dies Natalis II*.

As noted earlier, after Hanson retired in 1964 as Director of the
Eastman School, his reputation deteriorated badly. He was accused
of having provincialized the Eastman School by imposing his
euphonious musical style on the young composition students, while
excluding from the school proponents of more "progressive"
approaches of which he disapproved. His music, as epitomized by
the "Romantic" Symphony, was scorned by those in the musical
community old enough to have encountered it, as well as by others

who knew only its subtitle and reputation. With the Eastman recording series no longer active, few were aware that the septuagenarian composer was still creatively active. Therefore, when the New York Philharmonic announced a series of commissions to celebrate the orchestra's 125th anniversary in 1968—during the single decade of the twentieth century least sympathetic to the Neo-Romantic aesthetic—the inclusion of a new symphony by Howard Hanson was met with some derision. (This was the same decade when even Leonard Bernstein felt compelled to write an essay to justify—or apologize for—the composition of a straightforward, accessibly tonal work like the *Chichester Psalms*.) Presumably his participation was elicited more as an acknowledgment of his half-century of dedication to the cause of American music than as a tribute to his creative work. The composer was invited by music director Leonard Bernstein to conduct the premiere himself.

What the audience heard was a skillfully crafted work in a defiantly Neo-Romantic style—not the unctuousness of the "Romantic" Symphony, but a more tempered expression, not unlike the music Samuel Barber was composing at the time, strengthened by a stern, Sibelian demeanor. The Sixth Symphony comprises six short, concise movements, played without pause. Apart from its central *Adagio*—a wistful, poignant, typically Hansonian outpouring of full-breathed lyricism—the symphony is cool in tone, dry in sonority, spare in texture, stark in gesture, occasionally harsh in harmony, and relatively attenuated in tonality. Indeed, its language must have surprised those listeners unfamiliar with the composer's later music. On the other hand, the work is orchestrated with Hanson's characteristic brilliance, boasts two driving *scherzi* not unlike those found in Symphonies 3 and 4, and a triumphant, affirmative finale. ("A small, intimate soul surviving in the framework of cynicism and strife," was Hanson's own verbal interpretation.[35]) However, as in most of his other works nominally in the genre, the Sixth lacks the qualities of organic development and dialectical continuity essential to a true symphony and is more a succession of episodes in contrasting tempos and moods, despite the use of a unifying three-note motto: "the Perfect fifth with a major second on top of it. C-G-A with all of its variations, permutations, and extensions. That was to some extent conscious."[36]

In 1969, Hanson turned once again to the poetry of Walt Whitman, this time his *Mystic Trumpeter*, fashioning a fifteen-minute work in which the delivery of the text is shared alternately by a spoken voice and by a mixed chorus, accompanied by the orchestra. Whitman's passionate poem posits the notion of a ghostly trumpeter who bears witness to the charm of the medieval past, to the intensity and power of love, to the unspeakable horrors of war, and, finally, to the possibility of limitless joy in the time ahead. In the section dealing with the power of love, Hanson draws upon a motif that figures prominently in the second movement of his Sixth Symphony (and appears in other works from this period as well). The text is particularly well suited to the composer's musical temperament, with its vigorous language, fervent idealism, and its tendency toward overstatement, and he renders it into a satisfying expression of exuberant affirmation with a vitality remarkable in a work created by a composer in his midseventies. Indeed, this work, first performed at the University of Missouri, Kansas City, in April 1970, leads one to reflect that despite Hanson's advanced age and the stylistic evolution that is inevitable in a creative figure active for more than half a century, certain fundamental qualities remained constant in his work. In addition to its exuberance and vitality, there is a fundamental authenticity and directness of expression—with aspects both clear-cut and clean-cut—that make his body of work so convincing, deeply rewarding, and worthy of serious attention, whatever its undeniable limitations.

Hanson's later output gives the impression of being divided among religious works, secular works with poetic or literary reference, and abstract, theoretical works. Yet they do not really differ that significantly in compositional approach, as Hanson used his interval-projection technique to generate scale forms as melodic and harmonic source material in writing most of his later music—not just the works in which such methods are indicated by title or program notes. Furthermore, those works, such as *For the First Time*, in which the compositional technique seems to be the dominant issue tend to be as entertaining and accessible as any of his other works.

Another case in point is the Suite for Piano, Winds, and Percussion that Hanson composed in 1972, with the alternate title *Young Person's Guide to the Six-Tone Scale*. This work, less than half an hour in duration, comprises thirty-five short pieces intended to illustrate "*every possible category* of the six-tone scale."[37] The scale forms are divided into seven subcategories according to the interval featured, and the pieces—extremely short and epigrammatic, needless to say—are presented in orderly succession. Yet the collective impact of the Suite, first performed at the Eastman School in November 1972, is not at all didactic, nor is it profound by any means. Rather it is a most pleasantly refreshing diversion, drawing upon a virtually limitless imagination to create a kaleidoscopic array of musical images.

In 1974, Hanson returned to the spiritual realm for a choral/ orchestral work called *Lumen in Christo*. The composer prepared two versions, one for mixed chorus, the other for women's voices only, with a text compiled from several sacred sources, all touching upon the subject of "light." The work makes explicit reference to well-integrated quotations taken from the music of both Haydn and Handel. Its strikingly arresting opening is followed by a setting of "In the beginning" that sounds like Hanson's gloss on the first movement of Leonard Bernstein's *Chichester Psalms*. (Hanson openly expressed his admiration for the music of the celebrated composer-conductor.[38]) The second half of the work proceeds more slowly, with simple musical ideas that aim for a lovely, ethereal serenity but run the risk of sounding vacuous in a less than sensitive performance. *Lumen in Christo* was first performed at the Nazareth College of Rochester in October 1974.

Hanson returned again to the concert band medium in 1975 to compose *Laude*. Consisting of a chorale melody with eight variations and a finale, the work is similar in form and proportion to *Dies Natalis*. However, the later work is much more constrained in character and its variations more limited in stylistic range, although some passages are quite compelling. In the finale, the theme is transformed into the chorale from the composer's Third Symphony. Hanson made a shorter version of the work the following year, including the best of the variations, and entitled it *Fanfare and Chorale*.

Hanson's three final major works, while revealing little moderation of ambition, display an unfortunate diminution of both inspiration and formal judgment. The first of these is an oratorio called *New Land, New Covenant*, which represented the composer's most large-scale effort since the opera *Merry Mount*. The work was conceived and commissioned by a group of religious leaders under the aegis of a consortium of Presbyterian churches to mark the American Bicentennial in 1976. The explicit purpose of the work was to elaborate the religious principles that served as the implicit foundation, through a covenant with God, for the creation of the United States as an earthly Paradise of freedom and democracy. The work's text was compiled by the theologian Howard Clark Kee, who drew upon the writings of Isaac Watts, T. S. Eliot, John Newton, the Bible, and the Declaration of Independence.

Approaching his eightieth year, Hanson took on the task of shaping a large oratorio for solo soprano and baritone, a narrator, mixed chorus, children's chorus, organ, and orchestra. More than an hour in duration, the work comprises five large sections: I. Creation and Fall; II. New Exodus, New Covenant (1620); III. The Great Awakening (1750); IV. New Order of the Ages (1776); and V. Renewing the Covenant (1976). Much of the music is adapted from seventeenth- and eighteenth-century hymn tunes and chorales, whose conventional diatonic contours are of minimal interest to those outside the Protestant frame of reference. Hanson's original contributions maintain a simple directness that prevents them from conflicting with the character of the hymn melodies but, aside from a few touching passages, are generally quite tepid and without much musical interest of their own. The motif mentioned earlier that appears in the 1964 setting of Psalm 6 plays an important role throughout the work, and a choral motif from *Merry Mount* is also heard more than once. The premiere of *New Land, New Covenant* took place in May 1976 in Bryn Mawr, Pennsylvania.

The following year Hanson undertook what is most appropriately and poignantly regarded as his valedictory work, Symphony no. 7, "A Sea Symphony." In so doing, he turned one last time to Walt Whitman, the poet toward whose work Hanson gravitated so strongly and frequently. Indeed, with five works set to Whitman texts, it is likely that Hanson identified himself with the poet in more than a superficial way. Perhaps Whitman's glorification of the individual and his exuberant identification of himself with the explosion of positive energy that was transforming America during the late 1800s, along with his fervent belief in democracy as the means of unleashing human potential to the fullest, all reverberated with Hanson's own sense of the America he understood and loved. He may also have viewed his own dedication to universal music education and his (perhaps idealized) role as the embodiment of and advocate for musical humanism as analogous to Whitman's exaltation of a poetic humanism. Hanson chose three selections from *Leaves of Grass* as the text for his final symphony, and lines such as "Joyous, we too launch out on trackless seas, Fearless, for unknown shores on waves of ecstasy to sail . . ." suggest something about the composer's state of mind at this time in his life.

"A Sea Symphony" was completed in 1977, in commemoration of the fiftieth anniversary of the National Music Camp at Interlochen, Michigan. The eighty-one-year-old composer conducted the premiere in August of that year. Hanson had enjoyed a long association with this institution, which had even chosen "the theme" from his "Romantic" Symphony to end its concerts for many years.

From the opening of the first movement, the symphony's undulating, wave-like musical gestures convey a sense of "the unbounded sea." With an amazing similarity to the "Romantic" Symphony, the same ascending three-note motto motif is introduced, building to a powerful climax before the chorus has made its first entrance. However, such picturesque gestures, rolling and heaving textures, the images they suggest, and the moods they evoke comprise essentially all there is to the movement. Although there are some impressive sonorities, there is virtually nothing that might be viewed as musical substance. The second movement, containing the line "Now voyager—sail thou forth to seek and find," does have some lovely moments. Laden with autobiographical implications, the third movement, "Joy, shipmate, joy!," is hard for anyone steeped in Hansoniana to apprehend dispassionately. It begins with impressive vigor until "the theme" makes one last reappearance, perhaps as a symbol of pride in his own achievement, or perhaps as a gesture of farewell to his friends and admirers. As the movement surges forward, there is some true contrapuntal development until the familiar timpani pulses appear, pointing the way toward one final, ecstatic climax.

Hanson's final work, *Nymphs and Satyr*, is a short ballet suite in three movements, scored for chamber orchestra and completed in 1979. A bit of an anticlimax after the two preceding works, it is quite flimsy in substance. A lengthy opening section features the warmly undulating waves of sound of which Hanson had grown so fond during his later years. A brief central *scherzo*, originally planned as a *Fantasy* for clarinet and chamber orchestra, is based on what might be described as a bucolic Swiss-flavored mountain tune. Hanson reportedly used to sing the tune to his dog. The final section, originally a *scherzo* for bassoon and orchestra, returns to the ingratiating spirit of the opening for a gentle valediction.

CONCLUSION

Howard Hanson died on February 26, 1981. The *New York Times* obituary stated unequivocally, "Both as a composer and as a polemicist, Dr. Hanson stood for a tradition that most of his influential colleagues considered dead."[39] Perhaps the most ruthlessly objective indication of his significance within the academic music community shortly after his death—not just as a composer, but as an educator, administrator, and general statesman—is the amount of space devoted to the text of his entry in the *New Grove Dictionary of American Music*, published in 1986. In comparison with such contemporaneous figures as Virgil Thomson, who was allotted thirty-eight inches, Roger Sessions, who was allotted forty-six inches, and Roy Harris, who was allotted forty-five, Howard Hanson was deemed worthy of a little more than eight.

During the late 1980s, Gerard Schwarz, music director of the Seattle Symphony Orchestra, announced a new series of recordings to be released by Delos International. The series was to feature the leading contributors to the American symphonic repertoire of the twentieth century through comprehensive recorded surveys of their music. The composer whose music was chosen to inaugurate the series was Howard Hanson. The enthusiasm with which these recordings were received by the press suggests how dramatically the tide of fashion had turned and how receptive the public might be for unfamiliar music that would invite their affection rather than repel their advances. Following is a sample of the critical reassessment that began to take place with the appearance of these new recordings:

> Surely enough time has now passed for us to reexamine and reevaluate the entire catalog of Howard Hanson's compositions. Like so many victims of the 12-tone wave, he does not deserve the neglect the past few decades have inflicted upon him.[40]

> Hanson's simple diatonic language, his strong, clean-shaven orchestration and his tendency toward uncomplicated heroism are never pretentious, always sincere, very American.[41]

> One of Hanson's most characteristic and enduring qualities as a composer is the visceral, seamless flow of his melodic lines—so free as to sound almost improvisatory. It is precisely this melodic urgency that

> drives the symphonic argument along, and it is amazing how sure and well developed the technique was here in a symphony [the "Nordic"] written when he was still only in his early twenties. This is confident, generous, beautifully made music, richly (and sensitively) scored.[42]

> I hardly care that Hanson was enamored of the best Romantics of his era—Sibelius, Grieg, Rimsky-Korsakov, Tchaikovsky, Dvorák, and (surprisingly) early Debussy. For the results are nearly as good as many of his models—so good, in fact, that if these symphonies weren't American they would probably be standard repertory items.[43]

> Howard Hanson can be described as the American Neoromantic composer *par excellence*. . . . The early Hanson symphonies . . . are splendidly effusive, gorgeously orchestrated, rich in harmonic texture.[44]

> He was one of the last great romantics in the tradition of Dvorák and Sibelius, and anyone who enjoys those two composers should find most of his work appealing.[45]

Perhaps the most balanced and thoughtful summary comment about Hanson was offered barely a year after his death by composer and critic David Owens: "Hanson stood behind tonality and the conservative musical ideal to the end. But the best of his works . . . are more than merely indulgently appealing tonal music. The coincidence of Hanson's aural and dramatic sensibilities made for very effective pieces, and when his conveying of conviction did join forces with his masterful sense of orchestral depth and tonal beauty, the results were memorable and compelling."[46]

NOTES

1. Joseph Machlis, *Introduction to Contemporary Music* (New York: W. W. Norton & Co., 1961), 414.
2. David Russell Williams, *Conversations with Howard Hanson* (Arkadelphia, Ark.: Delta Publications, 1988), 83.
3. Williams, *Conversations*, 84.
4. Williams, *Conversations*, 84.
5. Williams, *Conversations*, 25–26.
6. Allen Cohen, *Howard Hanson in Theory and Practice* (Westport, Conn. and London: Greenwood Press, 2004).
7. Williams, *Conversations*, 82.

8. Williams, *Conversations*, 67.

9. Williams, *Conversations*, 65.

10. Neil Butterworth, *The American Symphony*, (Brookfield, Vt.: Ashgate Publishing Co., 1998), 79.

11. Williams, *Conversations*, 6.

12. Harold Schonberg, Review, *New York Times* (1 March 1968).

13. Williams, *Conversations*, 77.

14. Williams, *Conversations*, 34.

15. Williams, *Conversations*, 14.

16. Williams, *Conversations*, 16.

17. Williams, *Conversations*, 13–14.

18. Williams, *Conversations*, 5.

19. Lawrence Gilman, Review, *New York Herald Tribune* (11 February 1934).

20. Olin Downes, Review, *New York Times* (11 February 1934).

21. W. J. Henderson, Review, *New York Sun* (12 February 1934).

22. Gilman, Review.

23. Downes, Review.

24. Williams, *Conversations*, 32.

25. R. M. Campbell, Review, *Seattle Post-Intelligencer* (30 October 1996).

26. Melinda Bargreen, Review, *Seattle Times* (29 October 1996).

27. Cary Smith, Review, *Tacoma News Tribune* (30 October 1996).

28. Williams, *Conversations*, 15.

29. "Koussevitsky Lauds Hanson," *Rochester Times-Union* (11 December 1939).

30. Elliott Carter, "American Music in the New York Scene," *Modern Music* (1940): 97.

31. Williams, *Conversations*, 7.

32. Frederick Fennell, "The Eastman Wind Ensemble and the American Composer," *Pan Pipes* (January 1955): 19.

33. Howard Hanson, Record Liner Notes, Mercury SR-90267, 1961, reprinted in Mercury 434 370–2, 1996.

34. Howard Hanson, Record Liner Notes, Mercury SR-90357, 1963, reprinted in Mercury 434 370–2, 1996.

35. Richard Freed, Record Liner Notes, Turnabout TV-S 34534, 1973.

36. Williams, *Conversations*, 6.

37. Donald Hunsberger, Record Liner Notes, Mercury SRI-75132, 1979.

38. Patricia Ashley, "Howard Hanson," *Hi Fi/Stereo Review* (June 1968): 55.

39. Donal Henahan, "The Hanson Legacy," *New York Times* (28 February 1981).

40. Paul Moor, Review, *Audio* (December 1989): 142.

41. Bernard Holland, Review, *New York Times* (6 August 1989).

42. Edward Seckerson, Review, *Gramophone* (March 1990): 1604.

43. K. Robert Schwarz, Review, *ISAM Newsletter* (November 1989).

44. David Hall, Review, *Stereo Review* (September 1989): 126.

45. Joseph McLellan, Review, *Washington Post* (3 January 1993).

46. David Owens, "Inside 20th-Century Music: Howard Hanson," *Christian Science Monitor* (11 August 1982).

SELECTED BIBLIOGRAPHY

Ashley, Patricia. "Howard Hanson." *Hi Fi/Stereo Review* (June 1968): 47–55.

Cohen, Allen. *Howard Hanson in Theory and Practice.* Westport, Conn. and London: Greenwood Press, 2004.

Hanson, Howard. "Flowering of American Music." *Saturday Review* (6 August 1949): 157–164.

Henahan, Donal. "The Hanson Legacy." *New York Times* (28 February 1981).

Owens, David. "Inside 20th-Century Music: Howard Hanson." *Christian Science Monitor* (11 August 1982).

Perone, James E. *Howard Hanson: A Bio-Bibliography.* Westport, Conn.: Greenwood Press, 1993.

Williams, David Russell. *Conversations with Howard Hanson.* Arkadelphia, Ark.: Delta Publications, 1988.

ESSENTIAL DISCOGRAPHY

Chesky CD112: Symphony No. 2, "Romantic" (RCA Sym. Orch., Charles Gerhardt, cond.); www.chesky.com.

Delos DE-3092: Symphony No. 3; *Fantasy Variations* (Carol Rosenberger, piano); Symphony No. 6 (NY Chamber Symphony; Seattle Sym. Orch., Gerard Schwarz, cond.); www.delosmus.com.

Delos DE-3105: *Lament for Beowulf* (Seattle Sym. Chorale); *Merry Mount*—Orchestral Suite; Symphony No. 4, "Requiem"; *Serenade; Pastorale* (NY Chamber Symphony; Seattle Sym. Orch., Gerard Schwarz, cond.); www.delosmus.com

Delos DE-3130: Piano Concerto (Carol Rosenberger, piano); Symphony No. 5, "Sinfonia Sacra"; *Mosaics*; Symphony No. 7, "A Sea Symphony" (Seattle Sym. Chor. and Orch., Gerard Schwarz, cond.); www.delosmus.com.

Delos DE-3160: *Lux Aeterna; Dies Natalis; The Mystic Trumpeter* (James Earl Jones, speaker); *Lumen in Christo* (Seattle Sym. Chor. and Orch., Gerard Schwarz, cond.); www.delosmus.com.

Naxos 8.559072: Symphony No. 1, "Nordic"; *Pan and the Priest; Merry Mount*—Orchestral Suite; *Rhythmic Variations* (Nashville Sym. Orch., Kenneth Schermerhorn, cond.) *www.naxos.com*.

Vittorio Giannini: Photo by Nicolas Flagello, provided courtesy of Dianne Flagello.

4

Vittorio Giannini

Few composers fit the label "traditionalist" as accurately as Vittorio Giannini. Deeply imbued at an early age with the aesthetic values and compositional techniques of the European musical heritage, he devoted his life—as both composer and teacher—to applying these principles to his own music, and to passing them on to the next generation of serious music students. Composed at a time that virtually defined itself by its rejection of traditional values, little of Giannini's music was taken seriously by the music profession during his lifetime, although his meticulous craftsmanship commanded considerable respect and his personal warmth and magnetism earned him great affection. Yet no less demanding a critic than Virgil Thomson could write, "[Giannini's] talent has long been known as phenomenal, and now . . . he writes like a master, . . . with such fine skill and such pretty taste that no one can deny him a place among the authentic composers of our time. By following none of the contemporary trends, in fact, he has arrived at a highly individual position."[1] Giannini was a composer who could state, in all sincerity, that his creative work was motivated by, "an unrelenting quest for the beautiful, with the humble hope that I may be privileged to achieve this goal, if only for one precious moment and share this moment with my listeners."[2]

BIOGRAPHY

Vittorio Giannini was born in Philadelphia's Italian American community in 1903, to a family already notable for its musical activity. His father, Ferruccio, was a successful operatic tenor, immigrating to the United States from Tuscany in 1885. He was a stern, conservative, but rather charismatic patriarch, who set high standards for his family. In addition to his singing career, he recruited musicians from Italy to form an Italian American band that toured professionally and made several recordings; many of its members later found their way into the Philadelphia Orchestra. Ferruccio's wife, Antonetta, had been a professional violinist. Vittorio was the third of four children: his oldest sister Euphemia (1895–1979) became an operatic soprano, enjoying a long teaching career at the Curtis Institute; his second sister Dusolina (1902–1986) became one of the world's leading divas during the 1930s and 1940s; his younger brother Francesco (1908–1982) left a career as a professional cellist to become a psychiatrist.

Young Vittorio began taking piano lessons from his mother when he was five; violin and theory studies soon followed. After four years he had progressed so far that he was awarded a scholarship to study at the Verdi Conservatory in Milan. There, under his mother's supervision, he and his sister Euphemia lived and studied for four years (1913–1917). Although his study centered around the violin, Vittorio also showed an interest in composing, and a steady stream of original pieces began to appear.

Returning to the United States, Vittorio completed his basic general education in Philadelphia while continuing his efforts at composition. In 1920, he completed an ambitious *Stabat Mater* for soloists, chorus, and large orchestra, conducting the first performance of the work—indeed, the first major performance of any of his works—at the Philadelphia Opera House later that year. Not long after, Antonetta Giannini took both Vittorio and Dusolina to New York to pursue their musical training. Vittorio was introduced to the director of the graduate program at the Juilliard School and in 1925 was awarded a scholarship to study composition there, under Rubin Goldmark, while pursuing his violin studies with Hans Letz.

It was about this time that Giannini met Karl Flaster, a young news reporter with higher literary aspirations, while they were waiting together at a bus stop. The two became friends and began to collaborate on writing songs. Thus began a creative partnership that continued for the rest of their lives and went on to include several operas. They wrote their first song together, "Tell Me, Oh Blue, Blue Sky," in 1927; it became their most popular song and is still heard on recital programs more than seventy years later.

In 1931, the year after he completed his studies at Juilliard, Giannini married a pianist named Lucia Avella. The following year— eleven years after Howard Hanson—he won the Prix de Rome, which enabled him to return to Italy for another four years, accompanied by his new wife. Using this opportunity to concentrate on composition, he completed an ambitious, full-length opera, *Lucedia* (with a libretto by Flaster), a symphony, a cantata called *La Primavera*, and a piano concerto.

Having already made a considerable impact on European audiences, sister Dusolina attempted to use her influence to interest some of the major opera companies in *Lucedia*, a tragedy of doomed love based on an old Indian legend. The Munich National Opera proved to be receptive and mounted the work in October 1934. (Earlier that year, Bloch's *Sacred Service* had its premiere in Turin and Naples, and Hanson's *Merry Mount* was produced by New York's Metropolitan Opera Company.) After the premiere, Flaster described the experience of working with Giannini: "He possesses stupendous vitality, energy, and ambition. Music pours from him and to work with him is exhausting, yet uplifting, enervating, yet strengthening."[3] Although Flaster's libretto came under criticism, the music was well received, and subsequent productions were discussed. Giannini even met with Mussolini to discuss the possibility of an Italian production, but nothing materialized. Several years later, the orchestral score and parts were destroyed during the Allied bombing of Munich, and the opera has never been mounted again.

The favorable reception of *Lucedia* in Germany only served to enhance Giannini's growing reputation in the United States. In November 1935, he conducted the premiere of *Primavera*, an hour-long cantata scored for vocal soloists, chorus, and orchestra and comprising more than a dozen sections, each touching upon an aspect of the season of spring. The performance was broadcast over the NBC radio network. Before he completed *Lucedia*, Giannini had received a commission to write a symphony in commemoration of Theodore Roosevelt, as part of the opening ceremonies for the New

York State Theodore Roosevelt Memorial in January 1936. Completing the work in 1935, Giannini conducted the premiere, which was broadcast over the NBC radio network. Its first public performance took place three months later, in Rochester, New York, under the direction of Howard Hanson. In 1937, a twenty-three-year-old Rosalyn Tureck presented the premiere of Giannini's Piano Concerto in New York City, with Leon Barzin conducting the National Orchestral Association. Perhaps prompted by his successful fulfillment of the Roosevelt Memorial commission, the International Business Machine Corporation (IBM) invited Giannini to compose another symphony, this one to celebrate the January 1938 opening of the new IBM World Headquarters in New York City. The composer conducted the CBS Symphony Orchestra in the premiere performance, which was a highlight of the opening ceremonies and was broadcast over several different radio stations.

Thanks partly to Dusolina's persistence, Giannini enjoyed further European successes during the 1930s as well, until international tensions began to indicate that war was imminent. In 1937, she was soprano soloist in the Vienna premiere of her brother's large Requiem Mass, completed the previous year. And in 1938, the Hamburg Staatsoper introduced Giannini's next opera, an adaptation of Hawthorne's *The Scarlet Letter*, for which Flaster had provided the libretto. The production was conducted by Eugen Jochum and boasted Dusolina as Hester Prynne, Joachim Sattler as Arthur Dimmesdale, and Hans Hotter as Roger Chillingworth. The audience at the premiere demanded thirty curtain calls, and the reviews were enthusiastic. Subsequent productions were discussed, but the work has not been heard again.

On his return to the United States, Giannini began to devote some of his attention to teaching the skills of musical composition. Having developed his craft through arduous drills and exercises, along with diligent study of the repertoire, as practiced in Europe for centuries, Giannini felt an obligation to pass along the techniques he had mastered to the next generation and also to serve as something of a spiritual mentor to those about to enter the field as professionals. In 1939, he joined the faculty of the Juilliard School, and, in 1941, the Manhattan School of Music as well.

By the late 1930s, Giannini had developed a reputation as one of America's leading composers of "old-fashioned," romantic vocal music. The Columbia Broadcasting System (CBS) commissioned him to write two works as part of a new program that presented short operas composed especially for radio broadcast. Giannini responded with an adaptation of *Beauty and the Beast* in 1938 and a work called *Blennerhassett* in 1939. By this time he and Flaster had written about a dozen songs, and several were appearing with some frequency on recital programs. In addition to "Tell Me, Oh Blue, Blue Sky," others, such as "Sing to My Heart a Song," "It Is a Spring Night," and "There Were Two Swans," won favor as well. These songs were championed by such well-known singers as Giovanni Martinelli, Jan Peerce, and later, Eileen Farrell, Leonard Warren, and even Mario Lanza.

In 1941, Giannini attempted to interest Flaster in a plan for an operatic treatment of the life of Jesus. (Though described as a very "spiritual" person by those who knew him, Giannini never practiced the Roman Catholicism into which he was born.) Flaster had become discouraged and pessimistic about his career, however, and worked slowly and halfheartedly on the project. A letter written by composer to librettist during this period captures something of the spirit of the man, while illustrating the sort of counsel he gave to students experiencing the self-doubt and insecurity that face so many young artists who receive little tangible encouragement or positive feedback after investing significant time and effort:

> Dear Karl, you must know that people like you and me are not for this age. Our bodies are living in the present, our thoughts are in the future. Your poems, my music, are the products of an honest, straightforward, and deep feeling. Today this is not fully appreciated. It matters not. If our production is of value time will do us justice; if not, we have at least the virtue of having been honest with our gift. . . . Our reward would be the artistic accomplishment and if it turns out first rate, the joy of having created a masterwork.[4]

Nevertheless, after years of struggling with the project, Flaster gave up and Giannini completed the libretto himself.

During the late 1940s, Giannini was invited to serve as Dean of the Advanced Division of the Brevard Music Center in North Carolina. This position served to familiarize the composer and the arts administrators of North Carolina with each other—a development that was to have significant consequences later on.

Giannini had mused over the idea of basing an opera on one of

Shakespeare's plays for some time. In fact, he had drafted a scenario for an operatic adaptation of *The Taming of the Shrew* while he was still in the final stages of composing *The Scarlet Letter*. Unable to find a suitable librettist, he decided to work on it himself, with the help of his former student Dorothy Fee. Interrupted by several other projects, he did not complete the opera until 1950, but *The Taming of the Shrew* has proven to be his most celebrated work: The opera was first presented by the Music Drama Guild of Cincinnati and the Cincinnati Symphony in January 1953, under the direction of Thor Johnson, who was becoming a vigorous champion of Giannini's music. The opera was next seen via color telecast on the NBC television network in March 1954, in a production conducted by Peter Herman Adler, with John Raitt and Susan Yager in the leading roles. As the first opera to be telecast in color, *The Taming of the Shrew* drew considerable public attention and won a special award from the New York Music Critics Circle. The opera has been performed many times since then and was recorded commercially as well.

Giannini's marriage to Lucia had ended in divorce in 1951. Two years later he married a young harpist named Joan Adler, who had recently graduated from Juilliard. In 1956, Giannini further increased his teaching responsibilities by joining the faculty of the Curtis Institute of Music. This same year, he completed the short score of *Christus*, now a tetralogy of operas.

During the 1950s, Giannini became aware of the relatively sudden emergence of the symphonic band and its smaller counterpart, the wind ensemble, as proficient musical media flourishing in American colleges and universities. These ensembles, eager to dispel pejorative images of bands as loose aggregations of undisciplined amateurs, displayed voracious appetites for challenging original compositions. A vital new repertoire was being created by many of America's leading composers, and Giannini—perhaps recalling fond childhood memories of the concerts given by his father's band—seized the opportunity to make his own contribution, producing five works for band, including his Symphony no. 3, which he composed in 1958. This symphony has become a staple of the band repertoire, and is, without question, Giannini's most frequently performed work.

The 1960s proved to be a difficult time for Giannini, more for personal than professional reasons. Indeed, in many ways his career was at its apex, despite the fact that his romantically styled operas were received less and less charitably during these musically icono-clastic times. However, he was still receiving important commis-sions, such as the Ford Foundation grant that sponsored the composition of *The Medead* in 1960, considered by many to be one of his greatest works. The Ford Foundation also commissioned *The Harvest*, a *verismo*-style opera for which Karl Flaster supplied the story as well as the libretto. Premiered by the Chicago Lyric Opera in November 1961, the work received what was probably the worst critical response of his entire career. The same year, Giannini com-pleted a comic opera, called *Rehearsal Call*, based on a play by Fran-cis Swann. The work was commissioned by the Juilliard School, where it was produced in February 1962.

The following year, Giannini was invited to serve on a commis-sion to consider the founding of an ambitious arts academy in North Carolina. Such an institution would serve as an artistic training ground for the entire southern United States. The study concluded with a decision to establish the North Carolina School of the Arts; in 1964 Giannini was assigned the task of developing the curriculum and hiring the faculty and was offered the opportunity to serve as its first president. In order to fulfill these responsibilities, he was forced to relinquish his teaching positions at the Juilliard School, the Manhattan School, and the Curtis Institute.

But he did accept an invitation from Peter Mennin to head a new project, to be administered through Juilliard but financed by the U.S. Office of Education. Known as the Juilliard Repertory Project, the plan was to develop a broad curriculum for schools all over the country by selecting examples of the finest music, drawn from five centuries, to serve as pedagogical material. The curriculum would include folk music from many countries as well as "classical" music; new music would also be commissioned especially for this program.

But Giannini's health was not good. Something of a bon vivant, he frequently indulged his fondness for elaborate dinners, expensive cigars, and fancy European sports cars. He had already suffered one heart attack, but he had difficulty modifying his lifestyle. In 1963, his second wife announced that she wanted a divorce, which left him devastated. Many of the works he composed during the 1960s reflect—with greater or lesser explicitness—the turbulence of this period in his life. Double-bass soloist Gary Karr recalls, "Giannini wrote his *Psalm 130* for me during the period when his young wife was divorcing him. He told me that he was so much in love with her that he found it impossible to sleep, so during those agonizing nights, he poured his heart out into this work."[5]

The North Carolina School of the Arts opened in September 1965, with Giannini as its president. That year, despite the myriad responsibilities entailed in guiding a new school through its first year, and the attendant emotional pressures, he managed to complete a full-length operatic adaptation of the Greek play *Edipus* and began work on an *opera buffa*, *The Servant of Two Masters*, based on a play by Carlo Goldoni. *Servant* was to be presented by the New York City Opera in 1967. In November 1966—during the North Carolina School's second year of operation—Giannini suffered a fatal heart attack while in New York for the Thanksgiving break. He was sixty-three years old. With no children, he left his considerable estate, acquired through shrewd investments in real estate, to the North Carolina School.

At the time of his death, Giannini was known chiefly as one of America's leading teachers of the traditional skills of musical composition. Serving concurrently on the faculties of the Juilliard School, the Manhattan School of Music, and, later, the Curtis Institute for many years, he was regarded with great respect, affection, and admiration as something of a "father-figure" for a whole generation of young composers, many of whom went on to develop significant careers of their own. Alfred Reed, John Corigliano, David Amram, Nicolas Flagello, Thomas Pasatieri, and Adolphus Hailstork are just a few of the better-known composers who polished their skills under Giannini's guidance. His appointment as founding president of the North Carolina School of the Arts acknowledged his position as one of the nation's leading figures in arts education. Although he regarded himself primarily as a composer, he did not use his institutional affiliations to promote his own music, as did Howard Hanson, for example, so that his works never achieved widespread recognition. His own musical output was viewed largely as a footnote to his role as an educator and was generally dismissed as the "old-fashioned" byproduct of his "academic" orientation.

MUSIC

If Howard Hanson may be regarded as the standard-bearer for the style known as *Neo-Romanticism*, then Vittorio Giannini might be characterized as the avatar of what might be termed *Traditionalism*. The two concepts can be distinguished by noting that while both the form and content of Hanson's music are aligned with the principles of Romanticism, as opposed to Classicism, Giannini, on the other hand, developed a language that embraced principles and practices associated with the Baroque (and even pre-Baroque at times) and Classical, as well as Romantic styles, while rejecting Modernism in its many manifestations. In light of their points of both similarity and difference, a further comparison between the two is useful and even illuminating.

Certainly the music of both composers is accessible to the general listener: each was concerned with communicating to an audience, and each used a vocabulary and syntax familiar to the average concertgoer. But Giannini's career lacked the high visibility of Hanson's, which benefited from his position as director of a major music institution for at least four decades not to mention a recording project that managed to include virtually all his major works. Giannini also never had a major "hit"—a work performed widely by well-known orchestras and conductors—as Hanson did with his "Romantic" Symphony. When compared with such contemporaries as Copland, Thomson, and Harris, Hanson appears to represent a distinctly less American, more European mode of expression; but when compared with Giannini, Hanson's American qualities are clearly discerned, not only its style of orchestration, with its emphasis on winds and percussion, but also its rather simple, hearty, and straightforward optimism. By comparison, Giannini is quite thoroughly European in his orientation—in his use of classical forms, in his orchestration, and in the articulation of his phraseology. And if Hanson showed a predilection for choral music and other media suited for grand statements, alongside his seven symphonies, Giannini's interests were more broadly distributed, with songs as well as operas, chamber music as well as symphonies. Though the outputs of both composers are marked by a degree of unevenness in quality, Hanson's deficiencies in craftsmanship are offset by his music's strong sense of "personality," whereas Giannini's compositional skill has rarely met with criticism, while the question of whether he ever developed a truly distinctive voice of his own has been his chief area of vulnerability.

While Hanson's music seemed to build on several specific sources of inspiration, Giannini's influences are harder to specify, as his music is more broadly rooted in the entire European heritage. Yet some particular affinities do emerge: Puccini was clearly a model for his approach to vocal writing, while his treatment of the orchestra owes a great deal to Richard Strauss. Giannini also reflects some of the spirit—if not the language—of Rossini, in the strong *buffa* vein that runs through his creative personality. When one looks more deeply, one also senses an affinity with César Franck, in his romantic treatment of Baroque forms, and with Brahms, in his diligent formal coherence.

When considering such matters as originality versus derivativeness, one must remember that a composer who sets out to devise his own idiosyncratic vocabulary and syntax will sound "original" and "individual" far more readily than will one who chooses to embrace a more conventional language. But that does not mean that a composer of the latter type lacks his own voice, but rather that greater familiarity with his music is necessary before that voice may be discernable. To a thoroughgoing traditionalist like Giannini, the pressing aesthetic issues that concerned most of his colleagues—the quest for originality, the alleged exhaustion of tonality, the search for a uniquely American musical language—were utterly irrelevant. It is not as though he set out to create something "original," and instead produced music reminiscent of others. To his way of thinking, concerns like originality were "red herrings" that reflected insufficient knowledge and skill and a lack of respect for one's predecessors. For Giannini, all the answers lay in the unbroken chain of Western musical tradition, stretching back to Palestrina and before and evolving organically through the centuries. Thus the chromaticism of Wagner and his followers, for example, did not represent the death knell of tonality, but rather a means of expanding expressive possibilities, to be absorbed within the composer's palette of techniques. Revering the heritage of the past, he viewed his own work as a humble contribution to it, as well as a means of expressing his inner self, and he expected to be evaluated on the basis of his craftsmanship and of the sincerity and authenticity of his expression. Reminiscences of other composers were simply a form of homage. As he himself put it, "I try to carry on, amplify and evolve the great principles developed and established by the Masters and apply them to today's harmonic expansion and wider tonal horizon. . . . I believe in using all the compositional techniques the art has acquired up to the very latest."[6]

Unfortunately, Giannini did not keep a complete list of his own works, nor did he date his scores as a matter of course. Many of his works have remained unpublished, many others have gone out of print, some were left incomplete, and some were never orchestrated. Some titles have appeared in listings but the music has not been located. In short, there is no reliable chronological accounting of Giannini's creative work. This chapter, building on the efforts of others, is an attempt to provide a greater degree of accuracy and comprehensiveness than has previously appeared in print.

Giannini's output, which comprises approximately sixty-five works, does not fall into distinct creative periods, as do the outputs of many composers. Rather, his works might be considered to reflect three different, but overlapping, phases of emphasis. The first phase, extending from the 1920s to the early 1940s, shows a primary emphasis on vocal music—especially, operas and songs—of richly romantic character; the second phase, roughly from the early 1940s through the late 1950s, is characterized by an emphasis on instrumental music in classical and Baroque forms, often light and diverting in tone, but with a warm, romantic core; the third phase, comprising the last six years of his life, is marked by the emergence of a somewhat new voice, a Neo-Romantic Expressionism, as in the later works of Bloch—dark, intense, relatively dissonant and less clearly tonal, and much deeper in its emotional range. However, note that these phases are not mutually exclusive: that is, Giannini composed chamber and orchestral works during the first phase, as well as operas and songs; and he continued to write operas during the second phase; and he continued to write diverting instrumental music during the third phase.

Most Representative, Fully Realized Works

The Scarlet Letter (1937)
Symphony no. 1 (1950)
The Taming of the Shrew (1950)
Christus (1956)
Symphony no. 4 (1960)
The Medead (1960)
Antigone (1962)
Psalm 130 (1963)
Variations and Fugue (1964)
Symphony no. 5 (1964)

First Phase (1920s through Early 1940s)

As noted above, Giannini's first creative phase indicates a primary focus on vocal music—chiefly, six operas, two large choral works, and more than a dozen songs—and embraces the 1920s through the early 1940s. However, other works appeared during this period as well, such as his String Quartet and Piano Quintet (both 1930), Piano Trio (1933), Piano Concerto and Woodwind Quintet (both 1934), two symphonies (1935, 1937), Organ Concerto (1937), and Two-Piano Concerto (1939). In these early works, Giannini unabashedly adopted the language and spirit of European music from the late nineteenth and early twentieth century at its most extravagantly emotional, but without the darkly neurotic quality that characterizes much of the music of that period. In this Giannini shares much in common with his older contemporary Erich Wolfgang Korngold. But whereas Korngold's roots are chiefly Austro-Germanic, enriched by both Italian and French elements, Giannini's roots are primarily Italian, enriched by Austro-Germanic and French elements. Giannini's greatest strength—and this was recognized from the outset of his career—is the ease and naturalness with which he could translate basic human emotions directly into music. These works continually take flight through soaring melodies, carefully conceived to rise in intensity from plateau to plateau. It is this quality that accounts for the enduring popularity of composers like Tchaikovsky and Puccini, and posterity seems to suggest that it outweighs any number of compositional weaknesses that may be adduced. In Giannini's case, the chief weakness of his early large-scale works is a creative largesse that borders on fulsomeness. His own voice is first detectable in the vocal works, while in the instrumental works he often seems to remain close to antecedent models.

The early songs on which Giannini collaborated with Karl Flaster were examples of a sentimental genre fashionable from the late 1920s through the early 1950s. Such English-language songs served to leaven vocal recitals, especially on programs directed toward broader audiences, as in the case of those singers who performed frequently on radio. Though not truly aspiring to the high aesthetic standards of the "art-song," these less pretentious efforts, set to texts that verged on the mawkish, drew upon the enriched chromatic harmony found in the more serious works of the recent past and called for the refined vocal production demanded by *Lieder* as well as opera, though making less stringent demands. Ernest Charles, Charles Gilbert Spross, Richard Hageman, Roger Quilter, and Olive Dungan are some of the composers who contributed to this genre. Typically, they would select texts that highlighted some eternal truth, inspiring homily, romantic agony or ecstasy, or otherwise fragile sentiment, and expand them into passionate outpourings that built to grand climaxes. The Giannini-Flaster contributions, of which the most fully consummated were noted earlier, represent this genre at its best. Generally their songs utilized a clearly tonal harmonic language, enriched by chromatic alterations, although some (e.g., "It is a Spring Night") drew upon recent harmonic innovations from France.

Giannini and Flaster completed their first opera, *Lucedia*, in 1934. They based the work on what was supposedly an old Indian legend. In a striking parallel to Hanson's *Merry Mount*, the plot involves the doomed love of a virgin entrusted with tending a sacred flame and Evol, a young man who has become infatuated with her after she appears to him in a vision. After the unfortunate couple is discovered by the townsfolk, they are imprisoned and then set adrift in a small boat to die on the open sea. Giannini and Flaster worked on the opera for several years, completing it just months before its premiere. The work is structured as a Prologue followed by three acts, each divided into two scenes. The orchestration is rich and densely textured, unified by a series of leitmotifs, while the chorus is sometimes subdivided into as many as seven or eight parts.

Critic Herbert Peyser was sent to Munich to cover the premiere for the *New York Times*. After attending several performances he commented on the work astutely and at length. His primary observations are those that would follow performances of Giannini's music throughout his life and afterward as well. Beginning with some devastating criticisms of the libretto, Peyser remarks on the "sheer copiousness" of the music: "There is virtually enough music—beautiful music—in *Lucedia* to outfit a second opera. I can think of no operatic work by an American . . . that approaches this one in melodic lavishness and lyric fluency, in spontaneity, in whole-souled sincerity, in consummate mastery of musical means." He then goes on to express reservations about its lack of "originality" and its indebtedness to its predecessors. But he adds, "Above all, [Giannini] understands the value of sustained vocal lines, broad in sweep and wide in trajectory. He writes for the voice with an instinct for the true idiom that betrays his Italian ancestry. Every-thing 'sings' in *Lucedia*—the glowing orchestra quite as consistently as the people on the stage.'"[7] Whatever the reservations, these are strong claims for the first opera of a thirty-one-year-old composer.

As noted, Giannini's instrumental music from the early 1930s shows somewhat less individuality. His Piano Quintet in F-sharp minor (1930), for example, a leisurely three-movement work of about a half-hour duration, is something of a compromise between a melody/texture/emotion-based approach and the more formal developmental requirements of the Austro-German aesthetic. In this it resembles the sort of chamber music composed by Ernest Chaus-son during the 1890s or—even more so—that of Ernst von Dohnanyi from the 1910s.

Giannini composed his Piano Concerto while he was also working on *Lucedia*. It shares its key (a largely diatonic D minor), its dimen-sions, and even some of its thematic contours with the first concerto of Brahms. However, its character is far more emotionally volatile than Brahms ever was, even at his most unrestrained, and the pre-ponderance of diaphanously billowing *arpeggios*, rather than tightly contrapuntal textures, is more French than German in manner. Much of the concerto's bulk derives from Giannini's tendency (even-tually—but never fully—curbed) to overdevelop, especially via long chains of sequences, throughout every section of a composition. In this work in particular, he is also extremely generous with opportu-nities for the soloist to elaborate the material by means of the full arsenal of conventional virtuoso pyrotechnics. The work is cyclical in construction, clearly unified by the motifs presented at the outset, and while the overall texture is relatively simple, the thematic mate-rial is combined and manipulated with a thoroughness that is almost compulsive. The overall character of the concerto is extrava-gantly emotional, from its grimly portentous opening through its moments of almost saccharine delicacy and preciousness.

There is no evidence that Giannini's Piano Concerto was ever per-formed after its 1937 premiere in New York, although it was well enough received. After noting the current fashion for emotional restraint in music, Francis Perkins opined that "the opulence and expansiveness of Mr. Giannini's score proved welcome. He did not hesitate to dwell upon frankly expressed melodies, while his orches-tral coloring proved warm and vivid."[8] Similarly, Robert Simon found it "full of juicy melodies, and it has a healthy virtuoso bounce." However, both critics found its length excessive. Simon concluded, "A little chopping, lopping, and dropping will clean up the Giannini concerto, and pianists who want a 'real concerto,' one that comes off paper and gets to work on an audience, will find an answer in this composition."[9]

Giannini's next major work was the first of those seven he identified as "symphonies." The first two were not numbered, and the third, completed in 1950, he called (for no known reason) "No. 1." The first, completed in 1935, he identified as *Symphony, "In Memoriam Theodore Roosevelt."* Like the Piano Concerto, it is cyclical in construction and clearly—even diatonically—tonal, this time in G minor, its four expansive movements comprising a duration of about an hour. Again its considerable length is due more to excessive—at times redundant—development than to unfocused meanderings. The symphony is conceived along the lines of a character portrait in dramatic, Late-Romantic style, and its explicit program speaks of a "Death theme," a "Destiny theme," and the like. Its concept is reminiscent of a work like Strauss's *Ein Heldenleben,* although its solemn tone is more suggestive of Gliere's *Ilya Murometz* or, especially, the Swede Ture Rangström's *Symphony, "In Memoriam August Strindberg."* As with the Piano Concerto, there is no evidence that the symphony was ever performed again after its public premiere in Rochester.

Not long after the premiere of *Lucedia,* Giannini set to work on his large-scale *Requiem,* a comic opera in one act called *Not All Prima Donnas are Ladies,* and a number of other works, including several major collaborations with Karl Flaster. The most significant of these was an adaptation of Nathaniel Hawthorne's famous novel *The Scarlet Letter.* (Coincidentally, Hawthorne was also the source for the libretto of Hanson's opera *Merry Mount.*)

The two-act opera was completed in 1937, in time for an auspicious premiere in Hamburg the following year. By this time, the composer seems to have begun to discipline his tendency toward prolixity and redundancy. The event was again documented in the *New York Times* by Herbert Peyser, who found the work "something of a milestone in the history of American opera," and "a very considerable advance" over *Lucedia* in the way that it "moved in a straight line from point to point" with "practically no excess bulk and no unwarranted extravagances." Though qualifying his reaction with questions about its "originality," Peyser concedes the emergence of "a personal quality hitherto not conspicuous in Mr. Giannini's music and one discerns in it a kind of profile." He goes on to assert, "Above all, this music is a wholly honest, a wholly sincere expression of a nature refreshingly true to itself, that scorns to force its growth and development by recourse to idioms and agencies foreign to it. And it is music which flows spontaneously, which sings and invariably 'sounds.'"[10]

Lest one wonder whether Peyser's enthusiasm was idiosyncratic, rather than representative, consider the comments of critic Geraldine deCourgy:

> [Giannini] has assimilated much from successful predecessors, but even so the score was by no means an empty imitation of banal formulae. It was rather the free unfolding of a spontaneous melodic gift that thinks primarily in terms of the human voice and one that accepts tradition as an excellent thing without seeking to make new rules for himself or for others. . . . Though the music contained nothing new and sought and attacked no constructional problems, it pressed on with charm and continuity, and in the straightforward manner of the born and nonpioneering minstrel embraced all the gleaming instrumentation, opulent tone and surging outward-folding melodies that are the soul of music to every Italian with a song in his heart. And Giannini must be counted one of these.[11]

And yet *The Scarlet Letter* has never been produced again. If one can look past the clichéd phraseology of these notices, one cannot help but wonder—especially in view of the way the oft-bemoaned inability of American composers to produce viable operas has become a critical cliché itself—how it is that a work received as favorably as this has never been reconsidered and revived.

After he had completed *The Scarlet Letter*, Giannini turned his attention to a commission from the IBM Corporation to compose a symphony in celebration of the company's new World Headquarters in New York City. An outgrowth of the erstwhile IBM motto "World Peace Through World Trade," the "IBM Symphony" was to be a work of art as well as a self-congratulatory corporate memento, while also conveying a particular politicoeconomic message. The result—hardly a symphony—is a twelve-minute symphonic movement in three connected sections, unified musically by a fragment from IBM's theme song "Ever Onward." In view of the many considerations involved, it is surprising that the work is as effective as it is. Giannini seemed able to accept the various a priori constraints and worked within them to produce a composition true to his own personal Neo-Romantic style. The opening section conveys a sense of urgency and agitation, supposed to represent the troubled international situation; a lush, warmly lyrical second section is intended to represent the search for peace and love; the bustling third section suggests busy industrial activity; and a potpourri of national anthem fragments implies a spirit of international cooperation, all of which culminate in an obligatory triumphant finale.

After returning from the European production of *The Scarlet Letter*, Giannini turned to another commission: this time, from the Columbia Broadcasting System, who were interested in a short opera suitable for radio broadcast. He responded with an adaptation of the fairy tale *Beauty and the Beast*, with libretto by Robert Simon. The success of this effort, broadcast in 1939, led to another commission from CBS later the same year. This time, working with librettists Philip Roll and Norman Corwin, he adapted an actual episode from American history (involving Aaron Burr's conspiracy to overthrow the American government) into a romantic melodrama called *Blennerhassett*. Composer and librettists were well aware of the ever-present danger that one dull or graceless moment could move the listener to change the station. Both works—similar in their musical approaches, despite different subject matter—have subsequently been produced on the stage, with successful results. Each demonstrates the composer's remarkable ability to create within a duration of less than thirty minutes a concise music drama that contains all the necessary elements: strife, romantic passion, conflict, emotional peaks, all conveyed through gripping, gratifying music, deftly woven together through contrapuntal cross-references, in such a way that the audience leaves humming. Consider Bernard Holland's comments in the *New York Times* after a staged production of *Blennerhassett* more than half a century after its original broadcast and a quarter-century after the composer's death. After the still unavoidable references to Giannini's "amalgam" of the music of others, Holland adds:

> Still, one can't help being impressed by the grace and symmetry with which his stylistic borrowings are arranged. The vocal lines pour as thickly and smoothly as sloe gin. The climaxes are perfectly calculated. There is not a single stumble during the dramatic interchanges of this

five-person cast. Giannini's absolute confidence with other people's ideas constitutes an originality all its own. It is also a far cry from some of the clumsiness of his colleagues today.[12]

Second Phase (Early 1940s through 1960)

As mentioned, during the early 1940s, Giannini—now settling into New York City's academic musical life—turned his compositional attention away from operas and songs and toward an increased concentration on instrumental music. But there were other changes in emphasis as well: Instead of the grand scale and inflated romantic rhetoric of his operatic and instrumental works from the 1930s, most of the pieces from the early 1940s through the 1950s reveal a clearer, more concise approach to form, a moderation of emotional content, greater rhythmic regularity and textural simplicity, and a somewhat freer treatment of tonality. In short, Giannini arrived at his own adaptation of "Neo-Classicism," one that eschewed the biting dissonance, brittle sonorities, and emotional detachment of Stravinsky and his followers and reflected instead an ingratiating spirit of lighthearted geniality. Giannini also began to pay increased attention to matters of practicality, with regard to both performance forces and ease of execution. Increasingly aware of the burgeoning demand for high-quality repertoire of intermediate difficulty created by post–World War II America's emphasis on music education in the public schools, Giannini began to provide his own form of *Gebrauchsmusik*.

Somewhat ironically, the usefulness and appeal of this music resulted in something approaching popularity for a number of the pieces. Indeed, these have become Giannini's most frequently performed works and have essentially defined his creative personality for the musical public, although they represent only one aspect of his art. The irony is that their formal clarity and genial tone have led more demanding critics to dismiss these pieces as rather pedestrian efforts—skillfully crafted but reflecting neither emotional depth nor a truly individual style. Applied to the instrumental works of Giannini's second creative phase, these criticisms are not without some justification. Much of this music may indeed have no deeper meaning or purpose than simply to offer a pleasant diversion. And, in truth, his work is not as immediately identifiable moment to moment as is, say, Hanson's or Creston's. However, the essential core of Giannini's music is found in his slow movements. In them can be found certain distinctive melodic, phraseological, and harmonic features that gradually, with greater familiarity, emerge as Giannini's true voice. These features include a fondness for lines that highlight the interval of the fourth, a particular movement between a minor tonic and its submediant (heard as early as "Tell Me, Oh Blue, Blue Sky"), chords in which the bass notes are dissonant with the chord above, much use of *appoggiaturas* and suspensions, and—most of all—a way of spinning long melodic lines by developing motifs in phrases that build gradually and consistently through increasing emotional plateaus over a long span of time.

Although Giannini reduced his concentration on vocal music during this second phase, he did not abandon it altogether. And there is little doubt that his best-known and most highly regarded work is, indeed, his seventh opera, based on Shakespeare's *The Taming of the Shrew,* completed in 1950. The libretto fashioned by the composer and Dorothy Fee uses Shakespeare's own words, for the most part, although some of the lines are taken from *Romeo and Juliet* and one of the sonnets. As Giannini later recounted:

> It was necessary to enlarge the love element between Bianca, the younger sister, and Lucentio for a lyrical contrast needed about half way through the play. This actually called for additional text, and to try to match the quality of Shakespeare's verse was an obviously impossible task. I do not remember now how or when the idea of using lines from some of his other plays occurred to me, but I found that some of *Romeo and Juliet* fit perfectly. A similar situation arose in the last act. Kate needed a monologue where she could express the transformation taking place within her (which I felt was brought about largely because she had fallen in love with Petruchio). Again, after a search through Shakespeare's writings, the text for this solo was found in the Sonnets. The ending of the play needed to be altered, for in an operatic version it was necessary to have a lyrical situation where Kate's taming and Petruchio's love for her, despite his extraordinary actions, could be expressed in a love scene and duet. For this scene, additional text was also found in the Sonnets.[13]

The Overture immediately sets the buoyant, ebullient tone of the opera, while introducing most of the themes and motifs that pervade the work and provide its basic material. Despite the sparkling *opera buffa* exuberance that characterizes much of the work—especially Act I—the music is subtly conceived throughout, the orchestra creating a continuous symphonic development into which the voices—while dominating the sonority—are thoroughly integrated. This is the essence of Giannini's mature operatic style: free and uninhibited Italianate lyricism emerging from and soaring above a richly Straussian orchestral fabric intricately woven from a small number of unifying motivic elements. In keeping with the work's cheerful good humor, the harmonic language is straightforwardly tonal—even diatonic much of the time—although moments of romantic ardor expand with lush, chromatic opulence.

Among the work's high points are the effervescent three-part *fugato* among Lucentio, Tranio, and Biondello in Act I; Lucentio and Hortensio's respective attempts to court Bianca while disguised as tutors in Act II, Scene 1; the passionate love scene between Lucentio and Bianca, also in Act II, Scene 1; Katharina's aria in Act III; and the glorious finale of the opera, beginning first with a male quintet in a confused melange of mistaken identity, which is then resolved in a richly lyrical sextet involving the two couples and the two fathers, Baptista and Vincentio, and finally concluding with an ardent love duet between Katharina and Petruchio.

Virgil Thomson attended the opera's Cincinnati premiere in 1953 and commented:

> The Taming of the Shrew' is a strong work, a practical work; a highly professional achievement that holds the attention by musical means and that communicates dramatically. I suppose this is the definition of an opera, a real opera . . . a perfect opera. It has a good plot and its words are Shakespeare's. But it tells its story through music, vocal and instrumental; . . . It also represents an achievement in the field of today's major operatic need, which is English-language opera. In this sense it is a work of "advance," in spite of its stylistic old-fashionedness. . . . The libretto . . . is compact, expeditious, seems to have no major faults. His musical setting also has a clear trajectory, falls in a virtually perfect curve from its farcical beginning to its romantic close, and the effectiveness with which its dramatic line is sustained is due . . . to the composer's skillful exploration and equilibration of the musical opportunities offered. But the air-borne quality of the opera is most of all a result of sustained musical inspiration. . . . A sort of symphonic continuity involving thematic developments and transformations gives formal coherence, makes a musical shape of each scene, each act, the whole work. This thematic and orchestral elaboration points up the story, of course, colors its emotional content and underlines its dra-

matic syntax. The vocal lines chiefly follow rather than lead it, though they do become the center of attention in tender moments. . . . Dramatically it is strong and musically it is masterful. . . . its melodic charm constant, its orchestral sound delicious. It is a professional piece of work that communicates and is built to wear. One suspects that it might stand up even in the great houses. It rather asks for grand execution, in fact. . . . It is also by its vast energy and high musico-dramatic competence and by its sweet warmth of sentiment born for the big time. . . . For Giannini's possession and exuberant exercise of all these qualities let us today be thankful.[14]

(In view of Thomson's enthusiasm, it is remarkable that Giannini's name does not even appear in the composer-critic's book *American Music Since 1910,* published in 1970!)

In 1954, *The Taming of the Shrew* was telecast nationally. Olin Downes, writing in the *New York Times*, compared it favorably with Stravinsky's *The Rake's Progress*. The opera has enjoyed many subsequent productions throughout the country and has been consistently well received by audiences, if often somewhat begrudgingly by critics. Nicholas Tawa recalls, "I myself attended a Boston performance of the opera in 1960 and witnessed a huge audience of around 9,000 people go wild over its potency, vivid impact, alternating moments of charm and ardor, and luscious sounds. . . . [Yet] local reviewers castigated the composer and abused the work."[15] Soon after its premiere, Giannini devised an "orchestral suite," which serves to give broader exposure to the opera's most melodically appealing music.

The other significant operatic venture of Giannini's second compositional phase was probably the most ambitious creative effort of his entire career: the tetralogy *Christus*. He had initially presented the idea to Karl Flaster in 1941 and attempted to interest him in writing the libretto. But Flaster, discouraged and pessimistic, was unable to complete the task, so Giannini undertook it himself. Working on the project intermittently for some fifteen years, he completed the four operas in 1956, intending them for performance on consecutive nights. Calling for a large cast, including chorus, dancers, and so on, none of the constituent parts of *Christus* has ever been performed, nor is it certain that the orchestration was ever completed. However, Giannini played through it on the piano for Thor Johnson, who declared it to be the composer's masterpiece. Nicolas

Flagello, a student and, later, close friend of Giannini, was familiar with the tetralogy and echoed Johnson's sentiments. The operas are entitled *Nativity* (later changed to *Herod*), *Ministry*, *The Triumph*, and *Resurrection* (alternately called *The Passion*).

The chief instrumental works of Giannini's second phase are the first four of his numbered symphonies. The First, originally entitled *Sinfonia*, was completed in 1950 and had its premiere the following year by the Cincinnati Symphony Orchestra, under the direction of Thor Johnson, to whom the work was dedicated. Cast in one large movement in *sonata allegro* form, the symphony is built essentially from one thematic idea, which sprouts two other significant motivic fragments. The yearning, wide-arching character of this theme colors the entire character of the work, which exhibits a constant ebb and flow of unresolved emotion. Indeed, its exhaustive thematic development, culminating in an elaborate double fugue, combined with its ceaseless emotional intensity, all contained within a tight and relatively concise structure, make it one of Giannini's most powerful and fully realized works from this period.

Giannini's Symphony no. 2 was commissioned—as was Hanson's *Song of Democracy*—in honor of the fiftieth anniversary of the Music Educators National Conference. Completed in 1955, the work again bears a dedication to Thor Johnson, who was instrumental in arranging the commission. The three-movement symphony is highly representative of Giannini's music from this period: vigorously extroverted outer movements applying classical forms with the straightforward clarity of textbook examples, framing a warmly romantic slow movement redolent of a poignant nostalgia. One of the motifs that comprise the first theme of the first movement is dominated by the interval of the fourth, which Giannini used frequently—both melodically and harmonically—during this period to produce a "cooler" effect than that created by expanded triadic structures, to facilitate more casual modulations, and to create a less tightly focused sense of tonality. Much of the development during the outer movements harnesses the motoric momentum of quasi-Baroque thematic patterns. The symphony was premiered at the MENC convention in Chicago in 1955, under the direction of Joseph Maddy. Composed with young musicians in mind, it has remained a favorite of student orchestras ever since.

Giannini composed his Third Symphony in 1958, in response to a commission from the Duke University Band and its conductor Paul

Bryan, who gave the premiere the following year. His second contribution to this medium (he had composed *Praeludium and Allegro* earlier the same year), it is unquestionably Giannini's most often performed work and has become an enduring staple of the serious band repertoire. Its musical substance suggests it as the band counterpart to its orchestral predecessor in its clarity of form, simplicity of texture, geniality of expression, and its evocation of the freshness of youth. In four movements instead of three, the first places a hearty theme, expansively thrusting upward via a series of fourths, in opposition to a more warmly introspective second theme. Again, much of the development is based on motoric chattering patterns derived from the first theme. Similar to the previous symphony, the second movement evokes a melancholy, nostalgic mood. The third movement is a softly understated *scherzo*, while the fourth movement calls upon the band's martial associations, with an exuberant march somewhat reminiscent of similar efforts by Sir William Walton. Along with the sunny disposition and apparent straightforwardness of works like the Second and Third Symphonies, the immediacy and durability of their appeal is the result of considerable subtlety in motivic and harmonic relationships and even in voice leading.

Giannini's Symphony no. 4 aims toward a tighter integration of materials and a more serious level of expression than its two predecessors. The three-movement work was completed in 1960 and dedicated to Jean Morel, who conducted the first performance with the Juilliard Orchestra in May of that year. Like the Second and Third Symphonies, the Fourth opens with themes—three in this case—of widely contrasting character: the first, restless and tonally vague; the second, tender and warm; and a closing theme, passionate and triumphant. However, a closer examination reveals that all the thematic material of the symphony is derived from the first movement's opening theme, which is based solely on a series of ascending fourths and descending fifths (disguised by octave shifts) and includes all twelve tones. From the very opening of the work, the familiar conventions of *sonata allegro* form take place on the surface of a densely concentrated developmental fabric of contrapuntal interrelationships. The second movement is the emotional core of the symphony, with an opening theme that displays far more chromatic range than the composer's norm and a central section that blossoms into a gorgeously impassioned melody. The final movement begins in the character of a *scherzo* in Giannini's familiar *buffa* mode, dominated by intervals of the fourth and fifth and permeated by references to the symphony's chief thematic ideas. A slow epilogue brings a reprise of the melodic material from the second movement, building to a grand apotheosis, before a short coda recalls the *scherzo* material and brings the work to an end.

In his Fourth Symphony, Giannini achieved the dual accomplishment of a tightly shaped developmental structure and an emotionally gratifying work in the symphonic subgenre of mid-twentieth-century American Neo-Romanticism at its most balanced and cohesive, if not at its most personal or deeply profound. As such, it is probably the work in which Giannini's aesthetic aims come closest to those of Howard Hanson. A comparison between this work and Hanson's Sixth Symphony (composed seven years later) is apt and illuminating, highlighting the composers' stylistic similarities and differences, as well as their respective strengths and weaknesses. It is difficult to avoid the conclusion that Giannini displayed a formal mastery in his Fourth Symphony that Hanson never approached, while providing all the dramatic intensity and luxuriant lyricism that gives the older composer his appeal.

In addition to the operatic and symphonic works described above, Giannini's second creative phase also includes two sonatas (1940, 1944) for violin and piano, one (1946) for violin solo, and one for flute and piano (1958); concertos for violin (1944) and trumpet (1946); and the first (1953) of three orchestral divertimentos. Most of these pieces are conceived along similar lines as the Second and Third Symphonies. The second phase also reveals the composer's fondness for the Baroque style, which he imbued with a romantic warmth in works such as the *Concerto Grosso* (1946) for string orchestra, *Variations on a Cantus Firmus* (1947) for piano, *Frescobaldiana* (1948) for orchestra (based on several of the Italian composer's organ works), *Prelude and Fugue* (1955) for strings, and *Prelude and Fughetta* (1957) for piano. All these pieces vary in the appeal of their materials and the degree to which their unfolding extends beyond the routine. This period also saw the appearance in 1951 of *A Canticle of Christmas*, commissioned by Thor Johnson, who led the premiere at the Cincinnati Symphony Orchestra's Christmas concert later that year. Scored for baritone solo, chorus, and orchestra, this ingratiating but substantial and skillfully crafted work is built primarily on motifs from "Adeste Fidelis," which does not make its presence clearly known until the end, when the audience is invited to sing along.

Third Phase (1960–1966)

Around 1960, Giannini began to plumb a deeper, darker vein of expressive content, which he articulated through an intensification of his musical language. However, this change applied to only some of his new works. Others—for example, *Divertimentos nos. 2* and *3* (1961, 1964), the comic operas *Rehearsal Call* (1961), and *The Servant of Two Masters* (1966) and the *Dedication Overture* (1964) for band— continued in the manner of the second phase.

The works of the third phase are notable for their more serious— even tragic—subject matter and expressive implications, their fluent manipulation—and, at times, relative attenuation—of tonal stability, except at important structural junctures, and their wide-ranging harmonic flexibility, incorporating greater extremes of dissonance, as required by the work's expressive needs. This greater dissonance is achieved chiefly through the incorporation of unresolved *appoggiaturas* into the harmonic structure and by expanding the triadic harmony via polychords. Bringing his rhetoric closer to the Expressionism discussed in relation to Ernest Bloch, the intensity of these works, heightened by their density of motivic development and their concentration of mood and emotion, lend stature to Giannini's identity as an artist, while revealing unprecedented levels of depth within his expressive range.

The first composition to display this new mode of expression is *The Medead*, a four-movement monodrama for soprano and orchestra, commissioned by the Ford Foundation on behalf of soprano Irene Jordan. Miss Jordan introduced the work in October 1960, with the Atlanta Symphony conducted by Henry Sopkin. Following the terms of the commission, she gave subsequent performances with other major American orchestras that season and the next. With a text prepared by Giannini himself, the work—rather like a hybrid of symphony and concert aria—conveys the basic elements of the Greek tragedy through Medea's own words. The first movement opens at a pitch of near-hysterical intensity, immediately introducing several short motifs that permeate and unify the entire work. The extraordinary level of intensity is sustained throughout the movement, as the enraged Medea pours forth the story of her betrayal by her beloved Jason, for whom she has borne two sons. Jason is now about to marry the daughter of Creon, King of Corinth. In the dirge-like second movement, Medea invokes the aid of the witch-goddess Hecate in devising a plan for avenging her betrayal. This section introduces a motif, based on a falling minor-third in a cretic metrical pattern, that will reappear in the composer's Fifth Symphony, where it will play a significant thematic role. The third movement begins as Medea triumphantly reveals her plan for vengeance. In a pastorale of ironic sweetness, she describes how the golden crown and lavish gown she has bestowed upon her rival burst into flames, quickly devouring both the bride and her father. But Jason has somehow managed to escape the flames and is now likely to take his two sons from Medea. In the fourth movement, a somber ground bass, she reveals the ruthless action she has taken: to prevent Jason from stealing her children from her, she has murdered them as well. (A fascinating analysis of Giannini's treatment of leitmotifs in this work can be found in Myron Silberstein's essay "An Interpretation of Giannini's *Medead*."[16])

The initial performances of *The Medead* were fairly well received, despite the work's defiant disregard of then-current musical trends. Harold Schonberg wrote, "Mr. Giannini's work quite literally starts with a bang. A fortissimo attack and a crash of cymbals lead right into the harrowing story. There is nothing new about Mr. Giannini's philosophy of music, or his Wagnerian orchestra, but he handles the medium with a good deal of personality and conviction. He also has a feeling for the rhythm of the English language, and his prosody was extremely accurate."[17] In the opinion of Miles Kastendieck, "Giannini has met squarely the setting of Euripedes' story of jealousy and revenge. Moving in and out of tonality as the quality of emotion dictates dissonant expression, Giannini writes some puzzling pages. One of the finest moments occurs when Medea tells of the death of Creon and his daughter in the third part."[18] Jay Harrison found *The Medead* to be "a gripping piece of 'mood music.' . . . It establishes character and keeps that character alive through a wholly expert use of the voice and a climactic use of the orchestra."[19] According to Harriet Johnson, the score was "by far, Giannini's most dissonant and incisive opus. . . . There is more force and depth in this work than I can remember in any of his previous works."[20]

Despite the favorable response, *The Medead* was hardly heard again during the ensuing years, although it was regarded by those few familiar with his *oeuvre* as one of Giannini's best, if not his greatest, work. In its projection of profound emotional content, distilled and intensified through the expert handling of a symphonic process by which abstract musical ideas unfold in a continuous, logical, multilevel development, all directed toward the same expressive ends, *The Medead* stands as one of the supreme masterpieces of American Neo-Romanticism. Its utter neglect is one of the greatest casualties of the wholesale banishment of this body of repertoire that took place during the later 1960s. Still unavailable on recording, it remains largely undocumented and unknown to all but a few specialists some four decades after its composition. It was revived in 1990 at the Manhattan School of Music, where it was sung by Johanna Meier, with Gunther Schuller conducting the Manhattan Symphony. By this time Giannini, was all but forgotten, and James Oestreich, writing in the *New York Times,* felt it necessary to identify him for the reader, describing him as "a skilled composer in a conservative post-Romantic idiom that fell out of fashion at midcentury but might thrive in today's climate if given wider exposure." He described *The Medead* as "an impressive creation in an operatic mode that owes something to Verdi, . . . but far more to Wagner. The German composer's influence is apparent . . . in the entire cast of the piece, the way it sets the voice afloat on an orchestral sea and challenges it to surmount the surging waves."[21]

Giannini completed two operas in 1961. The first of these, *The Harvest*, was commissioned by the Ford Foundation for presentation by the Chicago Lyric Opera, which introduced the work in November of that year. Not a true example of the composer's third phase, the opera's style might be described as twentieth-century *verismo*, with a rural setting in the American southwest, around the year 1900. The plot was the creation of Karl Flaster, who worked with Giannini on the libretto. It was to be their final collaboration. The O'Neillian story involves three brothers, their blind father, and the wife of one of the brothers. The two other brothers are filled with desire for her, as is their father. By the end of the opera the father has murdered the woman and one of his own sons. Marilyn Horne played the role of the woman.

The distinguished auspices under which *The Harvest* was created and launched drew a good deal of attention to its premiere. The initial impact of the work was described and evaluated in copious critical commentaries, many of which seem tainted by hidden agendas.

For example, Claudia Cassidy, known for her harsh judgments as well as for her antipathy toward members of the Chicago Lyric Opera administration, softens her blows by acknowledging that "Mr. Giannini can write pleasant music." But as for *The Harvest*, the first act is "bad Puccini, his second frightful Copland, and his third ghastly Montemezzi."[22] Former Giannini student Roger Dettmer seems to be struggling with palpable Oedipal ambivalence in his reaction to the work. He describes the opera as:

> technically more adept, perhaps, than "Susannah" or "The Saint of Bleecker Street," or "The Ballad of Baby Doe," but all the same irreparably and astonishingly trivial. . . . As drama it suffers from a bad libretto, as old fashioned in expression as it is in situation. As music it suffers from kinship with innumerable film scores by less gifted others of the Wagner-Strauss persuasion. . . . Coming from a man of Vittorio Giannini's stature, . . . whose "The Taming of the Shrew" is the finest opera I know by an American composer, . . . it was doubly saddening to encounter.[23]

Indeed, the reactions to the work seem so divergent that it is difficult for one who did not attend the production to glean more than a vague impression of it. On the one hand, Don Henahan could write, "The libretto was pure soap opera of daytime television genre, innocent of even the pretensions of art, and the score met it on its own ground from start to finish. . . . The essential trouble . . . lay not in cast or libretto, but in the music. Where it was not pointless it was thunderingly obvious and repetitious."[24] On the other hand, the critic for *Musical America* writes, "The best music of Vittorio Giannini has been overlooked for so long by all but a few on his native soil that it is both difficult and distasteful to report the failure of his [latest opera]." He insists, "What afflicts *The Harvest* . . . is simply a bad libretto," adding, "For the very reason that Giannini is a musical prosodist without equal in the Americas, every outlandish declaration is audible."[25] Perhaps the most moderate comments are the most valid and reliable, as when Robert C. Marsh writes, "Among American operatic composers Vittorio Giannini rates as an old experienced hand." He describes *The Harvest* as:

> a violent drama of love and lechery which sails to its tragic climax on waves of chromatic tonality. . . . [It] impressed one as an American opera in the tradition of European realism, a score with some genu-

inely effective moments, but a work of less impact than such kindred scores as Janácek's 'Jenufa' or Leoncavallo's "Pagliacci." The music of "The Harvest" is appropriate to the action, strongly melodic, consistently craftsmanlike, and admirably suited to the theater. It was well scored, and the performance was well played under the composer's direction. One could complain that the idiom was not significantly different from that of Mr. Giannini's earlier works, but this was predictable. A little more melodic invention would have improved the effect of certain of the scenes, however.[26]

The year 1961 also saw the completion of *Rehearsal Call*, a work of vastly different tone and style. Based on a farce by Francis Swann, the opera concerns the various schemes of six eager young actors who find themselves living in a New York City brownstone, one floor above a successful Broadway producer. The score is light and playful, in Giannini's *buffa* vein, and filled with musical "in-jokes." *Rehearsal Call* was introduced at the Juilliard School in February 1962 under the direction of Frederic Waldman.

Once again the work received critical responses ranging from the damning-with-faint-praise variety to the patronizing and the snide. After the carping—predictable by now—about Giannini's having cobbled his musical language from the styles of others, Harold Schonberg wrote, " 'Rehearsal Call' makes no pretense at being big stuff. It is frankly thin, frankly adolescent, frankly derivative. But if nothing else, it is professional in its workmanship. Mr. Giannini knows the human voice and how to write for it. He has composed a three-act opera that should go over big in the workshop circuit (small cast, no chorus, one set, medium-sized orchestra)."[27] The comments of Paul Henry Lang were somewhat more pointed:

> Mr. Giannini's special talent is a sort of pronouncedly Italianate operatic lyricism of the Giordano-Cilea-Puccini lineage though without any recognizable personal qualities. . . . In his earlier works [he] proved himself an accomplished opera composer . . . and his skill remains no less apparent in "Rehearsal Call." He is versatile and has good theatrical instincts but, lacking a guiding star, too ready to be content with the mere exercising of his versatility. . . . Unfortunately, even allowing for the high school caliber of his libretto, in his handling of this modern comedy he remains thoroughly old-fashioned, . . . and is altogether content with eclectic gestures and old and tried recipes.[28]

What emerges clearly from a consideration of the critical responses to Giannini's music over the course of three decades is the realization that the casual, unfocused attention given to a single hearing of a new work is insufficient to engender insights beyond the most obvious and superficial. One is continually reminded of Brahms's oft-quoted response to the remark that his First Symphony owed a great deal to Beethoven's Ninth: "Any fool can see that."

In 1962, two years after completing *The Medead*, Giannini undertook a very similar effort: Though beginning as an opera based on the story of Antigone, the work eventually took shape as another monodrama for soprano and orchestra—this one in three movements, with a musical approach along much the same lines as the earlier work. However, there is no evidence that *Antigone* has ever been performed.

Giannini's next major work was entitled *Psalm 130* and was scored for double-bass (or, alternatively, cello) and orchestra. It was composed in 1963 for double-bass virtuoso Gary Karr, who gave the first performance in August of that year at the Brevard Music Center in North Carolina, under the direction of John Christian Pfohl. The work is an abstract, rhapsodic commentary on the Psalm ("Out of the depths my soul cries out . . .") that has inspired composers from the tragically short-lived Lili Boulanger to the Czech protégé of Dvořák, Vítezslav Novák. The solo instrument functions as a tortured protagonist, crying out against the orchestral backdrop, somewhat similar in conception to Ernest Bloch's *Schelomo*, with which it also shares its tragic emotional attitude and, to some degree, its harmonic language (as does *The Medead*). The work is based largely on a motif—presented at the outset—that outlines a minor-seventh chord. Despite the improvisatory effect created by its rhapsodic structure, it falls roughly into three sections—the opening and closing, proclamatory, agitated, and anguished, while the central section is poignant and meditative. Like *The Medead, Psalm 130* is one of Giannini's most personal, deeply moving, and fully realized works, although it has rarely been performed.

The year 1963 also saw the composition of Giannini's Piano Sonata, another work that used an especially harsh, dissonant harmonic language and brittle textures to evoke a feeling of great emotional turbulence, especially in the first movement. The opening boldly proclaims a three-note motif that saturates the polyphonic texture of the entire movement, while reappearing in the others as well. Several additional motifs are introduced during the exposition of this movement, all of which contribute to its unremittingly agitated character; even the subordinate theme seems to wail in despair. All this material is subjected to a lengthy and rigorous development until a major climax is reached during the recapitulation, after which the movement ends in snarling defiance.

The second movement is a lament whose character is unmistakably funereal and whose thematic material bears some resemblance to the motifs introduced in the first movement. After some elaboration of this D-minor dirge, there is a sudden shift to D-flat major, and a new melody, marked *"con gran dolcezza e tenerezza,"* is heard, ending the movement with a Mahlerian poignancy.

The meaning of this episode—and, perhaps, of the sonata as a whole—may be illuminated by recalling that 1963 was the year that Giannini's second marriage ended in divorce. That year Giannini also composed what proved to be his last song, entitled, "To a Lost Love," to his own text. There the D-flat melody from the sonata appears, set to the following words:

> If you must go, my love,
> Go not in bitterness;
> Go with a gentle sadness.
> I, with tears in my eyes,
> Give you one last kiss on the lips,
> As a token of my love that shall abide with you forever.

The final movement of the sonata has the character of a *scherzo-toccata,* propelled by a driving triplet figure in perpetual motion. At the center of the movement the meter shifts and the three-note motif from the first movement reappears, now pressing forward with grim determination. Then the opening triplet material returns, leading to an intensified treatment of the three-note motif and carrying the movement to a decisive close.

In 1964, Giannini composed *Variations and Fugue,* which proved to be his last work for band as well as his finest and most serious in conception, although it has never attained the popularity of the Third Symphony. Commissioned by Purdue University, it was first performed in May 1965 and is the most strictly formal of the composer's three most fully realized late works (the other two being *The Medead* and the *Psalm 130,* whose main motif is quoted several times in the band piece—possibly with symbolic significance). Utilizing as its theme a chord progression with bass line very similar to that which served this purpose in the *Variations on a Cantus Firmus*, the *Variations and Fugue* might be described as a third-phase reconsideration of some of the compositional issues addressed in that 1947 work for piano solo. It is also an especially thorough elaboration of Giannini's use of polychords in his most serious late works. But despite its tight structure and developmental density, the composition unfolds over a moody, expressively lyrical, and dramatic course, ending with a fugue that culminates in a climax of overwhelming power. The fugue subject—based on the theme used in the variations—is in the shape of a wedge, created by gradually expanding the intervals between each successive note upward and downward.

During the same year Giannini also composed his Symphony no. 5 on a commission from the Phoenix Symphony Orchestra, who gave the premiere in April 1965 under the direction of Guy Taylor. It is difficult to experience this work without hearing in it the composer's contemplation of his own mortality, as it displays a morbidity whose extravagance is comparable to that of Tchaikovsky's "*Pathétique* Symphony," although Giannini's death was still two years away. The Fifth Symphony, more than half an hour in duration, is a one-movement structure whose several sections roughly comprise the standard components of the classical prototype, framed between a prelude and postlude. The lugubrious prelude introduces the falling-minor-third motif that had appeared in the second movement of *The Medead*. Here it takes on an unambiguously funereal character, heard over a rocking pattern of juxtaposed fifths that outlines a minor triad with added minor-sixth. This motif drives the entire symphony, whose emotional character is unremittingly dolorous throughout, punctuated by climactic outbursts of almost unbearable *angst* before finally coming to an end in defeat without redemption. Again one is reminded of Ernest Bloch, one of the few composers whose musical language was capable of accommodating such extreme emotional expression. Yet even in his most bitterly pessimistic works, Bloch typically reached some degree of acceptance or, at least, resignation. However, it is not by its cloud of doom or its emotional extremism that the symphony is weakened, but by an excessive reliance on such heavy-handed devices as sequential repetition by rising minor-thirds. Despite the work's many passages of power and eloquence, these devices tend to create an unconvincing, blustering effect, as if the composer's intention to outdo all prior attempts in his quest for the ultimate musical expression of grief outstripped his own capacity for musico-emotional evocation.

In view of the tragic tone of so many of Giannini's late works, it is worth bearing in mind that the same year that saw the appearance of the *Variations and Fugue* and the Symphony no. 5 also saw the creation of the *Dedication Overture* and the *Divertimento no. 3*, both works of generally cheerful import. And while his next opera was a full-length adaptation (never performed) of the Greek tragedy *Edipus*, for his last major effort Giannini turned once more to the *opera buffa* genre in an adaptation of *The Servant of Two Masters*, a play by the eighteenth-century master of *commedia dell'arte*, Carlo Goldoni. Bernard Stambler prepared the libretto. Typical of its genre, the plot involves confusing relationships, disguises and mistaken identities, misunderstandings, and various romantic complications. Giannini had essentially completed the opera two weeks before his death on November 28, 1966, although he had yet to compose an overture. The premiere by the New York City Opera took place as scheduled in March 1967. During the preceding weeks, Giannini's student, colleague, and close friend Nicolas Flagello composed an overture based on the opera's main themes, but conductor Julius Rudel felt that the work was self-sufficient without one and chose not to use it.

The posthumous production of *The Servant of Two Masters* was fairly well received by the press. Harold Schonberg wrote, "Giannini was a conservative composer and an eclectic, but he was skillful and knew a great deal about writing for the voice. A professional in the best sense of the word, he had an ear responsive to the prosodic patterns of the English language, and there are none of the awkward-sounding accentuations that mar the work of more important composers."[29] The *New Yorker*'s Whitney Balliett commented, "[The] music proved to be unpretentious and eminently singable. . . . If it is at fault in any respect, it is in being too unpretentious, . . . The total effect, however, was entertaining, melodious, and visually pleasing."[30] Somewhat less enthusiastic was Herbert Weinstock, who wrote, "The eager, hard-working cast . . . were kept in unceasing, distracting motion by [the stage director]. Was that nervous over-activity an unconscious attempt to cover up the fact that Mr. Giannini's music lacks distinction or, sadly, any but very occasional low-intensity interest?"[31] Perhaps the most favorable reaction came from Ron Eyer, who found the work:

a gem, semi-precious perhaps, but still a gem. . . . The score . . . is straight out of the romantic opera tradition via Puccini. There are few dissonances to disturb the mellifluous flow of continuous melody and there are no set pieces, as such, although the principals do have opportunities for some soaring duets and other ensemble combinations. Giannini was no modernist, but he knew how to write for voice and orchestra and this opera may stand as the best memento of his distinguished career.[32]

CONCLUSION

Giannini's death was deeply mourned by his many students and close friends, and his contributions to music education—especially his most recent accomplishment as founder of the North Carolina School of the Arts—were acknowledged and praised highly. His own creative work, however, was regarded with—at best— patronizing tolerance for its staunch traditionalism.

A number of factors complicated—and continue to complicate— any serious, comprehensive assessment of his contribution as a composer. One is that Giannini's musical identity was split among several subcultures—two especially—that rarely intersect with each other: One is the world of opera, where Giannini identified his own chief contributions as a composer. But that is a milieu notoriously inhospitable to new works and condescending toward those composers who dare to compete with its icons. The other is the arena of music for bands and wind ensembles. This is the domain that offered the warmest welcome to Giannini's music and continues to keep his music and his name alive. But the band community is quite isolated from the other musical subcultures, which tend to regard it as aesthetically inferior and its leading creative figures as hacks and mercenaries. A second factor, already noted, that has hindered a more comprehensive understanding of Giannini's artistic contribution is the greater attention given by performers to works of his second creative phase—works that do not always represent his deepest artistic expressions. A third factor that has been a particular hindrance since Giannini's death has been the reluctance of his descendants to promote, publicize, or gain exposure for his works, or to cooperate with others who wish to do so. In fact, they have in some cases—for reasons that remain quite unknown—prevented such exposure from taking place. Many of Giannini's manuscripts remain locked away in bank vaults in North Carolina, their legal custodians oblivious to their artistic value, unfamiliar with the practices of the music world, and indifferent to the interest shown by performers or scholars.

For these reasons, as well as the fact that his reputation never achieved a comparable degree of prominence during his lifetime, Giannini's music has not enjoyed the revival of interest and reassessment that Bloch's and Hanson's have undergone. However, since 1990 there has been increased interest in works other than the pieces for band. As previously noted, *The Medead* was revived in New York City in 1990, as were both *Blennerhassett* and *The Taming of the Shrew* in 1991. Although not a single new recording of Giannini's music was released between 1970 and 1990, since the latter year there have been two recordings of *Variations on a Cantus Firmus*, a second recording of the Symphony no. 3, and first recordings of the Piano Sonata, *Concerto Grosso, Prelude and Fugue* for strings, and *Prelude and Fughetta* for piano. There has also been an entire compact disc devoted to twenty-four songs with texts by Karl Flaster, and selections from these songs have been recorded by such well-known vocal artists as Thomas Hampson, Roberta Alexander, and Ben Heppner. These recordings have been well received, without many of the routine qualifications made during the composer's lifetime.

Reviewing a recording that included both the *Concerto Grosso* and the *Prelude and Fugue*, Mark Lehman of the *American Record Guide* wrote, "Giannini has only a couple of pieces now in the catalog. . . . His early music is almost never played, yet the 1930 Piano Quintet (which combines stylistic elements from Brahms, Fauré, and Puccini) is a masterpiece. . . . He wrote once-popular operas as well as concertos, symphonies, and sonatas—all of them richly melodic, warmly and openly romantic, and crafted with old-fashioned skill."[33] Reviewing the same recording, English critic Rob Barnett wrote, "Giannini's Concerto Grosso is the blessed antithesis of the desiccated neo-classical tendency that swept bloodlessly through the twentieth century. It is a work of passion, power and warmth."[34] Lehman also commented on a recording of two piano works, "These premiere recordings of [Giannini's] tiny *Prelude and Fughetta* and full-scale *Variations on a Cantus Firmus* (from 1947) continue the discovery of an undeservedly forgotten composer who remained devoted to tonal harmony, traditional form, and old-fashioned romantic emotion—all of them evident in these two piano pieces."[35] Reviewing this same recording in *Fanfare*, Peter Rabinowitz compared the Giannini *Variations* to a Franck work also included: "Anyone who relishes the fusion of Baroque structure and post-Wagnerian harmony that marks the *Prelude, Chorale, and Fugue* (or, for that matter, the amalgam of voices in the Bach-Busoni *Chaconne*), should respond enthusiastically to Giannini's 1947 *Variations* . . . which is more extroverted in its bursts of virtuosity and denser in its harmonies than the Franck, but surprisingly similar in the intensity of the pressure it puts on its formal procedures."[36] A similar acceptance of what the music *is*, rather than what it is *not* is found in Adrian Corleonis's review of the Piano Sonata: "The epithet 'accessible' usually applied to Giannini . . . is appropriate in the sense that [his] music embodies no arcane procedures, but it misleads in point of the pithy, challenging utterance of [the sonata]."[37]

At the time of this writing, none of Giannini's most significant works is available on recording, and those few examples of his music that are form a spotty and misleading representation at best. Of the composers featured in this study, he is the one who has benefited the least from the post-1985 revival of interest in the American Neo-Romantics and therefore can be cited as the one whose work is most urgently in need of exposure and reconsideration.

It is not surprising that some of the most sympathetic assessments of Giannini's compositional stature come from those who were most familiar with his works. Composer Robert Parris concluded his article "Vittorio Giannini and the Romantic Tradition" with the following: "The strength of Giannini's music lies in its warmth and unaffectedness as well as in its technical *expertise*. . . . It is the expression of a man who believes in what he has to say and who has mastered all of the techniques necessary for its utterance."[38]

Michael Mark noted in his doctoral dissertation *The Life and Works of Vittorio Giannini*, "Giannini was a reactionary who preferred the tonality and structural balance of the music of his father's time. He neither ignored nor shunned the innovations of twentieth-century music, but used them only to a limited extent in his own music. That he was successful is due to the combination of exceptional musical talent and complete honesty in creativity."[39]

Composer-critic Arthur Cohn wrote:

Because Vittorio Giannini is concerned with the emotional wealth of music he is a romanticist; in that his form and structure have qualities of the Beethoven-Brahms school he is a classicist. Such paradox is possible. Giannini is an unabashed composer, writing fertile, fresh melodies . . . with the support of fully tonal harmonies (which might be termed conventional); the goodness of diatonic harmony will never wear out. But he is no neoclassicist of pandiatonicism, or neoromanticist aping the ancient Wagnerian cult. He is, frankly, a 20th-century composer using the well-sharpened tools of the 19th century.[40]

It is appropriate to conclude with a reminiscence by Bernard Stambler, librettist of *The Servant of Two Masters*. Stambler recalled with affection "[Giannini's] incredibly alert warmth which moved him in everything he did, a warmth shaped by an integrity that was both old-world and old-fashioned." Like a Tuscan peasant, he had "a strong sense of continuity with his father's and grandfather's way of getting things done: the peasant does his tasks in his own way, but the grandfather's way is always somewhere in the back of his mind, and the possible source of the best solution to a problem. . . . [For Vittorio] the styles and forms of the past existed as alive and real—components of the vocabulary he kept discovering and manipulating to express what he wanted to say."[41]

NOTES

1. Virgil Thomson, Review, *New York Herald Tribune* (8 February 1953).

2. Quoted in Notes on *Taming of the Shrew*, New York City Opera Program Book (13 April 1958).

3. Anne Simpson and Karl Wonderly Flaster, "A Working Relationship: The Giannini-Flaster Collaboration," *American Music* (Winter 1988): 389.

4. Simpson and Flaster, "A Working Relationship," 398.

5. Gary Karr, Email to this writer (9 June 2000).

6. Michael L. Mark, "The Life and Works of Vittorio Giannini (1903–1966)," (D.M.A. diss., Catholic University of America, Washington, D.C., 1970), 37.

7. Herbert Peyser, Review, *New York Times* (11 November 1934).

8. Francis D. Perkins, Review, *New York Herald Tribune* (23 March 1937).

9. Robert Simon, Review, *New Yorker* (3 April 1937).

10. Herbert Peyser, Review, *New York Times* (3 June 1938).

11. Geraldine deCourgy, Review, *Musical America* (July 1938).

12. Bernard Holland, Review, *New York Times* (28 February 1991).

13. Vittorio Giannini, "Shakespeare's Musical Training," *Music Journal* (June–July 1958): 8.

14. Virgil Thomson, Review, *New York Herald Tribune* (8 February 1953).

15. Nicholas Tawa, *American Composers and Their Public* (Metuchen, N.J.: Scarecrow Press, 1995), 167–168.

16. Myron Silberstein, "An Interpretation of Giannini's *Medead*," *Pittsburgh Undergraduate Review* (Fall 2002): 86–106.

17. Harold Schonberg, Review, *New York Times* (1 November 1961).

18. Miles Kastendieck, Review, *New York Journal American* (1 November 1961).

19. Jay Harrison, Review, *Music Magazine/Musical Courier* (December 1961): 40–41.

20. Harriet Johnson, Review, *New York Post* (1 November 1961).

21. James Oestreich, Review, *New York Times* (30 September 1990).

22. Claudia Cassidy, Review, *Chicago Sunday Tribune* (26 November 1961).

23. Roger Dettmer, Review, *Chicago's American* (27 November 1961).

24. Don Henahan, Review, *Chicago Daily News* (27 November 1961).

25. Unsigned Review, *Musical America* (January 1962): 120.

26. Robert C. Marsh, Review, *Christian Science Monitor* (9 December 1961).

27. Harold Schonberg, Review, *New York Times* (16 February 1962).

28. Paul Henry Lang, Review, *New York Herald Tribune* (16 February 1962).

29. Harold Schonberg, Review, *New York Times* (10 March 1967).

30. Whitney Balliett, Review, *The New Yorker* (28 March 1967): 124.

31. Herbert Weinstock, Review, *Opera* (May 1967): 385.

32. Ron Eyer, Review, *New York Herald Tribune* (10 March 1967).

33. Mark Lehman, Review, *American Record Guide* (July–August 1995): 113.

34. Rob Barnett, Review, *Classical Music on the Web* (May 2001), http://www.musicweb.uk.net/classrev/2001/May01/flagello2.htm.

35. Mark Lehman, Review, *American Record Guide* (November–December 1996): 254.

36. Peter Rabinowitz, Review, *Fanfare* (November–December 1996): 248.

37. Adrian Corleonis, Review, *Fanfare* (September–October 1999): 218.

38. Robert Parris, "Vittorio Giannini and the Romantic Tradition," *Juilliard Review* (Spring 1957): 42.

39. Mark, *Giannini*, ii.

40. Arthur Cohn, Review, *American Record Guide* (April 1964): 853–854.

41. Bernard Stambler, "A Remembrance of Vittorio Giannini," New York State Theater Program Book (9 March 1967): 9–11.

SELECTED BIBLIOGRAPHY

Mark, Michael L. "The Life and Works of Vittorio Giannini (1903–1966)." D.M.A. diss, Catholic University of America, Washington, D.C., 1970.

Parris, Robert. "Vittorio Giannini and the Romantic Tradition." *Juilliard Review* (Spring 1957): 32–46.

Peyser, Herbert. "Giannini's 'Lucedia.'" *New York Times* (11 November 1934).

Peyser, Herbert. "New Giannini Opera." *New York Times* (3 June 1938).

Price, Jeffrey W. *The Songs of Vittorio Giannini on Poems by Karl Flaster.* Dubuque, Iowa: Kendall/Hunt Publishers, 1994.

Silberstein, Myron. "An Interpretation of Giannini's *Medead.*" *Pittsburgh Undergraduate Review* (Fall 2002): 86–106.

Simpson, Anne and Karl Wonderly Flaster. "A Working Relationship: The Giannini-Flaster Collaboration." *American Music* (Winter 1988): 375–408.

Stambler, Bernard. "A Remembrance of Vittorio Giannini." New York State Theater Program Book (9 March 1967): 9–13.

Thomson, Virgil. "Music and Musicians." *New York Herald Tribune* (8 February 1953).

"Vittorio Giannini, Composer, Found Dead Here." *New York Times* (29 November 1966).

ESSENTIAL DISCOGRAPHY

ACA CM-20011-11: 24 Songs of Vittorio Giannini on Poems of Karl Flaster (Jeffrey Price, tenor; Cary Lewis, piano).

Albany TROY-143: *Concerto Grosso; Prelude and Fugue* (New Russia Orch., David Amos, cond.); www.albanyrecords.com.

Connoisseur Society CD-4208: *Variations on a Cantus Firmus; Prelude and Fughetta* (Myron Silberstein, piano).

Phoenix PHCD-143: Piano Sonata (Tatjana Rankovich, piano); www.phoenixcd.com.

Reference RR-52CD: Symphony No. 3 (Dallas Wind Sym., Frederick Fennell, cond.); www.referencerecordings.com.

5

Paul Creston

The story of Paul Creston has the qualities of an American myth: an individual's triumph over deprivation, achieving fame and success; his subsequent decline; and his posthumous vindication. Born in poverty to an immigrant family and unable to finish his basic schooling, he took on the task of educating himself, determined to make a name for himself as a composer in the competitive and elitist world of classical music. Not until age twenty-six did he present his first work to the public, aligning himself with New York City's musical avant-garde. Less than ten years later he enjoyed the honor of having his music performed by no less than the NBC Symphony Orchestra under the direction of Arturo Toscanini. Henry Cowell wrote, "There is no one known to me who handles more expertly the traditional types of development of a musical germ [than Paul Creston]."[1] By age fifty, he was among the three or four most frequently and most widely performed living American composers of concert music. Yet by the time he was sixty, his major works were no longer played, his name kept alive by a handful of oddities of largely utilitarian value.

BIOGRAPHY

Paul Creston, christened Giuseppe Guttoveggio, was born in New York City on October 10, 1906, the younger of two brothers. His father, Gaspare Guttoveggio, a proud, hard-working house-painter, and his mother, Carmela, described as tender and caring, had emigrated from Sicily the previous year. Living on the lower east side of Manhattan, the family had little money but did manage to afford a ten-dollar piano on which young Joe (as he was called) could practice. He took piano lessons from a mediocre local teacher and also taught himself the violin by practicing on his brother's instrument. Almost as soon as he started playing the piano, Joe began to compose, although he attached no particular significance to the activity. Another of his interests was literature, and he had already begun writing poetry, short stories, and essays and had even started a novel by the time he reached his teens.

Entering New York City's DeWitt Clinton High School in 1919, Joe became acquainted with other musical teens and began to realize the inadequacy of his own training. He scraped up the money for piano lessons of a more professional caliber and worked for several years under G. Aldo Randegger. But concert tickets were beyond his budget, so Joe spent hours studying scores and reading textbooks in the New York Public Library. Around this time, he played the role of a character named *Crespino* in a school play. His schoolmates began calling him "Cress," and the nickname endured.

When he was fifteen, financial pressures at home forced Cress to drop out of high school and contribute to the household income. He landed a clerical job but was determined to continue his education on his own. Motivated and ambitious, he mustered the self-discipline to maintain a grueling schedule: working during the day, he practiced the piano in the evenings until 11 P.M., then concentrated on other studies until the early morning hours. Learning that Thomas Edison had managed on four hours of sleep, he decided that he could do the same, smoking ground coffee in a pipe to stay awake.

At the company where he worked, Cress became friendly with a secretary named Louise Gotto. Three years his senior, she also came from a poor Italian American family, one of twelve children. Sharing his artistic aspirations, she was studying modern dance with members of the Martha Graham company. The two began dating, and their friendship developed into a serious romantic relationship.

In the meantime, Cress moved on to other clerical jobs, then to a position as claims examiner for an insurance company. He even earned a diploma in the insurance field via a correspondence course.

This period was of great importance in shaping the personality of this determined young man. Through his independent study he satisfied his voracious curiosity, pursuing a variety of subjects that captured his interest—not just music, but also literature, foreign languages, and linguistics in general; homeopathic medicine, cryptography, and philosophy, including the occult, also attracted his attention. Not only did this habit lead to a lifelong passion for independent study, but it also resulted in what is essentially the opposite of a standard basic education: that is, a highly idiosyncratic landscape of erudition that formed the framework for his own philosophy. Questioning conventional and inherited wisdom, he painstakingly and systematically developed his own theories of music, embracing aesthetics, acoustics, harmony, form, notation, and—most of all—rhythm. As he later wrote, "I was greatly assisted in my studies by that force which Rameau called 'the invisible guide of the musician,' a force which guided me to the right book or author for the answer to the engrossing question of the day."[2] Cress's ideas were not limited to music, however: he also developed his own theories of religion, language, health and nutrition, and what might be called "proper living." The result was a personal style marked by an idiosyncratic individualism, remarkably coherent and consistent within the parameters of its own postulates but resistant—even impervious—to perspectives derived from other premises. Also—probably as a defense against the sense of inferiority he felt regarding his lack of educational pedigree—he developed an aggressive, pedantic, and somewhat pontifical personal manner. Or, as he put it, "I did not . . . always accept without question or challenge every dictum of the authorities. The result of such intense scrutiny was to mold me into an iconoclast."[3]

Seeking ways to earn a living as a musician, Cress considered working as a church organist and in 1925 undertook a year and a half of organ lessons with Pietro Yon. Not only did Cress take advantage of every chance to accompany church services, but he also sought and found opportunities to improvise organ accompaniments to silent movies. However, sound entered the movies just a few years later, and live musical accompaniments became obsolete.

In July 1927, Cress and Louise were married. Embarrassed for a long time by his own unwieldy, foreign-sounding name, he decided now to formally change it to Creston, choosing Paul as his first name on a whim. By now Louise was dancing with the Martha Graham

company, participating in their New York debut. Her work exposed
Paul to the world of modern dance, while sensitizing him to the
importance of rhythm.

Combining his literary and musical interests, Creston began writing articles on musical subjects, from practical advice for the bud-
ding pianist and essays on the performance of Bach to a theoretical
examination of music therapy. Most of these articles were published
promptly in music periodicals of the time, initiating Creston's lifelong practice of giving written verbal expression to his ideas on
music theory and aesthetics.

It was during the early 1930s that Creston finally decided to com-
mit himself to a career in music. Although he had undertaken no
formal study of music theory or composition, he decided to focus
on writing music professionally. Many of his early pieces were
experimental in nature, exploring a variety of techniques and ideas
in search of his own identity and compositional voice. He designated as his Opus 1 Five Dances for piano, which he had written in
1932. Shortly thereafter, his music came to the attention of Henry
Cowell, then an enthusiastic activist on behalf of the avant-garde.
Cowell was impressed by the authenticity, integrity, and seriousness of purpose he found in Creston's early efforts. In October 1934,
Cowell gave Creston an auspicious showcase at one of his "Composers Forum" events at New York City's New School for Social
Research. There Creston performed his 1933 *Seven Theses* for piano.
(He had already submitted several of them to Arnold Schoenberg in
support of a request to receive discounted tutelage from the recently
arrived emigré from Europe. Schoenberg rejected them because of
idiosyncrasies in Creston's notational system.) Cowell published the
Theses in his *New Music Quarterly* the following year and also
released a recording of Creston's Suite for saxophone and piano on
his New Music record label. Cowell's continued support contributed
significantly to the validation of Creston's aspirations as a composer.

During the economically depressed 1930s, Creston faced a difficult struggle in attempting to earn a living through composition,
especially without the benefit of any institutional pedigree or affiliation. He wrote pieces for dancers, worked as an accompanist, and
took a position as organist of St. Malachy's Church, which he held
for more than thirty years. By 1937, he had abandoned his compositional experimentation, having arrived at the musical language that

would serve him, essentially unchanged, for the rest of his life. He completed some twenty works during the 1930s, quite a few of which were played publicly. Two pieces for small orchestra were presented at the prestigious Yaddo Festival in Saratoga Springs, New York, and a number of chamber works were performed in and around New York City, often with the composer's own participation. In 1938, he was awarded the first of two Guggenheim Fellowships, ushering in a period during which his reputation spread rapidly.

In 1938—only six years after completing his Opus 1—Creston's *Out of the Cradle* for chamber orchestra was introduced by Howard Hanson at one of the Eastman School's festivals of American music. In December of that year, *Threnody*, Creston's first work for full orchestra, was introduced by the Pittsburgh Symphony, under the direction of Fritz Reiner. Eugene Goossens conducted the piece in Cincinnati soon thereafter, and then presented it in New York, where it was well received by critics and audience.

But the work that really catapulted Creston's name to national prominence was his Symphony no. 1. Completed in 1940, it was introduced the following year in Brooklyn, New York, by the NYA Symphony Orchestra, conducted by Fritz Mahler. In 1943, the symphony won the New York Music Critics Circle Award as the best new American work, having been selected over no less than Copland's *A Lincoln Portrait*, William Schuman's *Prayer in Time of War*, and Morton Gould's *Spirituals*. In their comments, the critics praised the symphony's unpretentious, straightforward directness of intent, its skillful workmanship, and its high-spirited mood. (In 1952 the same work also won first prize at the Paris International Referendum, among finalists that also included major works by Vaughan Williams, Pizzetti, and Rosenberg.) Leopold Stokowski extracted the *scherzo* movement and performed it alone at a number of his concerts during the 1940s, and even recorded it with the All-American Youth Orchestra.

During the late 1930s Creston served as accompanist for saxophone virtuoso Cecil Leeson. Developing a fondness for the instrument's unique characteristics, he composed two works—a sonata and a suite—which they featured on their programs. In 1941 he composed a full-scale concerto for saxophone and orchestra, shortly after completing one of the first "serious" works—a concertino—for marimba and orchestra. So began Creston's association with "neglected" instruments, which continued with virtuoso works featuring trombone and accordion in addition to several more pieces for saxophone. Although it probably would have surprised (and disappointed) him had he known it, these pieces have proven to be his most widely and most consistently performed compositions.

By 1942, two sons had joined Creston's family. In order to support them he supplemented his income through private teaching of piano and composition and by writing background music for radio. Throughout the 1940s he provided music for children's programs, mystery shows, and even a weekly religious program.

But the success of Creston's Symphony no. 1 led to further awards, as well as significant commissions and performances by leading orchestras, soloists, and conductors. In 1942, the *Choric Dance no. 2* was selected by Arturo Toscanini for performance by the NBC Symphony Orchestra. Three years later, Toscanini also led the NBC Symphony in *Frontiers*, a symphonic poem that had been commissioned by Andre Kostelanetz and premiered in Toronto in 1943. The following year, the New York Philharmonic gave the first performance of Creston's Saxophone Concerto under the direction of William Steinberg, with the twenty-five-year-old virtuoso Vincent J. Abato as soloist. One year later, the same orchestra, this time under Artur Rodzinski's direction, gave the premiere of Creston's Symphony no. 2. Both this symphony and its predecessor were then taken up by Eugene Ormandy, who performed them frequently during the ensuing seasons. During the 1944–1945 season, Pierre Monteux offered Creston's *Pastorale and Tarantella* at conducting engagements throughout the country. In 1948, the Hollywood Quartet performed Creston's String Quartet and subsequently recorded it. That same year a substantive article by Henry Cowell appeared in the *Musical Quarterly*, offering a laudatory but realistic appraisal of Creston's accomplishments as he entered his middle forties. In 1949, pianist Earl Wild introduced Creston's Six Preludes in New York, then gave the first performance of his Piano Concerto in Washington, D.C., the following year.

If the 1940s saw Creston's music achieve national exposure, the 1950s continued the trend, with performances overseas and more than thirty premieres as well. In 1950, Eugene Ormandy introduced Creston's Third Symphony with the Philadelphia Orchestra, then with other major orchestras. Having won the advocacy of Toscanini, Creston's early *Two Choric Dances* soon became one of his most popular works, performed by such conductors as Victor DeSabata, Guido Cantelli, and others of this stature. In 1954, the work was recorded by the Concert Arts Orchestra, under the direction of Vladimir Golschmann. In 1953, the Louisville Orchestra commissioned, premiered, and recorded *Invocation and Dance*, which quickly became another success with audiences. In 1956, the year he turned fifty, a national survey found Creston tied with Aaron Copland as America's most frequently performed living composer.[4] That same year he was elected president of the National Association of American Composers and Conductors, a post he held for four years. In 1957, George Szell and the Cleveland Orchestra performed the *Dance Overture*, which had been played the previous year by Cantelli with the New York Philharmonic. Szell also chose Creston to write a piece in honor of the Cleveland Orchestra's fortieth anniversary. The result was *Toccata*, brought to New York the following year by Leopold Stokowski. Pierre Monteux had become a major Creston advocate, performing the Second Symphony on American and international tours throughout the 1950s. By the end of the decade, this work had become established as one of the favorite American symphonies, along with Hanson's "Romantic," Barber's First, Harris's Third, Schuman's Third, and Copland's Third. In fact, during a visit to the United States in 1959, Dmitri Shostakovich named Creston as one of the American composers whose music was most admired in the Soviet Union.[5]

Perhaps Creston's most vigorous advocate among conductors was Howard Mitchell, then music director of the National Symphony Orchestra of Washington, D.C. Mitchell had been performing Creston's music ever since he assumed his position with the orchestra in 1949. He conducted the Second Symphony in concerts all over the world and led the 1952 premiere of the Symphony no. 4. Two years later, he led the orchestra in a recording, issued by Westminster, of Creston's Second and Third Symphonies—the first recording ever to contain two symphonies by one American composer. In 1955, Mitchell commissioned the Symphony no. 5, which he introduced in Washington, D.C., the following year. That year the conductor wrote an article entitled "The Hallmark of Greatness," in which he stated, "If a composer's message is to be considered great by people of other countries, the music must be of such significance in its glorification of the composer's own country that it speaks above and beyond national boundaries in a universal message that people

everywhere can understand. This hallmark of greatness characterizes Creston's music."[6]

During the 1950s, as television replaced radio as the central focus
of entertainment in American homes, Creston was one of the composers asked to supply background music for the new medium. He
now focused on music for informative documentaries, including
CBS's highly regarded *Twentieth Century* series, for which he composed fourteen scores. His music for the episode "Revolt in Hun-
gary" earned Creston the coveted Christopher Award in 1958.

Then, during the 1960s, almost as precipitously as it had
appeared, Creston's star began to fade. By this time he had been
appointed to the board of directors of ASCAP (in 1960) and the same
year received a State Department grant to give a series of lectures on
American music in Israel and Turkey. Indeed, he was in considerable demand during this time as a lecturer and guest conductor.
Nevertheless, two distinct shifts were taking place. One was that
performances of his music were occurring less in major metropolitan centers and more in the smaller cities of the American heartland.
A second shift was that his major works—symphonies and tone
poems—were being set aside in favor of the rousing overtures and
other festive pieces he had written on commission. A form of type-
casting seemed to be taking place, as such pieces were requested of
him with increasing frequency. Although, perhaps overly eager to
please, he may have encouraged this trend unintentionally at first,
he soon saw its effect on the direction his career was taking. In 1959,
he had boasted that he had enough commissions to occupy him
until 1965. He continued to receive commissions during the following years, but the sources were far less auspicious and for less ambitious projects. That is, instead of a commission from a major
orchestra for a substantial symphonic work, there were requests for
modest band pieces from small Midwestern colleges or music teachers' associations or for a short choral piece from a local church organization. Two notable exceptions were the symphonic poem
Corinthians: XIII, composed for Guy Taylor and the Phoenix Symphony Orchestra in 1963 and recorded two years later by the Louisville Orchestra, and the *Chthonic Ode*, written in 1966 for the Detroit
Symphony Orchestra and Sixten Ehrling, who took it with him on
his guest-conducting tours during the following years. These
proved to be two of Creston's most fully realized orchestral works.
He also took the opportunity to compose two ambitious, large-scale

works for piano solo, *Three Narratives* (1962) and *Metamorphoses* (1964). Not written on commission, these stand as his most significant compositions for piano solo, although they never enjoyed a virtuoso performance during the composer's lifetime. In 1964, Creston joined the faculty of the New York College of Music, his first formal position at an educational institution. Also during the early 1960s, Creston brought to fruition the theories he had been developing for many years regarding the rhythmic element in music. The result was the textbook *Principles of Rhythm*, published in 1964. (Another text, *Creative Harmony*, was never published.)

In 1968, disheartened by the sudden disappearance of his music from major concert and recital programs and by the loss of his former prestige, especially among the sophisticates of the Northeast, this lifelong New Yorker—then sixty-two—moved with his wife to Ellensburg, Washington, accepting a position as professor of music and composer-in-residence at Central Washington State College. He remained there until his retirement in 1975, enjoying the admiration of his less cosmopolitan colleagues and students, as well as frequent—if far from polished—performances of his works. One of Creston's major projects during this period was another book, this one an attempt to correct a variety of illogical practices in the conventional notation of rhythm. *Rational Metric Notation* was completed in 1973, although several years elapsed before it was published. Perhaps Creston's most ambitious project during the early 1970s was a ten-volume series of graded rhythmic exercises called *Rhythmicon*. This series, completed in 1974, illustrated his approach to rhythm, while preparing the piano student for the types of usage found in Creston's mature keyboard works. Most of the music composed by Creston during his Ellensburg years was undistinguished—largely reiterations of ideas and concepts explored in earlier works: a few modest choral settings and some rousing band pieces.

In 1976, the Crestons relocated to San Diego, California. His seventieth birthday was acknowledged by a number of orchestras, drawing increased attention to his work, and he was invited to participate in "Creston festivals" at colleges in various parts of the country. The American Bicentennial also prompted a few minor commissions—chiefly pops-concert novelties in which he recycled the familiar devices he had been using routinely for years. But much of his energy during the mid-1970s was spent nursing slights from various quarters of the music world, struggling to find a publisher for *Rational Metric Notation*, and pursuing such long-standing interests as naturopathic medicine and nutrition, aspects of linguistics, and the Rosicrucian religion.

At this point in his life, Creston was more interested in documenting his positions on theoretical matters than in writing music. After much frustration, he resigned himself to financing the publication of *Rational Metric Notation* through Exposition Press, which eventually issued the book in 1979. He also completed a *Theory and Practice of Rhythmic Patterns*, similar to *Rhythmicon* but designed to be playable on virtually all instruments, and began work on several additional monographs.

In 1979, Creston received the first of three commissions that brought much gratification to his final years: The Mirecourt Trio, in residence at Grinnell College in Iowa, requested a full-length piano trio. Not only did these artists provide a performance of the highest caliber the following year, but the event itself and the circumstances surrounding it were videotaped for the purpose of creating a documentary. The production, called "Paul Creston Meets the Mirecourt Trio," was shown on Iowa Public Television and then on San Diego's PBS station as well. Soon afterward, the Mirecourt Trio recorded the work for commercial release.

Later in 1980, Creston received a commission from conductor Gerard Schwarz on behalf of the Los Angeles Chamber Orchestra. Schwarz, who had studied composition with Creston during the early 1960s, wanted to honor the composer on his seventy-fifth birthday with the opportunity to present a major work that would be performed on both coasts—on the East Coast by the New York Chamber Symphony. The work, which features a solo cello, was called *Sadhana* and was first performed in Los Angeles in October 1981. Creston took the title from a book of the same name, subtitled *The Realization of Life*, by the Indian poet and philosopher Rabindranath Tagore (1861–1941), long a favorite of the composer. Both the California and the New York performances were reasonably well received, though most reviewers commented on the work's somewhat anachronistic style. Noting that it "could have been written 40 years ago," the *New York Times*'s Edward Rothstein described it as "a series of orchestral variations ripe with Romantic gestures, including harp sweeps, lush sonorities, climaxes breaking into silences and impassioned exclamations. The work didn't seem to earn its final sweetness, but it was so original in voice, well wrought and compellingly sincere, that for brief moments, musical history seemed undone."[7] During his final years, Creston commented to an interviewer that *Sadhana* represented his deepest feelings and was his own personal favorite among his works. "I reached my first musical plateau when I heard Bach's St. Matthew Passion. The second was Stravinsky's Rite of Spring. The third was Ravel's L'Enfant et les Sortiléges; and when I heard [Sadhana] performed, I realized I had reached my fourth plateau of musical experience."[8]

In July 1981, as soon as he had completed *Sadhana*, Creston turned his attention to another substantial commission, this one from the American Guild of Organists, which requested a major work for organ and orchestra. He had originally entitled it *Symphonia* for Organ and Orchestra, but he eventually decided to call it his Symphony no. 6, more than twenty-five years after the completion of his Fifth. The premiere took place in June 1982 at the Kennedy Center in Washington, D.C. James Moeser was the organist, and Philip Brunelle conducted the National Symphony Orchestra.

These were Creston's last significant musical compositions, although he continued to devote much of his energy to theoretical writing. In 1983, he completed a monograph that he entitled *Uncle Pastor and Maestro* ("Uncle Pastor" was an anagram of his own name that he had begun to use as an alter ego). This was a further examination of inconsistencies in the conventional notation of note values, presented through a whimsical treatment of the dialogue format. He then began work on an autobiography and on an analysis of his own musical language. However, despite his rigorous adherence to an elaborate regimen of nutritional supplements, he developed a malignant tumor in one of his kidneys, which was removed surgically in June 1984. While convalescing, he resumed work on his autobiography. But the cancer returned, and on August 24, 1985, Creston died. In the *New York Times* obituary, Will Crutchfield wrote, "Mr. Creston's works constitute perhaps the most consistent embodiment of the affirmative, lyrical, melodic strain that dominated American music in the 1930s and for a time afterward."[9]

MUSIC

Paul Creston's music is characterized by an earthy, robust vigor and an ingenuous, extroverted exuberance, stemming from a constant flow of kinetic activity. Creston often asserted that all music is in essence either song or dance, and—for his music at least—this is certainly true. Rarely is it meditative or introspective. Even in subdued moments a surging lyricism presses the music forward.

As Creston was given to making verbal explanations of his guiding aesthetic principles, it is useful to begin a discussion of his music with some of his own comments. The following statements were made early in his career and have been reiterated frequently in program notes and the like:

> I look upon music, and more specifically the writing of it, as a spiritual practice. . . . To me, musical composition is as vital to my spiritual welfare as prayer and good deeds; just as food and exercise are necessities of physical health, and thought and study are requisites of mental well-being. . . . My philosophic approach to composition is abstract. I am preoccupied with matters of melodic design, harmonic coloring, rhythmic pulse, and formal progression; not with imitations of nature, or narrations of fairy tales, or propounding of sociological ideologies. Not that the source of inspiration may not be a picture or a story. Only that regardless of the origin of the subject matter, regardless of the school of thought, a musical composition must bear judgment purely on musical criteria. Its intrinsic worth depends on the integration of musical elements toward a unified whole.[10]

> In the use of the materials of composition, I strive to incorporate all that is good from the earliest times to the present day. If modality serves the purposes of expression, I utilize it; and if atonality is called for, I utilize it with an equally clear conscience. I make no special effort to be American in my music. I work to be my true self, which is American by birth, Italian by parentage, and cosmopolitan by choice.[11]

Nearly twenty years later, Creston gave a talk in which he elaborated further on his aesthetic principles:

> I . . . consider music as a language: a language which begins where words end, a language much more precise, more effective and more indispensable than any verbal tongue of man. Being a language, it consequently has many uses, all equally indigenous. All I ask of any composition is that it fulfill its particular purpose for it to be considered good music whether it be a cradle-song, a military march or a symphony. I cannot agree with the ultra-purists or snobs who regard only

suites, sonatas, and symphonies as good music and any other type as an indignity.[12]

Although Paul Creston never identified himself as a "traditionalist" ("I consider myself an iconoclast or a maverick. I am an eclectic composer."[13]), his use of classical forms and the techniques of thematic development associated with those forms identify him as a traditionalist for the purposes of this study. Indeed, he voiced a virtual traditionalist manifesto when he stated: "I utilize in my music all that is good . . . from ancient times to the present so long as it is clothed in 20th century language. I am not and never have been a revolutionary. I believe that the accomplishments and experience of 400 years should not be discarded: they should be built on and developed; that, in musical developments there has never been revolution but evolution."[14]

Creston is classified as a Neo-Romantic because of his embracing of emotional expression as a fundamental purpose of music, although there are aspects of his work that diverge from the Romantic aesthetic. ("I do not compose to shock or to confound but to communicate expressions of joy or exhilaration or spirituality."[15]) His music is also tonal, in the general sense of employing the property of orientation around a particular key-center, although this key-center may change frequently and be absent during transitional passages. Creston, however, objected vehemently to the application of the term "tonal" in describing his music, preferring the term, "pantonal." ("My music is not tonal. I change keys constantly!"[16] See discussion of tonality in chapter 1.)

Although Creston began his career as something of a radical and ended it as a conservative, he liked to think of himself as a moderate: "In my music, as in my life, I have striven to abide by the Golden Symbol of Pythagoras, 'Go not beyond the balance.' In other words, I have tried to determine and follow the golden mean or happy medium, and to avoid extremes of any kind or nature. It is not surprising, then, that I have been called a radical by conservatives and a conservative by radicals; which gives me a great sense of justification and convinces me that I must be on the right track: maintaining the balance.[17]

Creston's list of works comprises 120 compositions in all genres and media except opera. However, unlike the course of development followed by most composers, Creston—after a brief period of experimentation—settled into a consistent and distinctly personal musical language that remained essentially unchanged for almost five decades. But there were differences in the ways he approached each compositional genre. That is, his symphonies and other major orchestral works diverged in style and tone from his concertos and other virtuoso vehicles, which were different from his chamber works, and so on. Within most genres, however, the compositions share a great deal in common. Therefore, instead of the chronological division into style-periods undertaken in treating the other composers presented in this volume, it is more useful in Creston's case to discuss the characteristics of his rather idiosyncratic musical language and then the ways that this language was applied in the different genre categories, as represented by a few characteristic works from each.

Stylistic Features

Between 1932 and 1936, Creston completed approximately ten pieces that reveal a degree of stylistic instability and uncertainty, as well as some modest experimentation. These works include a number of songs, some piano pieces (including the *Seven Theses* championed by Henry Cowell and a full-length sonata), a suite for saxophone and piano, a string quartet, and a short piece for chamber orchestra called *Out of the Cradle* (based on a poem by Walt Whitman—like Tagore, a lifelong favorite). *Seven Theses* (1933) are the most obviously experimental, exhibiting a harshly dissonant harmonic language, with little discernible tonality. As Creston notes in the score:

> These Seven Theses may be viewed as essays in contrapuntal devices and progressional meter. A particular harmonic interval is employed thruout [sic] a part (or voice) first with the idea of doubling the melody at other distances than the octave (as was done in Organum music which was doubled in fourth and fifths); and second for its harmonic potentialities when placed against the other voices, which are treated in free style. The meter of each thesis is rather a metrical sequence, instead of a static measure or an ever-changing measure.[18]

Creston pursued the notion of progressional meter (a repeated sequence of several different meters) in several of these early pieces, then seemed to abandon it. The parallelism (doubling of a line at a constant interval) continued to interest him, but within much more consonant harmonic contexts. In fact, parallelism at the major third plays an important role in the String Quartet as well as the Piano Sonata (both 1936). The Piano Sonata also reveals the influence of Scarlatti in its many thinly textured running passages. (Indeed, the combination in the Piano Sonata of Baroque texture and figuration, Impressionist harmony, and Romantic emotional temperament provides an early example of an apparent stylistic incongruity that became one of Creston's enduring characteristics.) Harmonic usages later abandoned can also be found in the early songs, as can some uncharacteristically somber moods. Creston's gift for setting English texts in natural speech rhythms appeared in these early songs as well. But by 1937, Creston seems to have completed most of his experimentation and had arrived at what was essentially his mature style.

The composers whom Creston identified as his chief musical influences were J. S. Bach, Domenico Scarlatti, Chopin, Debussy, and Ravel. He also often cited Stravinsky's *Le Sacre du Printemps* and the aesthetic perspective he absorbed through his wife's involvement with Martha Graham and modern dance.[19] These latter two sources of influence heightened Creston's interest in the rhythmic element of music:

> Concerning the more specific aspects of composition, I believe all the elements of music—rhythm, melody, counterpoint, harmony, form and tone color—should be given due consideration to attain the perfect balance of a good musical composition. This does not mean that one element may not be predominant in a particular work. It merely means that no element is completely ignored. The element that is consistently disregarded is that of RHYTHM. A student of composition is taught harmony and counterpoint and form. Sometimes mention is made of melody. But in the matter of rhythm he is left to shift for himself.[20]

Rhythm

Rhythm was the most important element of music to Paul Creston. Indeed, when asked about his compositional procedure, he often responded that he began with the rhythm, rather than the melody or harmony.[21] He wrote voluminously on the subject, presenting the core of his theory in *Principles of Rhythm*. In this text he defined his terms and developed his concepts in an orderly, logical progression, applying them to a broad spectrum of the repertoire. However, the aspect of concern to this study is Creston's treatment of rhythm in his own music. A key distinction drawn in his textbook is the difference between pulse and beat. Pulse refers to the recurrent oscillation indicated by the time signature; beat refers to the actual audible subdivision of a meter. In most music from the common practice period—though not all (the exceptions provide Creston with many examples)—pulse and beat are identical. However, in Creston's music, extrametrical rhythm (i.e., when pulse and beat conflict, producing what is generally meant by the term syncopation) becomes a focal source of interest and delight, as pulses and beats interact and overlap in an array of patterns, all usually subsumed within one constant meter.[22]

The centerpiece of *Principles of Rhythm* is the series of paradigms that Creston called, "the five rhythmic structures." He had developed this concept at least two decades before the book was published, as his Six Preludes (1945) for piano were composed at least partially to provide a clear example of each structure (plus one in which they are combined). Creston traced these patterns of rhythmic organization back to the Renaissance. However, in the twentieth century—especially with the advent of *Le Sacre du Printemps*—such practices moved to the compositional foreground. But while composers like Stravinsky and Bartók used these techniques in passages where a specifically "rhythmic" effect was desired, Creston integrated them into his music as an intrinsic part of the rhythmic flow. This is true not only in lively, dance-like passages, but in slow, lyrical moments as well. Furthermore, Creston's maintenance of a regular meter as a superstructure differs from the more frequently encountered practice of changing meters—and this difference is more than a matter of notation. It is the integration of continually shifting accents and patterns within the frame of reference of a constant underlying pulse that makes Creston's treatment of the rhythmic element so distinctive.

Creston was fond of rhythmic *ostinati* (i.e., repeated patterns) and used them frequently, either as accompaniment or as what he called a "cumulative ground bass." In the latter, a rhythmic *ostinato* is presented and established; another is then superimposed above, then another, up to as many as eight different simultaneous rhythmic patterns. The result of these superimposed *ostinato* patterns may be either polymetric (different meters simultaneously) or polyrhythmic (different simultaneous subdivisions of one meter), or both. Examples of the cumulative ground bass occur in the orchestral works *Frontiers*, Symphony no. 2, *Chant of 1942*, *Invocation and Dance*, and in the symphonic poem *Walt Whitman*.

Harmony and Melody

Creston's harmonic language is almost as personal and recognizable as his approach to rhythm. As noted earlier, he described his music as "pantonal," for he felt that its fluid harmonic motion prevented it from establishing a stable key-center.[23] However, his refusal to acknowledge tonality in his music was rather overstated, as tonal centers are often present for entire phrases. Nevertheless, there are also frequent passages in which a tonic cannot be precisely identified, or is clearly avoided. Yet even during these passages the music rarely sounds like what the typical concertgoer thinks of as "atonal." This is because of Creston's use of what has been called "smooth dissonance," that is, harmony consisting largely of dominant-quality chords—usually dominant-sevenths, dominant-ninths, augmented-ninths, and augmented-elevenths, and, at times, major-sevenths and major chords with added sixths and ninths. The dominant-quality chords rarely resolve until the end of a passage or movement, and then, virtually never to the tonic implied by the dominant. The melodies move freely above, their tonal implications often contradicted by the harmony. This profusion of unresolved dominant-quality chords contributes to the ardent, surging quality of the music. The result is what Creston termed "pantonality." (Arnold Schoenberg also used the term "pantonal" in describing his very different music.)

As one might expect, the preponderance of expanded triadic harmony gives Creston's music a distinctly French quality, and one recalls the composer's own citation of Debussy and Ravel as chief influences. However, his preference for chords in root-position creates a fuller, richer sonority, while his emphatic gestures and heavily accented rhythmic patterns, his massive scoring with plentiful doubling, and his relatively sparing use of diaphanous or translucent textures sets Creston's music far apart from that of the Impressionists, while lending it a distinctly American flavor.

Another association noted in some reviews and program commentaries involves a similarity between Creston's harmonic language and that of some of the jazz, film scores, and Broadway musicals of the 1940s and 1950s. This undeniable overlap, obviously intensified by his copious use of syncopated rhythms, has led to the mistaken belief that Creston actively contributed to those genres. However, this coincidental resemblance was quite annoying to Creston, who insisted that his harmonic practices were clearly derived from his theories of pantonality, which were, in turn, based on acoustical principles. He claimed to have minimal knowledge or interest in commercial musical genres.

Interestingly, notwithstanding Creston's avowed pantonality, virtually each of his works ends with a major triad (as do inner movements, except for the occasional cadence on a major-seventh chord, which he conceptualized as a minor triad, reinforced by the major third below the root). However, as mentioned above, his final cadences are rarely the traditional dominant-to-tonic variety. More often the outer voices resolve in contrary motion, as in the conventional augmented 6th-to-V progression. This cadence has much of the effect of a perfect cadence, because of the presence of the leading tone. Another cadential pattern favored by Creston entails resolving a dominant-quality seventh-chord on the fourth degree to the tonic; in fact, examples can be found of dominant-seventh or -ninth chords on virtually all scale degrees resolving to the tonic. Frequently, in order to give more weight to the final cadence of a large-scale work, Creston used a sequence of several such chords, linked by a common tone that becomes an increasingly higher member of the chords, until the tonic is sounded. However, it is important to note that Creston's cadences bear no relation to any sort of key scheme or overall tonality. They simply function to conclude the work emphatically and with finality. Indeed, key schemes play virtually no role in Creston's music.

The prevalence of unresolved dominant-quality chords—or pantonality—in combination with his strongly accented rhythmic patterns is largely responsible for creating the distinctive "Creston sound." However, in a number of the composer's later works, thematic and dramatic factors are less strongly contoured, while pantonality becomes a continuous harmonic context. The result is a neutrality of affect that leaves the music vulnerable to the criticism of relying on the routine application of pat compositional formulae.

Creston often stated that after he determined the rhythmic structure of a new piece, he would then devise the harmony, from which he would extract a melody. This perhaps partially explains why Creston's melodies rarely display the spontaneity or independent identity of a typical aria or song by Giannini or Barber. Though they may be spun out in long, fluid lines, with *rubati* built into the rhythmic values, they are—like Bloch's—conceived motivically and developed accordingly. Depending on a work's character and style, these melodies may vary from modal simplicity to considerable chromatic, pantonal complexity. Creston's fondness for Gregorian chant is evident as early as 1936, when an original melody in "Gregorian style" served as the basis of the slow movement of his String Quartet. Actual Gregorian chant melodies as well as original melodies in Gregorian style recur frequently throughout Creston's music.

Orchestration and Texture

Creston's orchestration is essentially a thorough application of the traditional principles of scoring, as practiced by European composers of the late nineteenth and early twentieth centuries, with particular attention paid to acoustical theory. As his harmonic language is based to a large extent on the natural overtone series, Creston's scoring also tends to approximate the spacing of the overtones, producing the rich, full texture noted earlier. As might be expected, percussion batteries tend to be large and active.

Except in polyrhythmic or polymetric passages, Creston's textures tend to be homophonic. Fugues, and even *fugato* passages, are infrequent, and when they do occur, they are usually brief. Similar to them, but more consistent with Creston's style, is the cumulative ground bass technique described above in the section on rhythm. (A melodic, as opposed to rhythmic, example of this technique is the Introduction to the Symphony no. 2.) Perhaps Creston's most characteristic texture places a soaring melody in the strings and woodwinds against pulsating chords in the brass, usually in a distinctive, irregular rhythmic pattern. However, solos are also common, typically accompanied by one instrumental choir.

Creston's orchestration is usually sectional, with a particular scoring combination maintained for an entire passage, as opposed to the common Impressionist practice in which instruments enter briefly and then disappear, creating a kaleidoscopic effect. In Creston's music, that technique is limited to the dance-like sections of a work.

Creston wrote a great deal of virtuoso music for solo instrument and orchestra. His solo writing in such works thoroughly exploits the idiomatic capabilities of the instrument, in the manner of the typical romantic virtuoso concerto. Much of Creston's virtuoso music showcases unusual instruments, such as the saxophone, accordion, trombone, marimba, and harp. Although most of these pieces are of less substantive interest and depth than his major orchestral works, they have become widely popular. In fact, some— for example, the Saxophone Concerto, Marimba Concertino, and Trombone Fantasy—have become internationally known staples of their respective repertoires. However, the popularity of these works to some extent identified Creston as a producer of "novelty concertos," thereby diminishing his stature as a "serious" composer among more sophisticated circles.

Formal Organization

The flamboyant impetuosity of Creston's musical gestures belies the orderliness and logic of his formal practices, both in works in which classical forms are utilized and in those whose formal designs are *sui generis*. Creston's treatment of classical forms was quite traditional. For example, his *sonata allegro* forms follow the eighteenth-century paradigm closely, aside from abbreviated recapitulations and the lack of importance placed on key relationships. Thematic development is quite thorough, even in pieces of lesser import.

Creston favored a developmental technique he called "tangential variation." This is the device, traceable to the Renaissance polyphonists, of using the beginning (or head motif) of a theme, but altering its continuation. Creston used tangential variation with particular effectiveness in his concertos and other virtuoso works, as well as in the "dance" sections of his prelude-and-dance pieces. In such works, his tangential variations bear a similarity in feeling to the improvisations of a jazz artist.[24]

As inventive as Creston's manipulation of classical forms may have been, some of his most effective formal designs involve works shaped according to an *ad hoc* concept. Many such pieces are through-composed, sectional structures, in which contrasting sections are based on transformations of one unifying theme. This sort of design allowed Creston to express his feelings about extramusical subjects through music, but without sacrificing the economy, clarity, and coherence of autonomous or absolute structures. Perhaps Creston's most remarkable compositional gift was his ability to create music that sounds spontaneous and natural, but, on closer inspection, reveals a subtle logic underlying virtually every measure.

Most Representative, Fully Realized Works

Symphony no. 1 (1940)
Symphony no. 2 (1944)
Fantasy for Trombone and Orchestra (1947)
Symphony no. 3, "Three Mysteries" (1950)
Walt Whitman (1952)
Symphony no. 5 (1955)
Janus (1959)
Three Narratives (1962)
Corinthians: XIII (1963)
Chthonic Ode (1966)

Discussion of Works

Paul Creston's musical output falls roughly into five main categories. These subdivisions are not discrete, however, as many works contain elements of more than one category. Nevertheless, they represent a useful way to grasp the range and dimensions of Creston's creative expression. The main categories comprise: 1. Works of ambitious intent and serious character; 2. Festive and virtuosic works; 3. Neo-Baroque and Neo-Classical works; 4. The Prelude and Dance; and 5. Vocal and choral works.

A comprehensive study of Creston's creative output leaves the impression of a significant talent marked by considerable intelligence and originality, but whose ultimate achievement was compromised by limitations rooted in the structure of his personality. Remarkable indeed was Creston's early commitment to a course of intensive self-education, pursued tenaciously despite material deprivation, minimal encouragement from others, and a heavy burden of more mundane responsibilities. This rigorous self-directed study led him to develop a personal aesthetic philosophy tailored to his own artistic temperament and a musical language derived from this philosophy. A firm belief in his own talent and ideas enabled Creston to enter a competitive arena alongside others, many of whom enjoyed more advantages and opportunities than he. However, at some point the distinctive musical language he had developed and upon which his individual identity rested became a creative straitjacket, as he avoided deviations and excursions from his paradigms that might have otherwise provided variety and interest. Thus, what began as a personal aesthetic value system was gradually transformed into a defensive structure impervious to ideas not already accounted for by that value system. Without the infusion of new ideas, Creston's distinctive musical language became a stale formula whose only further refinement lay in the increased purity and precision of its own application. As a result, the works of his later years became increasingly sterile and vacuous.

Most of Creston's finest works are discussed in the first section below. These display the expressive range and idiosyncratic originality of his creative talent, while comprising some of the most distinctive examples of American Neo-Romanticism. However, many of the works in the categories that follow are more modest in their aspirations and appear to apply formulas developed early in the composer's career.

Perhaps the key to understanding Creston's creative personality lies in the psychological mechanism he developed to compensate for his lack of formal education. (He rejected the term "self-taught," preferring "self-learned." ["How could I teach myself something I didn't already know?"][25]) Pursuing his interests—musical and otherwise—on his own, he followed his curiosity, engaging in mental dialectics with the authorities he consulted, while serving as adjudicator of such imagined debates, as well as participant. This is a very different process from bringing one's questions, opinions, and points of disagreement to a respected mentor. Self-education may foster intellectual independence and the development of a purer, more uniquely personal point of view, but it does not facilitate as full an understanding of the prevailing conceptual context. A mentor, as the embodiment and representative of inherited wisdom, can explain, amplify, and clarify issues raised by the student and insist that the student grasp and master prevailing practices before rejecting them. On one's own, there is the danger that one will not fully understand the rationale behind what one is rejecting. Furthermore, lacking the advantages of fellowship, of comparing oneself with others holding similar aspirations, and of the social and professional contacts that a mentor and an academic community can provide, one develops the sense of being an "outsider," of being an unwelcome aspirant to an "in-group." The result is often a deep sense of inadequacy, of being at a disadvantage. Intellectual rigidity, arrogant defiance, defensive contentiousness, self-righteousness, and pomposity are often the residual effects of a lifetime of overcompensation. Such dynamics are likely to have contributed to the way Creston developed as a man and as a composer.

Works of Ambitious Intent and Serious Character

This category includes some works for orchestra and some for piano solo. Heading the list one might expect the six works Creston designated as symphonies. However, Symphony no. 2—his most representative and, arguably, greatest work—falls more logically in the fourth group and will be discussed there; Symphonies nos. 4 and 6 are more appropriately included in the second group. Nos. 1, 3, and 5 are discussed here, as are a number of other orchestral works that might be described as "symphonic poems."

As mentioned earlier, the Symphony no. 1 was the work that brought Creston's name to national prominence. Composed in 1940, the symphony may be seen as a bold statement of self-definition, an ambitious young composer's announcement of his presence on the scene, its classical design conveying a further sense of confidence. The basic features of his distinctive style are demonstrated as if on exhibition: the pantonal harmony illustrating a continuous evasion of tonal centeredness without the need for abrasive dissonance, the use of parallelism at the major-third as a further means of evading tonality without harshness, along with much use of syncopation and other forms of rhythmic manipulation. The work's four movements, entitled respectively "With Majesty," "With Humor," "With Serenity," and "With Gaiety," present four primary aspects of the composer's musical personality—aspects upon which he would elaborate for the rest of his career. The first movement is conventional in form, if distinctive in its content: a proudly Whitmanesque assertion of self, with a brash primary theme offset by a more subdued secondary theme whose sense of urgency is barely suppressed. The second movement is a *scherzo*, playful in character, with unexpected, off-kilter rhythmic tricks. The third movement is a fusion of sensual and spiritual yearning—a characteristic expression of the composer, similar to the "Gregorian Chant" movement of his String Quartet (1936). The finale is a rondo of joyful exuberance. As the work of a relative neophyte, the symphony is direct, concise, and clear as to its intentions and seems free of dogma, pretension, or self-indulgence, with nothing ambiguous or esoteric looming as a smokescreen. The Symphony's premiere took place in Brooklyn, New York, in February 1941. Fritz Mahler conducted the NYA Symphony Orchestra.

An early example of the composer's sectional treatment of the symphonic poem is *Frontiers* (1943), in which Creston attempted to pay tribute to "the vision, constancy, and indomitable spirit of the pioneers" who led the American migration westward. The three sections of the ten-minute work are intended to provide "a musical parallel of the moods" associated with this formidable venture, which are identified as "the vision, the trek, and the achievement." A wistful motif, presented at the beginning by a muted trumpet, is transformed during the three sections, unifying the composition. The most elaborate section is the second, representing "the trek."[26] A feeling of determination in the face of mounting adversity is suggested, as variants of the main motif are accompanied by an *ostinato* pattern—formed by subdividing a triple meter into a duple rhythm, juxtaposed against the metrical three-beat pattern—repeated with increasing intensity until it reaches a climax. This central section is framed by a brief but dramatic introduction and short epilogue of resolution. *Frontiers* was commissioned by Andre Kostelanetz, who conducted the premiere with the Toronto Symphony in October 1943 and led subsequent performances with many other orchestras during the next thirty-five years. *Frontiers* was introduced to American audiences in 1945, when Arturo Toscanini performed it with the NBC Symphony.

Creston's Symphony no. 3 was commissioned by the Worcester Music Festival. Completed in 1950, it was first performed in October of that year, by Eugene Ormandy and the Philadelphia Orchestra. The work bears the subtitle "Three Mysteries," after the three milestones of Jesus Christ. As the composer noted in the score, "Though it derives its inspiration from The Nativity, The Crucifixion, and The Resurrection, historic and mystic, the work is a musical parallel of inherent emotional reactions rather than a narrative or painting."[27] Once again, Creston attempted to dissociate his work from the notion of "program music" as a genre in which the music's structure is secondary to an extrinsic stimulus on which it depends for formal coherence. Insisting on structural autonomy in all his own works, Creston produced some of the most effective program music of the twentieth century. "Three Mysteries" is, in essence, a symphonic poem of sufficient scope, depth, and developmental complexity to be designated a symphony. Not only do their titles indicate the general subject matter of each movement, but Creston's own program notes go so far as to indicate an image or event associated with virtually each section within the movements. (For example, the first movement is subdivided into "Pastoral Night," "Shepherds' Fear," "The Annunciation," "The Propagation of the News," "The Adoration," and "Rejoicing.") Nevertheless, as Creston intended, the work is a brilliantly developed, fully independent musical structure.

The thematic material of the work comprises seven Gregorian chant melodies, whose own texts correspond appropriately to the sections in which they are employed. However, what is most notable—and controversial—about this symphony are its language and character, which are—Gregorian chants notwithstanding—"pure Creston." This is subject matter usually handled with ascetic reverence. The treatment is certainly reverent enough, but it is Creston's brand of reverence, and ascetic it is not. Rather, the modal chant material is subjected to rigorous development in the composer's characteristically robust, exuberant, and opulent manner. As Henry Cowell wrote, with remarkable insight and perspective, following the work's premiere:

> Our canons of musical taste today are still deeply affected by a millennium and a half of Gregorian practice. The farther a melody departs from these limitations the more likely it is to be called in bad taste. . . . The increasing harmonic dissonance and chromaticism of the 19th century were viewed by adherents of the older and purer tradition as an increase in musical immorality. Wagner dramatized this opposition by using dissonance and chromaticism to depict illicit love in the Venusberg music, in contrast to diatonic passages for the Christian knights. The 20th-century revival of the old church modes usually draws on other archaic elements in style, so that if a Gregorian melody is used, its surrounding musical atmosphere is often in appropriate taste. Creston pays no attention to any of this. He seems quite unaffected by the generations of attempts to separate in music God and the Devil, the

spirit and the flesh. Hand in hand with the actual Gregorian melodies
... rich 20th-century seventh and ninth chords abound, often following
each other chromatically. . . . There is no attempt to bring in dissonance
according to the principles of strict counterpoint, nor is there the least
attempt to curb the activities of the tritone, which interval of the Devil
seems to be one of Creston's favorites. . . . [Creston's approach is:] Gregorian melody served up with romantic passion, sometimes with
impressionistic instrumentation, with 20th-century dissonance and
rhythm; now and again atonal implications are found cheek-by-jowl
with the ecclesiastical modes. The result of Creston's insistence on
going his own way is that his combination of extremes has been
decried as so shocking as to be almost a violation of elementary musical decency. This opinion was widely expressed after the concert, even
by some who should have remembered that plainsong, in various periods of musical history, has been treated in non-liturgical music in the
style of the period without offending the sensibilities of its auditors.[28]

Three years later, however, Cowell reviewed the work's first
recording a bit less sympathetically, though no less perceptively:
"[Creston's] music is proper for the staging of the Passion Play
rather than for the Life of Christ itself. It is super-movie music, better than most actual movie music, but with the same approach to
the relation of music and events. It is the same sort of effectiveness;
and its weakness is an over-lusty, super-romanticized notion of
what constitutes feeling in musical sound."[29]

Cowell's comments are not unfounded. Yet the Third Symphony
is a personal statement, and the flesh-and-blood treatment truly
reflects Creston's individual conception of the subject matter. Moreover, the integration and development of the Gregorian themes are
quite intricate and ingenious—more so than their immediate effect
may suggest. Indeed, the central "Crucifixion" movement is probably one of the composer's most eloquent and deeply moving creations, centering around a mournful passacaglia that weaves two
Gregorian melodies contrapuntally, one of which is presented in
several metrical denominations simultaneously. But most of all, fundamental to the Neo-Romantic musical aesthetic is the principle that
intensity of conviction, sincerity of intention, and authenticity of
sensibility—controlled by rational and coherent formal structures—
are contagious and convincing to the sympathetic listener, despite
extremism in emotional expression.

Like Howard Hanson, Creston was strongly drawn to the poetry of Walt Whitman; indeed, seven of his works bear some relationship to Whitman and his writing. Perhaps the most notable of these is the symphonic poem entitled simply *Walt Whitman*, which includes some of Creston's most evocative and deeply felt writing. The work was commissioned by conductor Thor Johnson, who led the premiere in March 1952—the year of its completion—with the Cincinnati Symphony Orchestra. Creston developed his concept of the work by selecting four facets of Whitman's poetry and designing a tone poem whose four connected sections offer a musical interpretation of each of those aspects. The first section refers to Whitman's celebration of the individual and opens the work with a rugged swagger of self-assertion. The tone shifts markedly as billowing *arpeggios* herald the picturesque second section, celebrating Whitman's love of nature. Here a pastoral melody is passed among woodwind solos, accompanied by pulsating textures in the rest of the orchestra, which suggest with remarkable realism birds, insects, and other audible symbols of a verdant field. The mood shifts from a sultry, estival languor to a vigorous girding of self for the third section, which highlights Whitman's glorification of the challenge. This, the most abstract section of the work, features Creston's most complex treatment of the "cumulative ground bass" device, as *ostinato* patterns are gradually superimposed, until seven different simultaneous rhythmic patterns accompany a simple melody that grows increasingly louder. The effect suggests a distant goal that one can only approach gradually, after overcoming a multiplicity of obstacles. After a brief reminiscence of the work's opening, this section ends on a note of boisterous triumph, which fades rapidly into the final section, suggesting the poet's serene attitude toward death. Recalling some of the nature imagery of the second section, this subdued peroration is built around a poignant English horn solo, accompanied by shimmering figures in the strings. An almost palpable sense of peace, akin to the feeling of drifting slowly down a gentle stream, is felt, as the work's final moments reveal some of Creston's most imaginative orchestration.

In 1955, Creston composed his Symphony no. 5, commissioned by the National Symphony Orchestra of Washington, D.C., in commemoration of their twenty-fifth anniversary. The premiere took place in April of the following year, under the direction of Howard Mitchell. In his program note the composer wrote:

The keynote of the emotional basis of this symphony is intensity, and the feeling is generally one of spiritual conflicts which are not resolved until the final movement. All the thematic material stems from the series of tones presented at the very beginning by cellos and basses, evenly measured, but irregularly grouped. From these tones three definite, rhythmically patterned themes evolve: the first, aggressive and defiant; the second, lyric and impassioned (an inversion of the first theme); and the third, tender and poignant (played by the flute).[30]

Comparable to the Fifth Symphony of Vittorio Giannini, Creston's Fifth is the composer's chief example of a quintessential Neo-Romantic paradigm: the symphony as medium for the musical representation of a serious emotional crisis. But whereas Giannini's work is deeply tragic and ends in despair, Creston's belongs to the subcategory in which despair is overcome and a triumphant resolution is achieved. Also, Creston's music—like Giannini's but even more so—typically projects a heartily sanguine temperament; emotions like despair, anguish, and desolation are rarely encountered in his work. Again like Giannini's Fifth, there are instances in Creston's Fifth when the composer's intention to convey the ultimate in agitation and strife seems to outstrip his own creative resources, resulting in some unconvincingly bombastic moments. Creston indicated that his Fifth Symphony was prompted by an actual personal crisis, but never divulged its nature. One of his most ambitious works, the symphony illustrates his ingenious use of thematic transformation as a means of both structural and emotional coherence. For these reasons is the symphony discussed in some detail.

In three movements, the Symphony no. 5 begins in deep turmoil, as the lower strings present the work's thematic material, described above in the composer's note. Each successively higher string section enters in a faster rhythmic denomination, creating a turbulent sort of *stretto* effect, until the brasses defiantly snarl the movement's first theme (Ia), reinforced pugnaciously by the percussion. In classically concise *sonata allegro* fashion, the second theme (Ib) follows immediately—a pleading, wailing inversion of the first theme, played by the high strings. As these two themes are developed with great vehemence throughout the course of the movement, there is no respite from the vivid sense of struggle—indeed, violent conflict—until the recapitulation, when the second theme returns, now haughtily flaunting at least temporary victory.

The second movement begins with a linear statement in unison strings. This statement contains the essences of both of the main themes of the movement: the first, played by the oboe, begins with an ascending scale pattern; the second (IIb), which Creston identified as the third main theme of the symphony, introduced by the flute, begins with a three-note motif (an ascending half-step followed by a descending tritone) that gradually assumes primary importance for the remainder of the symphony. The two themes are developed in alternation, until theme IIb proclaims a woeful lament that culminates in the climax of the movement. The movement then comes to a close as the first theme is heard in a consoling English horn solo.

The third movement begins with a mighty outburst that aggressively proclaims a renewed sense of determination, as the plaintive theme IIb now appears assertive and forceful. A dance-like section follows, stealthy in character and in a five-beat meter, during which themes Ia and IIb are developed. As this section proceeds, the energy level (though ebbing occasionally for relief) and the developmental activity intensify, as theme IIb's three-note head-motif comes into increasingly clear focus. There is a sense that the work's fundamental conflict is gradually being resolved, as themes Ia and IIb interact contrapuntally. The IIb motif seems to function as a powerful weapon, as the movement conveys a sense of increasing mastery. Finally, the momentum increases, as the three-note IIb motif is whittled down to two notes, which then climb to the resoundingly triumphant final cadence.

In the early 1960s, Creston composed two major works for piano solo that exceed all his prior keyboard music with regard to technical difficulty, structural sophistication, and expressive complexity. The first is a set of three pieces, called *Narratives*, which he completed in 1962. Each *Narrative* is a freely developmental sectional form, rhapsodic in style, in which the composer's characteristic rhythmic intricacies are well integrated into the overall concepts, while fully exploiting the resources of the instrument. *Narratives nos.* 1 and 3 are pantonal in harmony and dramatic in character, with massive sonorities, virile gestures, and densely arpeggiated textures; *no.* 2 is lyrical and introspective, with a more clearly defined tonal center (and even uses a key signature). Its elaborately filigreed textures are reminiscent of the Impressionists. All three pieces use metrical signatures such as 6/12, 9/12, and 12/12, which were Creston's "corrections" of the conventional 6/8, 9/8, and 12/8, which he believed were based on long-standing misconceptions.[31]

If the *Three Narratives* represent the apotheosis of the more freely intuitive, spontaneous, improvisatory side of Creston's compositional personality, as applied to the piano, then his *Metamorphoses*, written two years later, represent the opposite pole: a large-scale keyboard work that illustrates his most disciplined, tightly structured, rational mode of composition. This work is a series of twenty variations on a twenty-eight-note theme that contains all twelve tones played at least twice, without an implicit tonal center. The angular theme is initially presented unadorned and unaccompanied, *senza espressione*, in even quarter notes. The variations that follow embrace the full range of Post-Romantic/Impressionistic keyboard figurations, as the theme is explored from a variety of perspectives, proceeding in successively more remote directions. In each of the first twelve variations, the theme is transposed up successive half steps. The subsequent variations present the theme in inverted form and embedded at times within vertical structures and other textures. The work achieves a dramatic climax on a low-register cluster-chord, which is followed by a haunting, neo-Gregorian treatment of the theme, bringing the piece to an ethereal conclusion. Despite the presence of all twelve tones in the theme, and the relative absence of tonal center thereby effected, *Metamorphoses* was not composed according to principles of serialism, although it does embrace a harsher harmonic vocabulary than Creston's norm, while avoiding the tendency toward grandiosity that often weakened his more ambitious efforts. Moreover, in this work Creston took the opportunity to explore the relevance and utility to his own music of an approach that was central to American composition at the time. In 1977, the work was choreographed by Tomm Ruud, in which form it was presented by the San Francisco Ballet.

Creston continued to explore aspects of the twelve-tone technique two years later in *Pavane Variations*, an orchestral work remarkably similar to the *Metamorphoses*. Commissioned by the La Jolla Musical Arts Society and its conductor Milton Katims for performance in August 1966, this is another set of variations on a twelve-tone theme. Creston explained his use of twelve-tone material by indicating that the stately, solemn character of the Pavane called for a theme whose expressive quality was rather cool and remote. But again, the composer emphasized that although he used a twelve-tone theme, the work did not follow serialist procedures.

In 1963, in between the *Three Narratives* and the *Metamorphoses*, Creston wrote an orchestral work he called *Corinthians: XIII*, taking its title from the New Testament chapter he described as "an apotheosis of love." In his program note the composer wrote:

> The work . . . is neither an exegesis nor a painting, but an emotional parallel of three manifestations of love: the love between mother and child, between man and woman, and between man and mankind. . . . [The composition is in three sections.] Since all manifestations of love are, in essence, one, a single theme . . . is the basis of all three sections. This theme, however, is transformed and developed differently in the second and third sections to fit the particular moods. Midway in the second section a short love dance is incorporated. In its transformation for the third section—love between man and mankind—the theme becomes, almost naturally and logically, the Gregorian melody "Salve Regina," which is utilized with a minimum of alteration.[32]

Once again exploring and commenting on several aspects of a concept by means of thematic transformation, Creston produced one of his most affecting and appealing works—reminiscent of the Symphony no. 3 in its content and treatment, but exhibiting a greater refinement of taste. Once again the influences of Debussy and Ravel are strongly evident in its rich harmonic language and luxuriant textures. *Corinthians: XIII* was commissioned on behalf of the Phoenix Symphony Orchestra, who gave the premiere in 1964 under the direction of Guy Taylor.

Creston turned once more to a sectional form unified by thematic transformation in 1966, in a major work of markedly different tone: *Chthonic Ode*, subtitled "Homage to Henry Moore." The work was commissioned by the Detroit Symphony Orchestra, and its premiere took place in April of the following year conducted by Sixten Ehrling. Concerning the work Creston wrote: "Chthonic is a term used by Sir Herbert Read in reference to Henry Moore's sculpture. It seemed an appropriate title for a composition written in homage to the great sculptor's work. Among the word's various connotations, the one I selected in this particular case is 'dwelling in or beneath the earth.'" Using the same process of conceptual analysis and musical synthesis he applied to the symphonic poem *Walt Whitman* and other such works, Creston continued:

> In Henry Moore's sculpture I see seven qualities which I have striven to incorporate in the music: vitality, restraint, primitiveness, humanism,

womanhood, monumentality and universality. These qualities determined the form of my piece: free sectional form in four distinct but
connected sections. The first section is based on the qualities of vitality
and restraint, the second on primitiveness, the third on humanism and
womanhood and the fourth on monumentality and universality. . . .
The task of paralleling Moore's art in music was a formidable challenge. I was encouraged to undertake the task by his philosophy of art
with which I concur completely. "All good art," writes Moore, "has
contained both abstract and surrealist elements—order and surprise,
intellect and imagination, conscious and unconscious."[33]

In keeping with the character of Moore's sculpture, the *Chthonic
Ode* features bold, aggressive gestures, harsh, massive sonorities,
jagged rhythmic figures, and what was probably the most dissonant
harmonic language ever employed by Creston. Only the final section, in its evocation of "monumentality and universality," suc-
cumbs to the composer's weakness for bombast and overstatement,
marring what is otherwise an imaginative, novel, and vividly compelling work.

The final work to be discussed in this section is one of Creston's
last and one into which he felt he had captured his deepest feelings
about life: *Sadhana*, for cello solo and chamber orchestra. Conductor
(and former student) Gerard Schwarz had commissioned the work
in honor of the composer's seventy-fifth birthday and conducted the
premiere in October 1981, with the Los Angeles Chamber Orchestra.
The title *Sadhana* is taken from a book of the same name, subtitled
The Realization of Life, by the Indian poet and philosopher Rabindranath Tagore (1861–1940). Like Walt Whitman, Tagore was a lifelong
inspiration to Creston (whose first song, "The Bird of the Wilderness" [1933], was set to a Tagore poem). Tagore's *Sadhana* was written in 1913 and was the prolific Nobel Prize–winning author's most
important philosophical work, elaborating the fundamental ideas of
the Hindu religion. Creston's *Sadhana* is structured along the lines
of a theme and variations. Each variation is identified with a chapter
of Tagore's book and attempts to express the moods and feelings
engendered in the composer by that chapter, and each features a different combination of instruments. An introduction presents the
"Sadhana theme," followed by a cadenza played by the solo cello,
after which the "variation theme" is heard. Twelve variations follow, with the "Sadhana theme" recurring in Variation VI. Toward

the end of the work, the cello cadenza reappears, ushering in the final variation, "Cantilena," based on the "Sadhana theme." Though the solo cello is featured prominently, it is never used virtuosically, nor does it dominate in the manner of a concerto. The variations display a wide range of moods and emotions, but create a gentler, more understated overall impression than most of the composer's major works.

Festive and Virtuosic Works

Creston composed a great many works of festive character for orchestra and band, as well as a large number of concertos and other pieces that feature a soloist's virtuosity. The two groups are discussed together here because they share many characteristics in common: a more limited emotional range, concentrating particularly on exuberant expressions of joy that at times verge on the manic (in faster sections), and on a warm, ardent lyricism (in slower sections). Rhythmic manipulations and felicities, though ever-present, tend to be simpler than in the works described in the previous section and are usually subordinated to other concerns, especially in the concertos, where the virtuosic element is dominant. Yet despite their embracing of grandly romantic gestures, the relatively flat emotional contour of the concertos links them also to the Baroque style—a trait that is even more salient in Creston's chamber music. In the festive works as well as in the concertos, forms are straightforward and conventional, although thematic development and motivic interrelationships are rigorous, despite their light, relatively casual tone. Because the works in this category are so very similar to each other, discussion of individual works will be limited to a few representative examples.

The chief works of festive character are the Symphonies nos. 4 and 6, *Dance Overture* (1954), *Toccata* (1957), and *Choreografic Suite* (1965)—all for orchestra; the band works *Celebration Overture* (1954), *Jubilee* (1971), *Liberty Song* (1975), and *Festive Overture* (1980); and *Hyas Illahee* (1969), for chorus and orchestra. The virtuoso vehicles comprise concertos for saxophone (1941), one piano (1949), two pianos (1951), accordion (1958), and two concertos for violin (1956, 1960)—all with orchestra. There are also concertinos for marimba (1940) and for piano with woodwind quintet (1969). In addition there are "fantasies" featuring piano (1942), trombone (1947), and accordion (1964) with orchestra. There are also a suite (1957) for organ, a rhapsody (1976) for saxophone and piano (or organ), and *Dance Variations* (1942) for coloratura soprano and orchestra.

One of the most artistically successful of Creston's virtuoso vehicles, and one that has proven to be of enduring interest to performers, is the *Fantasy* for Trombone and Orchestra. The work was composed in 1947 on commission from Alfred Wallenstein, who led the premiere the following year with trombonist Robert Marstellar and the Los Angeles Philharmonic. Like most of his works designated as a "fantasy," it is in essence a short concerto, its three sections condensed into one movement.

The work opens assertively and vigorously, introducing three motifs within the first few seconds. These motifs, developed with remarkable ingenuity, account for virtually the entire work, generating the solo material, the orchestral material, and even the accompanimental figures. The difficult solo part is developed largely through "tangential variation." This technique, the intensely syncopated rhythmic character of both the solo and tutti elements, Creston's distinctive harmonic language, and the context of associations surrounding the trombone as a solo instrument all contribute to a general feeling reminiscent of "progressive jazz."

The first section maintains a vigorous, kinetic rhythmic drive, a bit grimmer than Creston's norm. The second section is sweetly lyrical, although rhythmic asymmetries abound throughout, but remain in the background texture. The final section begins with a *fugato* featuring some especially difficult passages for the soloist before progressing to episodes of increasing intensity. A brilliant cadenza brings the work to an end in a blaze of excitement. With a duration of barely twelve minutes, Creston's Trombone *Fantasy* is a masterpiece of motivic economy and developmental integration. It has been a favorite challenge for serious trombonists throughout the world ever since it first appeared.

As noted earlier, Creston's concertos tend to share much the same scope, form, and expressive content, so a discussion of one—in this case, the Concerto for Two Pianos and Orchestra—will suffice. This work was composed in 1951, although it was not performed until 1968 when duo-pianists Yarborough and Cowan gave the premiere with the New Orleans Philharmonic, under the direction of Werner Torkanowsky.

The concerto comprises three movements. The first opens assertively, presenting several short motifs of distinctive character. These motifs are combined, transformed, and developed ceaselessly and exhaustively throughout the movement, running an expressive gamut from bouncy good humor to lyrical tenderness. Solo and tutti passages alternate in a manner suggestive of the Baroque ritornello approach, although the musical content is typically Neo-Romantic.

The second movement is sweet and gentle in character. Some of the thematic ideas are new, while others are derived from the first movement. Contrast is provided by a central episode built around a playfully wistful motif.

The third movement unfolds along the lines of a brilliant tarantella in *rondo* form. Again the music is tightly and logically structured, maintaining a concentrated focus on the thorough development of a few short motifs. A lively, exuberant tone is maintained throughout. As the final section approaches, the energy is further intensified, bringing the work to a dazzling conclusion.

What is most remarkable about this work—and about Creston's concertos in general—is that a casual listening leaves the impression of an utterly conventional virtuoso vehicle, light in aesthetic weight and suitable for performance at a pops concert or other "semiclassical" venue. Yet closer analysis reveals a structure of considerable developmental complexity and discipline, without a moment's irrelevant impulse. Once again, an impression of casual, light-hearted fun is enhanced and substantiated through strict and exhaustive adherence to logical, disciplined development of a small number of motivic elements. However, because Creston composed so many concertos and similar works, because they tend to resemble each other so much, and because some of them became his most frequently played pieces, their cumulative effect on his reputation was not solely positive. Although such works were usually received enthusiastically by audiences, they were often treated with scorn, even contempt, by critics. Indeed, while Creston's music was enjoying considerable attention and popularity, complaints that it was trite, routine, mannered, and riddled with overused gimmicks and clichés began to appear in more high-minded circles. Creston was even accused of pandering and opportunism. While some of this can be attributed to professional envy, there is no question but that Creston's creative thinking often lapsed into formulae and that this tendency became increasingly pronounced as he grew older.

Creston's Symphony no. 4 was also composed in 1951, several

months after the Two-Piano Concerto, and received its first performance in January of the following year by the National Symphony
Orchestra of Washington, D.C., under the direction of Howard
Mitchell. In four movements, the work maintains a joyful, exuberant
character throughout. As with Creston's concertos, some of the symphony's material resembles the sort of light or "mood" music heard
on radio and television during the late 1940s and early 1950s. Yet—
again, like the concertos—despite its frolicsome character, the
work's structure is tightly organized, with more developmental
intricacy than is apparent on the surface.

The first movement makes a nod to *sonata allegro* form, with a
slow, majestic introduction that introduces a basic three-note motif
that recurs during the work in a variety of guises. This slow introduction soon gives way to a lively exposition of the two main
themes, the first of which is clearly derived from the introductory
motif. The movement bounces along cheerfully and with unflagging
energy, developing its two themes rigorously, by means of continuous rhythmic manipulation and contrapuntal activity. Yet despite its
developmental rigor, the movement's effervescent character never
wanes. The second movement is a warm, gentle pastorale, complete
with a florid melody introduced by the flute, and a rocking *siciliana*
rhythmic accompaniment (based on the first movement's three-note
motif). A playful interlude is based on a subtractive rhythmic *ostinato* (4 + 3 + 2). The *scherzo* is jocular in character, based on a rhythmically irregular idea played *pizzicato* by the strings and a burlesque
theme introduced by the bassoon. A lush string melody serves as
the "trio" section. The finale is a jaunty *rondo* whose rollicking high
spirits are interrupted only by episodes of warm, ardent lyricism.

Although some critics complained of the symphony's "pops concert" tone, it was very successful with audiences and was Creston's
own favorite among his symphonies.[34] Performed with precision,
polish, panache, and conviction, Creston's Fourth serves as a full-
length, fully elaborated symphony readily accessible to even the
least sophisticated listener.

Creston's Symphony no. 6 proved to be his last major work. Commissioned to compose a work for organ and orchestra by the American Guild of Organists, he completed what proved to be a
symphony in 1981. The work received its premiere in June of the
following year by the National Symphony Orchestra, under the
direction of Philip Brunelle. James Moeser was the organ soloist. The

Symphony consists of one twenty-minute movement comprising four connected sections, each corresponding in character to the four conventional symphonic movements. In his program notes, Creston indicated that in this work he conceived the organ as both a solo instrument and as a second orchestra.

The symphony opens as the organ introduces the first theme, dramatic and majestic in tone. The orchestra then presents a lyrical second theme, whose character is poignant and yearning. These two ideas provide most of the material for the entire work. As the first section develops these two ideas, a buoyantly jovial mood is maintained, with relatively few rhythmic asymmetries. The second section is playful and *scherzo*-like in character. Here a favorite irregular rhythmic *ostinato* $(2 + 2 + 2 + 3)$ is heard—used also in the Accordion Concerto and other works—as accompaniment to a flowing, lyrical melody. The third section revives the material from the opening section, now casting it in a sweet, *cantabile* manner. A four-note motif from the first theme emerges, with a coyly pleading quality. This idea figures prominently in the remainder of the Symphony. The final section returns to the bouncy character of the opening, as a cumulative ground bass creates a contrapuntal texture in the strings. Rhythmic elements are emphasized, but again, they are not as irregular or asymmetrical as the composer's norm, aside from some gentle syncopation. As the symphony's various motifs are brought together, the lyrical second theme comes to the fore to lead a grand apotheosis.

Like his Fourth Symphony, Creston's Sixth is discussed in this section because of its relatively narrow expressive range and its generally festive tone. Rhythmic intricacies play a less significant role, and those that appear lack the pungency and "swing" of earlier examples. These qualities, together with less strongly contoured thematic material and more homogeneous use of pantonal, nonkey-centered harmony, produce the lessened expressive intensity and relatively diffuse, unfocused dramatic contour characteristic of a number of Creston's last works and suggest the routine application of stale formulae.

Neo-Baroque and Neo-Classical Works

Though a number of commentators who apply the term more broadly than does this writer have identified Creston as a "Neo-

Classical" composer, the strongly emotive quality of most of his major works and the extroverted grandeur and flamboyance of his gestures place him among the Neo-Romantics for the purposes of this study. Nevertheless, there is no question but that Neo-Classical, and even more so Neo-Baroque, qualities are found throughout his output. Compositions in which these elements figure prominently represent the third major category of Creston's creative work. Into this group fall most of his chamber music, as well as the *Partita* for Flute, Violin, and Strings (1937), the *Pre-Classic Suite* (1958) for orchestra, and the Suite for String Orchestra (1978). The chamber works comprise a String Quartet (1936), the Sonata for Saxophone and Piano (1939), the Piano Trio (1979), and suites for saxophone (1935), viola (1937), violin (1939), and cello (1956)—all with piano. There is also a suite for flute, viola, and piano (1953) and one for saxophone quartet (1979).

As with the previous category, most of the works in this group share many characteristics in common. All the works entitled "Suite" (including the *Partita*) are modeled on the Baroque suite and comprise either three or five movements (except for the Viola Suite, which has four), most of which are identified with one of the familiar dance paradigms (e.g., *sarabande*, *gigue*, and the like). Consistent with Baroque style, each movement displays a characteristic affect or, more accurately, type of rhythmic and textural activity, which remains constant throughout. Generally, a cheerful, optimistic tone prevails, alternating between vigorous or playful fast movements and warmly lyrical slow movements. Forms are clear and concise; development is continuous, but with fewer motivic complexities and interrelationships than in the other categories. Rhythmic intricacies and manipulations are simpler and less salient as well, although they do contribute to the lively, energetic quality of the music. The harmonic language is consistent with Creston's French-flavored pantonality. The combination of Baroque gestures and formal articulation with Impressionistic harmony results in music that at times resembles that of such French composers as Jacques Ibert and Jean Francaix, among others. Because of the great similarity in substance, style, and quality among Creston's music of this genre, an examination of two representative works—one early and one late—will suffice.

The Sonata for Saxophone and Piano is probably Creston's single most widely performed and best-known work and, indeed, is perhaps the one undisputed classic in the concert saxophone chamber music repertoire. Composed in 1939, the sonata was introduced in New York City the following year by Cecil Leeson, with the composer at the piano. One of the few works Creston actually designated a sonata, it differs from his suites in its use of Classical, rather than Baroque, forms, in the slightly more elaborate developmental processes of its first movement, and in the more potent character of its climaxes.

In three movements, the sonata opens vigorously, as the several distinct motifs comprising the first theme begin to undergo development at once. The lyrical second theme, whose contour resembles that of the opening motif, follows; immediately and with little relaxation of momentum, its accompaniment figure promptly joins the developmental texture. The harmony is pantonal throughout, although the lyrical passages rest briefly on temporary tonal centers. Rhythmic and developmental energy continue unabated, uninterrupted by any sort of recapitulation, until the movement comes to an end.

The second movement opens with a smoothly flowing melody in 5/4 that begins unmistakably in A major—until the first chord changes, immediately canceling such apparent tonal stability. (This melody may be seen as a direct outgrowth of the second theme of the first movement.) Passing through a series of parallel seventh-chords, the melody eventually returns to the key of A for its cadence. The movement unfolds as this melody grows, eventually achieving an intense climax before subsiding gently, accompanied by parallel triads in chromatic descent, back to its tonic of A.

The third movement is a brisk and perky rondo. Irregular and asymmetrical rhythmic patterns abound, creating patterns of overlapping interactions between the two instruments and bringing the Sonata to a vivacious conclusion.

Creston's Piano Trio dates from 1979, forty years after the Saxophone Sonata. It was commissioned by the Mirecourt Trio, who were in residence at Grinnell College and gave the first performance in Des Moines, Iowa, in April of the following year. Despite its having been composed while the composer was in his seventies, the trio shares much in common with the earlier work: its Impressionistic, pantonal harmony, its profusion of playful rhythmic irregularities, and its consistently genial tone (perhaps even more so than the Saxophone Sonata, whose energetic first movement displays a bit of an "edge"). The scoring of the later work calls Ravel to mind, but such a resemblance only serves to underline the vast temperamental difference between the hearty, vigorous good cheer of Creston and the exquisite delicacy and refinement of his French hero.

The Piano Trio comprises four movements. The first presents two contrasting thematic ideas in a rough approximation of *sonata allegro* form. The material is presented in smoothly etched counterpoint, but its development is less tightly concentrated than in the corresponding movement of the Saxophone Sonata. This section thus resembles a varied alternation more than a true development.

The second movement is a light-hearted *scherzo* in the form of a five-part *rondo*. The refrain is a playful idea presented *pizzicato*, while the two episodes are built around irregular rhythmic *ostinati*.

The slow third movement is entitled "Recitative and Aria." Creston conceptualized the cello as a "masculine" voice, whose assertions are answered by the violin, representing the "feminine" voice. The "Aria" that follows is really a duet between the violin and cello, mediated by the piano. As the two ideas are developed jointly, the first theme from the first movement makes an appearance. The movement achieves a passionate climax before subsiding.

The fourth movement suggests a lively *tarantella*—a favorite dance form of Creston's—but a more cheerful one than the norm for this paradigm. Several musical ideas appear in rapid succession: the central one, aggressive and heavily accented, provides a brief, dark contrast to the prevailing sunny mood.

The Prelude and Dance

The fourth category of Creston's work refers to a genre with which he is closely associated: the "Prelude and Dance"—a type of composition that he devised as early as 1938, in the *Two Choric Dances* but whose origin is traceable to Stravinsky's *Le Sacre du Printemps*. Creston described the *Two Choric Dances*—the first slow, the second fast—as "an abstract conception suggesting movements of a group of dancers." The use of the Greek-derived term "choric" carries an ancient or timeless implication. The second *Choric Dance* is preceded by a starkly portentous introduction that accumulates tension that is released at the start of the *Dance*. This became Creston's prototype for the Prelude and Dance.

Typically, such works retain the quality of an abstract ceremony of timeless provenance, beginning with an introductory section of dramatic, atmospheric, or recitative-like character. The Prelude usually builds toward a climax, the Dance beginning at the culmination point, with an aggressive statement of an *ostinato* rhythmic pattern that will serve as its basis. The Dance is a free, highly rhythmic development, often addressing the same thematic material presented in the Prelude. Although the meter of the Dance tends to be constant, there are numerous irregular and extrametrical subdivisions, often in simultaneous combination. Thematic development may be quite elaborate and ingenious. Although the energy level of the Dance may fluctuate, there is usually an overall gradual increase in intensity. In the more extended examples there is often a recapitulation of elements from the Prelude, before the piece comes to a wild and orgiastic conclusion.

Many of the pieces in this category use the title *Prelude and Dance*, while others bear related titles, such as *Pastorale and Tarantella* and *Invocation and Dance*. Pieces entitled *Prelude and Dance* were composed for orchestra, piano solo, accordion, band, and two pianos (Creston's last work). An orchestral piece called *Janus* is one of the most fully realized of the works in this category. However, the best-known and most elaborate example is the Symphony no. 2, perhaps Creston's most distinctive, most representative, and—many agree—greatest work.

The Symphony no. 2 was composed in 1944 and was first performed in February of the following year by the New York Philharmonic under the direction of Artur Rodzinski. Creston described the work as "an apotheosis of the two foundations of all music: song and dance."[35] It comprises two movements: Introduction and Song, and Interlude and Dance.

The Introduction begins with a statement of the symphony's main theme—a slowly undulating melodic line of twenty-seven notes, including all twelve chromatic tones—played by the cellos. This presentation, defining a general tonality of F with Phrygian implications, initiates a cumulative ground bass, as the violas, second violins, and first violins each successively contribute themes of their own. Within an overall meter of 12/8, the rhythmic design of each repeating line is fraught with different regular and irregular subdivisions, while their melodic shapes are floridly chromatic, without producing vertical structures that exceed the limits of "smooth dissonance." The resulting counterpoint is a rich texture of gliding lines, devoid of metrical accent. After this initial presentation, the four themes are further explored individually, until a unison restatement of the first (Main) theme brings the Introduction to a close, while reaffirming the F-Phrygian tonality.

The Song begins with a flute solo presenting the Main theme, whose intervals are altered to create a warmly diatonic melody in D-flat major (the Song theme), accompanied by a gentle woodwind figure (the Accompaniment motif) that originally appeared in the first violins during the Introduction. This section unfolds luxuriantly, as the Song theme, soaring with a passionate lyricism in richly fluid phrases of mounting intensity, is pressed forward by the now-surging Accompaniment motif. In a masterful example of Creston's developmental brilliance, virtually every element of this full-throated Song is traceable to the Main theme (via the Song theme), its melodic inversion, and the Accompaniment motif, although its articulation proceeds with the appearance of an utterly spontaneous lyrical effusion. The Song builds to a grandly majestic climax in the key of D-flat before subsiding into a mood of calm tranquillity.

The Interlude introduces the second movement, as the Main theme is heard, rhythmically altered so that its character is now aggressive and defiant. After some elaboration of this theme, an ominous *ostinato* in 2/4 (within an overall meter of 3/4), based on the Accompaniment motif, introduces a mysterious flute solo in which a variant of the Main theme is heard. The tension rebuilds until a restatement of the Main theme, played in unison, triggers the start of the Dance.

The Dance, in 3/4 meter throughout, opens with an emphatic, heavily accented statement of its basic rhythmic *ostinato*, a syncopated two-measure pattern $(3+2+3+2+2)$ illustrating the rhythmic structure Creston labeled "Irregular Subdivision Overlapping." After this pattern has established itself, it recedes into the background, taking on the melodic contour of the Accompaniment motif. Now begins an extended development of fragments of the Main theme—and of the viola theme from the Introduction as well—accomplished through a series of syncopated tangential variations that clearly resemble improvisational jazz "riffs." The Dance builds in intensity, as the tonality shifts frequently and new *ostinato* figures appear in conjunction with patterns heard earlier, all driving the concentrated motivic development forward through a series of climactic high points. Finally, the Dance seems to have spent itself, and trills in the upper strings and woodwinds accompany a rapid diminution of intensity and activity, leading to an abbreviated and modified recapitulation of the somber counterpoint from the first movement's Introduction. Then, beginning softly, three rhythmic *ostinati* heard previously during the Dance are reintroduced in succession, as the intensity begins to mount once more. Once these *ostinati* are established in an intricately interlocking cumulative ground bass, the Song theme, now transformed into a passionate melody in E-flat minor, soars above in the high strings. Once again the music attains an intense emotional pitch as the melody strives higher and higher, while additional instruments augment the rhythmic accompaniment. Finally, the music arrives at a tonality of G-flat major, as a percussion flourish presses the momentum forward to a final cadence. In its rich elaboration and thorough integration of a personal and original aesthetic concept into a cohesive work of great appeal, Creston's Second stands as a major landmark of American Neo-Romanticism and one of the most significant American symphonies of the 1940s.

Vocal and Choral Works

Although Creston composed many vocal and choral works, most of them lack the distinction of his instrumental works and few have made an impact of any significance on singers, choral conductors, audiences, or critics. One reason for this is that Creston's melodic lines—motivic and, by his own admission, harmonically derived— lack the lyrical focus that gives vocal music much of its appeal. Another factor is that neither vocal nor choral music lends itself to the sort of rhythmic manipulations that give Creston's music much of its interest (with one exception noted below), nor is it suited to the extroverted flamboyance characteristic of his creative temperament. Furthermore, the composer's preference for abstract texts of a philosophical or spiritual nature resulted in music of a consistently bland emotional character. Because of its negligible importance, this portion of Creston's output is discussed briefly and in summary fashion.

Creston's vocal and choral music is divided approximately evenly between sacred and secular pieces. Most are relatively short, although there are a few of more substantial proportions. Perhaps the most ambitious is *Isaiah's Prophecy* (1962), a half-hour Christmas oratorio calling for vocal soloists, chorus, and orchestra. Another is *The Psalmist* (1967), five psalm settings for contralto and orchestra. Hampered by the factors noted above, both these works suffer severely from monotony in both mood and in musical materials. Creston also composed four settings of the Roman Catholic Mass, one of which is a Requiem. These, however, are exceedingly modest works—short in duration, with diatonic—and sometimes Gregorian—melodies, consonant harmony, and largely homophonic textures. The results are surprisingly neutral in affective expression. The three-movement *Celestial Vision* (1954) for male voices a capella brings together texts representing three divergent spiritual perspectives: Dante's *Divine Comedy*, Walt Whitman's *Song of Myself*, and the Bhagavad Gita. However, the three movements, while differing somewhat with regard to rhythmic motion, use essentially the same harmonic language in reflecting virtually identical emotional terrains. Like most of Creston's choral music, textures are largely homophonic, which further restricts the music's range of expression—an expression, one might sadly add, that seems no better suited to the character of the texts than to matters far more mundane. The second movement of *Celestial Vision* is but one of a number of Whitman settings composed by Creston. Others include *A Song of Joys* (1955) for voice and piano, *Leaves of Grass* (1970) for mixed voices and piano, and *Calamus* (1972) for male voices, brass, and percussion. Despite the composer's professed admiration for Whitman's poetry, all these settings reflect Creston's most generic emotional vocabulary, yielding little focus or specificity to the feelings presumably engendered by the texts. (This is in strong contrast to the range of expression captured in the orchestral poem *Walt Whitman* discussed earlier.) The same is true of Creston's several Tagore settings.

A few of Creston's vocal works warrant mention as transcending the limitations characteristic of his compositions in this genre. One is the setting he composed in 1945 of Psalm XXIII. While displaying a sweetness that verges on the cloying, conveyed with a full-blooded emotionality that certainly violates later twentieth-century standards for the expression of spiritual feelings, this setting nevertheless reflects a sincerity and conviction missing from most of Creston's other vocal and choral works. The setting exists in versions for soprano with piano, organ, or orchestra; and for soprano solo, mixed voices, and piano, organ, or orchestra. Worthy of mention in the secular domain is a setting composed in 1964 of W. H.

Auden's *Nocturne*, scored for soprano and chamber ensemble. This work also brings a freshness and a specificity of expression that set it apart from the composer's other secular settings.

Perhaps Creston's most artistically successful choral work is *Hyas Illahee*, composed in 1969, shortly after his relocation to the state of Washington. In this three-movement work for mixed voices and orchestra the composer attempted to achieve a fullness of expression comparable to that found in his instrumental music. In order to accomplish this, he created a text consisting of only nonsense syllables, Chinook Indian words and interjections, and names of places in Washington and Oregon. Then, treating the chorus as a musical adjunct to the orchestra, rather than as the vehicle for a text, Creston was free to explore within this medium the use of rhythmic *ostinati* and other characteristic devices, producing a work with many of the qualities found in his "festive" pieces.

CONCLUSION

When Paul Creston died in 1985, he was known chiefly for the few works that had established themselves internationally in the repertoire: his Sonata for Saxophone and Piano, which had been recorded thirteen times, the Concerto for Saxophone and Orchestra or Band, the *Fantasy* for Trombone and Orchestra, the Concertino for Marimba and Orchestra, and several short pieces for band. His symphonies and other major works lay moribund, apparently forgotten. The only major orchestral works recorded since the 1950s were *Corinthians: XIII* by the Louisville Orchestra in 1965 and the *Two Choric Dances* by the Arizona Chamber Orchestra in 1979. The three major commissions of his late years—the Piano Trio, *Sadhana*, and the Sixth Symphony—seemed like isolated tributes to an elder statesman.

But, as in the cases of Hanson and Giannini, the 1980s began to witness a renewal of interest in Creston's music. Conductor David Amos, a vigorous advocate of American traditionalist composers, had already commissioned Creston's Suite for String Orchestra during the late 1970s. In 1982 he recorded the work, along with the same composer's *Chant of 1942*, with the Israel Philharmonic. In 1984 the Piano Trio was recorded by the Mirecourt Trio, who had commissioned the work. In 1990 Amos recorded the *Partita* with the London

Sinfonia. Then, the following year Amos conducted the Krakow Philharmonic in a recording devoted to three of Creston's major orchestral works: *Walt Whitman, Corinthians: XIII,* and the Symphony no. 2—the first new recording of a Creston symphony to appear in more than twenty-five years! The release was well received by the press. James Reel noted that "conductors had pretty much abandoned [Creston's] orchestral music." This new release appeared "just as it seemed Creston's legacy was about to be banished to the conservatory recital hall." He concluded, "this disc will prolong the Paul Creston success story. May the story never end."[36] Another fine Amos-conducted recording appeared in 1994—this one featuring Creston's Concerto for Two Pianos and Orchestra, in a stunning performance by the duo-pianists Joshua Pierce and Dorothy Jonas.

But David Amos was not the only conductor to take an active interest in Creston's orchestral music. Gerard Schwarz, the former student who had commissioned *Sadhana* in 1981, was now music director of the Seattle Symphony. During the late 1980s he had undertaken a major recording project to feature American orchestral music in performances by both the Seattle Symphony and the New York Chamber Symphony. Having started with Howard Hanson, he soon turned his attention to Paul Creston. Schwarz's New York performance of the *Choreografic Suite* prompted a sophisticated and insightful comment from *New York Times* critic Bernard Holland: "The orchestra has the top-heavy brass and grandiose gesturings of Hollywood movie music. Creston, like Bernstein, found a certain innocent beauty in the melodramatic, the slightly trashy and the sentimental."[37] Schwarz's first all-Creston recording was issued in 1992 and featured the Symphony no. 3, along with several shorter works. Karl Miller noted that "the music of Paul Creston has been all but ignored these last 40 years. It is a great pity, since he wrote so many fine works." While conceding that the program shows "some unevenness," he added, "When his music gets vigorous, it is terrific." For Miller, "The real treat in this collection is the *Invocation and Dance.* It is filled with all of the best in Creston's music—the reflection, the lyricism, and the explosive bombast."[38]

In 1993, Creston's widely performed but never-recorded Trombone *Fantasy* was released by the Swedish label BIS in a performance by the brilliant virtuoso Christian Lindberg. With an accompaniment provided by Sweden's Malmö Symphony, under the direction of American conductor James DePreist, this is perhaps the most fully consummated Creston performance ever to appear on recording.

The Creston revival continued the following year with Gerard Schwarz's second disc devoted entirely to music by the composer—this time, the Symphony no. 5, the aforementioned *Choreografic Suite*, and *Toccata*. The release was welcomed by Andrew Achenbach, who described it as "hot-blooded music, passionately essayed."[39] *American Record Guide*'s Mark Lehman wrote, "What a pleasure to hear Paul Creston's music in such splendid performances and full-blooded sound—especially after the dim and faded recordings he was subjected to in the LP era!" Lehman described Creston's music as "full-blooded and robust, with the insistent rhythmic drive, soaring themes, rich harmonies, brassy orchestral splendor, and unsubtle drama of World War II-era film scores." Quite perceptively, he added, "We are no longer so close to it to worry about its unfashionableness. Moreover, the forthright exuberance of its *allegros* and open sentiment of its *andantes* are given more depth and interest than their conventional surface might at first reveal by the composer's use of rigorous thematic transformations to unify his expansive structures, as well as his remarkable ability to create fascinating textures by superimposing catchy rhythmic patterns."[40] The same year, Greenwood Press published a volume on Creston, compiled by Monica J. Slomski, in its series of "bio-bibliographies" of American composers.

Then, in 1995, the third recording of Creston's Second Symphony appeared, part of the Detroit Symphony Orchestra's survey of American music, led by Neeme Järvi. Justin Herman called it "a valuable release: the jewel of the Chandos American Series."[41] In 1999, as part of a deluxe ten-CD special edition, the New York Philharmonic released Pierre Monteux's live-concert performance from 1956 of the Second Symphony. That same year the gifted Yugoslavian pianist Tatjana Rankovich presented an entire compact disc devoted to traditionalist American music, including first recordings of Creston's Piano Sonata and Six Preludes, as well as music by Vittorio Giannini and Nicolas Flagello. This recording was favorably received in both the American and the British press, as well as by Internet critics. Mark Lehman was again one of the most articulate, commenting on the Piano Sonata: "A work with this combination of virtuosity, tunefulness, drama, and color offers much to both performers and audiences,"[42] while Steven Schwartz noted that although the Preludes were conceived as rhythmic studies, "these highly poetic, even fun pieces stand as far from the normal image of 'study' as one can get. Each prelude makes an expressive point as well as a technical one."[43] Then, in 2001, a recording featuring Creston's early *Seven Theses*, along with his 1964 *Metamorphoses*, was released, both works brilliantly performed by pianist Peter Vinograde. Rob Barnett commented about the *Metamorphoses*, "Now this is the sort of work that would make a coup for an up-and-coming young pianist in one of the world's piano competitions. . . . A lovely and unfashionable disc. It may yet play its part in stirring rising generations of pianists to take a 'dangerous' turn and shake the piano establishment."[44]

But perhaps the recording that most definitively heralded the revival and reassessment of Creston was a 2000 release on the widely distributed Naxos label offering new readings of the composer's First, Second, and Third Symphonies. The performances featured the National Symphony Orchestra of the Ukraine, conducted by Theodore Kuchar. (This recording will presumably be followed by another comprising the remaining three symphonies.) Three critics presented their views via a veritable symposium on the British website Classical Music on the Web. While disputing the relative merits of the works' different recorded performances, the three were unanimous in their praise for the music. Rob Barnett concluded his comments: "Snap up this bountifully complete and inexpensive disc and open your symphonic shutters just a little wider." Describing the first movement of Symphony no. 2 as "the mark of a composer at the zenith of his powers—technically in command and emotionally eloquent," he called the symphony as a whole, "a work to set beside the great symphonic works of 1940s USA."[45] For Lewis Foreman, "the high point of this programme is Creston's Third Symphony, surely one of the all-time greats of American symphonism."[46] David Wright, who was dissatisfied by the performances of the Ukrainian orchestra, began his review, "I have known and loved these symphonies for over forty years." He then, quite accurately, quotes the composer's assertion that Howard Mitchell's performances of the Second and Third Symphonies fully embody his own intentions. However, describing the Third Symphony as "a deeply-felt personal and original religious quest," he showed a misunderstanding of Creston's view of the work, when he added, "it is a 'factual' music-picture not an emotional one." Wright apparently overlooked the composer's comment, printed in the score, that "the work is a musical parallel of inherent emotional reactions rather than a narrative or painting." He concluded his comments by averring, "These are great symphonies, probably some of the best American symphonies of all."[47]

NOTES

1. Henry Cowell, "Paul Creston," *Musical Quarterly* (October 1948): 533.
2. Paul Creston, Letter to this writer, 10 June 1981.
3. Paul Creston, Letter to this writer, 10 June 1981.
4. Howard Mitchell, "The Hallmark of Greatness," *Musical Courier* (15 November 1956): 10.
5. "Amity is Voiced by Shostakovich," *New York Times* (25 October 1959).
6. Mitchell, "The Hallmark of Greatness," 10.
7. Edward Rothstein, Review, *New York Times* (20 October 1981).
8. A. Duane White, "Paul Creston," *Music Clubs Magazine* (Spring 1983): 28.
9. Will Crutchfield, Obituary, *New York Times* (25 August 1985).
10. Paul Creston, Letter to Henry Cowell, 11 January 1948, quoted in Cowell, "Creston," 534–535.
11. Creston, Letter to Henry Cowell, quoted in Cowell, "Paul Creston," 538.
12. Paul Creston, "A Composer's Creed," lecture delivered at Central Washington State College, Fall 1967, 15; published in *Music Educator's Journal* (March 1971).
13. White, "Paul Creston," 29.
14. Paul Creston, speech delivered in Lancaster, PA, upon receipt of Lancaster Composers Award, 19 April 1970.
15. Creston, speech delivered in Lancaster, PA.
16. White, "Paul Creston," 29.
17. Creston, speech delivered in Lancaster, PA.
18. Paul Creston, *Seven Theses* (New York: New Music Press, 1935); reissued by Shawnee Press, Delaware Water Gap, PA.
19. Paul Creston, Letter to this writer, 11 August 1970.
20. Creston, "A Composer's Creed," 16.
21. Creston, "A Composer's Creed," 16.
22. Paul Creston, *Principles of Rhythm* (New York: Franco Colombo, 1964).
23. Paul Creston, Letter to this writer (25 September 1971).

24. Paul Creston, "Principles of Melodic Construction," unpublished notes, sent to this writer, June 1975.

25. Daniel Cariaga, "Moderation Works for Composer Creston, 74 + ," *Los Angeles Times* (1 October 1981).

26. Paul Creston, Program Notes, 1943.

27. Paul Creston, Program Notes, *Symphony No. 3* (New York: G. Schirmer, 1950).

28. Henry Cowell, Review, *Musical Quarterly* (January 1951): 78–79.

29. Henry Cowell, Review, *Musical Quarterly* (October 1954): 625.

30. Paul Creston, Program Notes, 1956.

31. Paul Creston, *Rational Metric Notation: The Mathematical Basis of Meters, Symbols, and Note-Values* (Hicksville, N.Y.: Exposition Press, 1979).

32. Paul Creston, Program Notes, *Corinthians: XIII* (New York: Mills Music, 1963).

33. Paul Creston, Program Notes, 1966.

34. Paul Creston, Letter to this writer, 11 March 1970.

35. Paul Creston, Program Notes, 1945.

36. James Reel, Review, *Arizona Daily Star* (17 May 1991).

37. Bernard Holland, Review, *New York Times* (8 October 1991).

38. Karl Miller, Review, *American Record Guide* (November–December 1992): 108.

39. Andrew Achenbach, Review, *Gramophone* (October 1994): 3.

40. Mark Lehman, Review, *American Record Guide* (September–October 1994): 120.

41. Justin Herman, Review, *American Record Guide* (January–February 1996): 99.

42. Mark Lehman, Review, *American Record Guide* (November–December 1999): 118.

43. Steven Schwartz, Review, *Classical Net* (2001), http://www.classical.net/music/recs/reviews/p/phx00143b.html.

44. Rob Barnett, Review, *Classical Music on the Web* (August 2001), http://www.musicweb.uk.net/classrev/2001/Aug01/CoplandCreston.htm.

45. Rob Barnett, Review, *Classical Music on the Web* (June 2000), http://www.musicweb.uk.net/classrev/2000/June00/creston.htm.

46. Lewis Foreman, Review, *Classical Music on the Web* (June 2000), http://www.musicweb.uk.net/classrev/2000/June00/creston.htm.

47. David Wright, Review, *Classical Music on the Web* (June 2000), *http://www.musicweb.uk.net/classrev/2000/June00/creston.htm.*

SELECTED BIBLIOGRAPHY

Barnett, Rob, Lewis Foreman, and David Wright. Review of Creston Symphonies 1–3. *Classical Music on the Web* (June 2000), http://www.musicweb.uk.net/classrev/2000/June00/creston.htm.

Cowell, Henry. "Paul Creston." *Musical Quarterly* (October 1948): 533–541.

Creston, Paul. "A Composer's Creed," lecture delivered at Central Washington State College, Fall 1967; published in *Music Educator's Journal* (March 1971): 36–39, 91–93.

Creston, Paul. *Principles of Rhythm.* New York: Franco Colombo, 1964.

Creston, Paul. *Rational Metric Notation: The Mathematical Basis of Meters, Symbols, and Note-Values.* Hicksville, N.Y.: Exposition Press, 1979.

Creston, Paul. "The Structure of Rhythm." *Clavier* (November 1971): 15–20.

Crutchfield, Will. "Paul Creston, 78, a Composer of Symphonies." *New York Times* (25 August 1985).

Mitchell, Howard. "The Hallmark of Greatness." *Musical Courier* (15 November 1956): 9–10.

Slomski, Monica. *Paul Creston: A Bio-Bibliography.* Westport, Conn.: Greenwood Press, 1994.

Tull, Fisher. "Paul Creston: An Interview." *Instrumentalist* (October 1971): 42–44.

White, A. Duane. "Paul Creston." *Music Clubs Magazine* (Spring 1983): 26–29.

ESSENTIAL DISCOGRAPHY

ASDisc: *Two Choric Dances*; *Dance Overture* (NBC Sym. Orch., New York Philharmonic, Guido Cantelli, cond.).

BIS CD628: Trombone Fantasy (Christian Lindberg, trombone; Malmö Sym. Orch., James DePreist, cond.); www.bis.se.

Delos DE-3114: *Out of the Cradle*; *Partita* (Scott Goff, flute; Ilkka Talvi, violin); Symphony No. 3, "Three Mysteries"; *Invocation and Dance* (Seattle Sym. Orch., Gerard Schwarz, cond.); www.delosmus.com.

Kleos 5121: Concerto for Two Pianos and Orchestra (Joshua Pierce, Dorothy Jonas, pianos; Nat'l. Sym. Orch. of Polish Radio/TV, David Amos, cond.); www.heliconrecords.com.

Music & Arts CD-934: Piano Trio (Mirecourt Trio); www.musicandarts.com.

Naxos 8.559034: Symphonies Nos. 1, 2, 3 (Nat'l. Sym. Orch. of Ukraine, Theodore Kuchar, cond.); www.naxos.com.

Naxos 8.559153: Symphony No. 5; *Toccata*; *Choreografic Suite* (NY Chamber Symphony, Seattle Sym. Orch., Gerard Schwarz, cond.); www.naxos.com.

Phoenix PHCD-143: Piano Sonata; Six Preludes (Tatjana Rankovich, piano); www.phoenixcd.com.

Phoenix PHCD-149: *Seven Theses*; *Metamorphoses* (Peter Vinograde, piano); www.phoenixcd.com.

Samuel Barber: Photo provided courtesy of G. Schirmer

6

Samuel Barber

Samuel Barber might be viewed as the "poster-boy" of American Neo-Romanticism—the one composer featured in this study whose music attained a level of international recognition almost impervious to the shifts of musical fashion. Naturally inclined from childhood toward musical composition as an expression of personal moods and feelings, he maintained this aesthetic perspective throughout his creative life. The beneficiary of significant advantages from the start, he was born into a cultivated, affluent family already blessed with two prominent musicians eager to nurture the development of their talented young relative. While still in his teens Barber was introduced to influential patrons who soon facilitated the presentation of his music to some of the world's most prominent conductors. At the age of twenty-six, he composed one of the most beloved, frequently heard compositions in the repertoire of American concert music, familiar to many who have never been present at a classical venue. From that time on he remained one of America's two or three most frequently performed composers, his career marked by virtually uninterrupted success, while most of his works enjoyed the advocacy of the world's most celebrated soloists and conductors. When the adherents of Modernism gained power and influence during the late 1950s and 1960s, Barber encountered his first taste of failure, as his previous success and the apparent ease with which it was won marked him as a member of the scorned "establishment." Though his reputation was tarnished by the

243

stigma of *bourgeois* complacency, his most popular works never suffered neglect; and while he spent the last fifteen years of his life
nursing the wounds caused by critical disparagement, the ensuing
two decades have witnessed the revival of his reputation and the
acceptance of nearly all his music into the active repertoire.

BIOGRAPHY

(For the section on Barber's biography I am indebted to Barbara B.
Heyman's *Samuel Barber: The Composer and His Music*.[1] Her study,
rich in factual detail, is a useful resource for those who wish a more
elaborate account of the composer's life.)

Samuel Osmond Barber II was born in 1910 in West Chester,
Pennsylvania, a conservative, affluent community some thirty miles
from Philadelphia. His father, Roy, was a physician, descended
from one of the town's most prominent families. An esteemed member of the community, Dr. Barber was a trustee of the local Presbyterian church, as well as president of the school board. His wife, Daisy
Beatty, traced her American ancestry back to the 1700s. Her sister
Louise (1871–1947) was one of the world's leading operatic contraltos during the first two decades of the century; she was married to
Sidney Homer (1864–1953), a Boston-born composer who had studied with Chadwick and Rheinberger. Homer's art-songs were highly
regarded during that same period. Young Sam had a sister Sara,
three years his junior.

The straitlaced character of his nuclear family and the surrounding community was offset by the colorful artistic life to which he
was exposed by his aunt and uncle. At the age of six Sam accompanied his uncle Sidney to see his aunt perform in *Aida* opposite
Enrico Caruso at the Metropolitan Opera. Not long after this he
began writing down his own tunes, assisted by his mother. Already
in evidence was a preference for melody, as well as a lifelong predilection for melancholy moods (one of his first piano pieces was entitled *Sadness*).

When he was nine Sam began piano lessons with William Hatton
Green, a respected local musician who had studied with Lesche-
tizky. Around this time the young musician set forth the course of
his life in an often-quoted note to his mother: "I have written this to
tell you my worrying secret. Now don't cry when you read it

because it is neither yours nor my fault. I suppose I will have to tell it now without any nonsense. To begin with I was not meant to be an athlet [*sic*]. I was meant to be a composer, and will be I'm sure. I'll ask you one more thing.—Don't ask me to try to forget this unpleasant thing and go play football—*Please*—Sometimes I've been worrying about this so much that it makes me mad (not very), Love, Sam Barber II."[2]

The following year Sam composed the first act of an opera, with a libretto written by the family's Irish cook. When he was twelve he took the liberty of showing his compositions to his uncle. Homer validated Sam's creative intentions with sober, earnest advice, initiating a role as the young composer's chief mentor that he willingly continued to fulfill for the rest of his life. "There is no doubt you have the making of a composer in you," he wrote.

> There are three things you must aim for definitely. The first is the development of a taste that should, in time, amount to a passion, for the best in music in all forms. . . . Your whole life will be influenced by the forming of your taste in the next few years. . . . The second . . . is to have a good teacher in composition. . . . The third thing is that you should master a practical instrument. . . . You must not think that you can fool with music and get anywhere. Sooner or later you will have to do hard work, and you will make more rapid progress now than when you are older.[3]

Two years later, Homer counseled the young adolescent:

> If you write naturally and spontaneously, you will develop a style of your own, without being conscious of it. It is the unconscious charm that is so elusive and valuable, in art, as in Life. . . . Everything depends . . . on the development of your taste and the refinement of your sensibilities. If you think of music from the point of view of sensationalism and publicity, your work will show it. If you learn to love the poetic undercurrent and the subtleties of beauty and spirituality which have been expressed in music, your work will show it just as much. The wonderful thing about art is that a man can conceal nothing; it reveals him as naked and unadorned.[4]

And just a few years after that, "It takes some courage to go into an art which shows you as you are, and no doubt many wonderful souls have shrunk from the ordeal and refused to put their real emo-

tions into art form for others to know."[5] Those familiar with Barber's subsequent development will appreciate just how deeply the
young composer took his uncle's advice to heart. Throughout the
probing, reflective correspondence they maintained for the next
twenty-five years, Homer continued to emphasize the importance of
naturalness, sincerity, and taste. Barber remained a lifelong advocate of his uncle's songs and inherited the older man's fondness for
Celtic poets such as James Stephens, not to mention Yeats and Joyce.

Despite the skepticism with which his parents initially viewed
Sam's fervent musical aspirations, his uncle's validation and encouragement soon won their support. Realizing that he needed the stim-
ulation and challenge of a wider network than their local town
could provide, his father arranged for the fourteen-year-old to
spend Friday afternoons in Philadelphia at the newly opened Curtis
Institute of Music. His portfolio of original work, now quite large
and varied, impressed the school faculty, and he was found to be a
personable fellow, despite his somewhat aristocratic manner. He
began studying composition with Rosario Scalero (1870–1954),
whose rigorous traditionalism was compatible with the counsel he
was receiving from his uncle. His other major teachers were Isabelle
Vengerova (piano) and Emilio de Gogorza (voice). He was to remain
with all three teachers until the 1930s.

During his early years of study in West Chester, Sam had participated in local recitals, and as early as 1923 his sister had sung several of his songs at a church performance. In 1926, his family
arranged a program devoted entirely to music by the young composer. The concert, which took place at their home, was attended by
an audience of a hundred. The following year he graduated from
high school, near the top of his class. A song he wrote as the school's
alma mater is still in use today.

Although Barber was impressed by the sophistication of many of
the Curtis students, no one made as great an impact as a young man
who had just arrived from Italy in 1928. His name was Gian Carlo
Menotti, and the two soon developed an intense romantic relationship that was to last for many years. Menotti also became his most
trusted critic and remained so for the rest of his life.

The next years were fruitful and rewarding for Barber. In 1928, he
composed a violin sonata that won the Bearns Prize (although later
he was to withdraw the work). He attended concerts of the Philadelphia Orchestra regularly, preparing for them in advance by study-

ing the scores to be performed. These concerts, then under the direction of Leopold Stokowski, exposed him to a wide variety of new and unfamiliar repertoire. An avid reader, Barber pursued an interest in literature, while attempting to teach himself several foreign languages. During the summers, Menotti escorted him to Italy, where the two continued their studies with Scalero. Menotti also introduced his companion to Cadegliano, the village where he had spent his childhood.

In 1931, Barber graduated from the Curtis Institute, fulfilling his composition requirements with the *Overture to "The School for Scandal."* By this time he had already completed dozens of songs, the *Serenade* for string quartet, the setting of Arnold's *Dover Beach* for baritone and string quartet, and a full-length piano concerto (which he subsequently withdrew). Soon to follow were the Cello Sonata and *Music for a Scene from Shelley.*

In 1933, Barber won a second Bearns Prize for *"School for Scandal,"* which afforded him the opportunity for a more extended stay in Europe. However this sojourn prevented him from attending the first performance of an orchestral work of his own: That August the *Overture* was performed in Philadelphia by Alexander Smallens and the Robin Hood Dell Symphony Orchestra. The work was heard by an unusually large and appreciative summer audience, initiating the pattern of auspicious premieres, enthusiastically received, that propelled his career forward for many years.

During that summer, on a rather brazen whim, Barber and Menotti appeared without invitation at the island villa of Arturo Toscanini in Lago Maggiore. To their considerable surprise, they were welcomed warmly and invited by the maestro to come again. On subsequent visits they often found themselves in the company of other musical luminaries—Toscanini's son-in-law Vladimir Horowitz, for example. The informality of these encounters made them ideal opportunities for the sort of networking that would prove enormously fruitful throughout Barber's career. On such a visit Toscanini invited the young composer to submit one of his works to him for possible performance. However, it was several years before Barber decided that the moment was right.

When he returned to the United States, Barber gained the interest and attention of Mary Curtis Bok, the wealthy patroness who had founded the Curtis Institute. She decided to take a hand in promoting the young composer's career, introducing him to a number of influential figures, among them Carl Engel of the publishing firm of G. Schirmer. Engel immediately offered to publish several of Barber's newly completed compositions.

In 1935, Barber finally had the opportunity to hear one of his orchestral works performed, when the New York Philharmonic gave the premiere of *Music for a Scene from Shelley*, under the direction of Werner Janssen. In an interview connected with this event, the twenty-five-year-old composer made a telling statement about his intentions that clearly guided his development as an artist, while linking him aesthetically with the other composers featured in this study: "My aim is to write good music that will be comprehensible to as many people as possible, instead of music heard only by small, snobbish musical societies in the large cities. Radio makes this aim entirely possible of achievement. The universal basis of artistic spiritual communication by means of art is through the emotions."[6]

To supplement his income from composing, Barber had been attempting to develop a career as a vocal recitalist. Radio offered an opportunity for him to pursue this plan, and through this medium he soon presented vocal recitals, some of which were heard nationwide. Their success led to a series of weekly broadcasts on which he accompanied himself at the piano in repertoire drawn from the seventeenth to the twentieth centuries. Also in 1935, RCA invited him to record *Dover Beach* with the Curtis String Quartet. He seized the opportunity, although he had never sung the work in public. The result, accomplished in only two run-throughs, interrupted halfway through for a side-change, was meticulously executed and highly expressive and remains a valuable musical, as well as historical, document. In May, Barber was awarded the Prix de Rome, as "the most talented and deserving student of music in America," which enabled him to spend two full years in Europe.[7]

It is difficult to grasp the incendiary speed with which personal advantages and fortuitous historical circumstances converged with the authentic appeal of his music—to critics as well as to audiences—to propel Barber's career forward from age twenty-five on. Not only was Louise Homer performing her favorites from among her nephew's songs, but soon former fellow student Rose Bampton was as well, carrying his name forward as her own celebrity mounted. Yet even then, reservations were expressed about the conservatism of his style. No less astute a commentator than Aaron Copland wrote, "Barber writes in a somewhat out-moded fashion, making up in technical finish what he lacks in musical substance. So excellent a craftsman should not content himself forever with the emotionally conventional context of his present manner."[8] On the other hand, developing and remaining true to his own personal, richly expressive creative voice brought him wide popular acceptance without his having to embrace vernacular musical styles, as did Copland and so many others in their efforts to broaden their appeal.

During his stay in Europe from 1935 through 1937, Barber completed the op. 10 settings of James Joyce, as well as his Symphony no. 1. However, before this work had its premiere in Rome late in 1936, Artur Rodzinski, who had met Barber several years before at Curtis, had already promised to conduct it with several major orchestras during the seasons to come. Later that year Barber also completed the first draft of his String Quartet. (On September 19, 1936, he wrote to his cellist friend Orlando Cole, "I have just finished the slow movement of my quartet today—it is a knock-out!"[9]) The next year saw the composition of an orchestral work entitled *Essay*.

Back in the United States in 1937, Barber moved into an apartment in New York City with Menotti. There he was able to enjoy the fact that his *Overture to "The School for Scandal"* was played twice in one week: by the New York Philharmonic under Barbirolli and by the visiting Cleveland Orchestra under Rodzinski. Early in 1938 he finally responded to Toscanini's offer to consider his music for performance, submitting to the maestro both his newly completed *Essay* and the *Adagio* movement of his String Quartet, which he had extracted and arranged for string orchestra at the suggestion of his devoted and prescient friend Gama Gilbert. To Barber's delight, the conductor agreed to perform both pieces with the NBC Symphony later that year—the first American works he was to feature on his NBC broadcasts. Both were great successes, the *Adagio* going on to become the most widely known piece of concert music composed by an American, perhaps rivaled only by Gershwin's *Rhapsody in Blue* and Copland's *Fanfare for the Common Man*. It was performed at the funeral of Franklin D. Roosevelt and has been heard at similar occasions ever since; it has served to evoke a quiet sadness in movies, and has even been used in television commercials.

At the time, however, Toscanini's performance of the two pieces by Barber prompted considerable controversy. Generally regarded as the world's leading conductor, the Italian maestro was known for his antipathy toward American composers. His choice of Barber as the first native-born composer he was to champion drew considerable notice. And although his performances were enthusiastically received by the audience and praised by critics, they infuriated proponents of Modernism. Activist Ashley Pettis wrote a letter to the *New York Times* in which he described Barber's music as "dull" and "utterly anachronistic as the utterance of a young man of 28."[10] This prompted a series of heated exchanges debating whether or not American music had to embrace "a contemporary idiom" in order to be legitimate and worthy of performance.

During the late 1930s, Barber accepted a teaching position at the Curtis Institute, forming and conducting a madrigal chorus, for which he composed *A Stopwatch and an Ordnance Map*, the three *Reincarnations*, and several other pieces. However, he was not fond of teaching, and his students could sense his disdain, so shortly after being elected to the National Institute of Arts and Letters—at age thirty, the youngest recipient ever—he retired from teaching to concentrate almost exclusively on composition. (Already one of America's two or three most frequently performed composers, he was now able to support himself by his works alone.) His main projects at this time were a second *Essay* for orchestra and a violin concerto, commissioned by Samuel Fels, founder of the Fels Naptha company, for his violin-playing adopted son Iso Briselli. The story of the commission has become a favorite of program annotators: Fels tried to rescind the commission when Briselli claimed that the third movement was unplayable. Barber arranged a private reading at Curtis and enlisted violinist Herbert Baumel to prove that the work was indeed playable. The Violin Concerto went on to become another one of the composer's enduring successes.

After several years of working and reworking its material, Barber completed a second *Essay* for orchestra early in 1942. Barely a month after it was finished, Bruno Walter conducted the premiere with the New York Philharmonic. Another positive reception led to an immediate flurry of further performances, conducted by George Szell, Eugene Ormandy, and others. It was shortly after this that Barber and Menotti purchased—with the help of Mary Curtis Bok—a large house in Mount Kisco, New York, which they named "Capricorn." Joined there by their good friend, poet Robert Horan, they made Capricorn a center of intellectual, cultural, and social life for a whole network of talented creative artists.

In September 1942, while involved in planning an experimental film with Howard Hughes, Barber was inducted into the Army Air Force. Stationed in Fort Worth, Texas, he was deeply distressed to have his composing curtailed. Nevertheless, he seems to have felt an obligation to contribute to the war effort and enlisted some of his more illustrious colleagues—Serge Koussevitzky among them—to advocate that he be permitted to fulfill his patriotic duty by writing music that would unify the nation in the spirit of victory. These efforts proved successful, and he responded to requests for "war music" with such pieces as the *Commando March.*

Then, in 1943, Barber hit upon the idea of a patriotic symphony dedicated to the Air Force, a work that "would best express the mood, the adventure, the vivid action of the individual Army flying man."[11] Looming as precedent was Dmitri Shostakovich, whose "Leningrad" Symphony had become such a symbol of the Allied struggle that his name had become virtually a household word. Presenting the idea to his superior General Barton Yount, whose wife was an enthusiastic music lover, Barber was given approval to proceed and was even permitted to work on the composition at home in Mount Kisco. The only stipulation was that he appear at West Point for bi-weekly presentations of the latest portions of his work-in-progress. He pursued the work with great enthusiasm, convinced it would be his best, while the Army flew him around the country from airfield to airfield, in order to inspire within him the appropriate sentiments. At one point, disappointment was expressed that the *Flight Symphony* (as the military had dubbed it) had not included "new technical devices" to reflect the innovative technology employed by the Air Force. So Barber agreed to incorporate into the work a sound produced by an "electronic tone generator," designed especially for the purpose by Bell Labs, to simulate a radio beam.

All these circumstances were heavily publicized in the media, with much attention focused on the work's propagandistic power, so that its first performance was anticipated with great excitement. The premiere of the *Second Symphony (Dedicated to the Army Air Forces)*—as it was formally identified—took place in March 1944, with Serge Koussevitzky conducting the Boston Symphony. The performance, broadcast nationwide, was received enthusiastically by both press and public, and listeners claimed to hear in the work representations of air-raids, planes taking off, and the like,

although, from the beginning, Barber denied any descriptive or programmatic intentions. The work continued to garner tremendous
publicity, as other allies expressed interest in performing it, and
many subsequent performances and broadcasts took place during
the months that followed.

The army was extremely proud of having engendered this work.
General Yount called Barber "a great musician and . . . a fine, patriotic citizen," while General Matthew Arnold called the symphony
"one of the most outstanding contributions to musical literature that
has come out of this war era. . . . The enlisted man . . . will take great
pride in knowing that one of his own fellow soldiers is responsible
for this fine work."[12] Barber had hoped that the symphony's success
might reduce his military responsibilities, and this indeed came to
pass, as he was permitted to work on his *Capricorn Concerto* in
Mount Kisco. But, although he was also granted an early discharge,
he did have to defer a number of exciting composing opportunities
because of military obligations.

In January 1945, the celebrated virtuoso Vladimir Horowitz introduced three of Barber's *Excursions*, a group of short piano pieces in
quasi-vernacular style that he had been tinkering with during the
past few years. Later the same year, he was commissioned by NBC
to compose some orchestral music to accompany a radio show. The
result was a short orchestral piece called *Horizon*. At this time he was
also working on a cello concerto that had been commissioned at the
suggestion of Serge Koussevitzky for cellist Raya Garbusova, who
would present the work the following year with the Boston Symphony.

During the 1940s, modern dance pioneer Martha Graham was
actively commissioning scores from many of America's leading
composers to use in her choreographic works. Introduced to Barber
through their mutual friend Robert Horan in 1945, Graham
expressed interest in Barber's composing music for a work on the
subject of Medea. The result of this collaboration was the score to
Graham's *Cave of the Heart,* which Barber subsequently transformed
into the ballet suite *Medea*, then later condensed into a shorter work
entitled *Medea's Meditation and Dance of Vengeance*. Using a much
harsher harmonic language than that found in his previous works,
this music initially drew a mixed reception, disappointing those
who expected only comforting romanticism from Barber, while
pleasing those who had been urging on him a more adventurous

spirit. In its later, more condensed form, this music has become another of the composer's most successful orchestral pieces.

Barber had discovered the writing of James Agee during the 1930s, having set his poem "Sure on This Shining Night" in 1938. He had also become familiar with the poignant, poetic prose passage entitled *Knoxville: Summer of 1915*, which had appeared in the *Partisan Review*. Early in 1947, soprano Eleanor Steber approached Barber with a request for a work with orchestra that she would present with Koussevitzky and the Boston Symphony. Saddened by the death of his Aunt Louise, and by the rapidly deteriorating health of his father, Barber was struck by the way Agee's reminiscence of a parent's death "expresses a child's feeling of loneliness, wonder, and lack of identity in that marginal world between twilight and sleep."[13] Feeling a tremendous affinity with this passage, Barber decided to fulfill Steber's request with a musical interpretation of Agee's words.

Not until shortly after Barber completed his setting of *Knoxville* did the two men meet, and later on they became friends. Toward the end of his life, Barber reflected on their affinity, recalling that the scene conjured in those words:

> struck me as something very like my own childhood had been. . . . Agee and I were the same age and of similar background, we both had back yards where our families used to lie in the long summer evenings, we each had an aunt who was a musician. I well remember my parents sitting on the porch, talking quietly as they rocked. And there was a trolley car with straw seats and a clanging bell called "The Dinky" that traveled up and down the main street. A lot of odd coincidences. Agee's poem was vivid and moved me deeply, and my musical response that summer . . . was immediate and intense. I think I must have composed *Knoxville* in a few days.[14]

In 1948, commissioned by Richard Rodgers and Irving Berlin to write a major piano sonata to be premiered by Horowitz, Barber went to Rome to concentrate on the work. Rarely able to compose with ease, Barber encountered creative "blocks" periodically throughout his career, but the one he faced while working on the sonata was especially severe. Finding Rome too distracting, he returned to the States after several months. Here he was sidetracked by numerous details involving upcoming performances and publications. By 1949, having completed three movements, Barber decided to conclude the work with the slow movement. Horowitz, who offered plenty of advice throughout the process of composition, balked at this notion and insisted on a virtuoso finale. Not until Horowitz's wife (Toscanini's daughter) accused him of being creatively "constipated" did Barber hit upon the idea of ending the work with the Latin-flavored fugue, which he completed in a matter of days.[15]

Toward the late 1940s, Barber began to seek opportunities for conducting his own works. Although he had been dismissed from Fritz Reiner's conducting class at Curtis with the verdict that he "would never make a conductor,"[16] Barber reasoned that his own participation in the performance of his music might draw to it greater attention and interest. Then, in 1950, London/Decca invited him to come to England and conduct recordings of three of his major works with the New Symphony Orchestra of London. Though he saw this as a promising opportunity, he felt the need for some preparation, arranging for an intensive regimen of lessons from conductor Nicolai Malko. Following Malko to Copenhagen, Barber hired the Danish Opera Orchestra for a series of practice sessions, building his technique as well as his confidence. He retained Malko as coach during the actual recording sessions, which took place in December of that year.

The London sessions, which included the Second Symphony, the Cello Concerto, and the *Medea* ballet suite, went very well. Barber wrote to his family, "I am absolutely delighted about the whole venture. . . . [The head music director] says I am the only composer he knows—and he knows them all—who can conduct his own works and wishes me to do further work for them."[17] Shortly afterward, Barber went on to Germany, where he conducted several highly successful concerts of his own works. Returning to the United States in the spring of 1951, he conducted the Boston Symphony in his Second Symphony. Though well received, this performance brought his foray into conducting to an end.

Asked toward the end of his life why he gave up conducting, Barber replied:

> Because on-stage I had about as much projection as a baby skunk. Projection, nerves—and I got bored of rehearsing my own music. . . . Oh I suppose there's something to be gained from hearing a composer conduct his own work. My tempos could be definitive. But generally, I

don't believe composers make very good conductors. . . . By the time I [conducted my Second Symphony in Boston] I knew exactly where the violas were going wrong, and where I'd have to make them do it over and over, very slowly. Now how can you remain interested in doing that, whether it's your own music or not?[18]

Appointed vice president of the International Music Council of UNESCO, which met in Paris, Barber spent considerable time in Europe during the early 1950s. In France, he became friendly with Francis Poulenc and composed his *Mélodies Passagères* for the Frenchman ("I've rarely been that close to another composer").[19] He also composed a diverting group of short pieces, called *Souvenirs*, for piano, four hands, which he had intended to play at parties with his close friend Charles Turner, whom he had met through Gore Vidal. Shortly thereafter Lincoln Kirstein suggested that Barber orchestrate these pieces as the basis of a ballet. Barber agreed, and George Balanchine choreographed the work.

In 1953, Barber completed settings of a group of texts written by tenth-century monks, which he called *Hermit Songs*. (It was about this time that he received news of the death of his uncle Sidney, upon whose remarkably wise counsel and warm support Barber had continued to rely throughout the years of his early maturity.) Searching for the optimal singer to present the songs at the Library of Congress premiere, he settled upon a young black woman who had been attracting attention for her performance in *Porgy and Bess*. Leontyne Price proved to be a fortuitous choice, performing them many times and inaugurating a musical partnership that endured for many years.

Perhaps Barber's most significant work of the early 1950s was a commission from the Koussevitzky Music Foundation: a group of choral settings with orchestral accompaniment of the profoundly visionary religious poetry of Sören Kierkegaard. Its 1954 premiere in Boston, conducted by Charles Munch, with Price as soprano solo- ist, was followed immediately by many other auspicious perform- ances, in the United States and abroad.

By the mid-1950s, the view of Barber held by the mainstream clas- sical-music community might be represented by the following: "Samuel Barber, perhaps the most frequently performed American composer of stature living today, possesses the rare faculty of being able to touch greatness and the heart of the listener at the same time."[20] As America's leading melodically oriented traditionalist, Barber would have seemed a likely candidate as an opera composer, and indeed, he had been receiving suggestions for years that he try his hand at this most demanding genre. However, Barber had many misgivings about taking on such a project, and, though he had discussed possibilities with Thornton Wilder, Dylan Thomas, James Agee, and others, he had a difficult time finding a subject that seemed right for him. Menotti, feeling that he knew best what would suit Barber, proposed an idea of his own, influenced by the stories of Isak Dineson, which Barber enjoyed. Barber accepted Menotti's proposal to write the libretto, but complications with the latter's own ongoing projects created long delays in his completing the task.

The successful European performances of *Prayers of Kierkegaard* only drew further attention to Barber's opera-in-progress. Most propitiously, the Salzburg Festival expressed interest in mounting the work's premiere, although that honor was reserved for New York's Metropolitan Opera Company. While anxiously awaiting a completed libretto, Barber fulfilled a commission from the Chamber Music Society of Detroit with *Summer Music*, for woodwind quintet.

Finally, during the summer of 1956, Menotti completed the libretto for what would be *Vanessa*, and Barber devoted the rest of the year and most of the next to completing the work, selecting the cast, and helping to prepare the production. *Vanessa* was to be the first new American work produced by the Met since 1947, and only the twentieth since the company debuted in 1883. Barber's first choice for the title role had been Maria Callas, but she declined. His second choice, Sena Jurinac, backed out only six weeks before opening night. Eleanor Steber then agreed to take the part, despite the short notice. The other roles were sung by Nicolai Gedda, Rosalind Elias, Regina Resnik, and Giorgio Tozzi. The conductor was Dmitri Mitropoulos.

The premiere of *Vanessa* in January 1958, was a spectacular success. Barber's bow was met with "deafening delirium" from the audience,[21] while the critical response was equally favorable. Later that year the work was awarded the Pulitzer Prize, and the composer was nominated to the American Academy of Arts and Letters. That year the Metropolitan took *Vanessa* to Salzburg, with essentially the same cast as the New York production. Here the reception was less uniformly positive, the contemptuous remarks of some critics anticipating the kinds of comments that accompanied the decline in Barber's reputation that was to become more widespread within the decade. ("The work was hailed by American critics . . . as a great new American opera; but public and critics on this side of the ocean could detect neither greatness nor novelty in the opera. . . . There is hardly anything in this music that has not been said in a better, and more modern, way by Leoncavallo, Puccini, d'Albert, and Richard Strauss."[22]) However, despite the grumblings of spokesmen for the avant-garde, *Vanessa* was considered a great success.

On the heels of *Vanessa*'s triumphant premiere, Barber completed a number of smaller projects, among them a brief operatic sketch called *A Hand of Bridge*, composed to another libretto by Menotti for presentation at the Festival of Two Worlds, a new summer program inaugurated by Menotti in Spoleto, Italy. He also fulfilled another commission from the Koussevitzky Foundation for an orchestral work that was presented at the Boston Symphony's Christmas concert in 1960, as well as a request from Mary Curtis Bok for a piece to celebrate the donation of a new organ to Philadelphia's Academy of Music. For the occasion he composed *Toccata Festiva* for organ and orchestra.

During the late 1950s, plans were under way for the creation of a new arts complex in the center of New York City to be called the Lincoln Center for the Performing Arts. William Schuman, one of the guiding forces, would leave his position as president of the Juilliard School to become the center's first director. The vast new complex was to house the Metropolitan Opera, the New York Philharmonic, the Juilliard School, the New York City Opera, a library for the performing arts, and other related institutions. Scheduled to open during the early 1960s, Lincoln Center—located in one of the world's artistic capitals—would be a showcase for the most significant artistic talent of the day, but works by New York's most celebrated artistic figures would presumably be highlighted initially. Many new works were commissioned for the occasion, and, as one of America's most distinguished composers, Barber was a natural choice to be featured prominently. Indeed, he was asked to provide several new compositions for the opening seasons: the first was a commission from G. Schirmer to write a piano concerto in celebration of their hundredth anniversary, with a premiere to take place during the opening week of Philharmonic Hall, as the New York Philharmonic's new home was first named; the second was a

concert scene for soprano and orchestra. And, after the success of
Vanessa, Barber seemed the most likely composer for Met director
Rudolf Bing to approach for a work to open the new opera house.
Within a year after the premiere of *Vanessa*, Bing began to pressure
Barber for a commitment.

However, in 1961 Barber's sister died, leaving him despondent
and unable to compose. He began to spend increasing periods of
time in Europe, and even built a chalet in the Dolomites of northern
Italy. In 1962, he was invited to the USSR—the first American composer to attend the Congress of Soviet Composers. Returning to the
United States, he attempted to address his first two Lincoln Center
commissions: the Piano Concerto and *Andromache's Farewell*. But
progress was slow. John Browning, whom Barber had met in 1956,
agreed to be the soloist in the concerto and the composer worked
closely with him, tailoring the work to his particular strengths. Even
Vladimir Horowitz was given the opportunity to offer input.

Andromache's Farewell was completed soon after the concerto.
Thomas Schippers, who was to conduct the New York Philharmonic
in the premiere, recommended Martina Arroyo as soloist. (Schippers was, for a time, one of Barber's most sympathetic interpreters,
although he expressed some personal distaste for the man: "Sam
and I have never gotten along. . . . Our wavelengths have never
met."[23] However, Schippers's advocacy was cut short by his death
in 1977 at age forty-seven.) Barber accepted Schippers's suggestion,
and worked closely with the soprano, even to the point of selecting
the gown she would wear. The premieres of the two works were heralded with considerable publicity and were reasonably well
received by both audiences and critics. Indeed, the Piano Concerto
won the 1963 Pulitzer Prize and the 1964 Music Critics' Circle
Award; Browning recorded the work and performed it some fifty
times between 1962 and 1964. However, by this time a schism was
developing between audiences and the popular press on the one
hand, both of whom recognized Barber as one of America's foremost living composers, rivaled only by Aaron Copland, and the self-
appointed "high-brow" press and academic world on the other,
who scorned him as the quintessential "establishment" composer,
darling of the *bourgeois* artistic institutions, who pandered to the
reactionary yearnings of the "middle-brow" public for music with
melodies they could enjoy. On the one hand, for example, Jay S.
Harrison called the prize-winning concerto "the best piano concerto

ever written by an American," adding, "Every dazzling phrase, every wild-eyed scale, every contortionist figuration comes alive as part of the whole."[24] Yet B. H. Haggin found the same work "another characteristic product of this composer who is no creator—one in which he uses a lot of notes in the gestures of saying the impressive things he doesn't really have to say."[25]

It was around this time, in 1964, that G. Schirmer's director, Hans Heinsheimer, happened to mention to Barber that the once highly publicized Second Symphony was not fulfilling the high expectations initially held for it. Apparently, despite its tremendous wartime success, and the fine recording Barber had conducted in London in 1950, the work's popularity seemed to lag behind that of his other major orchestral works. One factor might have been the general withdrawal of support among major orchestras and conductors from native symphonic music, as the international serialist movement, whose leaders scorned music with deliberate national appeal, became increasingly influential. Or perhaps Barber's retreat from the heartfelt lyricism that had brought him such popularity alienated his audience once wartime passions had subsided. In any case, Barber is reported to have replied, "It is not a good work. . . . Let's go back to the office and destroy it."[26] Heinsheimer described how the two men proceeded to tear up all the performance materials they could find. Although Barber decided to salvage the second movement, retitling it *Night Flight* after a book by Antoine Saint-Exupery, the symphony as a whole remained dormant for the rest of his life.

Meanwhile, ever since Rudolf Bing had begun pressing Barber to accept the challenge of writing an opera to open the new Met, the composer had been considering a variety of subjects, among them works by Tennessee Williams, James Baldwin, and Henry James; even *Moby Dick* was a serious candidate, as friends and acquaintances offered suggestions of their own. One of Barber's first decisions was that the work would be designed to feature Leontyne Price. There was a general feeling that the subject matter should be "American." Menotti was fervently hoping to write the libretto, but his contribution to *Vanessa* had come under so much criticism that many were attempting to discourage Barber from a repetition of that situation. An American subject would militate against Menotti's participation. Considering the profusion of input proffered, the high visibility of the event, and the composer's generally reticent nature, his seemingly glib response to questions as to why he had agreed to take on such a task—"Because I realized none of my friends would speak to me if I didn't"—may well have been true.[27]

Eventually Barber followed a suggestion reportedly made by Thomas Schippers (according to Richard Dyer) and chose for his subject Shakespeare's play *Antony and Cleopatra*, undertaking the libretto himself. However, a crucial step was taken in 1964, when Bing invited Franco Zeffirelli to step in as librettist, stage designer, and director of the new opera—a decision of which Barber learned only from a newspaper article. Evidently Zeffirelli was excited by the prospect of a grand extravaganza with parallels to *Aida*, and began shaping the opera in a direction quite different from what Barber had envisioned. Although Barber moved into a Tuscan villa so that he could work intensively on the libretto with Zeffirelli, the two men somehow continued to pursue their divergent interpretations in tandem. As the deadline approached, Barber was working feverishly on the music, calling on the gifted Neo-Romantic composer Lee Hoiby for assistance in the final stages. Rehearsal time was limited, relative to the enormity of the project, although Price and Justino Díaz (as Cleopatra and Antony), honored to participate in such a momentous event, were well prepared.

Opening night, September 16, 1966, was a disaster. *Life* Magazine called it, "Culture's Big Super-Event." It was attended by an audience of 3,800, including the First Lady, Governor Nelson Rockefeller, Ferdinand Marcos, with 3,000 more standing outside. Harold Schonberg wrote, "It was quite a spectacle, situated on the cosmic scale somewhere above the primeval atom, the original Big Bang, and somewhere below the creation of the Milky Way . . . a big, complicated package: big, grand, impressive and vulgar; a Swinburnian mélange of sad, bad, mad, glad; rich and also nouveau-riche; desperately aiming for the bigger and the better."[28]

"On that memorable night, just about everything went wrong," wrote John Gruen. "The production—devised, directed, costumed and co-authored by Franco Zeffirelli—heaved and creaked under the massive weight of mammoth stage sets, live horses and goats and what seemed a cast of thousands; light cues misfired with disastrous results (Leontyne Price as a black Cleopatra made her first entrance in total darkness and could not be seen); the Met's new revolving stage, a vital factor in the short-scene structure of the opera, failed to revolve."[29]

English critic Sydney Edwards wrote, "Everything about *Antony and Cleopatra* . . . seemed right until the curtain went up. . . . In the event, the opera was tragically overshadowed by almost everything else. A New York show-off night of a magnificence that only the richest city in the world could provide, the TV cameras and radio reporters, the huge crowds lining the roads outside, diamonds enough to rescue Britain from debt forever."[30]

With the passage of time other perspectives began to emerge. Richard Dyer noted, "Probably no other operatic premiere in history has been as extensively covered in the international press. It was therefore the press rather than the opening-night public that created the lasting legend of the failure of *Antony*," pointing out that each act had been interrupted by applause, and that the performance was followed by fourteen curtain calls.[31]

Some five years after the debacle, Barber himself commented:

> What I wrote and envisioned had nothing, but nothing, to do with what one saw on that stage. Zeffirelli wanted horses and goats and 200 soldiers, which he got, and he wanted elephants, which he fortunately didn't get. The point is, I had very little control—practically none. I was not supported by the management. On the other hand, management supported every idea of Zeffirelli's. Then, of course, there were all those mishaps of a first night in a new house. I was simply the major victim of all that."[32]

Years later, in his memoirs, Rudolf Bing admitted, "Zeffirelli was—we all were—somewhat doubtful about the music, and over-produced the opera."[33]

The morning after the premiere, Barber sailed for Europe, ignorant of the reactions in the press, until he began to receive condolence notes from friends. Realizing the severity and viciousness of the criticism, he became quite depressed, vowing that he would never compose again. Meanwhile, relations between Barber and Menotti had become strained. The latter had been deeply hurt by his exclusion from the Metropolitan Opera project; also, Menotti had adopted a son whom Barber regarded with some distaste. Gradually their lives drifted apart, although they remained friends until Barber's death.

In 1967, Barber's mother died. Depressed and increasingly dependent on alcohol, he turned down several commissions, including a request from the Philadelphia Orchestra for a major work commemorating the bicentennial of the city of Philadelphia. He remained preoccupied by the failure of *Antony and Cleopatra* and even began to consider some of the more substantive criticisms seriously, in spite of himself. He then began toying with the idea of a revision. In 1968, he fashioned two of Cleopatra's arias into a concert piece. Recorded soon after by Leontyne Price, these excerpts served to alert the public to the quality of the music lying dormant in the neglected opera. He also composed a cycle of five songs for Price, which he called *Despite and Still*.

In 1969, Barber hired a young Spanish aesthete by the name of Valentin Herranz as his personal assistant. Herranz became the composer's closest companion and source of emotional support for the rest of his life. During the following years, Barber completed his last major work, a large cantata called *The Lovers*, based on poetry by Pablo Neruda. Dedicated to Herranz, the work suggests a painful recollection of failed romantic involvements. The work's initial performances in 1971 by the Philadelphia Orchestra under Eugene Ormandy were well received, but so unfashionable was Barber at this time that the work was not played again during his lifetime. Interviews with the composer during his later years reveal a petulance and sarcasm that suggest how difficult it was for him to endure a degree of critical disaffection for which a lifetime of adulation had left him unprepared.

During the early 1970s, Menotti began to press Barber to sell Capricorn. Although the house in Mount Kisco had become a financial liability, Barber retained an intense emotional attachment to it, regarding it as a private sanctuary, as well as a symbol of his relationship with Menotti. The eventual sale of the house in 1973, together with the division of the household, intensified Barber's depression. He often referred to himself as "homeless," although he had taken an apartment near New York's Lincoln Center.

It was during these very years that Barber agreed to collaborate with Menotti on a thorough restructuring of *Antony and Cleopatra*. An offer by Peter Mennin to mount the revision at Juilliard in early 1975 helped to focus their efforts. In its new form the opera was generally well received, and commentators began to reconsider the composer's responsibility for the work's initial failure.

But Barber's drinking had gotten worse, to the point where his intellectual functioning became impaired, and his weight was becoming a health liability. He tried Yoga and Zen Buddhism, and entered treatment with a psychiatrist who specialized in alcoholism. At the same time he accepted enormous fees—said to be the most lavish offered any composer to date[34]—for commissions that he could only fulfill with flimsy trifles.

Toward the late 1970s, Barber showed signs of recovery. In 1976, he was awarded the Gold Medal from the American Academy and Institute of Arts and Letters. Two years later, he was feted by friends at a grand birthday party. But later in 1978, he was diagnosed with lymphoma. That summer he began work on an oboe concerto commissioned for Harold Gomberg and the New York Philharmonic. However, chemotherapy and periodic hospitalizations prevented him from making headway. By 1980, he had completed the slow movement in short score, entitling it *Canzonetta*, and leaving the orchestration to Charles Turner, his former student and close friend for almost thirty years. In September, he went to visit Menotti in Scotland, where he suffered a stroke. Herranz brought him back to New York, where he remained in the company of friends until January 23, 1981, when he died.

The following day the *New York Times* carried an obituary on its front page, testifying to the dominant position his name still held. "Samuel Barber, the American composer who twice won the Pulitzer Prize and whose Adagio for Strings became one of the most popular works in the orchestral repertoire, died yesterday in his Fifth Avenue apartment after a long illness. He was 70 years old," began Donal Henahan's lengthy appreciation. "Throughout his career, Samuel Barber was hounded by success. Probably no other American composer has ever enjoyed such early, such persistent and such long-lasting acclaim."[35]

Shortly after his death, his friend and editor Paul Wittke commented perceptively, "Always elegantly dressed and urbane in manner and speech, [Barber] seemed to belong to the world of Henry James and Edith Wharton. But . . . beneath the aristocratic surface of his cosmopolitan gaiety lived a most private, dedicated, and disciplined man. His wit was a line of defense against a deep-rooted melancholia . . . passion and resignation are inherent in everything he composed."[36]

Ten years before Barber's death, a revealing interview with John Gruen appeared in the *Times*, in which the composer discussed his career with some candor. Several comments from that interview serve as a telling epitaph: "I guess . . . I've had a wonderful life being [an American composer]. It's true I've had little success in intellectual circles. I'm not talked about in the *New York Review of Books,* and I was never part of the Stravinsky 'inner circle.' In Aaron Copland's book, *Our American Music,* my name appears in a footnote. . . . In fact, it is said that I have no style at all but that doesn't matter. I just go on doing, as they say, my thing. I believe this takes a certain courage."[37]

MUSIC

The primacy of melody, mood, and emotion in the music of Samuel Barber, relative to abstract formal considerations, identifies him as a "Neo-Romantic" composer. In this his work resembles that of Howard Hanson, more than that of the other composers treated in this study. However, Barber's music reveals far more breadth of expressive range, depth of feeling, refinement of sensibility, and compositional craftsmanship than that of the senior Nebraskan. Perhaps what is most remarkable about Barber's achievement is not just the magnificence of his greatest works, but the large proportion of his output that reaches this high standard. This partly accounts for its overwhelming and continually growing popularity, as does its striving—at least in the early works that continue to be most favored—toward the expression of "beauty" as this term is understood by the average music lover, along with a self-perpetuating streak of good fortune. Barber's art is fundamentally "literary" in nature; that is, not only does a large proportion of his output—actually, more than half—make explicit reference to actual works or genres of literature, but its emphasis on mood and feeling, often evoked by texts that appealed to him, is descriptive, rather than purely self-expressive, as in the works of Nicolas Flagello, for example. In this sense, Barber's work bears the closest fundamental relationship to film music, albeit that of an extraordinarily fine sensibility, capable of projecting such moods and feelings into music with uncanny appositeness.

The fine craftsmanship often attributed to Barber is more a matter of "good taste" than of contrapuntal wizardry, structural complexity, or unexpected thematic transformations or other types of developmental sleight-of-hand. Following the guidance of Sidney Homer, Barber was concerned with formal balance and expressive effectiveness (i.e., achieving precisely the expressive goal intended, and in the most effective way, devoid of excess, overstatement, or other *gaucherie*). As John Browning wrote, "Grand philosophical pronouncements are not to be found in this music. Rather, Barber's language is that of the poet—swift changes of mood and a pervading melancholy and loneliness conveyed on a sumptuous harmonic tapestry. There is a passionate sensuality which never lapses into cheap sentimentality or vulgarity. An almost infallible taste governs every note."[38]

Barber's output is relatively small, comprising only about forty-eight works. However, nearly all of them have entered or are in the process of entering the standard canon of repertoire actively performed. Most commentators have asserted that the composer's style remained essentially unchanged throughout his career. Even Barber himself said, "I really don't think my style has ever changed, except perhaps in details due to text."[39] However, a thorough examination of his output points to three distinct style periods of unequal duration. In fact, the aesthetic concerns addressed in each of these periods may be viewed as corresponding to the basic developmental stages of life: an early period representing the composer's artistic "childhood," lasting through 1942; an exploratory or experimental "adolescence," lasting until about 1952; and a period of maturity or "adulthood," comprising the remainder of his career.

Though Barber's musical language is thoroughly rooted in that of the late nineteenth-century European masters, his works display fewer overt reminiscences of his predecessors than do the other composers discussed in this study. In his early works, he succeeded in forging an identity of his own without rupturing the Late Romantic lingua franca with which he was comfortable. His own sensibility was so cosmopolitan that he was able to distill the generalized attitudes and principles of his romantic predecessors without allowing individual accents to upset the subtle balance upon which his language was based. Thus, while his piano textures may suggest the influence of Brahms, Barber's impetuousness is far from Brahms's stern, German formalism. Although his gentle modality, urbanity, and surface immediacy have often been described as French, his emotionalism and textural clarity distinguish his music immediately. Barber's spontaneous lyricism has often been characterized as Italianate, but it is far more refined and elegant than typical Italian melody. The elegiac character of his music, constrained by a digni-

fied reserve, suggests the tone, if not the actual style, of Sir Edward
Elgar, but the Englishman's imperial grandeur was foreign to Barber's more modest nature.

Most Representative, Fully Realized Works

Dover Beach, op. 3 (1931)
Symphony no. 1, op. 9 (1936)
Three Songs, op. 10 (1936)
Four Songs, op. 13 (1937–1940)
Reincarnations, op. 16 (1940)
Knoxville: Summer of 1915, op. 24 (1947)
Prayers of Kierkegaard, op. 30 (1954)
Vanessa, op. 31 (1957)
Andromache's Farewell, op. 39 (1962)
Antony and Cleopatra, op. 40: Two Scenes (1966)
Despite and Still, op. 41 (1968)
The Lovers, op. 43 (1971)

"Childhood": Early Period (until 1942)

Recently a number of pieces from Barber's teen years have come to
light, affording an opportunity to experience his creative voice from
the time before he defined himself as a professional composer.
These include *Three Sketches* (1923–1924) and *Fresh from West Chester*
(1925), all for piano solo. The earliest are cloying salon trifles to be
sure, but with a sense of grace remarkable in a thirteen year old. The
later pieces, along with songs like "A Slumber Song of the
Madonna" (1925) and "There's Nae Lark" (1927) show a notable
increase in sophistication and a memorable flair, free of any lapse in
taste or workmanship, despite their provenance as "parlor music."
Indeed, their irresistible "prettiness" and refinement anticipate *Souvenirs*, composed nearly three decades later, while providing a point
of departure from which to view the music that soon followed.

Barber's early period, or artistic "childhood," comprises his op. 1,
the *Serenade* for string quartet, completed in 1928, through his op.
17, the *Second Essay* for orchestra, completed in 1942, when he was
thirty-two years old. The strongest influence on Barber's early music
was that of Brahms, although this was pretty well digested by 1933.
These works are generally characterized by straightforward,

tonal—if modestly chromatic—harmony with little unresolved dissonance, a largely diatonic lyricism of rather genteel, high-toned cast, regular, metrical rhythm, and relatively simple textures. This is the music that brought Barber to prominence so quickly and secured his reputation as a major American compositional voice during the 1930s, and these remain his best-known and most frequently performed works. Many of them seem to suggest the tender vulnerability and touching innocence of childhood; perhaps it is these qualities that so many have found endearing.

The *Serenade* was composed while Barber was still an undergraduate at the Curtis Institute, where it was first performed in May 1930, by the school's string quartet. In three short movements, it is notable for displaying at such a young age the refined sensibility with which the composer remained so closely identified throughout his career. The fastidious character of this tepid nocturnal diversion is disturbed only by an occasional hint of morbidity reminiscent of Schoenberg's *Verklärte Nacht*. Today the *Serenade* is usually heard in an arrangement for string orchestra made by the composer in 1944, which adds body to an otherwise rather anemic expression.

Barber's Three Songs, op. 2, were composed between 1927 and 1934. Barber himself often performed them, as did fellow student Rose Bampton while she was building her career. The earliest of them, "The Daisies," clearly reveals its roots in the parlor-song tradition to which Barber was exposed during his youth (and to which Vittorio Giannini contributed notably during the same years). But these songs are also clearly the works of a young aesthete, displaying the restrained expression of elegiac emotions that was central to Barber's artistic personality. The essence of this sensibility, expressed with Brahmsian elevation of tone, may be heard clearly in the brief setting of A. E. Housman's "With rue my heart is laden." This is followed by "Bessie Bobtail," a chilling portrayal of a tortured vagrant woman possessed by religious demons. Clearly discernible in these songs is the extent to which Barber followed his uncle's dictum that the artist's primary obligation is to heed one's inner voice. In these and the other songs and choral settings composed throughout his twenties, he courageously exposed the vulnerability of his artistic soul. In this music there is often a strain of sadness, but a sweetness as well, along with a sense of fragility.

At age twenty-one, Barber composed what was perhaps his first great work—a deeply moving setting for baritone (or contralto) and string quartet of Matthew Arnold's *Dover Beach*. Rose Bampton was the soloist in the work's first performance at the Curtis Institute in May 1932. Barber's musical interpretation evokes a gloomy Victorian atmosphere appropriate to the poem while consistent with the young composer's aristocratic, hypersensitive temperament. The setting is precocious in the conviction with which it embraces and personalizes the high-minded despair of Arnold's poem, as well as in its emotional complexity: clinging with dread to a loved one while facing a world in which nothing is secure or certain and in which all that one values is on the verge of being overthrown— feelings with which Barber must have resonated as a young artist, as he witnessed the beginnings of an assault on the aesthetic verities he had been taught to trust. In its yearning for the security of the past he set forth psychological and emotional themes—made explicit in the texts that he chose—that he was to develop throughout his maturity. Considered alongside what he had thus far completed, *Dover Beach*, with its irregular phrase-lengths and chromatic melodies set almost atonally to consonant harmony, represents a remarkable leap forward into the realm of a more abstract, expressionistic use of music, relative to the straightforward tonality and symmetrical melodic phrases of the conventional song.

Barber later recalled:

> [The poem] fascinated me; it's extremely pessimistic—the emotions seem contemporary. "Dover Beach" is one of the few Victorian poems which continue to hold their stature; it is a great poem, in fact. Originally, I cut the middle part about Sophocles. Soon after *Dover Beach* was finished I played it at the Owen Wister house in Philadelphia, and Marina Wister exclaimed, "But where's the wonderful part about Sophocles?" (Conversation was at a high level at those grand Philadelphia houses—if you said "Sophocles" when you meant "Aeschylus" you simply didn't get another drink.) She was quite right, and so I wrote a contrasting middle section. The piece was the better for it. . . . Not long after I completed the final version . . . Vaughan Williams lectured at Bryn Mawr College, and I visited him there. I sang *Dover Beach* for him at the piano, and he seemed delighted. He congratulated me and said, "I tried several times to set 'Dover Beach,' but you really *got* it!"[40]

At about the same time as he composed his *Dover Beach* setting, Barber completed a full-length piano concerto, as well as two Interludes for piano solo, all of which he subsequently withdrew from his official work list. Premiered by Barber himself at the same May 1932 concert as that at which *Dover Beach* was introduced, the *Interludes* have been released posthumously, for public performance and recording. The first is slow and rhapsodic, lasting some seven minutes, while the second is brilliant and much shorter; both reveal the strong influence of Brahms's later pieces for piano solo, which may account for the composer's dissatisfaction with them. Yet with a mood and character that could only be attributed to Barber—in the words of Martin Anderson, "Brahms seen through Barber's eyes"[41]—the first Interlude is quite eloquent, with a lyrical warmth that makes a strong and lasting impression. As the short solo work in Barber's early style for which pianists have long wished, it has begun to appear frequently on recital programs.

For his graduation from the Curtis Institute in 1931, Barber composed an orchestral work: *Overture to "The School for Scandal."* Not intended to precede or accompany the actual play, the work purports simply to capture the merry, exuberant spirit of the eighteenth-century comedy by Richard Brinsley Sheridan. Maintaining a balance between scintillating playfulness and a winsome lyricism with remarkable facility, this graduation exercise has become, along with Leonard Bernstein's *Candide* Overture, one of the most popular curtain raisers in the American repertoire. Perhaps its most significant element, from the standpoint of Barber's stylistic development, is its secondary theme: a poignant diatonic melody, introduced by the oboe, clearly tonal but with a slight modal inflection. This is the first appearance of a type of melody—typically introduced by the oboe, bittersweet in character, though increasingly chromatic and complex in later works—that represents one of the composer's most distinctive and readily identifiable usages. The *Overture* was first performed in Philadelphia in August 1933 by Alexander Smallens and the Robin Hood Dell Symphony Orchestra.

Barber's first extended, full-scale work was his Sonata for Cello and Piano, composed in 1932. He wrote it for his good friend, the cellist Orlando Cole, whom he consulted frequently during the process of composition; Cole joined the composer in the sonata's first performance in New York City in March 1933. (This initiated a practice continued by Barber throughout his career, of tailoring a work to a particular soloist whom he involved closely in the process of composition.) The Cello Sonata is the last of his works that bears the strong influence of Brahms. Though superficially "classical" in form, the sonata embraces a romantic primacy of feeling through a sequence of mood-states, rather than the more classical sense of dialectical process and progression. Impetuous and noble in character overall, the first and third movements are alternately passionate and gentle and are quite extended in scope. The opening and closing of the second movement, which frame a *scherzo*-like middle section, are unmistakably Barberian in their melodic beauty. Unashamedly "old-fashioned," the sonata makes no concession to Modernism. A compositional approach that places so much emphasis on emotional expression and melodic beauty inevitably places a great responsibility on the appeal of local musical events—a burden that limits the durability of much nineteenth-century music. But, more than many of his musical antecedents, Barber had a prudent sense of taste and proportion—as well as an extraordinary melodic gift—that supported the intuitive nature of his art. Although technical matters, such as the balance between the two instruments, are sometimes handled awkwardly, the Cello Sonata has become one of the twentieth century's most widely performed works of its kind.

In 1933, Barber, then twenty-three, turned next to another short orchestral work, which he called *Music for a Scene from Shelley*. This rather cumbersome title is responsible for a plethora of misunderstandings and lengthy explanations, which are more tortuous than the music itself. Inspired by Shelley's *Prometheus Unbound*, the ten-minute piece is linked to a scene in which Panthea prompts her sister Asia (goddess of love) to hear the "voices in the air," suggested by the sounds of inanimate winds, seeking Asia's sympathy and love. The problem is not only that the reference is remote and tenuous: the music itself does not really capture the feelings suggested by the passage identified in Shelley's work—a point made by a number of the bolder commentators (W. J. Henderson saw the work as "suggesting some sort of catastrophe"[42])—although it is quite a powerful and evocative piece of music. Barber's first attempt at pure mood painting, *Music for a Scene from Shelley* evokes a sense of Gothic mystery as the main motif, four notes in a descending pattern, is heard against the backdrop of an undulating murmur. Although the motif undergoes little true development, reorchestrated and retextured repetitions at gradually increasing dynamic levels heighten the emotional intensity. As the work builds, a sense of terror and dread is conjured, suggesting the approach of some ominous apparition; other material is introduced, and the work builds to a blood-curdling climax before subsiding.

Music for a Scene from Shelley was first performed in March 1935, by the New York Philharmonic, conducted by Werner Janssen. More performances followed almost immediately, in Europe as well as in the United States. However, overall, the piece is somewhat less popular than Barber's other early orchestral works, probably owing to its consistently gloomy tone and its less sweetly melodious thematic content. Barber's exquisite sensitivity to mood enables him to achieve a powerful impact, but comparable sensitivity to dramatic pacing is required from the conductor in order to achieve the full effect. Although some commentators have described the work as "French" in sound, pointing to the influence of Debussy's *Nuages*, others have noted a similarity with Holst's *Neptune*. But these similarities are superficial, as the work's expressive content and musical realization are quite distinctive and not at all derivative. As a haunting evocation of mood, with little contrapuntal or motivic complication, the work would be an ideal cinematic accompaniment.

Although given somewhat less attention until recently, Barber's choral music—short a capella pieces as well as larger accompanied works—comprises some of his most deeply moving music, much of it religious, or at least "spiritual," in nature. The earliest examples included in his work list are a setting for unaccompanied women's voices of "The Virgin Martyrs," translated from an ancient Latin text, and a setting for unaccompanied mixed voices of Emily Dickinson's "Let Down the Bars, O Death." These two pieces, composed in 1935 and 1936 respectively, are grouped as Two Choruses, op. 8. In the second of these, in particular, Barber's use of harmony suggests both the purity of Renaissance choral writing and the intensity of Romanticism. Barber pursued this expressive duality in many subsequent choral works, such as the *Prayers of Kierkegaard*; it can be found in several instrumental works as well, most notably, the famous *Adagio* from his String Quartet.

Barber's largest and most ambitious work from the mid-1930s—and, perhaps, the greatest work of his early period—is the Symphony no. 1, which he wrote during his stay at the American Academy in Rome. The composition subsumes within one movement of approximately twenty minutes' duration four sections that represent the standard divisions of the conventional symphony: a boldly resolute opening, a skittish *scherzo* section, a slow, lyrical section, bittersweet and yearning, introduced by a characteristically poignant oboe solo, leading to a solemn *passacaglia*, which builds to a conclusion of stern determination. (Heyman presents persuasive evidence that Barber consciously modeled the structure of the work on the one-movement Seventh Symphony of Jean Sibelius.) Essentially monothematic, most of the work is based on the defiantly assertive motif in E minor with which it opens. The symphony is economical and compact, achieving a compelling expression of romantic lyricism and drama within a large, satisfyingly integrated formal structure. Its character suggests a protagonist's passionate emotional journey as he unflinchingly confronts life's diverse challenges. By dint of its affecting treatment of potent thematic material, the expressive course that it traverses, and the successful balance of energy throughout, the symphony is a masterpiece for a twenty-six-year-old composer. Few of Barber's subsequent efforts in abstract forms are as successful. Indeed, the First Symphony remains one of the greatest of American Neo-Romantic symphonies, following chronologically the 1922 "Nordic" Symphony of Howard Hanson (coincidentally, also a Symphony no. 1 composed by a twenty-six-year-old as the creative fruit of a Prix de Rome), and one of the greatest American symphonies of the 1930s. The work, which bears a dedication to Menotti, was first performed in Rome, in December 1936, by the Augusteo Orchestra (the same orchestra that had given the premiere of Hanson's "Nordic" thirteen years earlier), with Bernardino Molinari conducting.

Barber subsequently undertook a major revision of the work, which was completed in 1942. Even after the revision, however, congested string figurations occasionally submerge contrapuntal lines and blur the outlines of phrases, requiring extra attention from the conductor. Bruno Walter led the first performance of the revision in 1944 with the Philadelphia Orchestra, then with the New York Philharmonic, with whom he recorded the work shortly thereafter.

During the 1930s, Barber composed a large number of songs, many of which were not included in his published groups and omitted from his official list of works. During the early 1990s, Deutsche Grammophon issued a set of recordings, under the guidance of pianist John Browning, purporting to comprise Barber's "complete" songs. Among them were ten previously unpublished songs, included with the permission of Menotti, Barber's musical executor. Though two of them (mentioned earlier) predate Barber's opus 1, the others were composed between 1934 and 1937, and are therefore approximately contemporaneous with the op. 2, 10, and 13 groups.

One might infer that the composer did not judge them to be of the same quality as those in the published groups. The comprehensive survey indicates Barber's attainment of an exceedingly high standard of musico-poetic expression from op. 2 on; only one or two of the unpublished songs—"Of That So Sweet Imprisonment" and perhaps "Strings in the Earth and Air" (both James Joyce settings composed at the same time as the first two songs of op. 10)—warrant inclusion in their company. The others, while pretty enough, remain within the conventions and milquetoast sensibility of the English-language parlor song of the time.

Most of the songs Barber composed during the 1930s display the same emphasis on emotive melody as the contemporaneous instrumental works. The Three Songs, op. 10, composed during the years 1935–1936, comprise "Rain Has Fallen," "Sleep Now," and "I Hear an Army," all to texts from *Chamber Music* by James Joyce, and each provides a glimpse of one facet of love. "Rain Has Fallen," with its melancholy retrospective tone, is exquisitely poignant. "I Hear an Army," with its aggressive military imagery, can be a little overbearing within the intimate context of a *Lieder* recital. However, with the orchestrated accompaniment Barber supplied during the early 1940s, it is simply overpowering.

Barber composed his String Quartet later on during the same year as the Symphony no. 1. However, in contrast to the terse, streamlined structure of that work, the Quartet is one of Barber's most flagrantly episodic works—thoroughly lyrical and subjective, with virtually no acknowledgment of the principles of Austro-Germanic classicism usually conceded to the genre, even by composers committed to a romantic aesthetic outlook. Indeed, in both form and substance, it is one of the most essentially romantic string quartets in the repertoire, relying almost exclusively on the intrinsic beauty of its musical material and on the effectiveness of its discursive impulses. Fortunately, the material is unfailingly appealing and the composer's intuitions are sound, guiding it coherently and concisely so that its lack of a strong structure does not significantly weaken its impact. It is *sui generis*, and one either accepts it on its own terms or not. Barber's creative gift was so literary in nature that—with the exception of the First Symphony—he seemed almost incapable of mastering the techniques of organic growth essential in constructing large works of absolute music, unless guided in some way by a literary point of reference. In pieces like the String Quartet, Barber appeared to be floundering out of his element, as lovely ideas are linked together seemingly arbitrarily—the formal antithesis of the classical string quartet, despite its perfunctory nod to *sonata allegro* form. An alternation between major and minor harmonic coloration creates the distinctive bittersweet quality so characteristic of Barber's music from this period. The second movement is the famous *Adagio*, to which is appended an abbreviated recapitulation of the first movement. Originally Barber composed a third movement, which caused him great difficulty, as finales often did. The Quartet was introduced by the Pro Arte Quartet at the Villa Aurelia in Rome, the day after the premiere of the Symphony, in December 1936. After the performance, Barber continued to tinker with the third movement, and, after several more readings, eventually dropped it altogether. In 1938, he substituted the recapitulatory coda that now concludes the work.

The *Adagio* warrants its own discussion. As remarkable a stroke of genius as it may appear to be, the piece capitalizes on a fusion of spiritual purity and romantic sentiment similar to the approach used in the choral setting "Let Down the Bars, O Death" and in several subsequent works as well. The *Adagio* is, in a sense, a pseudo-Renaissance motet, in which a metrically irregular conjunct motif is developed pseudo-polyphonically, its sense of pathos intensified by dissonances derived largely from suspensions, *appoggiaturas*, and cross-relations. Though the approach suggests the sixteenth century in effect, the expressive profile points to a romantic elegy, as the piece builds in ardor toward a heartfelt climax, then recedes.

The *Adagio* was first played in an arrangement for full string orchestra by the NBC Symphony under the direction of Arturo Toscanini in November 1938. The conductor then took it on an international tour, and within a few years the *Adagio* had become something of a national threnody. During the following decades it was arranged for clarinet choir, for woodwind ensemble, and for organ; an arrangement set to the text of *Agnus Dei* was made for mixed chorus a capella. This version, with the chorus underlining the neo-Renaissance implications and quasi-ecclesiastical effect of the music, is exceedingly effective and is rapidly gaining popularity in its own right.

In 1982, the BBC asked a number of prominent musicians to comment on the *Adagio for Strings* as a "perfect piece of music." Aaron Copland said, "It comes straight from the heart, to use old fashioned terms. The sense of continuity, the steadiness of the flow . . . [are] all very gratifying, satisfying, and it makes you believe in the sincerity which he obviously put into it." William Schuman stated that "you are not aware of any technique at all. . . . It seems quite effortless and quite natural; . . . If the *Adagio for Strings* makes the effect that it does, it's because it's a perfect piece of music in the sense that the Mendelssohn Violin Concerto is a perfect piece of music. . . . The emotional climate is never left in doubt . . . when I hear it played I'm always moved by it."[43]

Sharing the NBC Symphony broadcast with the *Adagio for Strings* was the first of the three works entitled *Essays for Orchestra*—a genre created by Barber to identify short orchestral compositions that follow neither classical structures nor explicit literary programs. Essentially, they are varied successions of mood-states, or tone poems without programs—related motivically, but without the sense of abstract dialectical progression found in a symphony, although each is structured coherently enough to sustain interest throughout its brief duration. Though spaced unevenly throughout his career (1938, 1942, 1978), the three *Essays* provide something of a cross-section of Barber's stylistic evolution. The first two, written early on, hold an enduring place in the repertoire; the third, composed toward the end of his life, is well on the way to joining its predecessors. Their success is attributable to the direct and immediate appeal of their musical ideas as well as to Barber's unerring mastery in presenting them to maximum effect, without imposing upon them excessive structural rigors.

Essay no. 1 is typical of Barber's music from the 1930s: Cut from the same cloth as the First Symphony it opens with a somber, noble elegy whose throbbing pathos suggests the mood of the *Adagio* but with a more "human" feeling—one of the most eloquent, deeply felt passages Barber ever wrote. It is scored richly but simply, and its solemnity is set off neatly by a fleeting and gossamer-like *scherzo* section—somewhat nocturnal in character. Though not as inspired as the opening, this section, which resembles the *scherzo* episode from the Symphony no. 1, weaves together the work's two main motifs, before the opening returns for a final, rather abrupt peroration. The orchestral works from the 1930s—*Music for a Scene from Shelley*, the Symphony no. 1, and the *Essay no. 1*, in particular—were all composed when Barber was in his twenties and are among his most fully realized works: musical melodrama at its most elegant and fastidious.

Four Songs, op. 13, were composed between 1937 and 1940 and are perhaps Barber's best-known group of songs, largely because they include "Sure on this Shining Night," by far the most popular of his poetic settings—what might be termed the *"Adagio for Strings"* of his vocal output and one to which the term "beautiful" certainly applies. The popularity of this song prompted Barber to make an attractive choral arrangement, which highlights its canonic counterpoint. The op. 13 group is more of a miscellany than the op. 10 songs. In addition to the setting of the poem by James Agee (who also wrote the text Barber adapted for his *Knoxville: Summer of 1915*), it includes the solemn "A Nun Takes the Veil (Heaven-Haven)," a plea for solitude by Gerard Manley Hopkins, which also appeared in a choral version; W. B. Yeats's mischievous "Secrets of the Old," set in an impishly asymmetrical meter; and Frederic Prokosch's richly romantic, postcoital love song "Nocturne." The phraseology of this song bears a strong resemblance to that of "Rain Has Fallen" from the op. 10 group. Both "Nocturne" and "Sure on this Shining Night" are among the songs whose accompaniments Barber orchestrated several years later. The first performance of the op. 13 songs was given by soprano Barbara Troxell, with pianist Eugene Bossart at the Curtis Institute in April 1941; since then they have been championed by many leading singers.

A choral work dating from this period is a setting for double mixed choir a capella of Gerard Manley Hopkins's "God's Grandeur," completed in early 1938 for a performance that spring by the Westminster Choir. Over the course of his career, Barber set a number of texts on religious subjects, but they tended to be humanistic poetic expressions, rather than liturgical texts, or even truly religious poetry. The astute English musicologist Wilfrid Mellers observed, "The texts [Barber] set were seldom overtly religious, though they often celebrated the presumptive innocence of child or peasant. . . . Barber was on the mark in believing that the truth of his religious sensibility was inseparable from his awareness of the common heart of humanity."[44] While not without its magical moments, *God's Grandeur* does not reflect the consistency of inspiration found in the contemporaneous *Reincarnations*, although Mellers considers it to be Barber's finest choral work. It is interesting to note that a device appears in this piece involving overlapping entrances in sequence at lower pitch levels—an effect that also found its way some two years later—and to better advantage—in "Anthony O

Daly"—the second *Reincarnation*—on the words "After you there is nothing to do!" *God's Grandeur* is another of the works Barber decided to omit from his official work list, although it has enjoyed some posthumous attention.

Barber next turned to an abstract work of major proportions: the Violin Concerto commissioned by Samuel Fels. The work is notable for an abrupt shift in style and tone that distinguishes the first two movements from the finale. The Concerto opens with an immediate statement by the violin of the movement's main theme—a genial melody of brazenly diatonic lyricism. Serving as a foil for this melody, which dominates the movement, is a whimsical idea located chiefly in the woodwinds. This movement, largely relaxed and ingratiating in tone, is followed by an equally lyrical *Andante*, built around a melody of more bittersweet, poignantly nostalgic character, introduced characteristically by a solo oboe. In stark contrast to both these movements, the finale is a frenetic *perpetuum mobile*, couched in a tonal and harmonic language more harsh and brittle than was customary for the composer at that time—far more so than the two preceding movements. Though relentlessly energetic, the character of much of the material is playful and droll. The result is a sense of aesthetic inconsistency that has troubled critics since the work first appeared. However, more disturbing than this inconsistency is the finale's essential triviality, with virtuosic display seemingly its only purpose. The first two movements, though enormously appealing, are not terribly difficult, either technically or interpretively. The third movement, which precipitated the brouhaha surrounding the commission recounted earlier, is difficult technically, not interpretively, and is something of a throwaway. The main interpretive challenge is to balance the work: to make a conceptual distinction between the first and second movements, and to make the finale sound as though it has an artistic reason for being, beyond giving the soloist an opportunity to play fast—perhaps a lost cause. Nevertheless, a reasonably accomplished violinist can make a favorable impression with the Concerto, and a fine artist can do even more.

The Concerto's official premiere took place in February 1941, with Albert Spalding as soloist with the Philadelphia Orchestra conducted by Eugene Ormandy. However, the work was performed prior to that by Herbert Baumel at the Curtis Institute, with Fritz Reiner conducting the school orchestra. Critical response to the Concerto was uncharacteristically mixed. Olin Downes commented, "The violin concerto of Samuel Barber, a work ambitiously conceived, and written with honesty and talent, impresses at a first hearing as a form too big for the composer successfully to fill."[45] "There is certainly feeling for the long line but what goes into it is not very choice," opined Donald Fuller. "The first two movements have genuine, unaffected simplicity, yet the intimate quality is kept at such a low pitch that the fire almost goes out. The finale however throws all restraint to the winds. It is harmonically and rhythmically confused, stylistically out of keeping with the preceding material. Even the virtue of a rather pale unity is thus lost."[46] Though the work found favor with violinists, critics continued to express reservations. The English writer Malcolm Rayment commented, "The first two movements are lyrical and little concerned with virtuosity. This is left to the Finale, a fairly short and hectic movement in which the solo part is a perpetuum mobile. This rather brittle music . . . may seem out of place after the preceding movements."[47] "This work is a lovely poetic one, with the exception of its disturbing perpetual-motion finale in which Samuel Barber suddenly thrusts us into the disorienting atmosphere of the Second World War," observed David W. Moore. "It is Barber at his most touching and heart-warming."[48] Moore is not alone in attributing the work's shift in style to the outbreak of war that occurred between the composition of the second and third movements. But a more likely explanation is simply that dazzling finales were alien to Barber's temperament, and he continued to have difficulty producing them throughout his career. Critics' misgivings notwithstanding, Barber's Violin Concerto has gone on to become a favorite of violinists and audiences; it remains by far the most widely performed American violin concerto.

Although he did not enjoy teaching, the madrigal choir that Barber agreed to conduct at Curtis during the late 1930s seemed to provide a stimulus for his creativity in that medium. The short pieces he composed for chorus during that period are among his most sensitively expressed creations. In 1940, he set Stephen Spender's poem *A Stopwatch and an Ordnance Map*, just written the preceding year in response to the Spanish Civil War, for male chorus and timpani. The music returns repeatedly to a virile martial refrain among which are placed episodes of quiet, reflective lamentation. Imaginative, highly expressive use of chromatic melodic motifs and largely consonant harmony results in a brief, hauntingly understated assertion of pacifism. Barber conducted the Curtis Madrigal Choir in the work's first performance in April 1940. Five years later, at the suggestion of Leopold Stokowski, the composer added an optional brass ensemble to the scoring.

Also for the Curtis Madrigal Choir, Barber completed his three *Reincarnations* for mixed voices a capella in 1940. The poems are based on old poetic fragments collected and elaborated by Irish poet James Stephens (a favorite of Sidney Homer as well as of Barber). They provided further opportunity for the composer to draw upon elements associated with the old English madrigal while achieving a more flexible tonality without abandoning consonant harmony, thereby creating refreshing, gently modern reinterpretations of an antique genre. The opening of the first, "Mary Hynes," is light in texture and fleet in motion, with frequently shifting meters, in exultant praise of "the love of my heart." It concludes with a more subdued, reflective passage of gentle yet intricate counterpoint as the poet awaits "The Blossom of Branches" as she approaches "airily." The second setting, "Anthony O Daly," is a funeral dirge in which a lament in triple meter unfolds in imitative counterpoint over a single-note drone on E, chanting the name "Anthony" in a five-beat pattern that repeats throughout the song, until an anguished climax is reached. Following the somber open-fifth that ends the second setting on E, the A-minor triad, followed by an F-major triad, which begin the third setting, "The Coolin," create an effect of exquisite serenity. Largely homophonic in texture, with a lilting, dotted-note rhythmic pattern, Barber's characteristic shifts between major and minor coloration within a diatonic tonal context create a bittersweet undercurrent to a moment of utter romantic contentment. The *Reincarnations* are among the most fully realized and deeply moving of Barber's poetic settings. Their artistry and sensitivity have yet to achieve widespread appreciation.

Barber completed a second *Essay* for orchestra early in 1942, although he had been working and reworking its material for several years. The most remarkable features of the work are the wide range of emotional expression and the richness of developmental elaboration accomplished within the scope of ten minutes. Its structure comprises three main sections: a sort of "prologue," followed by a *scherzo*-like developmental section, which leads to a fervent, hymn-like apotheosis.

The opening section presents the work's two main themes: the first is a pentatonic theme introduced by the flute. Not unlike the opening section of Creston's *Frontiers*—a work of comparable scope and substance composed one year later—this theme conveys a sense of breadth and vision. The music gradually becomes more animated, leading to the second thematic idea, first heard in the violas, followed by the oboe, against a restless accompaniment in the flutes and clarinets. The energy level of the music continues to increase, as the second idea is developed. A stentorian restatement of the first theme in the horns, accompanied by rapid repetitions in the timpani, cellos, and basses, signals the end of the first section. A sudden loud chord ushers in the second section, as the clarinet and bassoon begin a skittish *fugato* based on the opening pentatonic theme, now transformed into a rapid triplet rhythmic pattern. This section and its material resemble the *scherzo* portion of the Symphony no. 1 and the second section of the *Essay no. 1*. Soon the second theme is added to the nervous polyphonic tapestry, and the two ideas undergo considerable development. Finally, the themes are heard—in reverse order—closer to their original guise, as the tempo broadens, forming a transition to the concluding section. This part is based on a third thematic idea, actually suggested barely noticeably by the brasses toward the end of the first section. This hymn-like theme begins softly but richly in the strings, gradually building in intensity, as the trumpets and horns add the opening pentatonic theme to the fabric. The hymn finally culminates in a triumphant affirmation whose sense of monumentality is remarkable for a work of such modest proportions.

Essay no. 2 may be regarded as the final work of Barber's early period, or as a transitional work into a period of "adolescent" experimentation, when he tried his hand at incorporating elements into his music that his colleagues were exploring successfully. Its lyrical primacy, solemn tone, and clarity of harmony, rhythm, and texture are characteristic of his earlier works. However, the pentatonic structure of the main theme, and its emphasis on the intervals of the fourth and fifth, give it an American flavor—devices new to Barber, but favored by many other composers at the time. Its breadth of utterance and reach for grandeur also link it to many other American symphonic works of the 1940s. The mood of the times was reflected in a comment made by critic Donald Fuller, shortly after the work's premiere: "[The *Second Essay*] is the best of this composer's work to date. I think Barber has been reading his Copland and Harris scores and it has been good for him. The horizon has also broadened, and he now appears capable of real thematic invention."[49]

The premiere of Barber's *Second Essay* took place in April 1942, one month after its completion, with Bruno Walter conducting the New York Philharmonic. One of the composer's most fully consummated shorter orchestral works, it was immediately picked up by George Szell, Eugene Ormandy, and others who promptly gave it widespread exposure. It has remained one of Barber's most popular pieces.

"Adolescence": Period of Exploration and Experimentation (1942 through 1952)

There is a clear stylistic and conceptual division between the works just discussed—through op. 17—and those that followed. Perhaps moved to self-doubt by criticisms that he was a hothouse reactionary, so to speak, "contemporary only in the sense that [he] is still alive,"[50] Barber—still only thirty-two years old—began an exploration of some of the compositional trends that were then engaging the attention of others, not unlike an adolescent's concern with peer approval and attraction to new behaviors discovered "outside the home," as it were. Chief among them was the Neo-Classicism of Igor Stravinsky, with its tart pandiatonic and polytonal harmony, irregular rhythmic patterns, and drier orchestration; he even dipped a tentative toe into twelve-tone writing. Now the rather humorless, somewhat straitlaced, genteel quest for "beauty" was amplified—not truly replaced—by a lighter, cooler, less personal vein of feeling. Barber's expressive palette also expanded to include touches of humor and irony, accented sometimes by hints of Parisian urbanity and at others by fashionable traces of Americana. In addition to the influence of Stravinsky and Copland, suggestions of the somewhat more playful, extroverted language of Menotti appeared in his compositions as well. All this brought Barber's musical language into the American mainstream of the time. Perhaps his most notable success from this period was the setting for soprano and chamber orchestra of James Agee's *Knoxville: Summer of 1915*. But many of the pieces from the 1940s, while never failing to display their composer's refined sensibility, are rather like adolescent affectations: artificial, lacking the very individuality, conviction, and sincerity that so distinguished Barber's earlier work. Nevertheless, much of this music was favorably received, and some pieces continue to be held in high esteem. And while this period of conformity with contemporary fashion lasted barely a decade, it served to broaden Barber's acceptance among those elements of the musical public—critics, in particular—who valued that which was *au courant*.

These differences are strikingly evident in the Two Songs, op. 18, composed in 1942–1943. The poems—"The Queen's Face on the Summery Coin," by Barber and Menotti's close friend Robert Horan, and "Monks and Raisins," by José Garcia Villa—are playful and lighthearted—quite different in style and character from the sort of texts to which Barber had been previously attracted. The music that he devised for them was equally uncharacteristic, as described above. The Horan setting displays a toying with major-minor harmonic conflicts that recurs in the next few works as well, most prominently in the Cello Concerto.

This was the period of World War II and Barber's military participation. One of the pieces he contributed to the war effort was the *Commando March*. Though not musically significant, the march was played widely and served to spread Barber's name and reputation into areas remote from his familiar social and aesthetic terrain. Though rather dainty for a military march, it is constructed with considerable sophistication, revealing harmonic subtleties that emerge felicitously in a well-executed rendition. The first performance took place in Atlantic City, New Jersey, in May 1943, with the composer himself conducting the Army Air Force Band. Soon afterward, Barber rescored the march for symphony orchestra, in which form it was introduced by Serge Koussevitzky and the Boston Symphony Orchestra in October of the same year.

But Barber's main contribution to the war effort was his Symphony no. 2, the surrounding circumstances of which were discussed earlier, in the biographical section. A distinct departure from anything the composer had attempted previously, the work initially known as the *Flight Symphony* opens stridently—even aggressively—before unfolding a sternly expansive theme whose spirit anticipates the corresponding moments of the Sixth Symphonies of Prokofiev and Vaughan Williams (both composed later). The movement is gripping throughout—taut, virile, solidly and tightly—if conventionally—structured, with rugged sonorities and angular rhythms. Quartal harmonies spiked with major and minor seconds abound, creating an abrasiveness that is never without expressive purpose. The composer's identity peeks through with a characteristically lyrical secondary theme introduced by the oboe. However, despite the superficial modernism of its harmonic language, the movement is simply a more roughhewn, yet still brilliantly executed, treatment of symphonic melodrama familiar from Barber's earlier works.

The second movement—which also exists as an independent work entitled *Night Flight*—purports to evoke the loneliness of the solo pilot. It is built around a slow, five-beat harmonic texture that functions somewhat like an *ostinato*. The use of "blue-notes" creates a more overtly Americana flavor, as an English horn solo evokes a wistful, nostalgic poignancy that Barber developed further in *Knoxville* and several other works. Polytonal passages occasionally suggest the style of Roy Harris.

The finale is the weakest portion of the symphony. Attempting to renew the sense of determination set forth in the opening movement, it subjects rather routine material of a martial cast to an exhortative treatment that rings false. (One of the main ideas anticipates the primary theme of the finale of the Piano Concerto, composed two decades later.) The movement is a sequence of episodes, with passages that verge on empty contrapuntal "note-spinning," at times suggesting the glibness of William Walton. The movement sounds increasingly forced and contrived as it draws toward the end, with a slow epilogue (added later) followed by a triumphant conclusion that lacks conviction.

A distinctly American quality, as yet rarely encountered in Barber's music, appears throughout the work. It is this quality—more the result of gestures and sonorities than of pseudonational melos—that links the symphony to the music of Copland, Harris, and others active at the time. Yet when one considers all the patriotic hoopla surrounding it, the symphony is remarkably free of self-consciously nationalistic or jingoistic appeal.

As reported earlier, the *Second Symphony (Dedicated to the Army Air Forces)* enjoyed a highly publicized and enthusiastically received premiere by Serge Koussevitzky and the Boston Symphony Orchestra in March 1944. Despite its dedication, the composer insisted all along that the symphony was not descriptive or programmatic in any way, regardless of the images it may have evoked in the minds of some listeners. Then, in 1946–1947 Barber undertook a substantial revision, which included replacing the electronic tone generator used in the second movement with an E-flat clarinet and changing the title simply to "Symphony no. 2." Somewhat ironically, the revised version had its first performance in Germany in December 1947, by the Berlin Philharmonic under the direction of American conductor John Bitter. It was this version that Barber recorded in London in 1950. But the question remains, what was it about this work that led Barber to withdraw it in 1964? Can we take his statement that "it is not a good work" at face value?

The Symphony no. 2 may not be the most authentic product of Barber's inner emotional life; its character is certainly far less personal and individual than most of the music he had composed thus far. But this does not necessarily diminish either its inherent quality or its effect on the listener. In it Barber explored a harsher, more athletic, and more extroverted type of expression than he had in the past. He also produced a reasonably strong symphonic structure—more ambitious and complex than its predecessor—and this was no minor accomplishment for a composer who was rarely at his best in large abstract forms. As is true for the Violin Concerto and for several other of Barber's extended instrumental works, the finale is significantly weaker than the preceding movements, but, as is also true of the Violin Concerto, the work's strengths ultimately outweigh its weaknesses on balance.

So why the withdrawal and destruction? It is not as if his other works are free of weaknesses. Not surprisingly for a period of experimentation, much of his music from the 1940s reveals flaws of one kind or another. One might argue that the works that immediately followed the Second Symphony—the *Excursions*, the *Capricorn Concerto*, and the Cello Concerto—are less successful artistically, but the composer did not feel the need to withdraw them. One plausible explanation is that Barber—essentially a quiet, private sort of person—found the demand to which his position of eminence subjected him that he produce "blockbusters"—that is, grand, highly publicized musical events—terribly intimidating. Although he certainly enjoyed his exalted position among his peers and the advantages and opportunities it afforded him, he dreaded this pressure. Aware to some extent that monumental statements were unnatural to his creative temperament, he undertook such efforts with serious misgivings. (Much the same factors were involved in the subsequent experience with *Antony and Cleopatra*, whose rejection, however, followed a somewhat different course.) The destruction of the symphony in 1964 was perhaps more a rash, impulsive act in symbolic repudiation of an alien offspring than an actual obliteration of the work itself. After all, the printed score and the 1950 recording had been available for some time and were widely circulated. Nevertheless, most of the orchestral parts were destroyed and the work was banned from recording or public performance.

However, in 1984, performance materials for the symphony surfaced in England, and the Barber estate was persuaded to grant permission for a new recording to be made. In 1989, the symphony was issued on compact disc in a new performance by the New Zealand Symphony Orchestra, under the direction of Andrew Schenck. This recording, widely praised by a new generation of critics and listeners, led to the symphony's revival. Today it may be regarded as one of the finest American symphonies of the 1940s, a work whose strength and power are readily apparent when performed with conviction.

Another stylistic departure for Barber during the early 1940s was a group of four short piano pieces that dabbled in vernacular American musical idioms. This sort of notion was very fashionable at the time, and many composers were producing similar pieces, Copland's *Four Piano Blues* being one of the better-known examples. Completed in 1944, Barber's aptly titled *Excursions* are sheer diversions, neither parodistic nor serious minded, although—quite like the *Commando March*—the workmanship and taste they reveal is far more meticulous than their actual aesthetic content. Stylistically sophisticated glosses on familiar American genres, they are incongruously tenderfooted in tone but highly effective pianistically: The first is a rather fastidious take on boogie-woogie, the second is a blues, the third is a sort of generic folk song that makes vague reference to "The Streets of Laredo," and the last suggests a hoedown played on harmonica, with touches reminiscent of *Petrushka*. Three of the four pieces were introduced by Vladimir Horowitz in Philadelphia, in January 1945, and represent his first foray into American music. The premiere of all four pieces was given in New York City by Jeanne Behrend, in December 1948.

In 1944, Barber was appointed to New York's Office of War Information. His first assignment in this position was the composition of *Capricorn Concerto*, named for the house that he and Menotti had purchased in Mount Kisco, New York, during the previous year. This work represents a more extreme break with his earlier music than any of the pieces just discussed. An example of true Neo-Classicism, the concerto is modeled along the lines of a *concerto grosso* and uses the same instrumentation as Bach's *Brandenburg Concerto no. 2*, with flute, oboe, and trumpet as solo instruments, set against a string orchestra. Light in texture and mood, with an overall feeling of detachment and "objectivity," the result is the aesthetic opposite of works like the Symphony no. 1 and the Violin Concerto. The strong influence of Stravinsky is so blatantly obvious in Barber's use of constantly shifting, "additive" rhythms, pandiatonic harmony, crisp, dry sonorities, and diminutive gestures, that a remark made in a letter to his uncle in 1948 concerning the Russian composer's *"very definite limitations"* (emphasis Barber's) is interesting to note: "With all Strawinsky's talent and imagination, his lack of lyricism and utter inability to work in more than small periods weigh heavily against him." These limitations, he felt, explain "why Strawinsky is not a great composer."[51]

The *Capricorn Concerto* is one of Barber's weakest works, from which his own musical identity is largely absent. It was first performed in New York City in October 1944, by the Saidenberg Little Symphony conducted by Daniel Saidenberg. Some commentators seemed to feel that this attempt to accommodate musical fashion represented an advance for Barber, "[exemplifying] strikingly what a productive study of Copland will do for a young musician who has been brought up in the tradition of big, fat sounds and pompous effects."[52] However, others reacted differently. Noel Straus commented, "Though it had nothing particularly original to impart and was largely episodic and fragmentary in its three divisions, it served its purpose well enough in rather inconsequential but clever fashion,"[53] while an unidentified *Musical America* critic found it "little more than a flip exercise of humorous rhythmic and instrumental formulas . . . which have been done far better at one time or another by Stravinsky, Shostakovich and their fellows."[54]

Similarly disappointing is Barber's next work, his second effort in the vein of a traditional virtuoso concerto, this one featuring the cello. Commissioned by a Rhode Island philanthropist for cellist Raya Garbousova at the suggestion of Koussevitzky, the concerto was completed in 1945. With a strong lyrical emphasis and a loose and leisurely formal expanse, it is more accurately characterized as

"Neo-Romantic" than "Neo-Classical," despite the use of a harsher harmonic language than that found in the Violin Concerto, for example. The cello writing is felicitous and idiomatic, though very challenging. However, despite tight motivic relationships, the work as a whole makes a rather diffuse impression, owing to long, discursive cadenzas and cadenza-like passages, and to expressive content that is surprisingly ordinary—especially in the outer movements, where the thematic material seems shallow and less genuine. Characteristically, the heart of the concerto is the second movement, which offers some appealing, heartfelt lyricism. An alternation between largely diatonic melodic writing and passages that twist chromatically anticipates the style of the very late oboe *Canzonetta*. The finale is largely routine and uninteresting, except for a strangely haunting, ominous passage built over a ground bass, which occurs twice.

Raya Garbousova gave the first performance of Barber's Cello Concerto in April 1946, with the Boston Symphony Orchestra conducted by Serge Koussevitzky. Although the work has gradually found its way into the instrument's active repertoire, it lacks both the intense conviction of the Violin Concerto and the formal strength and dramatic power of the Piano Concerto yet to come. Robert Sabin found the concerto "one of Barber's most labored, thematically dry and academically stilted scores. One searches almost fruitlessly for the color, the imaginative power and the eloquence he has achieved in his scores for the theatre and in other compositions."[55] As Albert Goldberg expressed it two decades later, "The trouble is that the musical substance hardly supports the technical hazards."[56]

However, in his next work Barber found the elements necessary to generate a deeper, more personal application of the Modernist materials and techniques he had been exploring. In 1945, he was invited by Martha Graham, whose highly regarded, revolutionary choreographic works had utilized music by many of America's leading composers (Copland had written *Appalachian Spring* for her the previous year), to participate in a collaboration with her. They agreed on a project based on the Medea story, and Graham arranged for a commission from the Alice M. Ditson Fund. The following year Barber completed a suite of nine short movements, scored for an ensemble of thirteen instruments, just under a half-hour in duration. Graham originally called the work *Pain and Wrath Are the Singers*, but immediately before the May 1946 premiere, changed the title to *Serpent Heart*. The following year she retitled it *Cave of the Heart*.

The concept underlying this collaborative work was a universalization of the psychological forces of jealousy and vengeance, rather than a literal retelling of the Greek legend. However, the ancient, exotic setting and the dramatic power of the emotions involved clearly inspired Barber's creative imagination (and anticipated such later forays into classical themes as *Andromache's Farewell* and *Antony and Cleopatra*). The result is a score of stark, gripping intensity, drawing from the composer some of the harshest, most dissonant music he ever composed. The work is no less redolent of Stravinsky than is the *Capricorn Concerto*, and, indeed, the spare, dryly acerbic sonorities produced by the small, woodwind-dominated ensemble only makes this influence more salient, while providing the sort of pregnant understatement well suited for choreography. Yet despite its astringency, there are some affecting melodic sections, as well as reflective moments of haunting mystery and exotic atmosphere. Interestingly, in the popular "Dance of Vengeance," Barber attempted the sort of primitivistic rhythmic orgy of which Paul Creston was a master, in which an irregular *ostinato* provides the basis for a wild dance sequence that builds in intensity to a frenzied, Dionysian climax. However, by comparison, Barber's mannerly reticence restrained him from fully exploiting the music's capacity for violent effect.

In 1947, Barber adapted the score for concert presentation, condensing some of the material, and expanding the orchestration to symphonic proportions. Now titled simply *Medea*, the concert suite was given its premiere by Eugene Ormandy and the Philadelphia Orchestra in December of the same year. The fuller orchestration enhances the power and richness of the sonorities, while lending additional color to the exotic effects. Reviewing the Philadelphia performance, Virgil Thomson welcomed "a Samuel Barber freed at last from the well-bred attitudinizing and mincing respectabilities of his concert manner,"[57] although more conservative critics and listeners bemoaned what they perceived as the composer's abandonment of "beauty." The *Medea* concert suite was one of the works recorded in London in 1950, under Barber's direction.

In 1955, Barber made yet another version of the *Medea* music—this one a single movement of less than fifteen minutes duration, scored for an even larger orchestra, entitled *Medea's Meditation and Dance of*

Vengeance. Despite much the same musical material, the impact of this version is quite different from that of the concert suite. Although the latter retains the dry, astringent, Neo-Classical bite of the original dance score, the new revision adds still more power to the climaxes and more opulence to the exotic atmosphere. The result is a work in the mature Neo-Romantic style that Barber unveiled during the early 1950s—a style that embraced much greater angularity and dissonance than appeared in the music of the 1930s. *Medea's Meditation and Dance of Vengeance* was first performed in February 1956, by the New York Philharmonic conducted by Dimitri Mitropoulos. It is in this form that the music is most often heard today, having become another of Barber's most widely performed orchestral works. However, the process of condensation resulted in the loss of a sizable amount of interesting and effective musical material whose absence is regrettable.

After *Medea,* Barber composed what is probably his most widely loved and admired work, with the exception of the *Adagio*: the setting for soprano and orchestra of a portion of James Agee's exquisite reminiscence, entitled *Knoxville: Summer of 1915.* (See the biographical section of this chapter for the many relevant parallels and coincidences shared by Barber and Agee.) Barber composed *Knoxville* on a commission from soprano Eleanor Steber, and Serge Koussevitzky had agreed to conduct the premiere. He knew that both singer and conductor wanted a work for full symphony orchestra, so that is how he scored it, although he would have preferred a more intimate ensemble. The premiere took place in April 1948—exactly one year after its completion—with the Boston Symphony Orchestra. In 1949, however, Barber rescored it for a small chamber orchestra, and that has become the definitive version.

The text, written in poetic prose, recalls a period during the writer's childhood surrounding the death of his father. The passage vividly and uncannily presents this recollection through the sensibility of the child. Barber's musical setting successfully captures this sensibility in all its nuances, evoking the bittersweet feeling of a childhood reminiscence by using a gentle, rocking motif as the basic thematic element. It is especially notable that while the emotional tone of retrospective nostalgia in recalling childhood innocence is typical of Barber, the musical setting embraces the fashionable, slightly acerbic, Stravinsky-based language of Neo-Classicism. As adopted by Copland and others, the crisp, woodwind-based sonori-

ties and pandiatonic harmony characteristic of this idiom, combined
with pentatonic melodies often inflected by "blue-notes," was
emerging during the 1940s as almost a lingua franca through which
to depict rural America. (Indeed, one is not surprised by Barber's
report that Copland had said to him, "I wish *I'd* found the text of
Knoxville first!"[58]). In short, although the emotional content of the
piece recalls Barber's artistic "childhood," the musical language is
another "adolescent excursion"—especially in its revised instrumentation—although the work's enormous popularity has misled
many listeners into viewing it as one of his most characteristic creative fruits. Furthermore, perhaps more than any of his other works,
Knoxville, with its innocent, slightly reserved, self-effacing lyricism,
has been a great influence on the vocal music of a subsequent generation of American traditionalist composers, such as John Corigliano
(in his early works), Lee Hoiby, Carlisle Floyd, and many others. So
perfectly does the musical setting capture and reflect the subtle
blend of memories, sensations, and feelings implied by Agee's eloquent prose, that the work may stand as the most apt fusion of text
and music to be found in the American repertoire.

   In October 1947, while working with Eleanor Steber in anticipation of the premiere of *Knoxville*, Barber set another Joyce text, this
one for soprano and piano, entitled *Nuvoletta*. The words, taken
from *Finnegan's Wake*, suggest a sort of death scene, presented in a
chilling blend of literal meaning, implication, and nonsense—all
conveyed in a light-hearted tone of flighty unreality. Barber aptly
captured this tone with a waltz-like treatment that includes much
high-lying *coloratura*. *Nuvoletta* is one of his relatively few compositions that suggest the musical influence of Menotti. It is revealing to
note that years later Barber cited this piece when he was asked by
an interviewer whether he had ever set a text he didn't fully understand. "I'm not unlearned in Joyce," he noted. "I've read quite a few
books on him. But what can you do when you get lines like 'Nuvoletta reflected for the last time in her little long life, and she made
up all her myriads of drifting minds in one; She cancelled all her
engauzements. She climbed over the bannistars; she gave a childy,
cloudy cry,' except to set them instinctively, as abstract music,
almost like a vocalise?"[59]

   At about the time he was composing *Nuvoletta*, Barber received a
commission from the unlikely duo of Irving Berlin and Richard Rodgers to compose a piano sonata in honor of the twenty-fifth anniver-

sary of the League of Composers. The premiere was to be given by Vladimir Horowitz. Barber had a great deal of difficulty finding an opportunity free of distractions in which he could concentrate on the sonata. Following his preferred approach, he worked closely with Horowitz, allowing him to offer his own input into the creative process. Not completed until 1949, the sonata was introduced by Horowitz at a recital in Havana, Cuba, in December of that year. He recorded the work for RCA the following year and performed it more than twenty times in recital during that season. Enthusiastically received by audiences, it was immediately hailed as a masterpiece by most critics and was soon programmed by dozens of pianists, newcomers as well as veterans, during the years that followed.

The Piano Sonata's success can be attributed partly to the stunning impact it makes as a virtuoso showpiece and partly to the void it filled in the repertoire. Despite the existence of piano sonatas by Americans such as MacDowell, Griffes, Ives, Sessions, Creston, Copland, and many others, none met the triple criteria of being fashionably modern in style, overtly expressive enough to appeal to the general listener, and virtuosic enough to function as a showpiece. However, so well did Barber's effort fill this void that it has continued to hold an exclusive place in the piano repertoire for more than half a century, effectively preventing any of the many comparable works composed during the ensuing years from gaining enough exposure to threaten its position of primacy as "the" American traditionalist piano sonata.

Barber's Sonata comprises four movements. The first is a tempestuous *sonata allegro* that, like the first movement of the Second Symphony, embraces a harshly dissonant, tortuously chromatic, texturally complex language in the service of a darkly emotional, intensely dramatic expression. This movement displays the first prominent use of a device that increasingly emerged as an enduring feature of Barber's mature language: descending sequences of fourths—perfect, augmented, and diminished—often serving as means of "cooling off" diatonic lyrical passages. (This usage might be compared with Vittorio Giannini's analogous embracing of the interval of the fourth during the 1940s.) The second movement functions as a *scherzo*, but with more of the character of an *intermezzo-burlesque*, light and gossamer-like. Returning to the tone of the opening, the third movement is a dark, lugubrious piece of "night music" whose somber tread suggests the inexorable build-up of a *passacaglia* without actually adhering to the form, as it reaches a towering climax and then recedes. The finale is a propulsive fugue, bristling with technical challenges, whose syncopated subject has intimations of Latin American dance music that emerge more clearly during some of the episodes, before culminating in a hair-raising coda.

Despite its undeniable effectiveness, a number of critics—admittedly a minority—have expressed reservations about the work. "It is a virtuoso's paradise, a real contemporary showpiece," wrote Harold Schonberg, "though one wonders how much of the praise is praise through default of contemporary composers of piano music."[60] Thirty years later, Max Harrison observed, "It has always seemed to me that this piece is pianistically rather more trouble to play than it is worth musically."[61] As is the case with others of Barber's works from the 1940s, much of the sonata seems contrived and lacking in true spontaneity. The first movement is weakened by ideas and effects that are not optimally realized on the piano, for example, emphasis on single notes in the instrument's middle register, which fail to project the power that seems required. This movement, agitated and impulsive, displays a complex, multilayered texture reminiscent of late Scriabin more than anyone else. As with that composer, the textures often seem overly congested, as the music scrambles frantically in too many different directions. The exceedingly difficult challenge for the pianist is to set and maintain a vigorous sense of purpose, while also delineating the many mood-shifts and textural elements within their relative relationships to each other. This is a goal that not even Horowitz was able to achieve.

The sonata's other major weakness concerns the matter of irreconcilable stylistic incongruities. The character of the four movements and their thematic ideas touch upon so many different styles that a certain uncomfortable heterogeneity seems inherent in the work. The finest large-scale, multimovement works of mature Neo-Romanticism are unified by a consistent, superordinating concept, such that individual movements, regardless of how they may differ from each other with regard to tempo, texture, thematic material, and so on, join collectively in conveying this concept. In other words, the movements "belong" together. From this perspective, the twinkly little *scherzo* and the flashy fugal finale, while providing conventional contrasts in mood, tempo, and pianistic challenge, are not consistent with or relevant to the overall meaning of the work, as proclaimed by the turbulent, restless first movement, and acknowledged by the gloomy eloquence of the slow movement. A reservation along these lines was noted rather hesitantly by Olin Downes, who confessed to having "a question in mind about this very interesting work. Is its second movement, the lightest of the four, really necessary? The same sonata in three movements, with the present scherzo omitted, would be ideal in length and completely coherent and consistent in its structure."[62]

Discussions of the Piano Sonata invariably comment on the presence of twelve-tone series that appear in several of its movements. However it is essential to understand that these ideas contribute to a chromatic effect within clearly tonal structures; their treatment in no way follows the principles outlined by Arnold Schoenberg, nor does it achieve the atonal effect intended by the Second Viennese School. Their use is thoroughly consistent with the Neo-Romantic view of tonality as an expressive continuum, rather than representing any sort of concession to the serial style (except perhaps as a private joke).

French poems by the German poet Rainer Maria Rilke inspired Barber's next stylistic "excursion," this one into a French-flavored realm of sensuality, although Barber insisted, "I certainly didn't try for a French tone."[63] Nevertheless, these songs—the composer's only foreign-language contributions to the genre—represent the emergence of a new dimension in his range of expression. Embracing the rich harmonic language of Impressionism, Barber developed a freer, wider-arching lyricism—less symmetrical, less diatonic, and less "proper" or constrained emotionally. Although this new freedom and sensuality can be heard in all five songs, perhaps the second song, "Un cygne," most clearly displays these qualities as they were soon to emerge as essential elements in Barber's mature style.

Three of the songs were completed in 1950 and presented in Washington, D.C., by Eileen Farrell, with Barber at the piano. He composed two more the following year, and the entire group of five *Mélodies Passagères*, which Barber dedicated to his friend Francis Poulenc, had its premiere in Paris, in February 1952, with baritone Pierre Bernac and Poulenc at the piano. The two presented the American premiere a week later in New York and recorded the group as well. Asked years later whether Poulenc had been fond of the songs, Barber replied, "Francis was a darling man, but he was enamored only with his own songs."[64]

What this study identifies as Barber's "adolescent" period of exploration and experimentation came to a close in 1952 with *Souvenirs*, six pieces originally conceived as party entertainment for piano, four hands. The music is an attempt to evoke a certain *mise en scène* recollected from the composer's childhood. As he stated with remarkable specificity in a note printed in the score, "One might imagine a divertissement in a setting of the Palm Court of the Hotel Plaza in New York, the year about 1914 . . . remembered with affection, not in irony or with tongue in cheek, but in amused tenderness." Although the specified year is somewhat early, Barber's mother apparently used to take him to the Palm Court of the Plaza for tea when he was young, so the emotional essence here is nostalgia once again. But instead of the bittersweet poignancy with which this feeling was imbued in his earlier music, here there is a certain delight in exalting the essential banality of the concept through an extravagantly elegant and sophisticated treatment—that is, the quality known as "camp," which originated within the homosexual subculture. This is another feature that emerged as an aspect of Barber's mature work. Although the aesthetic import of *Souvenirs*, with its origins in salon music, is certainly lightweight, its unerring sense of the style and ambiance it attempts to evoke, and the grace, panache, and epicene charm of the treatment, which brilliantly incorporates traces of both Ravel and Stravinsky into its tone of studied triviality, are undeniable throughout. And in one of the movements, "Hesitation Tango," an indulgently languorous surface barely conceals a sense of sinister danger in which Barber's dramatic power emerges with eloquent grandeur.

Before Barber finished the four-hands version of *Souvenirs* in 1951, Lincoln Kirstein, upon hearing several of the pieces, suggested that the music be orchestrated for choreographic use. Barber complied with his request, completing both the orchestration and a piano solo version in 1952. That same year the duo-pianists Gold and Fizdale received the composer's permission to arrange the work for two pianos. They performed and recorded their arrangement the same year. The following year the orchestral version was introduced by Fritz Reiner and the Chicago Symphony Orchestra. Not until November 1955 was it actually choreographed by Todd Bolender for the City Center Ballet in New York City.

"Adulthood": Music of Maturity (after 1952)

Around 1953, Barber's music entered a new phase, a period of maturity, when he no longer felt the need to embrace the fashionable compositional styles of the moment or to borrow from the languages of other composers, but instead arrived at a more personal language of his own. Leaving behind his experiments with vernacular idioms and Stravinskian Neo-Classicism, this new "adult" style was capable of embracing a range of expression much broader than the hypersensitive melancholia around which his early work had been centered. Now the tonal freedom and ambiguity and the textural complexity noted in the respective first movements of the Symphony no. 2 and the Piano Sonata were integrated with the sort of elegance and sensuality found in the *Mélodies Passagères*. Barber also revealed a growing taste for ancient Greek and Roman subjects, which he treated with a sumptuous exotic grandeur. He even embraced the frankly erotic, while remaining flexible enough to adapt to other new expressive challenges. The evocation of mood and atmosphere, enhanced by the heightened sensuality of impressionistic harmony and texture, played a more prominent role than before. While the tenderness, vulnerability, and spiritual purity of his early music were not abandoned altogether, they were juxtaposed within more complex expressive contexts, as in the 1954 cantata *Prayers of Kierkegaard*. As time went on, Barber often treated these feelings with irony, defensiveness, even decadence and self-pity, as he became increasingly aware during the antiaristocratic, self-consciously modernistic 1960s that the very success he had won at such a young age now caused him to be seen by many as an overindulged, superannuated child. Yet the bitterness and disappointment of his later years lent the best works from this time—*Andromache's Farewell*, *Antony and Cleopatra*, and *The Lovers*—an "adult" emotional complexity missing from the works that made him famous. Instead of recognizing the maturation of Barber's creative personality, however, many critics and listeners—still expecting the overt lyricism of the *Essay no. 1*, for example—viewed these later compositions as inadequate attempts to match his earlier successes. Thus the finest works of Barber's maturity still remain some of his least recognized and least understood masterpieces.

As mentioned earlier, Barber's Uncle Sidney had ignited within

him a strong taste for Irish poetry. Ireland was also the source of
Barber's paternal ancestry, and in 1952 he even made a visit, which
only intensified his fascination. Around that time he discovered
modern translations of texts originally written by anonymous Irish
monks during the Middle Ages. "They are small poems, thoughts
or observations, some very short, and speak in straightforward,
droll, and often surprisingly modern terms of the simple life these
men led, close to nature, to animals and to God," Barber wrote in a
note included in the published score. He was especially moved by
"that strange vision of natural things in an almost unnatural piety,"
quoting Robin Flower, who attributed such perception to "an eye
washed miraculously clear by a continual spiritual exercise." By
1953, he had completed a group of ten settings of these ancient texts,
which he called *Hermit Songs*, receiving a commission from the Elizabeth Sprague Coolidge Foundation. He chose the then largely
unknown Leontyne Price to introduce them at the Library of Congress premiere in October 1953, with the composer himself at the
piano. (She went on to perform the cycle at her New York debut
recital the following year and numerous times thereafter.)

The *Hermit Songs*, his op. 29, proved to be Barber's most ambitious
song cycle to date and remains, along with *Knoxville*, his most
widely respected vocal work. Unified by recurrent motifs, the songs
display considerable variety in expression, conveyed through a
broadly flexible language that combines some Neo-Classical features with more traditional harmonic usage and modal—sometimes
pentatonic—melody. Moods range from the wry and whimsical to
the intensely spiritual. Perhaps the most characteristic song of the
group is "St. Ita's Vision," which captures Barber's familiar idealiza-
tion of mother and child, as the nursing of the Baby Jesus achieves
a sense of ecstatic mystery by means of a simple folk-like melody.
Even more deeply moving is the rending of the mother-child bond
in the verbally terse "Crucifixion," expressed with heartbreaking
intensity and eloquence. "The Praises of God" reveals the unmistakable stamp of Stravinsky in its asymmetrical rhythms and disjointed
textures, while "The Desire for Hermitage" seems autobiographical
in the intensity of its yearning for solitude.

Barber had long felt attracted to the simplicity and sincerity of
Gregorian chant. A commission from the Koussevitzky Music Foundation provided an opportunity for him to combine this attraction
with an interest in the theological writings of the Danish existential-

ist Soren Kierkegaard. And, as in many of the works of his new "adulthood," it also gave him the opportunity to integrate within one work several of the diverse elements of his musical language. The result, *Prayers of Kierkegaard*, is a work unsurpassed in its consistency of inspiration, the coherence of its construction, and the personal depth of its expression. In his program notes for the work, which he completed early in 1954, Barber wrote, "The entire literary production of Kierkegaard is motivated by the intent of bringing men into a religious relationship with God, and through his writings one finds his three basic traits of imagination, dialectic, and religious melancholy. The truth he sought after was a 'truth which is true for me,' one which demanded sacrifice and personal response."[65] Elsewhere Barber indicated that what appealed to him about Kierkegaard was his belief in emotional intensity and commitment as the path toward spiritual enlightenment.

Choosing four passages from the theologian's writings, Barber shaped a cantata for vocal soloists, chorus, and orchestra in which four sections are integrated into one movement of approximately twenty minutes duration. The work opens with hushed male voices, "grave and remote," singing the work's simple motif in unison a capella, in the manner of Gregorian chant. The orchestra soon enters softly, building to a climax as the chorus sings, "But nothing changes Thee," in a magnificent homophonic statement conveying a grandeur not heard in Barber's work since the *Second Essay* of 1942. A contrapuntal elaboration leads to a restatement of the climax, leading directly to the second section, based on the words, "Lord Jesus Christ, Who suffered all life long that I, too, might be saved." This more personal idea is expressed through a warmly lyrical, pentatonic melody, quite typical of Barber and somewhat reminiscent of the "Crucifixion" melody from the *Hermit Songs*. Introduced by the oboe, the melody is then picked up by the solo soprano (Leontyne Price, for whom it was written, at the Boston premiere). The third section, "Father in Heaven, well we know that it is Thou that giveth both to will and to do," is set to pure, reverent triads, chromatically—rather than tonally—related, in the unaccompanied chorus, punctuated by gentle orchestral chords. This passage, reminiscent in its spiritual purity of some of the composer's choral settings from the 1930s, is followed by a contrasting section introduced by a solo tenor to the words, "But when longing lays hold of us, oh, that we might lay hold of the longing!" The tenor melody is highly chromatic, with wide, irregular intervals, and is accompanied by sparse, mysterious instrumental sonorities. Alto, then soprano solos enter in counterpoint, soon joined by the chorus, first divided, then building toward a stern, climactic statement in unison, which then explodes in a wild, rhythmically driving orchestral frenzy based on the initial motif. The "Jesus Christ" motif returns, calming down the commotion, until the subdivided chorus, voices hushed in awe-filled reverence, sing the words, "Father in Heaven!" in alternating patterns of perfect fifths, based on the initial motif, accompanied by bells. A fervent hymn in chorale style then brings the work to a conclusion of devout serenity.

The first performance of the *Prayers of Kierkegaard* was given by the Boston Symphony Orchestra and the Schola Cantorum, conducted by Charles Munch, in December 1954. The critical response indicates some recognition of the work's extraordinary quality, even relative to Barber's other music. Olin Downes wrote:

> The unrhythmical and free-metered recitation in carefully shaped recitative has the flavor of plainchant, reshaped, freely recast in forms of our own modern consciousness. Sometimes the music becomes nearly barbaric, and intensely dramatic in its effect. Polytonality is used freely, logically, with distinction. The instrumentation is intensely dramatic. The final chorale is no more an imitation of a Lutheran form, any more than the choral recitative comes from the Catholic direction. Universality is the suggestion, a universality that does not dismiss but includes inevitably the consciousness of the infinite mercy, the infinite tenderness, the cosmic design.[66]

Cyrus Durgin found it "deeply felt and very moving in effect . . . deserves to be repeated until it is familiar."[67]

Performances soon followed in other American cities and in Europe. A performance conducted by Massimo Freccia in Vienna, in the spring of 1955, was the first to meet with Barber's thorough satisfaction. Comments made in his travel log give further indication of how he viewed the work: "[The soprano soloist sang] with such purity and perfection of style, her voice soaring and disembodied, more unearthly than Leontyne's; . . . And Freccia . . . had all the correct tempos and succeeded in creating a mystical and at the same time passionate atmosphere . . . here at last was my work as I meant it to be, the chorus dominating, shattering, moving: not stodgy and oratorio-like. The deep German basses and altos and the sopranos with body, like trumpets, not like Thomas Whitney Surrette recorders!"[68]

Barber was soon to be immersed in the daunting task of writing his first opera. While he was waiting for Menotti to complete the libretto for *Vanessa*, he turned his attention to a commission from the Detroit Chamber Music Society, funded by contributions from subscribers. Drawing upon thematic material he had originally used in 1945 for background music to an NBC radio broadcast, he composed a short work in a single movement for woodwind quintet, entitled *Summer Music*. Although the piece was completed in 1956, its use of material from the previous decade, along with the crisp, dry woodwind sonorities, gives it something of the feeling of his other works from the 1940s. The music, a succession of episodes assembled rather casually into a loosely structured arch-form, evokes the gently bucolic whimsy associated with this particular medium, although its relaxed attitude belies the technical challenges it imposes on the players. Promptly championed by the New York Woodwind Quintet, *Summer Music* has gone on to become one of the most frequently performed American works in its genre.

Finally, after several years of preparation, Barber's eagerly awaited first opera was completed in 1957, in time for its Metropolitan Opera premiere the following January. *Vanessa* is a representative work of Barber's stylistic maturity: Right from its opening moments, which blaze with an angular assertiveness, the new Barber proclaims himself, its full-bodied, hypercharged Neo-Romanticism a far cry from the prepubescent melancholia of his early works or from the fashionably detached cleverness of his music from the 1940s. One hears echoes of composers—the limpid lyricism of Puccini, the swagger and indolence of Strauss—suggesting qualities previously foreign to his sensibility. But despite such reminiscences, the rich yet searing chromaticism that was to become Barber's own distinctive mature language—although not yet known to its first audience—is ever present.

The weakest aspect of *Vanessa* is Menotti's Chekhovian libretto—specifically, its foolish characters and their ludicrously improbable predicament. A note in the score indicates that the opera is set in "Vanessa's country house in a northern country, the year about 1905." In this baronial setting lives the middle-aged Vanessa with her elderly mother, who bears some undisclosed grudge against her daughter, and Vanessa's grown niece, Erika. Vanessa is awaiting the arrival of her true love, Anatol, who has been absent for many years. When the guest finally arrives, he proves to be the son (also named Anatol) of the now-deceased lover. Vanessa, vain and self-involved, simply transfers her abiding passion to the younger man. A charming but manipulative opportunist, he leads both women on, seducing (and impregnating) Erika while courting Vanessa. Erika, though initially enamored of young Anatol, soon sees him for the shallow fraud he is and spurns his hollow promises. Subsequently, Vanessa and Anatol announce their engagement, and Erika runs out into the cold to abort her baby. Finally, Vanessa and Anatol leave together, while Erika stays behind with her great-aunt, never having revealed her seduction or pregnancy to Vanessa.

It is difficult to understand how Barber managed to conceive such magnificent music to portray the plight of such repellent people. One expects to encounter touches of irony that might suggest some sense of detachment or imply a commentary on the proceedings. Yet Barber's music plays it straight and serious throughout. For example, the aria, "Outside this house the world has changed," in which Anatol reveals the shabby superficiality of his character, is one of the opera's most beautiful moments. Menotti's own comment in the score, "The story is one of two women . . . caught in the central dilemma which faces every human being, whether to fight for one's ideals to the point of shutting oneself off from reality, or compromise with what life has to offer, even lying to oneself for the mere sake of living," is utterly unconvincing as an explanation of the opera's psychodramatic crux. The fact—often recounted—that Menotti sprinkled the libretto with numerous "personal" references he knew Barber would appreciate, points once again to the notion of "high camp," that is, the serious treatment of extravagant or improbable subject matter.

Nevertheless, if one can accept the libretto on its own terms and tolerate it with the indulgence usually granted to opera plots, *Vanessa* offers many musico-dramatic high points to appreciate and enjoy: in Act I, Erika's touching "Must the winter come so soon," as the two women await their guest's arrival, followed by Vanessa's "Do not utter a word," addressed to the as-yet-unidentified visitor. Although its underlying psychology is peculiar, to say the least, this aria displays the highly chromatic, wide-ranging, yet essentially minor-key melodic line characteristic of Barber's mature style. Act II includes the aforementioned "Outside this house the world has changed," Anatol's ingratiating attempt to entice Erika to marry him, followed by a torrid orchestral passage as Erika painfully decides to renounce her suitor, overlaid by a hymn sung by a vocal ensemble heard wafting from the chapel, as the act comes to an end; in Act III, Anatol and Vanessa's ardent duet, "Love has a bitter core"; in Act IV, Scene 1, the passionate encounters leading up to the opulent orchestral Intermezzo based on the Act III duet, illustrating what Peter Rabinowitz has called "the intoxicating, but disorienting, mixture of sentiment and sinister decadence that gives this music its ambiguous power;"[69] then, finally, in Act IV, Scene 2, the Doctor's poignant aria, "For every love there is a last farewell," in which references to childhood are accompanied by reminiscences of Barber's consonant early style, followed by emotional confrontations that precede the justly admired canonic farewell quintet, "To leave, to break." The music is lushly orchestrated throughout and richly interwoven with sensuous motifs that, with increasing familiarity, gradually build a sense of unity and integration in one's mind.

As noted earlier, the response of both audience and critics to the premiere was overwhelmingly positive. *Time* called it the "best U.S. opera yet staged at the Metropolitan"[70]; Winthrop Sargeant felt that it was "the finest and most truly 'operatic' opera ever written by an American . . . one of the most impressive things . . . to appear anywhere since Richard Strauss's more vigorous days"[71]; Paul Henry Lang wrote, "Vanessa is a major contribution to the international operatic repertory. . . . Barber's mastery of the operatic language is remarkable and second to none now active on the Salzburg-Milan axis. . . . His vocal writing is impeccable and his handling of the orchestra virtuoso to a Straussian degree."[72] When a recording featuring the original cast was released that same year, William Olsen commented, "Never does Barber fail in the climaxes and seldom in the interim. The almost 'leitmotif' approach to Act 1 grows in stature in each act until it shreds the emotions in the Quintet of Act IV, which can be referred to as nothing short of a work of genius."[73]

Yet despite its success, *Vanessa* was dropped from the Met repertoire at the end of the season, and there have been only occasional performances during the intervening years. The Met mounted it again in 1965, which prompted Barber to make some revisions. Perhaps the opera's reputation was subsequently tarnished by the disastrous failure in 1966 of *Antony and Cleopatra*. In 1978, *Vanessa* was revived at the Spoleto Festival/USA, a production that was tele-

cast nationally the following year on PBS. Reviewing that production, Shirley Fleming wrote, "[*Vanessa*] has all the characteristics that
opera goers profess to yearn for today—abundant melody, luxuriant orchestration, an integrated thematic structure and above all an
utterly idiomatic approach to vocal writing."[74] "Some may argue
that Barber spreads an almost suffocating blanket of dark passion
over Menotti's slender melodrama," wrote John von Rhein. "Others
will find its heaviness absolutely appropriate for the subject. In any
case, 'Vanessa' is no dumber than a lot of Romantic works that have
found their way into the repertory, and its great surges of melody
head straight for the emotions of the audience."[75] Thomas P. Lanier
commented, "Barber's music provides an unleashing of lush, rich,
varied melody, which simultaneously conveys inner stirrings and
the outward expression that either embellishes them or masks them
behind a facade."[76] Considering the few productions *Vanessa* has
enjoyed during the past half-century in light of the comments it has
engendered suggests that the potential appeal of the opera has
barely been tapped.

During the next few years, while entering the early stages of work
on a number of major projects, Barber completed several shorter
works. While none of these contributed significantly to his overall
achievement, each fulfilled its modest intentions with skill and good
taste. In 1958, Barber complied with a request from an organist with
whom he was acquainted to compose a piece for the dedication of a
new organ at a church in Grosse Pointe, Michigan. The result was
Wondrous Love: Variations on a Shape-Note Hymn. The old modal
hymn melody, presented initially in a primitive harmonic setting,
has a haunting appeal, while the variations gave Barber the opportunity to experiment with some novel harmonic combinations.

Wondrous Love was followed by a short *Nocturne* for piano solo,
subtitled "Homage to John Field." Although barely five minutes
long and conventional in overall form, the piece, composed in 1959,
is as challenging technically as it is satisfying musically. A number
of commentators have noted the peculiarity of its subtitle, with its
tribute to the contemporary of Beethoven credited with the "invention" of the "nocturne," in light of the music's obvious debt to
Chopin. On the other hand, one might observe that its limpid lyricism bears an even stronger resemblance to Scriabin, another exponent of the "nocturne" genre similarly indebted to Chopin. Barber's
piano music often employed—probably coincidentally—the sort of

highly chromatic harmony and densely woven textures found in Scriabin's middle-period works. The *Nocturne*'s filigreed melodic line includes passages that contain all twelve tones but, as noted earlier, the strongly tonal harmonic structure ensures that such chromatic elaborations are perceived as sheer ornamentation. Though not yet widely known, this piece, like the early *Interludes*, is rich in musical substance, with much to offer pianists, as well as listeners, and is likely to be heard with increasing frequency as its reputation spreads. The *Nocturne* was first played in San Diego by John Browning, shortly after it was completed.

Written the same year as the *Nocturne*, was the short chamber opera *A Hand of Bridge*, for presentation during the second season of Menotti's Festival of Two Worlds in Spoleto, in June 1959. Menotti himself wrote the libretto, which uses a game of bridge as the backdrop for a series of four interrelated soliloquies, as the characters each express (through asides) personal thoughts they would not share with each other. The libretto also includes personal "in-jokes" understandable only to the men's close friends, while the music is satirical, in a Stravinskian manner, tinged with slightly jazzy accents. As a critique of the shallow relationships and stifling conformity identified with *bourgeois* American life during the 1950s, the piece recalls Leonard Bernstein's *Trouble in Tahiti*, written nearly a decade earlier. Although Barber's clever trifle—less than ten minutes long—is far less elaborate and far less poignant than Bernstein's forty-five-minute television opera, it has its share of moments both witty and touching.

Later that same summer, Barber composed a short piece for flute and piano to play with Manfred Ibel, a charismatic young German aesthete whom the composer had met the previous year. Originally called "Elegy," the piece is based on a simple, tender pentatonic melody, repeated several times with some variation. Although Barber expanded it several years later into the second movement of his Piano Concerto, the morsel was retitled *Canzone* and was published as an independent piece for flute or violin with piano accompaniment. In this form it has become a popular item on recital programs.

In 1960, Barber composed *Toccata Festiva*, to celebrate Mary Curtis Bok's donation of a new organ to the Philadelphia Academy of Music. An attractive if thoroughly conventional showpiece, it is the sort of work that most composers provide as a matter of course in earning their livings as "professionals," but which Barber's extraordinary success usually enabled him to avoid. It is interesting in this connection that the composer actually turned down his fee—gracious if understandable in view of the extraordinary benefits he had enjoyed as a result of Mrs. Bok's generous patronage over the years. The single-movement work is essentially a freely rhapsodic development of one major thematic idea, along with several subordinate motifs. It is remarkable in being one of Barber's few compositions that give the impression of having been assembled routinely from the sort of material that had been used successfully in previous works. Largely affirmative and jubilant in tone, but with some moments of nostalgic reflection that strongly resemble portions of *Knoxville*, some passages of stunning beauty, and an impressive pedal cadenza, the work leaves an altogether pleasing, but not terribly memorable, impression. The gala premiere took place in September 1960, with Eugene Ormandy conducting the Philadelphia Orchestra and Paul Calloway as the organ soloist.

Toccata Festiva was followed by another sort of "potboiler" typically produced by a journeyman composer—the piece suitable for performance during the Christmas season. *Die Natali* was the long-delayed response to a commission from the Koussevitzky Music Foundation. Subtitled "Chorale Preludes for Christmas," the work is most notable for its tasteful avoidance of the clichéd sentimentality, grandiosity, or garishness to which so many pieces of this kind succumb. Eight familiar carols are treated to ingenious but rather severe developmental variations featuring polytonal counterpoint, irregular rhythmic dislocations, and other processes remarkable for their subtlety and coolness of affect. (Barber later extracted and arranged his treatment of *Silent Night* as an organ solo.) The overall impression is surprisingly understated, so that the emotional climax, based on an original motif tangentially spun off from *Adeste Fidelis*, is moving and dignified, rather than overblown. The premiere was given in December 1960, by the Boston Symphony Orchestra, under the direction of Charles Munch.

Barber next turned his attention to three major works, each connected with the inauguration of New York City's imposing new cultural mecca, the Lincoln Center for the Performing Arts. The first of these was a piano concerto on which he had been working for several years, its premiere scheduled for the opening week of Lincoln Center's Philharmonic (now Avery Fisher) Hall in September 1962. Barber selected John Browning as his soloist and, in his fashion, worked closely with the pianist during the process of composition.

Barber's Piano Concerto is remarkable in its absorption of some of the "sound" and "feeling" of serialism within an unabashedly Neo-Romantic composition. This differs from works such as the Piano Sonata and the *Nocturne*, whose employment of twelve-tone material is utterly irrelevant to the serial style. (And it differs from such works of the late 1950s and early 1960s as the late quartets of Bloch, the Fourth Symphony of Giannini, and the *Metamorphoses* of Creston, in which each composer subjected twelve-tone material to his own characteristic treatment, as if to say, "See, I can write twelve-tone music and it still sounds like me.") In his Piano Concerto, without actually employing twelve-tone rows, Barber devised highly chromatic, nearly atonal thematic material, emphasizing wide-interval leaps, jagged, disjointed gestures, and irregular rhythmic groupings, and subsumed them within a conventionally structured virtuoso concerto, balancing such material with passages of lyrical passion and ferocious cadenzas, all of which culminate in highly dramatic climaxes. The first movement is a tempestuous, but formally straightforward *sonata allegro*. The piano begins with a statement of angular, chromatic thematic material in the manner of a solo recitative. The orchestra then introduces a passionate, wide-ranging, almost atonal theme. After some development, the oboe presents a gorgeous, if more conventional, secondary theme, infused with typically Barberian poignancy. The development of all these ideas is unusually elaborate and complex for Barber, before a hair-raising cadenza and a full recapitulation lead the movement toward a decisive conclusion.

The second movement is an expansion of the nostalgic, thoroughly tonal *Canzone* for flute and piano composed in 1959. The expansion fully retains the expressive essence of its source, adding nothing significant but further ornamented repetitions of the pentatonic melody in different keys, clothed in varying textures and instrumentation. A bridge figure based on the increasingly recurrent descending-fourths idea noted in other pieces separates the melodic repetitions. It is only the extraordinary appeal of Barber's melodies that enabled him to indulge in such redundancy.

The third movement is a propulsive five-part *rondo* in 5/8 meter, in the manner of a frenzied *toccata*. The main thematic idea was actually anticipated toward the beginning of the third movement of Barber's Symphony no. 2, although its overall presentation and treatment here strongly resembles the music of Prokofiev. The movement is enormously difficult to play, but creates a brilliantly exciting effect. As was so often the case, the finale had become a stumbling block for the composer and was actually completed only two weeks before the premiere! As noted earlier, the Concerto made a dazzling impact at its first performance, with the visiting Boston Symphony Orchestra conducted by Erich Leinsdorf.

Several critical responses to Barber's Piano Concerto were cited earlier. Perhaps one of the most provocative reactions, from the standpoint of this study, was made by Paul Henry Lang:

> Mr. Barber . . . is not a member of the avant-garde and in some quarters will be denounced as a "traditionalist." But what is tradition? The slavish imitator of the past denies the history of progress, denies his own age, and insults the very thing he pretends to imitate by misusing it. There is considerable difference between this sort of traditionalism and a true understanding of the continuity of creative endeavor. That a work is deliberately within a somewhat older style is not a flaw unless it fails to gather impetus from the artist's temperament in the proceeding. This concerto rises everywhere above the painstaking and the ingenious; its individual elements have importance in themselves and the whole is not greater than the sum of its parts.[77]

Lang's thoughtful justification of "traditionalism" in music might be applied to every composer in this study. However, its point of vulnerability is the phrase, "unless it fails to gather impetus from the artist's temperament," that is, unless the result fails to reveal the composer's own identity or personal contribution to what is otherwise simply an anonymous regurgitation of the past. The problem is that such a determination is subjective, depending on the knowledge, experience, and acuity of the person making the judgment. Evidently, Lang felt that Barber met his criterion, but that Giannini did not, as indicated by his review—written earlier the same year—of the opera *Rehearsal Call*, quoted in a previous chapter. But without objective criteria, the point becomes circular, and therefore specious, simply favoring the better known composer: that is, the more familiar the composer and his music, the more readily is his musical identity detected.

In any case, whether Barber's Piano Concerto is "the best piano concerto ever written by an American," as Jay Harrison (quoted earlier) stated, is difficult to confirm. Notable rivals are Peter Mennin's (1957), Vincent Persichetti's, and Nicolas Flagello's Third (both, like

Barber's, 1962). But Barber's, which had enjoyed 150 performances by 1969, is certainly the most popular, with the possible exception of the Gershwin. Indeed, it may be the most frequently performed concerto for *any* instrument composed after 1950.

Later in 1962, Barber completed *Andromache's Farewell*, an unstaged dramatic *scena* for soprano and orchestra. Commissioned by the New York Philharmonic, the work is based on an incident from Euripedes's *The Trojan Women*. Barber enlisted the poet John Patrick Creagh to create a text appropriate for a musical setting. The episode is set in Troy, which has been vanquished by the Greeks, who have slain all the Trojan warriors. Andromache, devoted wife of Prince Hector of Troy, must turn over her son to the victorious Greeks, who will slay him, before enslaving her as the concubine of Achilles's son. Barber turned this situation into a twelve-minute *scena* of harrowing intensity. The work opens with an explosive orchestral introduction that presents the work's main motif, while setting a mood of almost hysterical agitation. Somewhat analogous to the opening of the Piano Concerto, *Andromache*'s searing initial statement, slashing with jagged intervals of sevenths and ninths and angular motifs tumbling over each other in dissonant counterpoint, suggests the atonal expressionism of Alban Berg, before—within a few moments—settling into a clearly tonal anchor, as a strange, archaic atmosphere is created by double-reeds suggesting exotic scale forms. The soprano enters with a transformation of the opening motif into an impassioned, more typically Barberian, melodic line. Later on, a more subdued lyrical section is based on a secondary idea introduced by the oboe, then taken up by the soprano (to the words, "Oh dearest embrace"). This haunting, serpentine motif is hinged on a single, striking shift between two minor chords rooted a tritone apart. (The creation of a musical idea of potent expressive effect based on a single chord change is a technique Barber used again in subsequent works.)

In *Andromache's Farewell*, Barber returned to the mysterious and exotic language he had used in *Medea*, infusing it with sumptuous orchestral textures and lavish tone colors, including ample use of percussion, such as the whip, xylophone, and a variety of delicate bells. The appearance of a tragic yet noble grandeur reveals a new dimension to Barber's expressive palette, one that he would develop more fully in *Antony and Cleopatra*. In the earlier work the composer's extraordinary gift for evoking mood, atmosphere, and emotion with exquisite precision and nuance is turned to subject matter of considerable psychological complexity and ambiguity, as maternal anguish is expanded to mythic proportions, and proclaimed concisely but with great dramatic power in this masterpiece of Neo-Romantic vocal music. One of the great works of Barber's later years, it remains less well known, having been overshadowed somewhat by the attention surrounding *Antony and Cleopatra*. The premiere of *Andromache's Farewell* took place in April 1963. Soprano Martina Arroyo presented the extraordinarily difficult vocal part, with the New York Philharmonic conducted by Thomas Schippers. One of the commentators who praised the work after its premiere was Winthrop Sargeant—perhaps the most outspoken proponent of Neo-Romanticism among the better-known critics—who felt that this work "would be a logical jumping-off place for those who hope to continue in the grand manner of musical composition."[78]

Barber's pivotal work of the 1960s—indeed, one of the pivotal works of his entire career—was *Antony and Cleopatra*, the surrounding events of which were discussed earlier in this chapter. The highly publicized premiere opened the new Metropolitan Opera House at Lincoln Center in September 1966. The conductor was Thomas Schippers and the stage director (and librettist) was Franco Zeffirelli, with Justino Díaz and Leontyne Price in the title roles. Barber and Zeffirelli had agreed to shape the libretto from only Shakespeare's words—drastically pared down, of course. The work's fundamental theme is the conflict between the adult responsibilities of mature manhood, represented by the world of Roman politics, and the irresistible lure of erotic attraction, represented by Cleopatra, the queen of Egypt. These two forces—and geographical locations—are distinguished musically by characteristic treatments: the Roman music is stern and martial in character and rather formalistic in its articulation, with angular melodies and fanfares highlighting perfect intervals; the Egyptian music is languid in tone, luxuriously and sensuously orchestrated with exotic coloration, sinuous melodies, and lush harmonies that suggest Scriabin in his ecstatic moments. Interestingly, Act I, Scene 2, when Caesar and Antony confront each other in the Roman Senate, opens with music that Barber rescued from the beginning of his then-moribund Symphony no. 2. The "love motif" that runs throughout the opera is the composer's familiar interlocking-fourths motif, here ascending instead of descending. (It is notable that this motif also appears in *Vanessa*,

viz., the duet between Erika and Anatol at the end of Act I.) As originally structured, the opera proceeded as a succession of short
scenes, requiring smooth and rapid transitions.

Both composer and librettist later acknowledged that their con-
ceptions were at odds with each other—Barber attempting to create
a human drama and Zeffirelli designing a grand spectacle.
Although Barber attempted to accommodate Zeffirelli's plan to
some extent, their fundamental opposition—not just an opposition
of conception, but of personal temperament as well—proved to be
the work's undoing. The initial critical verdict was that the opera
failed on all counts. Aside from mishaps with the complex stage
machinery, the profusion of characters, locations, and scene changes
was found to detract from the work's thematic focus, while the
music was criticized as purely functional and uninspired, with
much empty declamation, but little of the lyrical expression that listeners were accustomed to expect from the composer. Especially
missed was the presence of a love scene, which seemed peculiar for
a work that hinged on erotic attraction. Most critics seemed to agree
that Act III was the most successful musically, but that it was a matter of too little, too late. In the words of *New York Times* critic Harold
Schonberg, the opera was "neither fully traditional nor fully modern; skillfully put together but lacking ardor and eloquence; big in
sound but stingy with arresting melodic ideas."[79]

The failure of *Antony and Cleopatra* took on a life of its own,
becoming a symbolic representation of the complacent irrelevance
of *bourgeois* cultural institutions in a time of social upheaval. Art, of
course, is subject to different criteria from those applicable to social
or political (or even moral) questions; thus inferences or extrapola-
tions cannot be made from one realm to the other. However, social
and political issues are easier to discuss than issues of aesthetics—
modern aesthetics in particular. As a result, artists are often discussed—in the general press as well as in casual conversation—on
the basis of their social "image" or affiliation—especially in times of
social polarization. By the mid-1960s a growing antiestablishment
feeling had begun to reach the most sclerotic cultural institutions, if
only in the form of that fatuous vanity that became known as "radical chic." Barber, comfortably enshrined in middle age, had become
an easy target for people who couldn't distinguish his music from
Aaron Copland's but who saw him as the well-fed beneficiary of
artistic complacency and social privilege—two unpardonable sins
according to the standards of "radical chic."

Despite the devastating emotional effect of the opera's failure on Barber, he soon began to reexamine the work and consider how it might be salvaged through revision. His first step was to create a concert piece from two of Cleopatra's key scenes: the first, "Give me some music" from Act I, in which she muses with self-satisfaction about her heroic lover; the second, "Give me my robe" from Act III, as she proceeds to place a poisonous snake to her breast, rather than be humiliated by the victorious Caesar. (Cleopatra's "death motif," incidentally, is another that hinges on a single harmonic shift, between the minor tonic and its submediant.) Framed by an orchestral introduction and a connecting interlude, the two excerpts make a stunning impact. Completed in 1968, they were recorded the following year by Leontyne Price, who represented them magnificently, thereby giving succinct, concrete evidence of the high quality of the music that lay dormant in the opera. Also apparent from these two scenes is the similarity of this music to Barber's previous work, *Andromache's Farewell*: its opulent orchestration, with touches of exoticism and suggestions of antiquity, its regal grandeur, serpentine chromaticism, and blistering, at times angular, intensity. Price's recording awakened an interest among admirers of modern opera, and of Barber in particular, in the possibility of a major revision of the entire work.

Barber finally enlisted Menotti's active participation, and the two worked intensively from 1972 to 1974 on a thorough overhaul of the work's structure. In the process, they condensed the action, eliminating several characters and many of the spectacular elements, in an effort to highlight the relationship between the two principals and the work's essential conflict. More than an hour of music was removed, while a love scene was added in Act II, with a duet, "Oh take, oh take those lips away," whose text was drawn from a different, but contemporaneous play. (This luxuriant music is based on the harmonic shift from a major tonic up to a major-quality chord built a minor-third above.) The revised version, with Zeffirelli's name removed from the libretto, was first presented in February 1975 by the Juilliard American Opera Center. Now the response was far more favorable, pointing the way to a production at the Spoleto Festival in 1983, which was released the following year on a recording that went on to win a Grammy Award.

From a later perspective, one can recognize the strengths of *Antony and Cleopatra* as well as its weaknesses, while contemplating the question of how it happened that the world's leading opera company invested enormous resources in bringing together two experienced, successful creative figures, along with legions of other gifted individuals, to produce an epochal work, and instead, gave birth to a disaster. The very notion of two celebrated artists working in tandem, yet pursuing two divergent visions—each fully aware of what the other was doing yet stubbornly persisting in his own vision—is almost operatic itself in the extravagance of its folly. One returns to Rudolf Bing's comment, quoted earlier—"Zeffirelli was—we all were—somewhat doubtful about the music, and overproduced the opera"—and wonders why they were doubtful. Of what? Barber's competence? His judgment? Perhaps, in light of the occasion, Zeffirelli's notion of a grand spectacle *was* the more suitable idea. But if they wanted that sort of blockbuster, why did they approach Barber in the first place? It was no secret that he didn't compose that kind of music. In spite of that, however, much of the "grand" music—the choral Prologue, for example—is gripping. Actually, the weakest aspect of the opera is the excessive declamation in the Roman scenes—those involving Caesar, for example. Regardless of how it is justified dramatically, lengthy declamation always detracts from an opera's impact. On the other hand, much of Cleopatra's music reaches the highest standards set by Barber in his finest mature works. Indeed, it might be argued that ultimately the work's most advantageous representation is through Cleopatra's "Two Scenes," as arranged for concert performance.

A good deal of the early criticism involved the work's failure to meet the high dramatic standards suitable for Shakespeare. Opera is an unwieldy, intransigent, and circumscribed art form, with few necessary or sufficient conditions for its success. Therefore it seems foolish to complain about unfulfilled theoretical ideals. What ultimately matters is what an opera does do—not what it doesn't do. And history certainly demonstrates that an opera rises or falls on its music. Few successful operas actually meet the highest standards of drama, yet the issue continually arises with regard to new operas. More relevant questions are: Does the music support and enhance the basic emotional tone of the drama? Does the music carry the dramatic progression without weighing it down? Is the music compelling and satisfying in its own right? Is the vocal writing practical and effective?

Applying these questions to the revised version of the opera, one

is likely to answer in the affirmative, perhaps with some reservations. The opera as it now stands is a torrid melodrama of sexual
obsession set against an exotic, ancient Mediterranean backdrop.
The music is affecting and engrossing for the most part, propelled
by a readily graspable dramatic and musical logic, a consistent style
and emotional tone, and plenty of musical lines that remain in the
memory. Sumptuously orchestrated, quite a few of its fifteen scenes
boast music of stunning lyricism and majestic nobility in Barber's
mature Neo-Romantic style. Furthermore, despite the cloud of failure that has hung over the work for decades, its music has left its
mark on much of the operatic and vocal output of younger American composers who have followed in the Barber tradition, from Stephen Sondheim to Thomas Pasatieri.

The next new work Barber composed, after the *Antony and Cleopatra* debacle of 1966, was once again designed for Leontyne Price: a
song cycle with the provocative title *Despite and Still*. Completed in
1968, the group was introduced by its dedicatee in New York City,
in April of the following year. A comparison of this cycle with, for
example, the op. 10 and op. 13 songs provides striking evidence of
the extent to which the composer's ability to reflect subtleties of
meaning and emotion had deepened over the course of three decades. The five songs that comprise the cycle seem riddled with autobiographical implications on a number of levels. Three are settings
of poems by Robert Graves—one of Barber's favorite poets. The
group opens with "A Last Song," taken from Graves's "A Last
Poem." The song addresses with some despair the compulsion to
continue writing piece after piece, beyond the point of creative
exhaustion. At that time in his life Barber frequently expressed the
wish to be done with composing. "My Lizard (Wish for a Young
Love)," which Barber changed from Theodore Roethke's "Wish for
a Young Wife," is a light-hearted song that seems directed toward
some of the young men whose intimate companionship the composer enjoyed. In setting Graves's "In the Wilderness" Barber
returns to his spiritual preoccupations. With the wide-ranging, yet
largely diatonic minor-key melody characteristic of much of his
later music, the song seems to recall both the innocent piety of several of the *Hermit Songs* and the dichotomous imagery of spiritual
purity and madness that Barber expressed in "Bessie Bobtail," from
the op. 2 songs. "Solitary Hotel" is a passage taken from Joyce's
Ulysses, written in a verbal shorthand that almost suggests a scene

from a movie script. Barber set it as a tango, with the vocal line standing apart, giving it a tone of wry detachment. The song is especially clever and appealing, with the affectionately satirical quality that Barber managed so deftly. This and the Roethke setting provide contrast to the three Graves songs, which touch on matters of more serious personal importance to the composer. The cycle's overall title comes from the last Graves setting, "Despite and Still." The title seems to suggest a statement of defiance—the composer's return to the musical battlefield after recovering from the severe wound of rejection, unrepentant and with his aesthetic values intact. On the other hand, the poem itself seems concerned with allegiance to an imperfect romance, in spite of alternative opportunities that may have arisen and been sampled. (One cannot help recalling the strains that had developed between Barber and Menotti during this period.) The song displays a passionate intensity that seems to summarize the cycle as a whole and reveals perhaps more vehemence than the poem conveys by itself. One finds in these songs the musical and psychological depth and complexity characteristic of Barber's later work, as well as the sense of disillusionment tinged with self-pity that marked his last years.

Also completed in 1968 were Two Choruses, op. 42, brief settings of two quite divergent poems for mixed voices a capella. Throughout his creative life Barber returned to religious themes, which elicited some of his purest, most deeply felt expressions. But he invariably preferred spiritually inspired poetry to standard liturgical texts. (The only exception is the ex post facto setting of *Agnus Dei*.) Laurie Lee's "Twelfth Night" uses religious metaphor to intensify and deepen its evocation of mood and atmosphere in describing a winter night. This poem elicited an especially haunting lyricism from Barber. The companion piece is a setting of "To be Sung on the Water," a poem of more secular, but no less evocative, mood and tone by Louise Bogan.

In 1971, Barber completed what was to be his final major work and one of the masterpieces of his mature period: a secular cantata entitled *The Lovers*, scored for bass-baritone solo, mixed chorus, and orchestra, based on poems by Pablo Neruda, the Chilean poet who was to win the Nobel Prize for literature the following year. In its vivid and intensely personal portrayal of the cycle of love, from lustful relish to resignation and despair, the work is a final display of the exquisitely precise emotional expression that was Barber's par-

ticular gift, the mastery of which he pursued and refined throughout his creative life. Dedicated to his young companion Valentin
Herranz, *The Lovers* comprises settings of nine poems in English
translation, some set for solo voice, others for various choral combinations, with richly luxuriant orchestral accompaniment. A little
more than half an hour in duration, the cantata begins with an
extraordinarily evocative orchestral introduction, which sets the
tone and mood, while introducing motifs that unify the work. With
details that uncannily suggest an image of sensual languor in an
outdoor tropical paradise, the introduction gradually accumulates
energy and force until it explodes in ecstatic agony, foreshadowing
both motivically and expressively the emotional course to follow.
The first five settings convey scenes and images of aggressive, masculine sexuality, erotic play against an exotic backdrop, serene postcoital bliss, and timeless sensual indulgence. It must be conceded
that these sections are not all equally compelling musically,
although the third, "In the hot depths of this summer," scored for
women's voices, displays the distinctive bittersweet beauty irresistible to so many listeners. The sixth setting, "Sometimes"—a very
brief quasi-*parlando*—represents the turning point of the cycle, while
the final three sections convey with unmatched eloquence the disillusionment and anguish of romantic loss. The eighth, "Tonight I can
write," is a baritone solo that culminates in the lines, "To think that
I do not have her./To feel that I have lost her," set to the climactic
melodic line from the introduction, thus providing a chilling apotheosis of the grief that frames the entire work. The final section,
"Cemetery of kisses," is a haunting choral epilogue that ends the
work in despair and resignation.

   Commissioned by the Girard Bank of Philadelphia (whose directors initially balked—so it has been reported—at the blatant eroticism of lines penned by the avowedly Communist poet), *The Lovers*
was first performed in September 1971. Tom Krause was the bass-
baritone soloist, with the Philadelphia Orchestra and the Temple
University Choir conducted by Eugene Ormandy. The critical reception was mixed. Typical was the comment of Andrew Derhen: "*The
Lovers* leans on any number of earlier Barber works without measur-
ing up to its predecessors or achieving stylistic solidarity."[80] However, other critics, such as Harold Schonberg, felt that the work
represented the composer "at his very best." He believed that it
would "help re-establish Mr. Barber's reputation as America's most

important lyricist.''[81] After its initial performances, the work languished, unperformed, for two decades. Not until 1991 was it revived by the Chicago Symphony Orchestra. At that time, program annotator Phillip Huscher predicted that *The Lovers* would eventually be regarded as "one of the truest examples of Barber's individual voice, and of music's timeless ability to convey deep personal emotion.''[82]

Also in 1971, Barber completed a short piece—really, little more than a sketch—for orchestra, entitled *Fadograph of a Yestern Scene*, after a quizzical line in Joyce's *Finnegan's Wake*. Barber's first purely instrumental work since the Piano Concerto, the piece was commissioned by the Alcoa Foundation for the opening of Heinz Hall in Pittsburgh. William Steinberg conducted the first performance with the Pittsburgh Symphony in September 1971. Barely eight minutes long, the piece opens with a characteristic oboe solo, against a backdrop of shimmering strings. The melody evolves as it is passed from one solo instrument to another, in a pure evocation of mood. Luxuriantly scored throughout, it is rather like an idyll, or perhaps a cinematic scene-without-words. In its absence of classical design, it might be likened to the composer's "essay" concept, except that it is devoid of either contrast or conflict, maintaining a consistently gentle, pastoral tone, tinged with the flavor of Sibelius. A thematic idea from the Second Symphony, also used in *Antony and Cleopatra*, recurs here, but so transformed in character as to be barely recognizable. There is also a theme that will appear again in the *Essay no. 3*. Although the piece is more tantalizing than satisfying, it illustrates the increased emphasis on mood and atmosphere—here, to the exclusion of virtually all other elements—evoked with extraordinary subtlety, elegance, and precision of instrumental coloration, with which much of Barber's late orchestral music is concerned. Appearing at a time when the composer's reputation was at its nadir and when its sensuous gestures and sumptuous sonorities were anathema to the critical community, the piece was contemptuously dismissed. "There is little that is viable, little that holds the attention," wrote Carl Apone. "This is more like a man doodling than digging. The language is hardly in the twentieth-century vocabulary, and future historians will puzzle at its place on the opening of a new hall in America in 1971.''[83]

In 1972, around the time he decided to undertake the major revision of *Antony and Cleopatra*, Barber composed his Three Songs, op.

45. They had been commissioned by the Chamber Music Society of Lincoln Center for Dietrich Fischer-Dieskau, at that time the world's most celebrated male exponent of the *Lieder* repertoire. Perhaps in reference to the German baritone's customary repertoire, Barber selected three European poems, albeit in English translation—the first and third from German, the second from Polish. However, the style and tone of these songs are essentially equivalent to those of the recent *Despite and Still* cycle, and the texts are similarly tinged with autobiographical implications. The first, "Now Have I Fed and Eaten up the Rose," sets a translation by James Joyce of a poem by the Swiss Gottfried Keller. Its obliquely death-related imagery becomes clearer upon consideration that the text is one of those set by Swiss composer Othmar Schoeck in his ambitious Keller cycle, *Buried Alive* (which had already been recorded by Fischer-Dieskau). Barber's mournful setting highlights a characteristically modal melody built around a minor triad with added minor sixth. The second, "A Green Lowland of Pianos," sets a poem by Jerzy Harasymowicz, translated by Czeslaw Milosz. It is the sort of image-laden, surrealistic nonsense poem (not unlike *Nuvoletta*) that occasionally appealed to Barber and that he set in his affectionately satirical manner. The third, a setting of Georg Heym, translated by Christopher Middleton as "O Boundless, Boundless Evening," is Barber's final contribution to the song repertoire. The poem is a resigned acceptance of the approach of death, which Barber sets with a floridly ornamented, poignantly retrospective expansiveness. Strongly valedictory in tone, it is the most strikingly Germanic music Barber had composed since the early 1930s, but the resemblance now is to Strauss—or, even more so, to Korngold—rather than to Brahms. The first performance of these songs was delayed, due to Fischer-Dieskau's illness, until April 1974, when the baritone presented them at Lincoln Center's Alice Tully Hall.

Occupied with the *Antony and Cleopatra* revision, and weakened by emotional and health problems, Barber did not produce another work until 1977, when he completed *Ballade*, a short test-piece for piano solo that had been commissioned by the Van Cliburn Foundation three years earlier, for its International Piano Competition. The *Ballade* suggests a nocturnal fantasy, atmospheric and mysterious in character. The outline of its basic motif—four descending steps—is almost identical to the main motif of the *Music for a Scene from Shelley*, composed more than forty years earlier. In the *Ballade*, the motif is presented in an intriguing harmonic context, pregnant with possibilities for development. Its unfolding during the outer sections of the piece is reminiscent of the music of Ernest Bloch, while the turbulent middle section recalls Scriabin. Unfortunately, however, with a duration of barely six minutes, the piece offers little more than a hint of possibilities that might have been pursued. While its approximate length was specified in the commission, the *Ballade* seems short breathed, its material reiterated rather than truly developed. As one more addition to the composer's relatively small solo piano output, it has been rapidly absorbed into the repertoire, but it is not a fully realized composition, and few pianists have been able to shape it into a satisfying whole.

For his last completed work, Barber returned to the concept of the *Essay for Orchestra*, which he had explored twice in the past. Commissioned by Audrey Sheldon, a wealthy admirer who committed suicide before the work's premiere, *Essay no. 3* was composed during the summer of 1978. It was first performed that September, as part of Zubin Mehta's debut concert as Music Director of the New York Philharmonic.

The *Third Essay* is longer and more loosely structured than its two predecessors, displaying the perfumed languor and luxuriant orchestration characteristic of Barber's later compositions. Like so many of these works, it is fundamentally an evocation of mood—a complex mood in which hedonistic pleasure is subtly blended with veins of ennui and remorse. But without the attention and understanding of a sympathetic conductor, certain undeniable formal weaknesses can render it unfocused and labored. The work opens with twenty-seven measures of percussion only, during which an irregular rhythmic motif is presented. As the other instruments enter, a jagged melodic contour emphasizing the interval of the fourth is added to the rhythmic motif, which bounces down and up the orchestra, picking up substance and momentum, as other tiny figures appear. This lengthy introduction appears to be something of a miscalculation: not only do details of pitch and rhythm fail to emerge clearly during the opening percussion passage, but the expressive effect of the entire section remains quizzical—is it ominous, grotesque, or playful? Ideas are presented, then seem to peter out, held together only by artifice. Whatever its intended character, this section proves to be a form of stage setting, as the atmosphere is gradually transformed to a more intimate mood of sultry sensuality, almost as if a camera has zoomed in from a panoramic view to focus on the protagonists of a torrid love scene. This scene—the main body of the *Essay*—is built around four lyrical ideas, all derived from the rhythm and/or the melodic shapes of the motifs heard in the introductory section. The first three are heard in relatively quick succession: the first is introduced by the strings, marked *appassionato;* the second, presented by the euphonium, first appeared several years earlier in the *Fadograph of a Yestern Scene;* the third, which emerges as the work's main melodic idea, is first heard as a sort of rippling melody in the violins and flutes; the fourth, yearning in character, is introduced a little later by the English horn, accompanied by the harps. Interspersed with occasional reminders of the more angular rhythmic and melodic motifs from the introduction, these ideas writhe in and around each other, gradually building in intensity. Finally, the third idea reaches an opulent climax in the full orchestra, marked "with exaltation." However, this climax, achieved chiefly through orchestration and texture, is somewhat obligatory in effect, with a frustrating paralysis of harmonic motion and consummation. The climax has barely subsided when the tempo increases, and the jagged material from the introduction reappears, bringing the work to an almost brusque conclusion. (Originally, the ending was even more abrupt; after the premiere, Barber extended it slightly.)

While Barber was still working on the *Essay*, he had already received a commission from Francis Goelet to compose an oboe concerto for the New York Philharmonic and its long-time first oboist Harold Gomberg. This would have been a fortuitous assignment for Barber, as he had favored the instrument throughout his career as the initial vehicle for many of his most beloved melodic ideas. However his failing health prevented him from writing any more than what would have been the work's slow movement. Realizing in 1980 that he would not live to complete the concerto, Barber suggested that the single movement stand by itself, with the title *Canzonetta.* Left with the piece in short score, his student and long-time friend Charles Turner completed a simple arrangement for string orchestra.

The eight-minute elegy proved to be a most touching farewell, unfolding a long-breathed, largely diatonic melody laden with sadness, its poignant suspensions and mournful *appoggiaturas* conjuring a bittersweet dignity that harks back to Barber's early period (e.g., the Violin Concerto, slow movement). After this long melody, which might be heard as a final lament of Barber's "vulnerable child," follows its serpentine course, it is punctuated by a rather insouciant, strangely Mahlerian *codetta*—chromatic, with prominent use of fourths—which provides touches of irony and bitterness. It is almost as if Barber's jaded, disillusioned "adult" were gently mocking the "child's" tender innocence. These two ideas are then repeated in abbreviated form, the first returning once more to bring the piece to an end. *Canzonetta* was not performed until December 1981—almost a year after the composer's death—when Gomberg played it with the New York Philharmonic, under Zubin Mehta's direction.

CONCLUSION

At the time of Barber's death his career and reputation had been at their nadir for fifteen years, since the failure of *Antony and Cleopatra*. Although a number of his works—the *Adagio for Strings*, *Knoxville*, the Violin Concerto, the Piano Sonata, several of the short orchestral pieces—had become sufficiently established in the active repertoire to be immune to shifts in fashion, the general status of his reputation among "serious" critics was that of a skilled craftsman who had won great popular and commercial success by producing ingratiating replicas of established masterpieces, which looked back nostalgically to simpler times, using a familiar musical language that flattered, rather than challenged, its audience (e.g., see quotation from review of *Fadograph*). But the ink on his obituaries had barely dried when a revival began—initially, not a revival articulated through analytical reconsideration, but, rather, through a burst of performances, as a younger generation of celebrity soloists and conductors embraced not only his established "classics," but other pieces that had been largely waiting on the sidelines. As has been illustrated throughout this study, a composer's death seems somehow to neutralize much of the bitterness and resentment that may surround him while still among the living; only then does the music itself achieve a more vivid profile than the person, rather than the other way around.

While Barber's posthumous revival occurred on too broad a scale to document in detail, several key events can serve as landmarks. In

1983, the revised version of *Antony and Cleopatra* was mounted at both Spoleto Festivals, in Italy as well as in the United States. A recording made from these performances was released in 1984 and won a Grammy Award. In 1986, Oliver Stone's film *Platoon* was released, which featured the *Adagio for Strings* prominently on the soundtrack, bringing the piece to the awareness of a younger general audience. In 1989, an all-Barber orchestral disc, featuring Leonard Slatkin conducting the Saint Louis Symphony, was released, followed by another, with the same performers, in 1991. Also in 1989, with permission granted by the Barber estate, a new recording of the Symphony no. 2 was released, in a performance by the New Zealand Symphony Orchestra, led by the gifted American conductor Andrew Schenck. This recording, widely praised by a new generation of critics and listeners, led to further performances and recordings of the work during the years that followed. With that release conductor Schenck initiated a major Barber recording project that culminated with the 1992 release of the premiere recording of *The Lovers,* coupled with the *Prayers of Kierkegaard,* in performances by the Chicago Symphony Orchestra and Chorus. That recording too was awarded a Grammy. Unfortunately, Schenck's ambitious project was ended prematurely by the conductor's death from cancer while he was still in his thirties. In that year David Zinman and the Baltimore Symphony also released an all-Barber orchestral disc, and Barbara Heyman's book *Samuel Barber: The Composer and his Music* was published by the Oxford University Press. In 1994, Deutsche Grammophon released a set of two compact discs, featuring soprano Cheryl Studer, baritone Thomas Hampson, and pianist John Browning in a comprehensive survey of all Barber's songs. In 1996, with the reissue of several highly regarded recorded performances conducted by Thomas Schippers, another staunch Barber advocate who died prematurely in 1977, Tim Page commented, "It was particularly unfair that Schippers should die right before the great surge of interest in the music of Samuel Barber (sadder still that Barber himself did not live to see it; he died in 1981, as his spectacular reappraisal was just beginning)."[84]

Today Barber's entire *oeuvre* is available on recordings, most of the highest artistic caliber, a statement that can be made about very few composers of the twentieth century. Many of his works have entered the active repertoire, and more are joining them continually. It is likely that most of his output will achieve the widespread popularity of the *Adagio, Knoxville,* and the Violin Concerto, simply because so much of it is comparable in appeal. At this writing (2003), according to statistics compiled by the American Symphony Orchestra League, Samuel Barber's is the most frequently performed American orchestral music, well ahead of that composed by Leonard Bernstein, Aaron Copland, and George Gershwin—the runners-up.

In *American Composers and Their Public,* Nicholas Tawa wrote:

> Barber's highly developed and sophisticated mind completely understood how great was the denigration that nineteenth-century romanticism has had to endure, as much because of its strengths as because of its weaknesses. From the public's point of view, modern composers miscalculated terribly when they quickly erected a wall between themselves and expression like Barber's by giving it a repugnant cultural stamp. There existed a cultural emptiness in twentieth-century life that militants, ready ferociously to attack intrusions from the reactionary camp, have not fully appreciated and which Barber's music fills. He, more than they, was conscious of the debasement of humane feeling that came from the radical camp. Moreover, he perceived that part of the void in people's existence could be filled with melody. Throughout his lifetime, Barber composed music distinguished by its unflagging songfulness. Music lovers found his genius for lyricism, its effortless spinning out and vast expressive amplitude, in few contemporary European and American composers. Add to this an acute sensitivity to structure and a coherent unfolding of the emotional content and one can understand the singular merit of his compositions in the opinion of the unbiased.[85]

NOTES

1. Barbara B. Heyman, *Samuel Barber: The Composer and His Music* (New York: Oxford University Press, 1992).

2. Quoted in Heyman, *Barber,* 7.

3. Quoted in Heyman, *Barber,* 18.

4. Quoted in Heyman, *Barber,* 37–38.

5. Quoted in Heyman, *Barber,* 513.

6. Quoted in Heyman, *Barber,* 130.

7. Quoted in Heyman, *Barber,* 134.

8. Aaron Copland, "Our Younger Generation: Ten Years Later," *Modern Music* (May–June 1936), reprinted in *Copland on Music* (New York: Doubleday, 1960), 160.

9. Quoted in Heyman, *Barber,* 153.

10. Ashley Pettis, Letter to *New York Times* (13 November 1938).

11. Laura Haddock, "Boston Hears Symphony Dedicated to the Air Forces," *Christian Science Monitor* (3 March 1944).

12. Quoted in Heyman, *Barber*, 226.

13. Samuel Barber, Interviewed by James Fassett, CBS (19 June 1949), quoted in Heyman, *Barber*, 279.

14. Phillip Ramey, "Samuel Barber at Seventy," *Ovation* (March 1980): 20.

15. Quoted in Heyman, *Barber*, 301.

16. Quoted in Heyman, *Barber*, 311.

17. Quoted in Heyman, *Barber*, 317.

18. Allan Kozinn, "Samuel Barber: The Last Interview and the Legacy," *High Fidelity* (June 1981): 46.

19. Ramey, "Barber at Seventy," 19.

20. Ray Ellsworth, "Americans on Microgroove, Part II," *High Fidelity* (August 1956): 61.

21. Paul Henry Lang, "New American Opera Is Hailed at the Met," *New York Herald Tribune* (16 January 1958).

22. Peter Gradenwitz, "New Music at the European Festivals," *Chesterian* (Autumn 1958): 52.

23. Quoted in Tim Page, Record Liner Notes, Sony MHK-62837, 1996.

24. Jay S. Harrison, Review, *Musical America* (December 1963): 178.

25. B. H. Haggin, Review, *New Republic* (30 January 1965): 31.

26. Hans Heinsheimer, "The Composing Composer: Samuel Barber," *ASCAP Today* (1968): 4.

27. Hans Heinsheimer, "An Opera Is Born," Metropolitan Opera Program Book (16 September 1966): 50.

28. Harold Schonberg, "Onstage, It Was 'Antony and Cleopatra,'" *New York Times* (17 September 1966).

29. John Gruen, "And Where Has Samuel Barber Been . . . ?" *New York Times* (3 October 1971).

30. Sydney Edwards, "Paste Amid the Diamonds," *Music and Musicians* (November 1966): 20.

31. Richard Dyer, Record Liner Notes, New World NW-322/23/24-2, 1984.

32. Gruen, "And Where . . . "

33. Quoted in Dyer, Record Liner Notes.

34. Kozinn, "Samuel Barber," 46.

35. Donal Henahan, "Samuel Barber, Composer, Dead," *New York Times* (24 January 1981).

36. Quoted in John Browning, Record Liner Notes, Deutsche Grammophon 435 867-2, 1994.

37. Gruen, "And Where . . ."

38. Browning, Record Liner Notes.

39. Ramey, "Barber at Seventy," 18.

40. Ramey, "Barber at Seventy," 19.

41. Martin Anderson, Record Liner Notes, Solstice SOCD-145, 1996.

42. W. J. Henderson, Review, *New York Sun* (25 March 1935).

43. Quoted in Heyman, *Barber*, 174–175.

44. Wilfrid Mellers, Record Liner Notes, ASV DCA-939, 1995.

45. Olin Downes, Review, *New York Times* (12 February 1941).

46. Donald Fuller, Review, *Modern Music* (March–April 1941): 168.

47. Malcolm Rayment, Review, *Records and Recording* (April 1975): 21.

48. David W. Moore, Review, *American Record Guide* (May 1980): 16.

49. Donald Fuller, Review, *Modern Music* (May–June 1942): 254.

50. Goddard Lieberson, Review, *Modern Music* (November–December 1938): 67.

51. Quoted in Heyman, *Barber*, 244.

52. Charles Mills, Review, *Modern Music* (Winter 1946): 74.

53. Noel Straus, Review, *New York Times* (9 October 1944).

54. Anonymous Review, *Musical America* (October 1944): 24.

55. Robert Sabin, Review, *Musical America* (August 1951): 30.

56. Albert Goldberg, Review, *Los Angeles Times* (20 April 1970).

57. Virgil Thomson, Review, *New York Herald Tribune* (9 December 1947).

58. Ramey, "Barber at Seventy," 20.

59. Ramey, "Barber at Seventy," 18.

60. Harold Schonberg, "Letter from America," *Gramophone* (March 1951): 219.

61. Max Harrison, Review, *Gramophone* (March 1981): 1212.

62. Olin Downes, Review, *New York Times* (26 November 1952).

63. Ramey, "Barber at Seventy," 19.

64. Ramey, "Barber at Seventy," 19.

65. Quoted in Heyman, *Barber*, 350.

66. Olin Downes, Review, *New York Times* (9 December 1954).

67. Cyrus Durgin, Review, *Musical America* (1 January 1955): 14.

68. Quoted in Heyman, *Barber*, 357.

69. Peter Rabinowitz, Review, *Fanfare* (November–December 1994): 198.

70. Anonymous Review, *Time* (27 January 1958): 59.

71. Winthrop Sargeant, Review, *New Yorker* (25 January 1958): 100.

72. Paul Henry Lang, Review, *New York Herald Tribune* (16 January 1958).

73. William Olsen, Review, *New Records* (October 1958): 10.

74. Shirley Fleming, Review, *High Fidelity/Musical America* (October 1978): MA43.

75. John von Rhein, Review, *Chicago Tribune* (29 May 1978).

76. Thomas P. Lanier, Review, *Opera News* (7 April 1979): 8.

77. Paul Henry Lang, Review, *New York Herald Tribune* (25 September 1962).

78. Winthrop Sargeant, Review, *New Yorker* (13 April 1963): 153.

79. Harold Schonberg, "Onstage, It Was 'Antony and Cleopatra,'" *New York Times* (17 September 1966).

80. Andrew Derhen, Review, *High Fidelity/Musical America* (January 1972): MA23.

81. Harold Schonberg, Review, *New York Times* (7 October 1971).

82. Phillip Huscher, Record Liner Notes, Koch International 3-7125-2 H1, 1991.

83. Carl Apone, Review, *High Fidelity/Musical America* (January 1972): MA25.

84. Tim Page, Record Liner Notes, Sony MHK-62837, 1996.

85. Nicholas Tawa, *American Composers and Their Public* (Metuchen, N.J.: Scarecrow Press, Inc., 1995), 136–37.

SELECTED BIBLIOGRAPHY

Browning, John. "Samuel Barber: The Songs [Record Liner Notes]." Deutsche Grammophon 435 867-2, 1994: 8–14.

Gruen, John. "And Where Has Samuel Barber Been . . . ?" *New York Times* (3 October 1971).

Heinsheimer, Hans. "The Composing Composer: Samuel Barber." *ASCAP Today* (1968): 4–7.

Henahan, Donal. "Samuel Barber, Composer, Dead." *New York Times* (24 January 1981).

Hennessee, Don A. *Samuel Barber: A Bio-Bibliography*. Westport, Conn.: Greenwood Press, 1985.

Heyman, Barbara B. *Samuel Barber: The Composer and His Music*. New York: Oxford University Press, 1992.

Kozinn, Allan. "Samuel Barber: The Last Interview and the Legacy." *High Fidelity* (June 1981): 43–46, 65–68; (July 1981): 45–47, 80–90.

Ramey, Phillip. "Samuel Barber at Seventy." *Ovation* (March 1980): 14–20.

Schonberg, Harold. "Onstage, It Was 'Antony and Cleopatra.'" *New York Times* (17 September 1966).

ESSENTIAL DISCOGRAPHY

Deutsche Grammophon 435 867-2 (2CDs): Ten Early Songs; Three Songs, Op. 2; *Dover Beach* (Emerson String Qt.); Three Songs, Op. 10; Four Songs, Op. 13; Two Songs, Op. 18; *Nuvoletta*; *Mélodies Passagères*; *Hermit Songs*; *Despite and Still*; Three Songs, Op. 45 (Cheryl Studer, soprano; Thomas Hampson, baritone; John Browning, piano); www.deutschegrammophon.com.

EMI Classics 7243 5-74287/8/9-2 (2CDs): *Overture to the School for Scandal*;

Cello Sonata (Alan Stepansky, cello; Israela Margalit, piano); *Adagio for Strings*; *Essay No. 1*; Violin Concerto (Elmar Oliveira, violin); *Essay No. 2*; *Excursions* (Margalit); *Medea's Meditation and Dance of Vengeance*; *Summer Music* (Baxtresser, Robinson, Drucker, LeClair, Myers); *Nocturne* (Margalit); *Canzone* (Baxtresser, flute; Margalit, piano); *Essay No. 3* (St. Louis Sym. Orch., Leonard Slatkin, cond.); www.emigroup.com.

Guild GMCD-7145: Two Choruses, op. 8; *Agnus Dei*; "Heaven Haven," "Sure on This Shining Night," fm. op. 13; *A Stopwatch and an Ordnance Map*; *Reincarnations*; "The Monk and His Cat," fm. op. 29; *Vanessa*: excerpt; *Wondrous Love* (Jeremy Filsell, organ); *Antony and Cleopatra*: two excerpts; Two Choruses, op. 42; *Chorale Prelude, "Silent Night"* (Filsell); "Happy Birthday" Variation (Filsell); (Cambridge University Chamber Choir; Thomas Adès, piano; Timothy Brown, cond.); www.guildmusic.com.

Koch International 3-7125-2H1: *Prayers of Kierkegaard*; *The Lovers* (Sarah Reese, soprano; Dale Duesing, baritone; Chicago Sym. Chorus and Orch., Andrew Schenck, cond.).

Naxos 8.559024: *Overture to the School for Scandal*; Symphony No. 1; *Essay No. 1*; Symphony No. 2 (Royal Scottish Nat'l. Orch., Marin Alsop, cond.); www.naxos.com.

Naxos 8.559088: *Adagio for Strings*; Cello Concerto (Wendy Warner, cello); *Medea*—Ballet Suite (Royal Scottish Nat'l. Orch., Marin Alsop, cond.); www.naxos.com.

Naxos 8.559133: *Commando March*; *Medea's Meditation and Dance of Vengeance*; *Die Natali*; Piano Concerto (Stephen Prutsman, piano; Royal Scottish Nat'l. Orch., Marin Alsop, cond.); www.naxos.com.

New World NW322/323/324-2 (2CDs): *Antony and Cleopatra* (Esther Hinds, soprano; Jeffrey Wells, bass-baritone; Westminster Choir, Spoleto Fest. Orch., Christian Badea, cond.); www.newworldrecords.org.

RCA Victor 7899-2-RG (2CDs): *Vanessa* (Eleanor Steber, soprano; Rosalind Elias, mezzo-soprano; Nicolai Gedda, tenor; Metropolitan Opera Chor. and Orch., Dimitri Mitropoulos, cond.); www.rcaredseal-rcavictor.com.

RCA Victor 09026-61983-2: Three Songs (w/Samuel Barber, piano); *Nuvoletta* (w/Barber); *Hermit Songs* (w/Barber); *Knoxville: Summer of 1915*; *Antony and Cleopatra*—Two Scenes (Leontyne Price, soprano; New Philharmonia Orch., Thomas Schippers, cond.); www.rcaredseal-rcavictor.com.

Solstice SOCD-145: *Fresh from West Chester*; *Three Sketches*; *Two Interludes*; *Excursions*; Piano Sonata; *Nocturne*; *After the Concert*; *Ballade* (Lilia Boyadjieva, piano).

Sony Classical MHK-62837: *Overture to the School for Scandal*; *Adagio for Strings*; *Essay No. 2*; *Medea's Meditation and Dance of Vengeance*; *Vanessa*—Intermezzo; *Andromache's Farewell* (Martina Arroyo, soprano); (New York Philharmonic, Thomas Schippers, cond.); *www.masterworksheritage.com*.

Nicolas Flagello: Photo provided courtesy of Dianne Flagello.

7

Nicolas Flagello

The story of Nicolas Flagello embodies both tragedy and pathos, but it is one whose broad outlines are not uncommon throughout musical history. Born to a musical family with deep roots in the culture of nineteenth-century Italy, Flagello displayed a significant talent early on, performing publicly as a pianist while still a child. A student—and later colleague—of Vittorio Giannini, Flagello was deeply imbued with the values and practices of European Late Romanticism. Reaching maturity during the late 1940s and early 1950s, he found the hard-edged Modernist styles then in ascendancy cold and impersonal and alien to his temperament. To many of those in positions of power and influence, his music seemed hopelessly out of date, fifty years behind its times. Driven by the idealism instilled in him by Giannini, he produced a prodigious body of work, with little concern for the practical exigencies of a composing career. Then, approaching middle age with little reputation and no means of financial support, he descended into a self-destructive course that alienated friends and allies, damaged his creative abilities, and eventually cost him his health. Only after serious illness had forced his withdrawal from public life did interest in his work and recognition of its merit begin to gather momentum.

BIOGRAPHY

Nicolas Flagello was born in New York City in 1928 into a family that had been steeped in music for generations. His father Dionisio was a successful dress designer and amateur oboist, and his mother Genoveffa had been a singer whose father (Domenico Casiello, a conductor and composer) was said to have studied with Verdi. Flagello's younger brother, Ezio, was to become a world-renowned operatic bass-baritone. The family had immigrated to the United States from Salerno, near Naples, but their strong ties to the homeland left the boys with a stronger identity as Italians than as Americans. Nicolas began piano lessons with a maternal aunt (a conservatory graduate) when he was three and began composing when he was eight. He also took voice lessons and learned to play the violin and several woodwinds, making such rapid progress on the piano that by the time he was seven his parents arranged for him to give public recitals. In addition to playing the piano, he also sang Italian songs as a boy-soprano and was billed as "Il Piccolo Caruso" until his voice changed. He continued performing on the piano throughout his adolescence.

During the late 1930s, friends of the family brought Nicolas to the attention of Vittorio Giannini, another American-born composer with strong ties to Italy, who was at the time enjoying major successes in both the United States and Europe. Giannini took the youngster on as a student in the manner of an Old World apprenticeship, teaching him the craft of composition through hours of drill and study and imbuing him with the ethos as well as the musical principles of the grand European tradition, from Palestrina through Puccini, Debussy, Rachmaninoff, and Strauss. This apprenticeship with Giannini developed into a close personal and professional relationship that lasted until the older man's death in 1966.

Growing up in the Bronx, New York, Nicolas attended Evander Childs High School, while playing violin in Leopold Stokowski's All-American Youth Orchestra. Despite the intensive musical training lavished on him as a child, his parents strongly opposed his pursuing music as a profession. Graduating from high school in 1944, Nicolas turned down a scholarship to study engineering at New York University, much to the dismay of his parents. By now he was committed to music as his life's work and decided to devote the following year to intensive piano study with Adele Marcus (1906–1995). In 1945, he enrolled at the Manhattan School of Music, where he resumed composition study under Giannini, while pursuing conducting with Jonel Perlea (1900–1970). He graduated in 1949, submitting a symphonic poem, which he called *Beowulf*, as his composition thesis. He thereupon joined the Manhattan School faculty himself, while pursuing his master's degree. This he completed the following year, with the composition of his Piano Concerto no. 1. Flagello conducted the work's premiere, with Joseph Seiger as piano soloist.

During the late 1940s and early 1950s, Flagello continued to make frequent concert appearances, performing regularly as piano soloist with the Longines Symphonette, a radio orchestra featuring "light classical" music; the ensemble became so popular during the 1950s that it made a series of national tours. Its conductor, Mishel Piastro (1891–1970), had been a violin student of Leopold Auer and was another Old World character who became a father figure for the young pianist-composer. Not until the mid-1950s did Flagello abandon his career as soloist in order to concentrate on composition and conducting. It was also in 1953 that he married a young percussionist named Dianne Danese.

In 1955, a Fulbright Fellowship enabled Flagello to spend a year at the Accademia di Santa Cecilia in Rome, where he studied with the elderly Ildebrando Pizzetti (1880–1968). There he was awarded an advanced diploma, completing a violin concerto and a large orchestral work, along with several songs and shorter pieces.

Thus Flagello's formative years were far removed from the Modernist mainstream that dominated American music during the 1950s and 1960s. The Modernists' emphasis on complex, quasi-mathematical techniques and their quest for originality were alien to both his temperament and his training. He was offended by their scorn for such traditional romantic values as emotional self-expression and by their contemptuous view of "accessibility" as a form of "selling out." The artistic climate of New York City in particular, with its proud identity as cultural trendsetter, was hardly a sympathetic environment for a young composer with traditionalist values, struggling to find acceptance for his creative efforts. The contempt and hostility that often underlay critics' responses to Neo-Romantic works at that time are clearly reflected in a review of Flagello's *Missa Sinfonica*, composed in 1957 and introduced that year by the orchestra of the Manhattan School. Composer-critic William Flanagan described the work as "conservative in feeling, purple in harmony, razzle-dazzle and a mite trashy in orchestration . . . nothing distinguishes Mr. Flagello's work from the standard concept of what is appropriate for Hollywood background music. . . . One wonders

what interest Mr. Flagello's piece could hold for anyone of cultivated, sophisticated musical taste."[1]

Conservatories, as the word implies, were somewhat less aligned
with the avant-garde in those days than were the music departments
of prestigious universities. As such, the Manhattan School offered
something of a haven for Flagello. There his talent was recognized
and he could rely on the emotional support provided by Giannini
and other older faculty members. Giannini imparted to his students
the belief that "true" creative musical talent was a gift bestowed by
God. Such a gift imposed on the beneficiary an obligation to the ideals of inner truth and personal authenticity, to be pursued with unstinting diligence, humility, and gratitude for having been thus
blessed. Such dedication might result in neglect, misunderstanding,
or disparagement; one may be tempted to compromise or to accept
defeat. But to yield to such temptation would be tantamount to a
betrayal of God. Flagello embraced this doctrine and attempted to
adhere to it, writing only the music that emanated from his inner
voice, appending to each score the initials *AMDG* (*Ad Maiorem Dei
Gloria*), and refusing to concern himself with practical considerations that might promote the exposure of his works.

By the time he turned thirty in 1958, Flagello had completed about
twenty-five works, including four operas, four concertos, and several large orchestral and choral pieces, as well as solo piano pieces,
songs, and other vocal music. However, hardly any of this music
had been played, aside from a few readings by the performing
ensembles of the Manhattan School.

Nevertheless, Flagello entered the 1960s with optimism, confident
that success lay ahead, despite the challenges of supporting a family
that now included two sons. His wife devoted herself to creating a
secure home life that would enable him to devote virtually all his
energy to creative work. Taking on increased responsibilities at the
Manhattan School, he conducted the orchestra and led opera productions and directed the school's division of general studies, as
well as teaching composition. Opportunities to conduct for recordings seemed to be increasing, in Italy as well as in the United States,
as his talent began to gain attention among professionals in the
music world. Promising opportunities stimulated his creativity, and
new compositions, revealing a greater stylistic maturity, appeared
at a rapid rate. Between 1959 and 1968, Flagello completed more
than thirty works, of which virtually every one—even a five-minute

contest piece for accordion—is a serious artistic statement. During
this period, his creative drive was so consuming that he often left
orchestral works in short score, postponing the orchestration until a
time when performance seemed imminent. (Unfortunately, this
practice resulted in a number of major works left unorchestrated at
the time of his death.)

One of the figures who took an interest in Flagello during the
early 1960s was Paul Kapp, a music publisher who had the good
fortune to own the copyright of the popular song "I Left My Heart
in San Francisco." Kapp decided to use the profits from this song
to form an ancillary company (General Music) and a record label
(Serenus) to promote serious living composers whose music
appealed to him. He chose Flagello as his flagship composer, as well
as conductor for his own and others' music, with an initial release
in 1964 of four all-Flagello discs, featuring some fifteen different
works. These recordings, issued in 1964, were well received by those
critics who gave them notice at all. Composer-critic Arthur Cohn
praised Flagello's:

> stimulating ingenuity in using harmonic materials . . . that are basi-
> cally familiar. The dynamic consequence of a composer's having no
> temerity in spinning a tune, shaping a generous hunk of melody,
> avowing a love for determinable balances, is exceedingly rewarding. It
> is not necessary to be a revolutionary. If a music manifests fresh
> melodicism, expressed by freed triadic prose and certified by rhythmic
> ripeness, it needs no apology. . . . The intervallic amalgamation indi-
> cates a romantic foothold with the drag and assertative value of pun-
> gent criss-crossed chromaticism: a full partnership that has stylistic
> propriety.[2]

Enos Shupp Jr., simply wrote, "If this is not great music, we will
gladly turn in our typewriter and quit."[3]

Despite the prevailing Modernist bias against traditional styles, a
number of critics were clearly impressed by what they were hearing.
In 1961, the Manhattan School Opera Theater mounted Flagello's
fourth opera, *The Sisters*. John Gruen described it as "first rate, at
least musically. Mr. Flagello has the gift of writing gratefully for the
voice, and his music has melodic sumptuousness. His orchestral texture is crystal-clear, and he knows how to underline dramatic
events."[4] Richard Freed, reviewing the first performance of Flagello's Violin Sonata, described it as "a well-constructed, highly

romantic work in three concise movements, ranging from a dark, impassioned dialogue for the two instruments to a warmly lyrical quasi recitativo to a humoresque-tarantella of almost diabolical brilliance. . . . [The performance] made the strongest of impressions for his sonata, which can be expected to be added to the general repertory."[5] And when the Manhattan School produced Flagello's fifth opera, *The Judgment of Saint Francis*, in 1966, Allen Hughes described it as "a new opera of some stature, considerable color and great volumes of sound,"[6] while *The New Yorker*'s Winthrop Sargeant called it "musically the most vigorous new opera I have come across in a long time. . . . [Flagello] has shown an unmistakable and totally unconfused talent for the operatic theatre."[7]

But these encouraging responses failed to lead to commissions, to further recordings, or to performances beyond the confines of the Manhattan School. Nor did Flagello's efforts to build a conducting career bear fruit, aside from some minor guest appearances and sporadic recording jobs. And Paul Kapp's cantankerous personality and his exclusive focus on unknown composers created distribution problems for Serenus records, which soon became almost impossible to find. Flagello was becoming bitter and pessimistic. Although he continued to voice Giannini's dictum that an artist must concern himself with only the creation of his art, and that popular success was an empty, meaningless pursuit, he nevertheless craved both respect and recognition. Yet in truth, Flagello did little to encourage more auspicious presentations of his work, simply stuffing manuscript after manuscript into a closet.

In 1964, Giannini arranged for Flagello to fill the position he was forced to vacate at the Curtis Institute. Giannini, as founding president, was hoping that Flagello would join him in North Carolina the following year, when the school was to open. In poor health, the older man did not expect to remain active very long and planned to install Flagello as his successor. But Flagello felt that residency in New York was essential for building his reputation and declined the opportunity.

Some of the difficulties Flagello faced in drawing attention to his work must be attributed to certain self-defeating aspects of his own personality. Within the social aristocracy that constitutes the world of classical music—including much of the audience and many of the professionals—a fawning, epicene personal charm and elegant manner often convey an artistic temperament more convincingly than does its actual creative manifestation. Flagello, not unlike Mozart, was an unfortunate misfit in this social milieu. His personal appearance betrayed a fondness for flashy clothes and accoutrements, and his verbal expression was stilted and awkward, heavily inflected with vestiges of his Bronx-Italian background. To conceal his discomfort and insecurity, he cultivated a brusque, unapproachable manner. The resulting persona seemed more appropriate to a gangster movie than to the concert hall. Furthermore, when musicians or listeners actually expressed interest in his work, he often rebuffed them with feigned indifference. (Such self-defeating behavior is not uncommon among composers who have endured years of neglect and disparagement: composers like Allan Pettersson and Kaikhosru Sorabji actually banned performances of their own music.) Inquiries from soloists and conductors—including some quite celebrated figures—went unanswered. For example, in a letter dated February 5, 1970, musicologist Nicolas Slonimsky wrote to Flagello, "For several years I have listened to your music . . . and admired it intensely. I simply cannot understand why your name is not in any book dealing with important twentieth-century composers, and why your works are so seldom played by major symphonic or chamber music organizations. I should like very much to include information on your major works [in new editions of several of my books]." There is no indication that Flagello ever responded to this letter.

Among trusted friends, Flagello was exuberant, earthy, and spontaneous and loved to recount extravagant tales of his own exploits. But presenting himself as a "serious composer" seemed an uncomfortable pretense to him, and he made little effort to inform friends and associates about his creative efforts. In fact, he expressed little interest when his music was performed, insisting that he derived no particular pleasure from hearing it. This casual, offhand manner led many of those close to him to regard his composing as a pastime of no consequence; often they were unprepared for the uncompromisingly serious tone of his work. Flagello himself was aware of these inconsistencies but had no explanation for them, appearing to be as bewildered by his own talent and the fruits it bore as were those around him. He would often say, "A composer has two sides to himself—one that he shows to others, and the other he brings out in his music."[8] And when asked why he composed, because he seemed so indifferent to having his work performed, he would shrug his shoulders and reply, "I don't know—I can't stop."

Then in his early forties, Flagello worked desperately to build a professional career—conducting operas in Italy and orchestras in South America, making recordings of movie themes, mood music, and Baroque music, making arrangements of light classics, managing music festivals in Italy, composing background music for TV commercials, and even ghostwriting for other composers. But there was still little interest or activity concerning his serious compositions. His despondence began to affect his personal life. After twenty years of marriage—perhaps because of a sense of shame and personal failure—he left his wife, who had consistently maintained her conviction in his genius. His creativity dwindled, as alcoholism and other self-destructive behaviors gradually ravaged his health and sanity. At this time, he began to fabricate a grandiose revision of the details of his life, one that corresponded more closely to his preferred self-image. As time went on he increasingly appeared to believe his own fictions.

Ironically, it was during this time that the de facto boycott of traditionalist music began to ease, and Flagello's music began to attract more widespread attention. In 1974, his oratorio *The Passion of Martin Luther King* was introduced at the Kennedy Center in Washington, D.C., by the National Symphony Orchestra under the direction of James DePreist, with brother Ezio as soloist, in what was probably the most prestigious event of his career. The work was generally well received by both audience and the press and was subsequently recorded and performed elsewhere by DePreist. Other conductors also took up the *Passion*, which has become the composer's most frequently performed work.

But Flagello was deteriorating, both mentally and physically. A fourth piano concerto and a choral work in commemoration of the American Bicentennial were begun, then abandoned, and by the mid-1970s he had almost ceased composing altogether. In 1977, he was forced to resign from the Manhattan School, after more than twenty-five years of service, leaving him without a regular source of income. In 1978, he married a younger woman, soprano Maya Randolph, but this relationship would last barely three years. By this time he was so consumed by financial, personal, and health problems that he could barely maintain an appropriate demeanor when circumstances required him to appear in public.

Yet the sudden rash of favorable interest in Flagello's music continued to grow and, to some extent, revived his creative energy. In

1979, his Symphony no. 2, "Symphony of the Winds" (1970), which had yet to be performed, came to the attention of band conductor and advocate Marice Stith. Stith led the Cornell University Wind Ensemble in the premiere and subsequently included it in his ambitious recording series. Stith then commissioned Flagello to compose another piece for the Cornell group. The result was *Odyssey*, his first major work in eight years. Introduced in Ithaca in March 1981, under the composer's direction, *Odyssey* was also released as part of the Cornell Wind Ensemble record series soon afterward. An audiovisual publisher used the premiere as an opportunity to produce an educational filmstrip about the creation and preparation of a new musical work. Called *Odyssey: The Birth of a New Work*, the production won an award at the National Educational Film Festival in 1982.

Later that year, Flagello was invited to Italy to conduct several performances of *The Judgment of St. Francis* at the Saint Francis Basilica in Assisi. A review in *Musical America* commented that the opera's "robust emotionalism is unflinching in its conviction, and its intensity is sustained by a sure sense of pacing, a natural flow of expressive melody integrated throughout the musical texture, and an ability to use voices, chorus, and orchestra to their maximum effect."[9]

Although this flurry of interest in his music was encouraging, the income it provided was nowhere near adequate to meet the ordinary expenses of living—even in the modest apartment in which he then resided. A small inheritance sustained him for several years, until he was faced with the humiliation of "borrowing" money from friends in order to pay his bills.

For years Flagello had been expressing interest in writing another opera, if only he could find a subject that appealed to him. Early in 1979, a friend suggested Eugene O'Neill's early Pulitzer Prize–winning tragedy *Beyond the Horizon* and gave him a copy of the play. After reading it, Flagello showed some interest in pursuing the notion, but those close to him were doubtful that he could muster the energy and concentration for such an ambitious project at this time in his life. Their skepticism was confirmed when a year of effort produced no more than a few measures. But he insisted that he was serious about the work, and—after another year and a half—he had completed one scene. However, he gradually became consumed with the project, and in April 1983, the full-length, three-act opera was finished, in short score. While he was writing the last two acts, he also composed *Quattro Amori*, a song cycle set to his own texts, for mezzo-soprano Barbara Martin, who presented it at Carnegie Recital Hall in April 1983.

During the early 1980s, Flagello's music came to the attention of the young Russian emigré Semyon Bychkov, then music director of the Grand Rapids Symphony Orchestra. Encountering the score to the Concerto for String Orchestra in a music store, he was intrigued by the work and performed it with his orchestra. The Concerto proved so successful that Bychkov then programmed it for performance in March 1983, with the Buffalo Philharmonic, where he was to assume the position of music director. Taking an interest in other Flagello works, Bychkov also led performances of the orchestral suite *Lautrec* in France as well as in the United States. As music director of the Buffalo Philharmonic, he scheduled two Flagello premieres for the 1985–1986 season: *Credendum* (1973) for violin and orchestra and a newly commissioned work.

Several members of the Amherst Saxophone Quartet had been present at the Buffalo performances of the Concerto for String Orchestra in 1983 and approached Flagello with the idea of a work for saxophone quartet and orchestra. During the following months, a commission was arranged and a premiere was scheduled for November 1985, five weeks after *Credendum* was to be presented. But *Credendum* had been left in short score, so Flagello now had the task of orchestrating it, in addition to composing the new work. However, the early dementia that was to end his career prematurely had already begun to interfere with his ability to carry out the routine activities of daily life, although—quite remarkably—he was still able to compose without obvious impairment. It was in this condition that Flagello, then fifty-six years old, began composing what was to be his last work, the *Concerto Sinfonico* for saxophone quartet and orchestra. Concentrating all his energy on the project, he managed to complete the work in short score by the end of 1984. He then faced the tasks of orchestrating both the concerto and *Credendum*. This proved to be a harrowing experience, as Flagello first refused to confront, then was forced to accept, the fact that he was losing his faculties. Worst of all, the deterioration had begun to affect his musical abilities, so that he was unable to manage the details of rhythmic notation, clefs, and transpositions. In a last-minute scramble, friends and colleagues pooled their efforts to ready the scores and parts for performance.

Despite many errors and discrepancies not noted in time, both performances took place as scheduled. Herman Trotter described the *Concerto Sinfonico* as "passionate, dramatic, and unremittingly serious, . . . with easily detected shape and a clear sense of purpose, with surgingly lyric lines, dense textures, and churning rhythms"[10]—amazing—but not unprecedented—that a work written under such desperate circumstances could make such a powerful and coherent impression.

Days after the performance Flagello was found wandering the street, unable to find his way home. His sons—now grown—were alerted to his condition and arranged for supervision and care. During the next few years, as his friends gradually withdrew from his life, his first wife, Dianne, assumed responsibility for his well-being. In 1990, his condition reached the point where he could no longer live on his own, and he was placed in a nursing home. There he remained for four years, mute and oblivious, until his death in 1994, the day after his sixty-sixth birthday. The *New York Times* obituary began, "Nicolas Flagello, an American composer and conductor who played a busy role in this country's postwar musical life, died yesterday in New Rochelle, N.Y." The notice went on to describe him as "a child prodigy and later a prolific composer," adding that his style, "which grew out of the Romantic tradition, became increasingly dissonant with the passing years but was still based on tonal centers and given to expansive expressions of emotion and big climaxes."[11]

Two months later, ex-wife Dianne, then director of the Manhattan School of Music's Preparatory Division, arranged for a memorial concert at the school, devoted to Flagello's music. Bill Zakariasen, writing in *The Westsider*, described the event as a "rewarding (if bittersweet) concert," and commented that Flagello's music "unfolds with direct, communicative ideas, strong emotional content and a thorough knowledge of all instruments, including the human voice—his first love."[12]

MUSIC

The music of Nicolas Flagello is a natural, almost instinctive expression of the basic feelings of earthy, flesh-and-blood humanity—love, hate, sorrow, hope, dread, and faith—in all their visceral immediacy. It might be viewed as a lament of existential loneliness—the loneliness of a stranger in his own time, the last member of a dying race. But it also speaks with the defiance of one who refuses to relinquish long-cherished values, who struggles to maintain spiritual purity in a world filled with fraudulence and cynicism. Its recurrent themes—the often futile quest for human solace, the inevitability of mortality, the power of compassion in the face of ceaseless strife, and faith in God as the only true source of consolation and salvation—are clearly depicted in such works as *The Judgment of St. Francis, The Passion of Martin Luther King,* and *The Piper of Hamelin.* But these themes can be felt intuitively in most of his other works as well.

Flagello's musical language represents an extension of the traditionalism of his teacher Vittorio Giannini: He never betrayed his loyalty to the aesthetic principles or elements of craftsmanship espoused by his mentor, nor did his own musical vocabulary ever diverge significantly from that of the older man. Moreover, he was capable of emulating Giannini's own style quite closely and did so frequently as a form of homage. Yet despite the undeniable similarity of their modes of expression, there are profound differences between the character of Flagello's mature artistic statements and that of Giannini's.

Flagello's earlier works—those composed before 1959—show a strong resemblance to the music Giannini composed during the 1940s and 1950s, while Giannini's later, more dissonant works show the strongest similarity to—and perhaps, even the influence of—the music of Flagello's maturity. There is no question but that in many works—especially those written during the 1960s—the two composers were using very similar musical materials to pursue very similar aesthetic and expressive goals. Yet distinct and significant differences between them may be clearly discerned by relating works of comparable scope and genre, for example, their respective piano sonatas (composed at approximately the same time), Giannini's *Concerto Grosso* (1946) versus Flagello's Concerto for String Orchestra (1959), and Giannini's Symphony no. 3 (for band, 1958) versus Flagello's Symphony no. 2, *"Symphony of the Winds"* (1970). Such comparisons highlight the extent to which Giannini tempered the emotionality of his music by diffusing it within classical structure and Baroque figuration and phraseology, in contrast to the more fundamentally direct, personal, subjective, yet extroverted character of Flagello's expression. This is not to suggest that Flagello's music is any less meticulously crafted than Giannini's, but that "generic" elements that might dilute the immediacy or intensity of impact were shorn away by the younger composer, so that every detail is directed toward enhancing the expressive effect. Flagello's work early on assumed a grander, more imposing posture than Giannini strove to achieve until he reached his final years. Perhaps what is most immediately salient about Flagello's music, traceable to his earliest compositions, is its elegiac, often tragic, emotional tone. Although Giannini's musical personality is, for the most part, warm and genial, Flagello's is gloomy, volatile, and explosive. Thus, if Giannini's music shows the influence of the Strauss of *Der Rosenkavalier*, Flagello's suggests the Strauss of *Salome* and *Elektra*.

Flagello was no more concerned with being "original" than was Giannini and thus freely acknowledged the impact of other composers on his artistic development. In addition to Giannini and Strauss, he often pointed to Brahms, whose tight formal logic and motivic integration were ideals to which he aspired. Flagello's musical style also reveals a treatment of the human voice as a vehicle for spontaneous emotion in the manner of Puccini, the flamboyantly virtuosic gestures and rich textures found in the piano music of Rachmaninoff, the sumptuous harmony and flexible, often modal, tonality of Debussy and Ravel, a grotesquerie reminiscent of Prokofiev, and even the dark, sinister orchestral colors of Bernard Herrmann. Cherishing the music of the past, Flagello sought to make his own personal contribution to the heritage he loved, in the language that was most natural to him, confident that the authenticity of his expression and the distinctiveness of his voice would emerge clearly.

One of the near-contemporary composers for whom Flagello averred admiration was Samuel Barber, and their shared primary emphasis on emotional expression, especially of a doleful cast, bears some comparison. Yet despite such affinity of content, their vastly different temperaments are clearly apparent in their music. If Barber's musical personality is elegant, refined, and literary, with a penchant for indulgent sensuality and a tendency toward a passive melancholia, articulated with precision and maintained with composure, Flagello's is relatively harsh, earthy, subjective, visceral, and restless, inclined toward vehement outbursts of anger and despair and articulated with broad strokes. Moreover, Barber's instrumental works often indicate a certain lack of interest in abstract developmental procedures, which often seem routine, obligatory, and extrinsic to his chief concerns. For Flagello, the process of composition was inseparable from formal development, and he seems to have relished the creation of ingenious formal structures.

A closer comparison may be drawn with Ernest Bloch, another composer whom Flagello greatly admired: The music of both composers is emotionally autobiographical and metaphysically speculative in essence, revealing grim, sober, and often pessimistic reflections on the human condition. Furthermore, their actual musical vocabularies are quite similar, in their fusion of several European Late-Romantic dialects into a cosmopolitan Expressionism that ranges between straightforward tonality and passages verging on atonality, depending on the needs of the work in question. Perhaps the feature that distinguishes them most clearly is one that is admittedly based in stereotype and cliché: Bloch's Jewish heritage is often apparent, through modal inflections suggestive of Hebraic melos, even in pieces that are ostensibly secular and universal in intent, while Flagello's ethnic heritage is reflected in its passionate emotionalism, expressed—even in purely instrumental works—through a theatricality suggestive of opera and a phraseology rooted in the Italian language. (It is worth recalling in this connection that Bloch's music enjoyed consistent favor in Italy, except during the period of Nazi influence.)

Another point of distinction between the two composers concerns Bloch's attraction to the traditional media of chamber music—string quartets and piano quintets as well as sonatas and suites—genres that held little appeal for Flagello, whose most characteristic medium is the composition for soloist with orchestra. Suggesting an individual bearing witness to life's spiritual and emotional torments, with the orchestra as empathic Greek chorus, this format, embracing the concertos, large vocal works, and other similar pieces, comprises approximately one fourth of Flagello's entire output.

Flagello's body of work includes approximately seventy-five compositions that fall into two major periods, separated by a brief transitional period: 1. an early period, ending in 1958; 2. a transitional period (1958–1959); and 3. a mature period, from 1959 through 1985. The survey that follows is more comprehensive in its inclusion of detail than the previous chapters, chiefly because so few of Flagello's works are generally known and so little information about them is available in any other published form.

Most Representative, Fully Realized Works

The Judgment of Saint Francis (1959)
Capriccio for Cello and Orchestra (1962)
Piano Concerto no. 3 (1962)
Dante's Farewell (1962)
Piano Sonata (1962)
Contemplazioni di Michelangelo (1964)
Electra (1966)
Te Deum for All Mankind (1967)
Symphony no. 1 (1968)
Credendum (1973)
Beyond the Horizon (1983)
Concerto Sinfonico (1985)

Early Period (until 1958)

Flagello's early period comprises some twenty-five works, dating from the mid-1940s through 1958, when he reached the age of thirty. The music from this period is clearly tonal, modeled unabashedly on the rhetoric and forms developed by the masters of the nineteenth century—Chopin, Liszt, and Rachmaninoff in the piano music, Puccini and Strauss in the operatic and vocal music. But what keeps the more ambitious of these early works from sounding like pale imitations is their intense conviction and authenticity of expression. Beyond his instinctive gift for fashioning powerful climaxes and surging, passionate melodies, Flagello placed considerable importance on structural values. As he gained confidence and maturity, successive works reveal increased attention to motivic economy, thematic integration, and true symphonic development, built upon contrapuntal substructures that reveal as much appreciation for the architecture of Brahms as for the passion of Puccini and the virtuosity of Rachmaninoff. This was the legacy of Giannini, yet even these early works reveal the traits, described above, that distinguish Flagello's compositional personality from that of his teacher and anticipate the works to come later. The most significant compositions from this early period are: the opera *Mirra* (1955), the Violin Concerto (1956), *Theme, Variations, and Fugue* (1956), Piano Concerto no. 2 (1956), and the *Missa Sinfonica* (1957).

Among Flagello's earliest compositions are a nocturne for strings, several short piano pieces, and music for brass ensemble. In 1949, as his "senior project" at the Manhattan School of Music, he composed his first work for full orchestra, a tone poem entitled *Beowulf*. Interestingly, aside from his operas, this proved to be Flagello's only venture into program music. Performed at the Manhattan School that year, under the direction of Harris Danziger, the twenty-minute work falls into three connected sections, unified by a motif heard on the oboe at the outset. The opening section, which Flagello called "A Typical Day in the Life of the People," develops this motif into a warm, surging melody reminiscent of Howard Hanson (but not at all like the Nebraskan's *Lament for Beowulf*), followed by a *scherzo*-like passage, and then by a slow, lyrical elaboration of the opening. The second section is a violent episode depicting Beowulf's "Fight with the Dragon." A long, reflective transition leads to a dirge-like peroration in triple meter, "Beowulf's Funeral." The work is characteristic of the composer in its dynamic emotionalism, with generously distributed climaxes, although blatant transitions and the obviousness of its episodic structure reflect his relative immaturity. Another weakness of this work—one found in many of the pieces from Flagello's "early period"—is a plodding rhythmic regularity, accentuated by pulsing, quarter-note accompaniments supporting symmetrical melodic phrases.

In 1950, Flagello submitted a piano concerto as part of the requirement for his master's degree from the Manhattan School. Joseph Seiger was soloist in the work's presentation to the public, while the composer conducted the school's orchestra. The concerto is thoroughly conventional in most aspects of its content, rhetoric, and form, demonstrating the young composer's mastery of the basic skills requisite in creating a virtuoso work in romantic style. In Flagello's early compositions, the tonality of thematic material is usually clear and straightforward, though it may become more unstable in transitional and developmental passages. The first movement, *Allegro maestoso*, is generally oriented in C minor and is built upon two themes: the first, solemn and assertive, preceded and accompanied by a persistent rhythmic figure; the second—first heard in F-sharp minor—mournful, with an irregular metric structure. These themes unfold predictably and are subjected to extensive, if rather routine, development, culminating in an elaborate cadenza. Instead of a literal recapitulation, both themes are combined in a *fugato*, which brings the movement to a conclusion.

The second movement, *Andante,* in the key of E-flat, displays an ardent lyricism, as it elaborates a gently poignant melody.

The energetic third movement, *Allegro con brio,* is another *sonata allegro* form, this time in the key of A major, built upon a theme in 6/8 with hemiola features, derived from the assertive theme from the opening movement and similar in shape to the main theme of the second movement. A secondary theme is built around ascending fourths. This material is developed extensively along conventional lines, until the arrival of the recapitulation—actually, a recapitulation of the entire concerto, as the finale theme is combined contrapuntally with the mournful second theme of the first movement. This culminates in a *coda* in accelerated tempo, bringing the work to a brilliant conclusion. The finale of the concerto bears a strong resemblance to the *Concerto Macabre* composed in 1944 by Bernard Herrmann for the film *Hangover Square.* Flagello was a great admirer of Herrmann's music in general and of the music for this film in particular. Yet despite such reminiscences, and despite its routine design, the sincerity of its expression and the solidity of its craftsmanship create a compelling and satisfying experience.

During the next few years, Flagello—performing regularly as piano soloist with the Longines Symphonette—composed a lightweight work for chamber orchestra, called *Suite for Amber,* dedicated to the conductor's pet dog. This was followed by two short pieces for symphony orchestra—*Aria Sinfonica* and *Overture Burlesca.*

Then in 1953, Flagello turned his attention to a large work for chorus and orchestra and another concerto, along with several songs and some short piano pieces. The choral work, entitled *Pentaptych,* comprised settings of five sacred texts from the Latin liturgy: 1. *Hosanna Filio David;* 2. *Cor Jesu;* 3. *Et Flagellis Subditum;* 4. *Stabat Mater;* and 5. *Jubilate Deo.* The choral writing was rich and impassioned, and each section built to an impressive climax. However, the work's cumulative effect was weakened by the plodding rhythmic regularity observed in a number of Flagello's earlier works. Although *Pentaptych* was never performed, the composer returned to it in 1968, immediately after the assassination of Martin Luther King Jr. Seizing the opportunity to create a larger work with a more personal focus, he used *Pentaptych* as the basis of an oratorio *The Passion of Martin Luther King.*

Pentaptych was followed by a concerto for flute. Entitled *Concerto Antoniano,* in honor of Saint Anthony, the father of Christian monasticism, the work shows a considerable advance in sophistication over the First Piano Concerto. Though its form still hews closely to conventional prototypes, the Flute Concerto is tighter motivically, with greater textural and contrapuntal complexity and a smoothly fluent coherence. Its chief sign of immaturity is a tendency toward overly deliberate, even labored, transitional passages—another weakness found in several of Flagello's earlier works.

The first movement, *Allegro moderato*, begins with a subdued introduction, in which an unaccompanied flute solo in D minor introduces two motifs that will serve as the thematic basis for the entire work. The orchestra enters softly, building in intensity, until the exposition proper presents the first theme, now in B minor, and in a whimsical guise, followed by the second theme (based on the second motif from the introduction), now heard in a sweet and delicate E major. Both themes are developed elaborately, moving through several changes of mood and tempo and culminating in an extended cadenza in two parts, separated by a haunting passage in which the flute is accompanied by only a harp. The cadenza is followed by an abbreviated recapitulation.

The second movement, *Andante comodo*, is a series of ornamental variations on a sweetly melancholy melody in A minor. A central section introduces a note of distress, before the mood becomes one of poignant acceptance, concluding the movement in A major.

The third movement, *Allegro con brio*, is the most elaborate structurally, while the nature of its themes and its overall *buffo* character are strongly reminiscent of Giannini. Its form is sectional, with suggestions of a *sonata rondo*, while a smooth coherence is maintained by a tight developmental focus on two motifs presented in the first two measures—one, emphasizing the interval of the fourth; the other, a conjunct turning figure that is a direct inversion of the second motif from the first movement. The opening section, which begins in B-flat, maintains a playful, lively tone while subjecting these two motifs to an extensive development. The second motif then undergoes a more subdued, reflective treatment in the second section, in an ambiguous E phrygian/A minor, marked *A Tempo più calmo*. The first motif then rejoins the second in a transition to the next section, extended by an improvisatory passage in which the flute treats both motifs, accompanied by mysterious triads in the strings. This leads directly into a fugal development in E, with the first motif as subject and the second as countersubject. A brief return of the second section serves as transition to a recapitulation of the first section, now in B minor, enhanced by further contrapuntal treatments of both motifs. In a grotesque, march-like coda, the second motif, propelled by a tritone-dominant, tauntingly reaffirms a concluding tonality of B, until a final flourish from the flute brings the concerto to an end.

The first performance of Flagello's *Concerto Antoniano* took place in Columbus, Ohio, in 1954. Claude Monteux was the flute soloist, and the composer conducted the Columbus Symphony Orchestra. The work was recorded ten years later, with Gary Sigurdson as soloist with the Orchestra Sinfonica di Roma under the composer's direction. Arthur Cohn described it as "a worthy contribution, with a first movement cadenza that truly climaxes the material, a contrastive slow movement, and a delightful finale—the music 'goes' and the flute is the perfect instrumental color for such lucidity."[13]

In 1954, Flagello completed his first opera, a one-act farce based on a play by Luigi Pirandello. Originally entitling it *The Cap*, he fashioned the libretto himself, retaining Pirandello's Italian setting. However, a year or two later he changed his mind and transplanted the setting to New England, around the year 1800, retitling the work *The Wig.* About half an hour in duration, *The Wig* involves six ludicrously caricatured characters engaged in mischief and trickery. The music again displays an *opera buffa* style strongly reminiscent of Giannini. The opera was not produced until November 1990, when the American Chamber Opera mounted the work with a reduced orchestration, prepared for the occasion by composer Anthony Sbordoni.

Also completed in 1954 was *The Land*, a song cycle comprising settings of six poems by Alfred, Lord Tennyson, for bass-baritone and chamber orchestra. Flagello composed the cycle for his brother Ezio, who introduced it in New York City the following year, under the composer's direction. In 1962, the brothers recorded the work in Rome, with a small instrumental ensemble. This recording, initially released during the early 1960s, has been reissued several times during the ensuing decades—most recently on compact disc in 1995.

Flagello's warm, luxuriant settings present a variety of contrasting moods, expanding Tennyson's simple verses in praise of birds, flowers, and seasons into a grand pantheistic statement, innocent in its fervor, which becomes explicit in the final song, "Flower in the Cranny." The entire cycle is unified by a single motif, first presented during an extended introduction, against an undulating instrumental backdrop suggesting waves of the sea. This motif, first heard in D minor, recurs in each song, often in altered form. At the end of "Flower in the Cranny," which has something of the character of a chaconne, this motif achieves a rapturous resolution in E major during an extended epilogue. The other poems in the cycle are "The Eagle," "The Owl," "The Throstle," "The Oak," and "The Snowdrop."

Flagello's mastery of orchestration was widely acknowledged, even if grudgingly by those unimpressed with his creative work. *The Land* gives first evidence of his ability, born of necessity, to convey, with only a small group of instruments, the effect of a full orchestra. The accompaniment of this song cycle achieves a remarkable richness and variety of instrumental color, although it calls for an ensemble consisting of only four winds and a group of strings, augmented by piano and celeste.

While he was working on the *Concerto Antoniano*, *The Wig*, and *The Land*, Flagello was also deeply immersed in what he later termed "my *Gurre-Lieder*," by which he meant the magnum opus of his early period, a full-length, three-act opera called *Mirra*. The composer again created the libretto himself, basing it on an eponymous play by the prolific writer who has been called Italy's greatest poetic tragedian, Count Vittorio Alfieri (1749–1803). *Mirra* (1786) is one of Alfieri's most highly regarded tragedies, a horrifying tale of incestuous love within the royal family of ancient Cyprus.

Mirra, Princess of Cyprus, has chosen Pereus, the Prince of Epirus, to be her husband. The marriage is to take place the following day, but, to the bewilderment of the King, Queen, and Pereus himself, Mirra seems visibly distraught. No one is able to elicit from her the reason for her distress. As the wedding is about to commence, preceded by an elaborate array of ritual ceremonies, Mirra becomes delirious and Pereus, convinced that she is rejecting him, becomes enraged and leaves. The remainder of the ceremony is canceled. Shortly thereafter, the King informs Mirra that Pereus has killed himself and, once again, he attempts to draw from her some explanation for her strange behavior. Finally, after much hesitation, Mirra ardently reveals the true object of her amorous desires: her father, the King himself. He recoils with horror at this revelation and she, inconsolably hopeless, takes a knife and plunges it into her own chest.

Completed in 1955, the opera is extravagantly romantic in style, brimful of emotional extremes, and utilizes a densely woven musical language that somewhat resembles Giannini's fusion of lush Puccinian lyricism with Straussian power and opulence. However, *Mirra* displays a highly charged volatility that distinguishes it from the more relaxed *bel canto* warmth found in the operas of Flagello's mentor. Although the cast includes only five principals, the work requires a large orchestra, full chorus, dancers, plus an on-stage band. Not surprisingly, *Mirra* has never been staged, although two orchestral excerpts have been extracted for concert performance, under the title "Interlude and Dance." Placed in reverse order from their appearance in the opera, the "Interlude" is taken from the prelude to Act III and sets a solemn mood, seething with passionate intensity, while the "Dance" is a wild, orgiastic frenzy that accompanies the ballet sequence from the abortive nuptial ceremony of Act II. The "Interlude and Dance" from *Mirra* was first performed by the Billings (Montana) Symphony Orchestra, under the direction of Uri Barnea, in November 1990.

In 1955–1956, Flagello spent a year in Rome on a Fulbright Fellowship, where he pursued advanced composition study with Ildebrando Pizzetti, at the Accademia di Santa Cecilia. His stay proved fruitful, resulting in a number of songs, a violin concerto, and a large orchestral work. Although Pizzetti's influence left little impact on Flagello's compositional style or technique, the *maestro*, then seventy-six, reinforced his student's proud awareness of his place in the continuity of Italian musical tradition. One of the songs Flagello composed during this period was *L'Infinito*, a setting of a poem of precocious philosophical cast by the nineteen-year-old Giacomo Leopardi (1798–1837). Pizzetti had asserted that the well-known poem was almost impossible to set, presenting an irresistible challenge to the young composer. A gloomy expression of humility and awe in the face of the Infinite, Leopardi's poem reveals a lofty yet pessimistic perspective that Flagello was coming increasingly to share, and his setting aptly captures its spirit. Although he initially set *L'Infinito* for bass-baritone and piano, the composer later arranged the accompaniment for chamber orchestra, in which guise it was recorded, along with *The Land*, by the Flagello brothers in 1962.

Another creative accomplishment from Flagello's year with Pizzetti was the composition of a violin concerto. Although he left the work in short score, and never even began the orchestration, the piano reduction is quite detailed. Many aspects recall the *Concerto Antoniano*, with an opening movement that is primarily lyrical in character, and a largely conventional—if typically rigorous— approach to form. Nevertheless the Violin Concerto exhibits greater textural complexity, as well as more thorough motivic integration and more sophisticated developmental procedures, than the earlier concerto.

The first movement, *Allegro giusto*, begins with a rather diffident statement of the slightly plaintive main theme by the solo violin, accompanied by gentle punctuating chords in the orchestra. Although the theme is diatonic, its tonality is ambiguous, suggesting a variety of different tonal centers as it unfolds chromatically. A full *tutti* statement of the theme highlights the minor triad with added major sixth and major ninth as a harmonic structure of importance, while confirming D minor as the primary tonality. Two other ideas are introduced during the exposition, the first of which is clearly derived from the main theme. The second, presented in A-flat minor, fits the role of a secondary theme, as it ardently surges through a variety of keys, though the primary theme thoroughly permeates the exposition. The presentation of the thematic material elides smoothly into the development section, as the treatment of the solo violin becomes more overtly virtuosic. As the development proceeds, the character of the work takes on some of the qualities of Flagello's mature compositional voice: densely contrapuntal development of the thematic material in the service of fervently melancholic expression, thrust forward from climax to climax by propulsive rhythmic patterns with little surcease. Predictably, the development leads to an elaborate cadenza—in two parts, as in the Flute Concerto, separated by a brief accompanied passage— followed by a recapitulation of the thematic material, its presentation somewhat altered.

The second movement, *Andante con moto*, is the earliest example of what is perhaps Flagello's most characteristic type of utterance: an impassioned outpouring of dolorous melody. Displaying a stepwise descent of a fourth, derived from the first movement's main theme, the melody establishes itself firmly in B minor, after a tentative, tonally ambiguous introduction. The melody is accompanied by a syncopated, pulsating rhythmic pattern, laden with *appoggiaturas*, that continues virtually without interruption throughout the movement.

The third movement, *Allegro comodo*, has the character and general shape of a *sonata rondo* with a tonal center of D. The primary thematic material is based on a triplet idea in perpetual motion, while the secondary theme again emphasizes the stepwise descent of a fourth. A syncopated rhythmic pattern serves as a third thematic idea. As the movement proceeds, these ideas are combined contrapuntally, and developed quite extensively, without any deviation from a fundamental focus on virtuosity. Flagello's Violin Concerto is a brilliant, fully consummated work, fusing three fundamental aesthetic values: densely integrated thematic development, passionate, uninhibited emotional expression, and untrammeled virtuosic display. In 2003 Anthony Sbordoni orchestrated the accompaniment, thereby preparing the concerto for performance.

Simultaneously with the Violin Concerto, Flagello produced a composition for large orchestra entitled *Theme, Variations, and Fugue*. This was the culmination of his year of study with Pizzetti and proved to be the most ambitious abstract, instrumental work of his early period. It is based on a doleful theme in B-flat minor, built around a descending minor triad, which is densely woven into a chromatic contrapuntal fabric. A secondary motif comprises a stepwise descending pattern. The nine variations that follow develop a wide range of affective attitudes, many of which—whimsical, farcical, sprightly, comical, ungainly—represent paths Flagello was rarely to pursue in the future, while others—mournful, resolute, warmly affectionate—he was to revisit again and again. The variations are followed by an elaborate fugue, with a jaunty subject based on the two motifs of the main theme. Beginning with a thorough, if rather orthodox, exposition and development, the fugue becomes increasingly expansive and "symphonic" in character. Finally the main theme, in its original, doleful guise, is introduced by the horn and cellos against running figures initially in just the violins and flutes, but gradually drawing in more and more of the orchestra. The work culminates in a monumental coda in B-flat major, stunningly orchestrated with lavish percussion and organ reinforcement. *Theme, Variations, and Fugue* has yet to be performed in public, although in 2003 Naxos released a recording, featuring the Slovak Radio Orchestra of Bratislava, conducted by the American conductor David Amos, as part of its "American Classics" series.

Upon his return to the United States later in 1956, Flagello turned his attention to another concerto—his second for piano and orchestra. In this work, he wholeheartedly embraced the familiar rhetoric of the romantic concerto, replete with thundering octaves, dreamy soliloquies, and cascading arpeggios that impart an almost "Hollywood" quality to throbbing melodies and fistfuls of virtuoso passagework that build to huge climaxes. Compared with his earlier concertos, the work at times reveals a sweetness verging on sentimentality. Yet despite its extroverted character, the Concerto no. 2 is brilliantly constructed, its entire substance derived from the six-note motif introduced by the piano at the outset. This motif, in a state of continuous metamorphosis and development, forms the basis of all three movements of the work.

The first movement, *Allegro giusto*, is an abbreviated *sonata allegro* form, featuring an animated first theme in C minor and a melancholy secondary theme in A minor. After these ideas are presented and elaborated in a variety of guises, the movement culminates in a tremendous climax that combines all the material heard thus far.

The second movement, *Andante giusto*, follows without pause, and features a warm, wistful melody in the woodwinds soon elaborated by the piano. Gradually this melody reveals itself as an inverted form of the concerto's opening motif. This is transformed into a stentorian statement, before melting into the movement's centerpiece—a variant of unabashed tenderness that rises to a luxuriant climax.

Once this outpouring recedes, a rather impish transition gradually leads to the finale: *Allegro quasi presto*. In contrast to the sweetness of the preceding section, this movement proclaims itself with a swagger, as the C minor motif from the opening movement now appears in C major. This theme is developed in alternation with a minor-key inverted variant of the basic motif through the full range of traditional virtuoso pyrotechnics. Finally, as the energy builds, the concentration of material intensifies, and all thematic elements are combined toward a grand finish.

Some time after completing the Piano Concerto no. 2, Flagello experienced misgivings about its cloying sweetness. Quite uncharacteristically, he returned to the score and revised the harmonic language in which the finale's primary material was couched, intensifying the transitional introduction with secundal dissonances and adding sevenths to the triadic harmony of the main theme, thereby creating a somewhat raucous, biting effect.

The Second Concerto still awaits its first public performance, although it was recorded—with these revisions—in 1995 by the Yugoslav pianist Tatjana Rankovich, accompanied by the Slovak Philharmonic of Kosice led by David Amos. After waiting forty years for its first hearing, the work was well received. Reviewing the recording, Paul A. Snook noted that it:

> gives off a kind of sophisticated sheen and accessibility that might lead a casual listener to think of Hollywood film scores of the 1940s. But a closer inspection reveals just how uncompromised and well written this music is—how naturally and compellingly it flows and evolves, all the while using time-tested methods of formal development but in freshly reconceived terms and always avoiding any suggestion of rhetoric or padding. In fact, even though Flagello's language . . . has been heard before, his way of harnessing it to serve his own expressive needs is wholly individual and never less than totally assured.[14]

British critic Bret Johnson observed that its "gratitude to Rachmaninov and Brahms is in no way a cloak for inadequate imagination; rather it is a springboard for a rare, extended display of brilliantly crafted invention, development and triumphant expostulation. Flagello sustains his line of argument assuredly and unselfconsciously. . . . Although he was only 28 when he wrote it, the Concerto's maturity and accomplishment make it immediately convincing."[15]

During the late 1950s, Flagello's wife Dianne was employed as a music teacher at a New York City junior high school. Among her responsibilities was the mounting of theatrical musical productions in which large numbers of untutored students could participate. There exists a whole repertoire designed for this purpose—mostly utilitarian efforts created by schoolteachers. While their creators may lack musical sophistication, they know how to tailor their pieces to the practical limitations and requirements of this rather circumscribed genre. Mrs. Flagello suggested to her husband that he try his hand at such an endeavor and introduced him to Christopher Fiore, who taught English at the same school. In 1957, the two adapted Washington Irving's classic story *Rip Van Winkle* as a two-act operetta for children. The cast includes twenty-five characters in addition to three children's choruses. The accompaniment is scored for school band with piano, but is viable with piano alone as well. While much of the music is limited by the capabilities of untrained children's voices and other constraints of the medium, the overture, a ballet sequence, and some of the vocal numbers display a warmth and tuneful exuberance reminiscent of Gian Carlo Menotti's most popular efforts.

The year 1957 also saw the completion of a major work for full orchestra, *Missa Sinfonica*. Although Flagello's personality and life-style were far from puritanical, religious feelings ran strongly within him and he attributed great importance to the role they played in his life. Indeed, he considered all his compositions to be fundamentally spiritual in nature—some pieces more explicitly than others. *Missa Sinfonica*—in five movements that correspond to the sections of the Roman Catholic Mass—was the most significant religious work of Flagello's early period. Each movement might be described as an orchestral motet based on a chant melody associated with that portion of the Mass. However, rather than creating a *stile antico*, or an attempt at a neo-Renaissance polyphonic style, Flagello—like Paul Creston in his Third Symphony—expressed his devotional feelings in his own personal musical language, with its ripely romantic gestures, rich harmonic framework, and opulent sonorities. Such an approach may be controversial, offending those who analogize (often unconsciously) the classical versus romantic dichotomy with spirituality versus carnality. (See the quotation from William Flanagan's review of *Missa Sinfonica* in the biographical section of this chapter. Is it far-fetched to view this vicious attack as an Irish Catholic reaction to an Italian Catholic mode of expression?)

As its title indicates, *Missa Sinfonica* reflects elements of both the Mass and the symphony. Of its five movements, the first, third, and fifth suggest hymn-like orchestral arias, while the second and fourth are rather *scherzoso* in character. Despite the year that appears on the score, the work shares many musical traits with the choral-orchestral *Pentaptych* of 1953. The slow movements in particular display a somewhat plodding metrical and phraseological symmetry, as the melodic lines ascend through predictable harmonic sequences to achieve naively ecstatic climaxes—all suggesting a somewhat earlier date of composition. Yet despite its weaknesses, *Missa Sinfonica* contains many passages touching in their heartfelt warmth and devotional innocence. The work was first performed by the orchestra of the Manhattan School of Music, under the direction of Jonel Perlea, in November 1957.

Transitional Period (1958–1959)

During the years 1958–1959, Flagello's language began to expand, as he ventured into different and sometimes deeper realms of expression. Some of these explorations led to "dead-ends" to which he never returned, while others pointed the way to further development. The most significant of these transitional works are the song *The Rainy Day* (1958) and the Concerto for String Orchestra (1959).

In 1958, Flagello completed *The Sisters*, a one-act operatic melodrama in two scenes lasting about an hour, with a libretto by Dean Mundy. Set during the early 1800s in "a town off the coast of Massachusetts," it depicts the jealousy and hatred that pervade a family of three sisters, two of whom are in love with the same man—a sailor—and their brutal father who will not tolerate any disobedience from his daughters. The libretto presents grotesquely exaggerated portrayals of sexually repressed archetypes: the sweet, innocent sister, the vicious, jealous sister, and the maternal, protective sister; the dashing, virile hero, and the cruel, tyrannically possessive father. Their foolish behavior follows a tangential, if generally predictable, course that ends as one of the daughters forces her sister off a cliff to her death.

The musical language of *The Sisters* is somewhat uncertain, veering between warm, ardent, Gianninian lyricism during tender, amorous moments, and more angular, irregular, dissonant passages when the father and the evil daughter are portrayed. But although the work is well integrated motivically, these opposing styles remain jarringly distinct. There is a poignant trio, a voluptuous love-duet, and several other lovely lyrical moments, as well as some solemnly evocative mood-settings, such as the *"Interludio"* that separates the two scenes. Yet despite these satisfying moments, the opera cannot be considered a fully realized success.

The Sisters was mounted by the Manhattan School of Music Opera Theater in February 1961, with the composer conducting and his brother Ezio in the role of the father. The reviews, as noted earlier, commented favorably on the musical aspects of the work.

Later the same year, Flagello composed a setting for low voice and piano of Longfellow's famous poem *The Rainy Day*. A lugubrious *ostinato* pattern first presented in B-flat minor permeates the piano accompaniment throughout most of the song. While setting a gloomy mood, the accompaniment suggests slowly falling rain-

drops, as the poet first describes the weather, then relates it to the
state of his life. The stable harmony and *ostinato* accompanimental
pattern are characteristic of the composer's earlier vocal music. But
with the passage introducing the words, "My thoughts still cling to
the smouldering past," the mood becomes darker still, as the harmonic rhythm quickens and the pattern that initially suggested rain-
drops now conveys something far more menacing. By the fourth
iteration of the phrase "dark and dreary," the ascending *ostinato* has
become hammerlike in its insistence before it suddenly breaks off.
Then, in seeming contradiction to the reassurance offered by the
lines "Be still, sad heart and cease repining; behind the clouds is the
sun still shining," the piano now throbs with mounting intensity, as
the bass line descends in contrary motion to the rising, increasingly
dissonant melodic-harmonic construction. The intensity becomes
almost unbearable until it culminates, after the word "shining," on
an F-dominant-seven with minor-nine and augmented-eleven—
perhaps the most powerful climax yet composed by Flagello. The
harmony returns to B-flat minor, and the original *ostinato* pattern
returns, for the concluding lines of the poem.

Why Flagello chose to set lines of consolation to music of such
harrowing anguish remains a mystery. However, in so doing he discovered a range and depth of musical expression that led him into
a new phase of creative development.

While he was composing his setting of *The Rainy Day*, Flagello
was also working on three pieces for piano, which he called *Symphonic Waltzes*. His first extended composition for piano solo, these
pieces were intended to evoke the feeling of Paris at the turn of the
twentieth century. The first, *Allegro movendo*, has a brash, raucous
quality, though it comes to a subdued conclusion. The second, *Lento
mosso*, is the sort of dark, haunted nocturne of which Flagello, pursuing a subgenre elaborated by Ernest Bloch, was to become a master. The third, *Allegro energico*, is festive in spirit, although it
culminates in a manic frenzy *a la* Ravel. What is most remarkable
and uncharacteristic about these pieces is that they represent an
excursion into the musical style of another time and place. In 1965,
Flagello returned to these pieces, orchestrating and transforming
them into a ballet suite he called *Lautrec* and removing the *Symphonic Waltzes* from his list of works. However, in 1992, the Flagello
family granted permission to pianist Tatjana Rankovich to present
the first performance of the waltzes at Weill Recital Hall in New York

City. She subsequently recorded them on a compact disc released in 1995.

Another such excursion into a less subjective style—at least, for two of its three movements—is the Concerto for String Orchestra, composed in 1959. A motoric regularity of pattern in the outer movements gives the work an uncharacteristic neo-Baroque flavor. The opening *Allegro misurato* sets a mood of grim determination, maintained throughout the movement. After an orthodox exposition the two main themes become intertwined in an elaborate development that delays the final recapitulatory statement until the coda.

For the second movement, *Andante Languido,* Flagello returned to the mournful sort of elegy he had explored in the Act III Interlude from *Mirra* and then again in the slow movement of his Violin Concerto. However, here the composer brings the prototype to fuller consummation—an outcry of anguish in which his most intimate, personal voice comes to the fore. In characteristic fashion, the movement begins tentatively, as successively more elaborate phrases build in intensity to a minor climax. All this serves as introduction to the slow, long-lined aria that follows, rising from the depths with a masterfully gauged ebb and flow until it reaches a towering apotheosis of despair before subsiding in resignation. The *Andante Languido* has been performed as a separate piece and in 1995 was recorded by the New Russia Orchestra conducted by David Amos.

The third movement, *Allegro vivace,* returns to the vigorous rhythmic character of the opening movement. It is essentially a five-part *sonata rondo,* built around an insistent, almost skittish, refrain. The main presentation of this refrain is followed by a contrasting episode in which a slightly melancholy tune appears over continuous running figures. (This tune gradually reveals an affinity to the secondary theme of the first movement.) After a restatement of the refrain, a second episode features an extensive fugal treatment of a fragment from the main theme, with the melancholy tune appearing as countersubject. After a final restatement of the refrain, the work comes to a spirited and decisive conclusion.

In 1964, Flagello conducted the Orchestra Sinfonica di Roma in a complete recording of the Concerto for String Orchestra. Reviewing this release, Arthur Cohn wrote, "The music is bold but re-creative, . . . The rhythm is exciting, penetrating, but never pants because it is breathless. Flagello's control of this aspect is perfect; it is also sensitive."[16] When Semyon Bychkov led the Buffalo Philharmonic in the Concerto for String Orchestra, Herman Trotter praised the work's "strength of utterance, sense of purposefulness and the linked logic of its extremely lyric line."[17] While Mark Lehman commented in his review of Amos's recording of the slow movement that, "Flagello's *Andante* can hardly fail to remind the listener of Barber's great *Adagio*," he added, "the surprise is that its nobility and power make it a worthy companion."[18]

Mature Period (1959–1985)

Although in retrospect Flagello professed no awareness of any change in his musical style or syntax, the arrival of a new, more mature compositional phase in 1959 is unmistakable. While hardly a concession to the values of Modernism, Flagello's mature style reveals a greater astringency: harmony is more dissonant, tonality is often quite unsettled—even atonal—for extended periods of time, lyrical lines are doled out more sparingly, rhythm is less symmetrical, and forms are tighter. Yet the music is still constructed along traditional lines, frequently utilizing classical forms, adhering to the basic principles of counterpoint and motivic development, and retaining clear tonal anchors to reinforce structural high points. Yet the change is not only a matter of language, but of content as well. The exuberant, sunny, joyful elements that had leavened his earlier music now all but disappeared, replaced by a dark, brooding quality at times turbulent, explosive, and cataclysmic. This subtle but significant shift moved his aesthetic identity away from a more conventional Neo-Romanticism and into closer alignment with the Expressionism of Ernest Bloch and the late works of Vittorio Giannini, upon which the younger man may himself have exerted an influence. In the music of Flagello's maturity, every element is tightly concentrated and focused toward the fullest, most intense realization of the intended expressive effect. While some pieces achieve ecstatic resolution, others yield only anguished epiphanies, and still others reach no sense of redemption at all. From this period came most of those works that might be considered Flagello's masterpieces: the opera *The Judgment of Saint Francis* (1959), the *Capriccio* (1962) for cello and orchestra, the Piano Concerto no. 3 (1962), *Dante's Farewell* (1962), the Piano Sonata (1962), *Contemplazioni di Michelangelo* (1964), the *Te Deum for All Mankind* (1967), and the Symphony no. 1 (1968).

Flagello was thirty-one years old when he completed the first work in which he demonstrated full mastery of his own compositional voice: his fifth opera, *The Judgment of Saint Francis*. Its subtitle, *A One-Act Opera in Rondo*, refers to its use of "flashbacks." Bishop Guido presides over an ecclesiastical court, where Francis (Francesco) is standing trial, accused by his father, a successful merchant, of giving away money and goods belonging to him. The work comprises seven scenes: The court and the musical theme associated with it represent the "refrain," while the "flashbacks," depicting the incidents leading to Francesco's conversion, represent the "episodes" of the *rondo*.

Flagello later recalled that during his period of study in Rome he had stayed briefly in the Umbrian town of Perugia. Hearing the church bells from the neighboring town of Assisi often called to mind the story of Saint Francis. "A musical phrase occurred to me, and I couldn't get it out of my mind. I became convinced that this *was* St. Francis' music."[19] It was this phrase that became the proclamatory seven-note fanfare that begins the opera and provides the musical substance of the entire work. Armand Aulicino's libretto depicts the familiar elements of the Franciscan legend: Francesco's refusal to acknowledge his father's authority, his kissing of a leper's hand, his visit to a dilapidated church where he experiences a divine revelation prompting him to give away his money, his period of seclusion in a cave, his imprisonment by his father in a rat-infested cellar, his decision to renounce his worldly life to serve God, and finally his delivery of the *Cantico del Sole*, the famous prayer of thanksgiving.

All this is presented through a tightly woven score lasting about an hour and a quarter, and calling for seven soloists, as well as a chorus and full orchestra. The music might be said to combine the violent emotional intensity of Strauss's *Salome* with the fervent piety of Puccini's *Suor Angelica*. Although it certainly boasts its share of lyrical moments, for the most part these emerge briefly from the dense orchestral texture within which they are interwoven. In contrast to Giannini's more relaxed, full-blossomed lyricism, Flagello's approach gratifies the listener's appetite frequently but only for short moments. This technique, which holds the listener's eager attention throughout, creates deep satisfaction when resolution is finally achieved. The score builds cumulatively, its unflagging emotional momentum and musical ardor punctuated by such highlights as an elaborate fugue in Scene IV—precisely where one might be expected in a traditional *rondo*—when Francesco gives his money to the priest of San Damiano, the reverent "Adoration" in Scene VI, when Francesco, alone in the cellar, prays contentedly, followed by the impassioned trio in which his mother and his fiancée Clara vow to follow Francesco in a life of service to God, the awed transfiguration of the chorus of townspeople in Scene VII, after they have witnessed the recounting of Francesco's conversion, and, finally, in the "coda," his hushed, pious soliloquy as he sings the *Cantico del Sole*.

In its embracing of such themes as the renunciation of worldliness in favor of a life devoted to brotherly love and the pursuit of spiritual truth—embodied in the life of a human being—*Saint Francis* captures some of the fundamental themes that underlie Flagello's creative work, crystallizing ideals to which he returned many times in other compositions. Although his own worldly life may not have approached these ideals, it is apparent that he viewed his artistic life and his work as a composer as a form of such self-renunciation.

The premiere of *The Judgment of Saint Francis* was given by the Manhattan Opera Theater at the Manhattan School of Music in March 1966. The conductor was Anton Coppola, and the celebrated basso John Brownlee took the role of the Bishop. As noted earlier, the reviews were generally favorable, and the performance was broadcast later that year. The next production of the opera took place at the Basilica of Saint Francis in Assisi, in July 1982, with the composer himself conducting.

During the late 1970s, Flagello was engaged to conduct an extensive and varied series of recordings for Peters International, with the Orchestra da Camera di Roma. As the only sample of his own music to be included in the series, he arranged the "Adoration" from Scene VI of *Saint Francis* for strings and harp, giving the vocal line to a solo violin. The recording has been reissued several times since its initial 1977 release, most recently in 1995 on compact disc.

Soon after *The Judgment of Saint Francis*, Flagello completed a short work for mixed chorus and orchestra, *Tristis est Anima Mea*. This dark, lugubrious work is perhaps the first of his compositions from which romantic lyricism is wholly absent. Its chief elements are stark open fifths, along with other, more dissonant chord structures, harsh, bell-like sonorities, and a simple motif that toys with the tension between a major- and a minor-third. These elements are developed through passages of densely chromatic counterpoint in alternation with spare-textured moments of eeriness. Despite its brevity, the work is stunning in its harsh, bleak power.

At this time Flagello began to produce new works—mostly abstract instrumental pieces—in rapid succession. Consistent in style and attitude, they maintain an extraordinarily high standard of artistry, while revealing particular sensitivity to the continua of tonality and harmonic dissonance as subtle gradients by means of which to control a work's emotional dynamics. Each of these pieces reflects the utmost seriousness of artistic intent, regardless of its scope, instrumental medium, or title. In fact, many performers and listeners have been perplexed by the uncompromisingly serious tone of works with titles like *Burlesca*, *Divertimento*, *Capriccio*, and the like; Flagello used these terms to indicate erratic or wayward formal designs, rather than a levity of tone or frivolity of content. These pieces are motif-driven, tightly woven and concise, but never mechanical or devoid of expressive content. Though largely atonal for long stretches, remote tonal references produce tensions that hold the listener's interest while guiding the character of the statement.

The first of two works completed by Flagello in 1960 was *Prelude, Ostinato, and Fugue* for piano solo. Its title—and even thematic material (in the *Ostinato*)—nods respectfully to Cesar Franck. The *Prelude* begins with a restless, searching quality, before building quickly to a massive climax and then subsiding. The *Ostinato* consists of a set of variations over an ascending minor scale, which functions as a *basso ostinato*, appearing in several different keys. Beginning with a melancholy lyricism, it too builds to a tempestuous climax. The *Fugue* is a propulsive piece that subsumes contrapuntal intricacies within a vehicle for virtuoso pianism. A three-voice exposition is followed by several developmental episodes, culminating in a chordal augmentation of the subject, marked *furiosamente*, which leads to a hair-raising coda. The work was recorded in 1964 by Elizabeth Marshall. Subsequent recordings have been made by pianists Joshua Pierce and Peter Vinograde, released in 1991 and 1997 respectively.

Also completed in 1960 was the *Divertimento* for piano and percussion. The work was composed at the suggestion of Paul Price, founder and conductor of the Manhattan Percussion Ensemble, in residence for many years at the Manhattan School of Music and a pioneer in establishing the percussion ensemble as a legitimate medium for serious music. Flagello explained his use of the title by stating his intention to compose a piece that would be entertaining to listeners and exhilarating to performers, despite its mood of sinister agitation. At the beginning of the first movement, *Preludium*, the piano introduces two motifs: a tritone and three adjacent descending tones outlining the interval of a third. These two ideas, together with their inversions, expansions, and contractions, become the raw material from which the composition grows. The *Preludium* and the third movement, *Toccata*, present brilliant episodes in which the piano, used in an aggressive, percussive manner, pursues a grim, breakneck course, propelled by driving, nervous rhythmic irregularities, while the ensemble provides coloristic punctuation. In the second movement, *Dialogo*, the ensemble—the vibraphone, in particular—steps to the foreground, creating a dark, ethereal mood against which the piano proclaims a dark, brooding soliloquy that ultimately builds to two explosive climaxes. This is the earliest example of a kind of brooding, largely atonal rumination to which Flagello was to return several times, in some cases developing such ideas into complete works.

The *Divertimento* received its first performance shortly after it was completed, with the composer as piano soloist, accompanied by the Manhattan Percussion Ensemble under Price's direction. Some thirty years later, in 1991, a performance of the work was released on compact disc, featuring the same ensemble and conductor, with Joshua Pierce as soloist.

In 1961, Flagello composed the first of the three works he designated with the term "sonata," this one for harp. Unlike many composers who alter their customary language when writing for harp, in an effort to accommodate the difficulty of making rapid chromatic shifts on the instrument, Flagello decided to write a major composition for the instrument without compromising his highly chromatic idiom. The result is a work of considerable musical substance, amounting to far more than the sort of decorative piece so often associated with the instrument, while making considerable demands on the performer. Composed at the request of harpist Lise Nadeau, the sonata is one of Flagello's most enduring successes, having been featured as a required piece at harp competitions throughout the world. In 1985, the work was recorded by the Canadian harp virtuoso Erica Goodman and released by the Swedish company BIS.

The first movement, *Maestoso quasi allegro*, opens with a stern vigor, strongly reminiscent of the opening of Bloch's *Concerto Grosso no. 1*. Retaining this character throughout, the movement is a straightforward *sonata allegro*, in which all the themes emphasize the intervals of a fourth and a seventh. As is often the case with Flagello's music, the second movement, *Lento*, is the expressive centerpiece of the sonata. Nocturnal in mood, it suggests a plaintive *sicilienne*, or even a waltz, which becomes increasingly troubled until a climax is reached, and the movement returns to the character and material of the opening. The final movement, *Allegro più possibile*, has the character of a brisk country dance. Loosely structured along the lines of a *rondo*, the movement maintains the sort of energetic rhythmic drive rarely required by works for harp, offset by contrasting material calmer in tone. Intensity builds toward a coda in which both thematic ideas are combined in a brilliant conclusion.

The Harp Sonata was soon followed by a work for flute and guitar entitled *Burlesca*. In a single movement of about ten minutes duration, the piece opens with a haunting nocturnal prelude in A minor, improvisational and introspective in tone, which returns at the end as a postlude. In between is a more active "burlesque," rhythmically and tonally flexible and grotesquely sinister in character. This section is based on a mode built from alternating whole and half steps, which Flagello associated with the indigenous music of the Mediterranean coast. He felt that this mode, sometimes called a "diminished scale," linked southern Italy to the Semitic cultures of the Middle East. (This scale form played an increasingly important role in Flagello's later music, but the *Burlesca* provides one of the earliest and clearest examples.) The two instruments engage in busy developmental interplay—sometimes contrapuntally intricate, at others, in the manner of voice-with-accompaniment. In 1964, *Burlesca* was released on a recording featuring flutist Gary Sigurdson and guitarist Pasquale Garzia. It has been performed numerous times, including in an arrangement for flute and harp. Another recording, with flutist Janet Ketchum and guitarist Peter Segal, was issued in 1979.

Amidst this series of instrumental works appeared a short choral piece: an a capella setting for mixed voices of *Virtue*, a metaphysical poem by the Elizabethan religious writer George Herbert (1593–1633). The poem treats a theme quite congruent with Flagello's spiritual preoccupations: the ephemeral nature of all things of beauty save the "virtuous soul," which "Like seasoned timber, never gives/ But though the whole world turn to coal,/Then chiefly lives." In addition to the poignance of its expression, the setting is especially noteworthy for the dissonance of its harmonic language, which highlights the moments of consonance that underlie the most crucial lines of the poem. However, the dissonant harmony, including quartal structures, staggered entrances, hocketed dovetailing, and chromatic voice-leading, all impose considerable difficulties in execution, in seeming disregard of the fact that the piece was published as part of a series designed for school choruses.

The year 1962 was the most fruitful of Flagello's career, during which he produced five new works—all of them serious in intent and ambitious in scope and substance. The first to reach completion was the *Capriccio* for cello and orchestra, perhaps the work in which the composer achieved fullest realization of the alternately brooding and explosive character he first explored in the second movement of the *Divertimento*. It is also probably the finest of the several major instrumental works in which Flagello dispensed with classical formal designs, devising a form determined solely by musical content and emotional intent. One of his masterpieces, it is a work of profound expression, individual personality, and concise, logical construction—orchestrated to achieve the fullest realization of its intentions, while also satisfying the requirements of a virtuoso vehicle.

The *Capriccio* begins and ends in a mood of somber gravity, and a haunted, gloomy atmosphere prevails throughout. Somewhat like Bloch's approach in *Schelomo*—and quite like Giannini's in his *Psalm 130*, composed the following year (1963)—the solo cello serves as a tormented protagonist, crying out against the backdrop of a richly evocative accompaniment scored for a modest-sized orchestra, with a large percussion section including harp and celesta. One of those compositions whose titles (as noted earlier) seem to belie their dark character, the fifteen-minute *Capriccio* pursues a complex, tortuous—and, indeed, tortured—psychoemotional course, its many connected sections forming an unpredictable sequence of shifting tempos and gestures, all of which join to produce a powerfully coherent statement. The work is unified by a single three-note motif—a rising second followed by a rising sixth—that, in its various inversions and fragmentations, pervades virtually every measure. While its beginning and ending establish a tonal center of C, further confirmed by harmonic signposts at crucial junctures, the *Capriccio* offers little sense of tonal stability. Its rhetoric is chiefly declamatory and recitative-like, with little that might be construed as lyrical melody. Stunning sound-images abound throughout, producing a wide range of eerie, unearthly, grotesque effects. The sequence of episodes leads to a menacing cadenza—motivically generated—which culminates in a climax of apocalyptic proportions. Finally, almost as an epilogue, the cello plays the most lyrical music to be found in the work, to an accompaniment of broken chords in the celesta and slow arpeggios in the harp. After such a harsh, unyielding course, this hint of lyricism and tonal clarity emerges with striking eloquence, creating an almost overwhelming sense of hopeless resignation, before the work fades away in motivic fragments without resolution, either spiritual or tonal.

Flagello's *Capriccio* was recorded in 1964 by cellist George Koutzen, with the composer conducting the Orchestra Sinfonica di Roma. Arthur Cohn praised its "keen sense of form," and added that "the orchestration is expert," and "the cello writing is beautifully arranged."[20] The work's first public performance took place in December 1966, when Koutzen performed it with the Chappaqua (N.Y.) Orchestral Association, again under the direction of the composer. However, there is no record of any subsequent public performance. It is perplexing and distressing that a contribution of this stature to a repertoire notably lacking in concerted works of quality and substance has failed to attract the attention of cellists. In 1991, the Italian recording was reissued on compact disc. English Internet critic Rob Barnett commented, "While the line between profound and gloomy can be difficult to discern Flagello treads it like a master. You can cut the atmosphere with a very broad shovel. The jagged shrieks of the orchestra at 3:33 recall the Bloch of *Schelomo* but this is a distinctive work of great power—Flagello has his own voice. The statement at 13:43 is one of major lyrical eminence. A work of extraordinary grip."[21]

While Flagello was completing the orchestration of the *Capriccio*, he was also working on a short setting for chorus and orchestra of the Latin *Te Deum* text. The music he composed was vehement and intense, challenging the chorus with dissonant, chromatic counterpoint, before reaching a subdued conclusion. Completing the draft in short score in February 1962, Flagello turned immediately to his next project, leaving the *Te Deum* untouched for several years. Then, five years later, prompted by the opportunity for a performance, he returned to it, expanding his conception and retitling it *Te Deum for All Mankind.*

Barely two months had elapsed before Flagello completed the draft of his next composition: the Piano Concerto no. 3. Although he never returned to orchestrate it, the work proved to be the most tightly organized and finely wrought of his concertos, comparable in stature to the other great American traditionalist piano concertos of the midtwentieth century—those by Samuel Barber (1962), Peter Mennin (1957), and Vincent Persichetti (1962). Similar in character to the *Capriccio*, the Piano Concerto no. 3 begins in the same somber frame of mind as that in which the earlier work ended. However, following the general formal model of the classical concerto, the later piece is somewhat more conventional in its effect. In fact, aside from the slow introduction and a solo cadenza that recurs throughout the first movement, the Concerto no. 3 follows rather closely the formal outlines and general approach of the Piano Concerto no. 2. For this reason a comparison of the two concertos—composed only six years apart—clearly illuminates the differences outlined above between Flagello's early period and his period of maturity.

As suggested, the Piano Concerto no. 3 is a dark, gloomy work, restless and agitated, frequently erupting into shattering explosions. It is based almost entirely on a single motif, a descending, four-note pattern heard first in the orchestra at the opening of the introduction, marked *Lento quasi adagio*. A short, ruminative cadenza leads into the *Allegro vivace ma giusto*, based on material derived from the opening motif. These ideas are developed and elaborated in a series of intensely charged episodes in various tempos. The tone is turbulent and aggressive, until a return of the opening cadenza leads directly into the second movement.

The *Lento andante* opens as the orchestra introduces a dusky statement of the main motif. The piano develops this into a gloomy nocturne whose dolorous tone is relieved by moments of bittersweet tenderness. This leads directly into a lugubrious "ghost-march," whose tortured mood culminates in a climax that seems to convey both triumph and despair.

The finale, *Allegro molto*, follows without pause. Its character might be described as a demonic "tarantella from hell," in which the concerto's basic motif predominates in clearly recognizable form. The movement pursues its alternately grotesque and tempestuous course, finally leading to a coda marked *Con più entusiasmo*, in which the intensity reaches a frenetic pitch as the concentrated development of thematic material is focused toward a decisive conclusion.

The Piano Concerto no. 3 remained untouched for more than thirty years, until pianist Tatjana Rankovich expressed interest in recording the work, together with the Concerto no. 2. Composer and music editor Anthony Sbordoni was enlisted to score the later work after he'd made an intensive study of Flagello's orchestration. He completed the task in 1994, and the following year both concertos were recorded by Ms. Rankovich, with the Slovak Philharmonic of Kosice, under the direction of David Amos. Although it is futile to speculate as to whether Sbordoni approximated the orchestration that Flagello "would have done," one can state confidently that Sbordoni's contribution is congruent with the composer's general approach, and well suited to the character of this work, which it animates with an ease and naturalness that mollifies any question of its authenticity or the legitimacy of its overall impact.

As with the Concerto no. 2, the critical response to the Third Concerto was overwhelmingly positive. Mark Lehman commented, "Tempestuous, ardent, bittersweet, sometimes gloomy or febrile, these two concertos—especially No. 3—infuse the old-fashioned piano-virtuoso vocabulary with astonishing potency."[22] Paul Snook felt that the concerto's "tumultuous incident and almost fatalistic ebb and flow seem to hint at some overwhelming personal catastrophe—either lived through or anticipated and in either case coming to a resolution that leaves the listener feeling exhausted but gratified."[23] Discussing both Concertos nos. 2 and 3, Adrian Corleonis concluded, "Flagello's piano concertos are among the most persuasively successful post-Rachmaninov essays in the genre—substantial, gripping, truculent, and the more compelling for having wrought lyrically arched triumph against the grain of the life we know."[24]

The first public performance of Flagello's Piano Concerto no. 3 did not take place until February 2000, when Peter Vinograde gave the premiere with the Owensboro (Kentucky) Symphony Orchestra, under the direction of Nicholas Palmer. Local critic Dwight Pounds described the work as "high *verismo* drama in a style not unlike that of Puccini and a mystery akin to that of Bartók. Flagello depicted this entirely tonal work with a wide range of emotions—conflict, love, agitation and pain . . . absolutely superb by any possible measure."[25]

Barely a month after completing the draft of the concerto, Flagello finished his next manuscript: a setting for soprano and orchestra of a portion of *Gemma Donati*, a monologue by the poet and literary scholar Joseph Tusiani. Tusiani's work portrays the great Italian poet and statesman Dante Alighieri through the eyes of his devoted wife, Gemma. The portion extracted by Flagello recounts Dante's nightmarish vision warning of danger to Florence, and his painful decision to leave his wife and children and depart for Rome on behalf of his city-state. Beginning and ending with a B-flat-minor accompaniment in triplet *arpeggios* that rises from the depths of the orchestra, Flagello's fifteen-minute dramatic monologue, entitled *Dante's Farewell*, is pervaded by the same shadow of gloom that enshrouds the other works that poured rapidly from his pen at this time. Though largely grave and sustained, the difficult vocal line has moments of tender, flowing lyricism as well as stark drama, and culminates in an extraordinary passage of rapid coloratura, with a climax on a high D. Another of Flagello's most powerful and intense works, *Dante's Farewell* was also left in short score, as he quickly became absorbed in his next composition, and it remained without orchestration at the time of his death. Although it has had several semi-public presentations with piano accompaniment, such a reduction can only approximate the evocative and dramatic mood-painting clearly intended for the orchestra. The accompaniment was eventually orchestrated by Anthony Sbordoni in 2003.

Dante's Farewell cannot be discussed without mention of the remarkable coincidence of the composition of this work with the composition of a work of comparable scale and similar style, also for soprano and orchestra, by Samuel Barber. His work, *Andromache's Farewell*, was commissioned for the opening season of New York's Lincoln Center. Its first performance took place in April 1963, while Flagello's work was completed in May 1962. In addition to the similarities just noted, both works are tragic in character and deal with classical literary subjects. However, as striking as this coincidence appears superficially, each work is deeply representative of the music written by its respective composer at the time. Perhaps the most interesting observation to be made is that during the 1960s both Flagello (*Dante's Farewell, Contemplazioni di Michelangelo, Electra*) and Barber (*Andromache's Farewell, Antony and Cleopatra*)—and Vittorio Giannini as well (*The Medead, Antigone, Edipus*)—were all drawn to classic literary subjects, which they treated with a torrid, emotionally extravagant Neo-Romantic musical style.

Quickly turning his attention from *Dante's Farewell*, Flagello set to work on another composition for piano, this time a sonata. Along with the Third Concerto, this substantial, three-movement work represents the composer's chief contribution to the romantic virtuoso solo-piano repertoire. Wholeheartedly embracing both the ethos and rhetoric of this heritage, Flagello imbued his sonata with his own distinctive emotional turbulence. Tightly constructed with an eye toward both expressive and motivic unity, all three movements are based on thematic material that emphasizes the interval of a half step. As is true of most of Flagello's music from this period, tonal centers are established as thematic material is presented, at major points of demarcation within movements, and at the ends of movements; however, at other times tonality is unstable and transitory.

The first movement, *Andante con moto e rubato*, is a standard *sonata allegro*, except that instead of the usual two themes, one idea in F minor, built from two short motifs, serves to fill the roles of both. This theme appears at times restless and searching, at others, bold and defiant, and at still others, introspective and ruminative.

The second movement begins with a soulful, recitative-like passage, which leads into a gloomy, nocturnal barcarolle—a type of mood-piece of which Flagello was especially fond. This soon builds to a tremendous climax, which then subsides in dark resignation.

The final movement, *Allegro vivace quanto possibile*, is a whirlwind perpetual-motion *toccata* that happens to be a full *sonata allegro*, two themes and all.

Another one of Flagello's most fully realized compositions, the Piano Sonata was first performed by Elizabeth Marshall at her Town Hall (N.Y.) debut in 1963, and she recorded the work the following year. Despite his previously cited praise for other works, Arthur Cohn was less impressed with the sonata, finding it to be "a stylistic ball that bounces in too many directions. The rhapsodic modulations of the opening are quite unacknowledged by the romantic sighs and furbelows of the second movement and totally unsustained by the perpetual-motion kinetics of the finale."[26] The work drew little attention during the next twenty-five years, until 1991, when it was recorded by Joshua Pierce. A performance by Peter Vinograde was then released in 1997, followed by another by Tatjana Rankovich in 1999. (This latter disc also included the sonatas of Paul Creston and Vittorio Giannini.) Now the critical response was more favorable. Discussing the sonatas of both Giannini and Flagello, Adrian Corleonis wrote:

Giannini's agitated anguish . . . and Flagello's embittered ecstasy of grief—set off by manic truculence—confront the listener with a knotted substantiality out of all proportion to mere length. Moreover, both works boil to conclusions without the facile amelioration of wholesome, feel-good sentiment. Indeed, one comes to admire in both composers the ready mastery of cyclically inflected sonata form that can make works so unflinchingly, elegantly cohesive of such explosive feelings.[27]

As it has become better known, the Piano Sonata has been compared with Barber's highly regarded and frequently performed essay in the form with regard to expressive intensity, concentration of form, and virtuosic elaboration. Steven Schwartz describes it as "full-blooded, virtuosic, Romantic music, although it manages to retain a modern harmonic outlook. The slow movement in particular is a killer. A barcarolle that works against type—most barcarolles are serene—it essentially howls from the depths. . . . I'd put it up there with the Barber piano sonata, a classic of American repertoire."[28] Comparing the two works, Mark Lehman commented, "Flagello doesn't quite have Barber's silken polish or virtuoso brilliance in figuration—but on the other hand is more sure of his own voice and thus, somehow, speaks with more urgency and conviction."[29]

The series of masterpieces that Flagello produced in 1962 was followed by a brief lapse with the composition of two pieces of more pedestrian quality: a short choral work with organ called *Tu Es Sacerdos* and a Concertino for Piano, Brass, and Timpani. The other creative fruit of 1963 was the Sonata for Violin and Piano. The first movement—*Andantino mosso*—is a *sonata allegro* form. Like the theme of the corresponding movement of the Piano Sonata, the theme of the Violin Sonata's first movement appears in several guises—initially, wistful and somewhat melancholy, but then transformed into an ardent, surging declaration. This theme is developed, along with other material, through a course that is alternately agitated and intensely lyrical.

The second movement opens with a bleak recitative in the violin, punctuated by tolling bell effects in the piano. As in the corresponding movement of the Piano Sonata, this is followed by an aria, *Movendo ma andante*, suggesting another dark, brooding barcarolle.

The brief finale is marked *Allegro giusto* and is a modified *sonatina* with the character of a burlesque in perpetual motion, bringing the work to a whirlwind finish.

Flagello's Violin Sonata had its premiere at Carnegie Recital Hall in May 1965. As noted earlier, the performance by violinist Carter Nice and pianist Anthony Makas was well received by the *New York Times* critic. But, never published, the work was not played again until 1980, when the composer himself accompanied his close friend violinist Walter Brewus at the Newport Music Festival. Critic Edwin Safford was "impressed," stating that the sonata "required no apologies for avoidance of the avant-garde. Flagello's structure, lyricism and unexpected turns were most convincing."[30] In 1987, the Violin Sonata was recorded by Eugene Fodor and Arlene Portney and in 1997 by Setsuko Nagata and Peter Vinograde. Again the critical response was positive. "How haunted this music, how restless the chromatic sighings," exclaimed Mark Lehman.[31]

The year 1964 was another productive one for Flagello, during which he composed two large vocal works, as well as several more modest items. Most important are settings for high voice and orchestra of four sonnets by Michelangelo (whose poetry was also set by Britten and Shostakovich). The first group of poetic settings written by Flagello in ten years, the *Contemplazioni di Michelangelo* represent a considerable advance in sophistication relative to *The Land*, for example, with regard to the rhythmic freedom and phraseological complexity of the vocal line, the integration of vocal line with accompaniment, and the textural and contrapuntal complexity of the accompaniment. As in the case of the *Cello Capriccio*, the orchestration achieves effects of remarkable richness and power, despite the use of an ensemble of only modest size.

Throughout his long life Michelangelo wrote more than 300 sonnets, madrigals, and other poetic examples, within which he imparted some of his most intimate, and also his most pessimistic, feelings. From this large group, Flagello selected four of those whose expressive content resonated with his own perspective, while also suggesting a sequence of commentaries on life and love, from youth to old age. The first setting, *"Come puo esser?"*, conveys the drama, volatility, and playfulness of young love. The second, *"Ben doverrieno,"* is the most extensive and deeply expressive portion of the work, with a scope that is truly operatic in its tragic grandeur. *"Ben fu"* stands in stark contrast—a light and exuberant piece with a brilliant sense of color that calls Respighi to mind. The final sonnet, *"Di piu cose,"* expresses the poet's faith in God as the source of spiritual redemption in the face of earthly misery. The mood of the music is gloomy and somber, building to a towering climax.

Flagello conducted the first performance of the *Contemplazioni* in February 1965, with soprano Donna Jeffrey and the Orchestra of America in New York City. He also recorded it in Rome that same year, with Nancy Tatum as soloist. The work drew praise from Enos Shupp Jr., who was impressed by its "fine vocal writing and superb orchestral accompaniments," finding Flagello "an enormously talented composer for voice."[32] In 1981, Flagello included the *Contemplazioni* on the program of a series of concerts he conducted in Peru, with his second wife Maya as soprano soloist. The local critic wrote, "Flagello has created inspired pages, with a grand spirit, solid formal structure, and an elaborate and interesting harmonic fabric."[33] The Roman recording was reissued on compact disc in 1991 and was reviewed some time later by Robert Cummings, who found the *Contemplazioni* to be "a most moving and powerful work."[34]

Simultaneously with the composition of the *Contemplazioni*, Flagello produced another group of poetic settings, this one distinctly different in style and tone, scored for high voice with chamber orchestra. Choosing six poems from William Blake's satirical collection entitled *An Island in the Moon* (1784), he created a song cycle characterized for the most part by a folk-like simplicity and good humor and with much lighter and more transparent textures. However, although his desire to pair the Michelangelo settings with a group of markedly contrasting character is understandable, Flagello was a far less graceful purveyor of wit than of more weighty expressive matters, and his efforts to evoke lighter, gentler moods were usually unsuccessful and sometimes in questionable taste. It is notable that the most successful songs in this cycle are the two that are more serious in tone: "O Father, O Father" and "Leave, Oh Leave Me to My Sorrows." Flagello recorded the Blake settings in Rome with Nancy Tatum, together with the *Contemplazioni*, for release in 1965. However the Blake songs were not included on the 1991 CD reissue.

Although the remainder of Flagello's music from 1964 comprises short pieces of less consequence, one may be chosen as illustration that the most inauspicious circumstances might draw from him artistic statements of considerable pith and substance. Commissioned by the American Accordionists' Association, Flagello composed a short piece for use by the Confederation International des Accordionistes as the required composition for the Coupe Mondial in 1965. Entitled *Introduction and Scherzo*, the five-minute piece begins with the slow, gloomy presentation of an ominous, irregularly descending motif within a context of uncertain tonality. This introductory material is elaborated into an ominous, almost diabolical statement thoroughly uncharacteristic of the type of expression associated with the accordion. The brief introduction leads directly into the *Scherzo*—really a dark, sinister waltz, of a sort that frequently captured Flagello's imagination—based on an inversion of the introductory motif. While providing the obligatory technical challenges expected of such a piece, it also displays the motivic concentration, unity of mood, and subtle regulation of harmonic dissonance and tonal stability that characterize Flagello's finest works. In 1991, in an effort to broaden its exposure, this writer arranged the *Introduction and Scherzo* for saxophone quartet, in which form it was published under the title *Valse Noire*.

In 1965, Flagello returned to the *Symphonic Waltzes*, the cycle of three pieces in French style that he had written for piano in 1958, now with the idea of orchestrating them and linking them together as a suite associated with the paintings of Henri de Toulouse-Lautrec. In reshaping the work, he composed a new movement to be inserted between the first and second waltzes and altered the rhythm and meter of the beginning of the final one to suggest a cancan. Finally, Flagello appended a verbal tag associated with Toulouse-Lautrec to identify each of the four movements. The first, called *"Paris—La Belle Epoque,"* is a musical portrait of the milieu that was not only the painter's home but also the social and psychological backdrop for his work. The music suggests a world in which gaudy, transitory pleasures provide escape from an inner emptiness of the spirit. *"L'Histoires Naturelles"* is Flagello's musical depiction of the menagerie that inhabited Lautrec's paintings—a slightly grotesque yet endearing circus, appearing helter-skelter in kaleidoscopic orchestral dress. *"Elles"* evokes the *demi-monde*, the sad nocturnal world of lost souls, the outcasts who emerge while the city is asleep. It was among the creatures of the *demi-monde*, especially its women, that Lautrec felt most at home. *"Moulin Rouge"* returns to the public scene: the glittering world of Parisian nightlife—the raucous dance halls and their forced gaiety, which Lautrec observed and captured in his art.

Though not a deeply personal work, *Lautrec* is lavishly orchestrated and makes a brilliant effect. It has been performed a number of times, in Europe as well as in the United States. Flagello recorded

the work in Rome in 1966, and shortly thereafter it was choreographed by the Alabama Ballet, who took the production on tour.
The Italian recording is one of those reissued on compact disc in
1991.

The other work completed in 1965 is a Suite for Harp and String
Trio. Also evincing something of a French flavor, the work's light,
diverting character and its scoring for a small chamber ensemble set
it somewhat apart from the rest of Flagello's output, as does a certain carelessness of structure. The Suite opens with a vigorous
"Petite Overture" in simple *sonatina* form. This is followed by a
gently wistful *"Valse,"* based on a piano piece originally composed
in 1953. The work concludes with a lively *"Rondino alla Giga."* The
Suite was released on recording in 1997.

Flagello completed one major work in 1966, along with several
short pieces composed largely with students and young musicians
in mind. One of these is a touching setting of Longfellow's poem
The Arrow and the Song, for mixed chorus with piano or harp. The
poem itself verges on sentimentality, and the lush harmonic warmth
of Flagello's poignant, heartfelt setting offers no resistance, recalling
the music he wrote during the 1950s.

But the most important work of 1966 is *Electra*, for which Flagello
returned once again to the combination of piano with percussion
ensemble. Calling for a much larger ensemble than that used in the
Divertimento, including celesta, harp, and more than forty percussion instruments, *Electra* is a more ambitious concept: a three-movement character study based on the Greek drama, in which the piano
represents the tragic heroine—somewhat like an operatic monodrama. Despite a degree of emphasis on texture, gesture, and timbre
unusual for Flagello, the work is quite similar to a piano concerto in
form, scope, and treatment. Within a straightforward *sonata allegro*
design, the first movement, entitled "Synopsis," depicts an emotional state of hysterical rage and an obsessive determination for
vengeance. The terse motif that erupts at the outset outlines a minor
triad in second inversion—the motif on which Richard Strauss's
opera *Elektra* (a favorite of Flagello's) is based. Within moments this
motif generates several related ideas that form the basis of the entire
work. One of these has a particular significance: an ominous, insistent motto outlining a diminished triad, which Flagello intended to
represent the heroine's monomania.

The second movement, "Lament," is a reflective soliloquy that suggests Electra's tormented devotion to her father. The haunted, nocturnal mood is enhanced by a variety of evocative sonorities produced by the enormous percussion battery.

In the third movement, Flagello followed Hofmannsthal and Strauss's precedent, ending the work with an ecstatic dance of revenge that culminates in Electra's fatal collapse. The "Death Dance" is a wild, frenzied *rondo* based, appropriately enough, on the *Dies Irae* motif in irregular meter, with references to the main ideas presented earlier.

The premiere of *Electra* was given by the Manhattan Percussion Ensemble, conducted by Paul Price with Flagello as piano soloist, in April 1966. The work has enjoyed a number of performances since then and was recorded by the same group, but with Joshua Pierce as piano soloist. This recording was released in 1991, on the same disc as the *Divertimento*.

In November 1966, Flagello's teacher, mentor, and beloved friend Vittorio Giannini died suddenly, four months before his last opera, *The Servant of Two Masters*, was to be mounted by the New York City Opera. Although the work was essentially complete, it lacked an overture, so Flagello decided to provide one, basing it on themes from the work and emulating Giannini's *opera buffa* style. Although the overture was completed in time for the production in March 1967, director Julius Rudel decided that the opera was self-sufficient without it and chose not to use it. Flagello retitled it *A Goldoni Overture* and conducted the first performance with the orchestra of his summer music festival in Maiori, Italy, in 1969. The overture was included on the recording made in 1995 with the Slovak Philharmonic Orchestra of Kosice, conducted by David Amos.

Later in 1967, Flagello turned his attention to another work for violin and piano, which he titled *Declamation*. A brilliant example of the concentration of materials and intensity of effect characteristic of his works from the 1960s, *Declamation* packs a remarkable density of musical activity into a mere nine minutes. All the thematic material is derived from the declamatory cadenza with which the work opens (hence, the title), and the solemn incantation that follows. The body of the work is an agitated *Allegro*, which subjects the motivic material to extensive development. The *Allegro* culminates in another, more elaborate, cadenza, followed by a return of the incantation, which brings the work to a majestic conclusion.

The premiere of *Declamation* was given by violinist Walter Brewus and pianist Edwin Hymovitz at Carnegie Hall in October 1968. It was not heard again until Eugene Fodor recorded it, along with the Violin Sonata, in 1987. A meticulous reading of the work by Setsuko Nagata and Peter Vinograde was released on compact disc in 1997. At about the same time, *Declamation* came to the attention of the celebrated violinist Midori and her accompanist Robert MacDonald, who selected it as the contemporary work to include on their spring 1997 tour of the United States, Europe, and South America.

Also in 1967, Flagello was invited to compose a work with which to conclude a festival concert featuring a chorus and orchestra comprising a select group of young musicians drawn from New York City's public high schools. In response he returned to the setting of the *Te Deum* he had drafted in 1962, now with the idea of expanding it by interspersing among the Latin text portions of abolitionist poet John Greenleaf Whittier's *Laus Deo*. Whittier's poem is a hymn in praise of God, expressing gratitude for the freeing of the slaves and an end to the Civil War. By so combining the two texts and composing a new, triumphant finale, Flagello transformed his abstract setting of the traditional Latin text into a vivid expression of homage to God, as well as a fervent hymn to the spirit of brotherhood. Still less than fifteen minutes long, the newly retitled *Te Deum for All Mankind* is another masterpiece of concentration and intensity and the finest of Flagello's choral works, including within its relatively short duration a great diversity of musical and expressive activity. Opening emphatically with a driving dotted-note rhythm (heard also in the first movement of the Third Piano Concerto and other subsequent compositions) that barely ceases throughout the entire work, the *Te Deum for All Mankind* includes tender, plaintive soprano solos, dense passages of dissonant choral polyphony, vehement homophony, a polytonal brass fanfare, mysterious *a capella* choral passages, and moments of poignant, heartwarming diatonic polyphony, not to mention several overpowering climaxes—all integrated seamlessly without any sense of stylistic disjunction.

The first performance of *Te Deum for All Mankind* took place at New York City's Philharmonic (now Avery Fisher) Hall in May 1969. Benjamin Chancy conducted the All-New York City High School Chorus and Orchestra; the chorus was prepared by John Motley, to whom the work was dedicated. Since that time the *Te Deum* has been featured as the concluding work at several similar youth-music festivals.

During the highly productive 1960s, Flagello was also immersed in the creation of a large-scale orchestral work in four movements—the first composition he chose to designate as a symphony. He composed the second movement first, in Rome, during the summer of 1964; the first movement was completed in February 1965, and the third and fourth in 1966. He finished the orchestration in January 1968, the year of his fortieth birthday. A brazenly unapologetic manifesto of an aesthetic ideal then at its absolute nadir with regard to musical fashion, it is Flagello's most ambitious abstract work and, in many ways, a definitive statement of both his artistic and personal identity. It is also a work of consummate compositional mastery and discipline, a virtual textbook of classic symphonic technique. Not surprisingly, he acknowledged as his model the Fourth Symphony of Brahms, a work that he held in great esteem, although its Olympian sobriety is far removed from the turbulence and desperation of his own composition.

Flagello's symphony opens boldly with a three-note motif—a descending fourth following by a descending second—that is the basis of the entire work. The first movement, *Allegro molto*, is an explosive *sonata allegro*, in which a violently agitated first theme is offset by a brooding, restless second theme, which ultimately achieves the major climax of the movement. The movement's sense of constant strife is engendered by frequent, heavily accented changes of meter.

The second movement, *Andante lento*, opens with recitative-like passages that gradually lead to the body of the movement, a long-breathed lyrical outpouring that ebbs and flows with the immediacy of an operatic scene, with the basic three-note motif woven throughout. Similar in conception to the slow movement of the 1959 Concerto for String Orchestra, this orchestral aria builds to a towering climax, before returning to the recitative-like passages with which the movement opened.

The third movement, *Allegretto brusco*, is an ironic *scherzo-and-trio* with grotesque and sinister undercurrents, based on an inverted form of the basic motif. (The second section of the *scherzo* is derived from the central portion of a Waltz in B minor composed for piano in 1953.) An eerie trio section offers a brief but unstable moment of respite, before the *scherzo* returns in modified form. This leads to a *stretto*, culminating in a wildly demonic outburst in which all the ideas of the *scherzo* are combined. The movement concludes on a note of uncertainty and anticipation that sets the stage for the mighty finale to follow.

The fourth movement, *Ciaccona: Maestoso andante,* opens with a majestic *tutti* statement that conceals a bass line created from an extended retrograde elaboration of the symphony's basic motif. The chaconne (in truth, what most references identify as a *passacaglia*) is built on that bass line. A series of nineteen strict variations begins with the solemnity customarily associated with the form but then becomes increasingly agitated, leading to a return of the opening majestic statement. Now a series of freer developmental variations follows, which create the effect of a poignant, bittersweet interlude. However the moment of tenderness soon turns ominous and tense, leading, after a total of twenty-six variations, to a vigorous fugue of which both subject and countersubject are transformations of the *passacaglia* bass line. The fugue proceeds, further developing all the movement's thematic material in increasingly concentrated fashion, rising to an intense emotional pitch. A *stretto* then culminates in a stark statement of the *passacaglia* theme, harmonized triadically, that is both triumphant and defiant, leading the work to an extremely hard-won conclusion.

The Symphony no. 1 was first performed in April 1971, with the composer himself conducting the symphony orchestra of the Manhattan School of Music. Michael Mark described the work as "a really notable addition to the literature. The work is beautifully expressive, doesn't meander, and is brilliantly orchestrated to boot. . . . Nicolas Flagello is a major talent and one looks forward to hearing him and his symphony continue to give pleasure to audiences the way they did this night."[35] However, the work was not heard again for twenty-two years, until it was played once more by the Manhattan Orchestra, this time conducted by David Gilbert, in October 1993.

There have been no further public performances of the symphony, although a recording featuring the Slovak Radio Symphony of Bratislava, conducted by David Amos, was released in 2003. Response to this recording was generally positive. Though Roger Hecht found the symphony to be "a worthy effort but not one of the great American symphonies,"[36] composer-critic Arnold Rosner called it "a major success," adding, "Here is true heart-on-sleeve emotional music, throbbing and crying out, in a personalized tonal and formally traditional language."[37] William Zagorski described it as "a strapping, brawny, yet concisely precise essay. . . . There is not an ounce of padding in this rigorously constructed piece. Everything is spun out from its opening motive, whose myriad harmonic implications are developed strikingly and seemingly effortlessly."[38] Adrian Corleonis found it to be "a gripping, powerful, grimly exhilarating work that stands shoulder-to-shoulder . . . with the later Prokofiev symphonies and the best of Shostakovich."[39]

Like the Fifth Symphonies of Paul Creston (1955) and Vittorio Giannini (1964), Flagello's Symphony no. 1 exemplifies the Neo-Romantic paradigm of the symphony as quintessential medium for the representation of serious emotional crisis. But unlike the two older composers, who had to strain the limits of their emotional vocabulary in order to embody feelings of such intensity, Flagello's musical personality was naturally suited for expressions of this kind. His Symphony no. 1 therefore looms as perhaps the consummate Neo-Romantic essay of this subgenre—indeed, along with the Symphony no. 7 of Peter Mennin, it may be the greatest of all American traditionalist symphonies.

The work that followed the tempestuous Symphony no. 1 was a *Serenata* for chamber orchestra, one of Flagello's few works of light, diverting character. It was composed in Rome during the summer of 1968 and received its first public performance the following year by the orchestra of a summer music festival in Salerno, conducted by the composer. The *Serenata* is structured somewhat along the lines of a Baroque suite. The first movement, "Psalmus," is a memorial to Giannini and captures something of the older man's warmth and tenderness of spirit. Toward the end of the movement the two main motifs from Giannini's *The Taming of the Shrew* are heard in the horn and the oboe. "Passe-Pied" is a rather jocular but grotesque rendition of an old dance form. The "Siciliana" that follows evokes not only the flowing dance rhythm characteristic of its ancestry, but also utilizes the Mediterranean mode described earlier in reference to the *Burlesca* for flute and guitar. The concluding "Giga" is the most spirited movement of the four, as well as the most musically involved. It consists of a lively opening section and a more relaxed contrasting section, each of which is heard twice, connected by a fugal transition the second time. The movement concludes with a joyful coda that combines both themes contrapuntally.

The *Serenata* was recorded in Rome under the composer's direction in 1968, shortly after it was completed, although this recording was never released until 1995. In the meantime a recording by the New Russia Orchestra, conducted by David Amos, had been released the previous year. Bret Johnson found the *Serenata* to be "one of [Flagello's] finest creations. The gently nocturnal Cantel-oubeian first movement soon yields to the gawky *Passe-Pied* and the even more nocturnal Siciliana. The concluding *Giga* could easily be by William Alwyn, but it is the breadth of Flagello's versatility that calls to mind so many other musical figures, rather than any craven imitation."[40]

Flagello had long admired Martin Luther King's dedication to the ideals of human justice and brotherhood and was deeply moved by the influential black leader's assassination in April 1968. The comment made by Pope Paul VI, upon learning of King's sudden mar-tyrdom, "I liken the life of this man to the life of our Lord," immediately galvanized Flagello's creative energy. Seeking a suit-able form of musical tribute, he recalled the choral-orchestral *Pen-taptych* composed fifteen years earlier and realized that restructuring the work around Martin Luther King would provide the human focus missing from the earlier work. He decided to com-bine excerpts from the speeches of the slain civil rights leader in alternation with the Latin liturgical texts, so as to suggest King as a latter-day embodiment of Jesus Christ. Indeed, the selections he chose from King's speeches concern the fundamental Christian val-ues of brotherly love, faith in God's omniscient goodness, and enduring hardship without succumbing to fear or vengeance, rather than more worldly social concerns. He set King's words in an expressive *arioso* consistent stylistically with the choral portions, in such a way that the vernacular solo element continually reverberates against the timeless spirituality of the Latin choral sections in a deeply moving synergy. Flagello ended the work with a heartfelt setting of a portion of the "I Have a Dream" speech, followed by the vigorous choral fugue "*Jubilate Deo.*"

Although the oratorio was completed in 1968, the premiere did not take place until February 1974, when James DePreist conducted the National Symphony Orchestra and the Cathedral Choral Society at the Kennedy Center in Washington, D.C., with the composer's brother Ezio as bass-baritone soloist. However, while preparing the work several months earlier, DePreist requested that Flagello omit the "I Have a Dream"/"*Jubilate Deo*" sequence. In DePreist's own words:

The music that accompanied the "I Have a Dream" segment was so incredibly beautiful that it captured the spirit of the words, but in a crucial sense it did not capture the contrast of the context of those words—that it was necessary to have a march to the Capitol to make those words, that dream, a reality. I told [Flagello] it needed to be more bittersweet to evoke the experience more fully. I said this cautiously; I said he could tell me that if I wanted a different ending, I could write it myself. But to my surprise, he said he understood my point. So we talked about how I felt the spirit of the work would be better encapsulated in a new finale based upon a return to the theme of the third movement. Even though that was my idea, the ending was fully his because he wanted something more elaborate than a literal recapitulation. I was grateful to Nic to be magnanimous enough to allow an interloper to provide an idea like that, and I have felt since that time a commitment to labor on behalf of that piece.[41]

Years later, Flagello conceded that DePreist's suggestion improved the work's effectiveness, but he remained fond of the "I Have a Dream"/"*Jubilate Deo*" sequence. In 1976, he began to compose another choral work, to be called *Psalmus Americanus*, which would incorporate this material, but the project was never completed.

Including four of the five sections from the early *Pentaptych*, the final version of the *Passion of Martin Luther King* reflects many characteristics of Flagello's ultra-Romantic 1950s style—more deliberate pacing, greater metrical regularity, more consonant harmonic language, and an unambiguous sense of tonality. As always, the orchestration is sumptuous and virile, with no stinting on the climaxes, and the choral writing is gorgeous, with especially exquisite part writing in the "*Cor Jesu*" and "*Stabat Mater.*" The solo settings of King's words are apt—although, admittedly, the refined *bel canto* approach is a far cry from the robust rhetoric of black evangelical preaching. In truth, despite the extravagant grandeur of the music, this is a very personal, almost mystical, interpretation of Martin Luther King, rather than a work of social consciousness. And, although it has proven to be Flagello's best-known and most frequently performed piece, it is not without significant weaknesses: In addition to the aspects attributable to its early date of composition, the pacing of the work lacks variety, with too many consecutive passages of slow music. In short, it is considerably less successful artistically than the similarly conflated *Te Deum for All Mankind*.

Nevertheless, the *Passion* has been received well by audiences and has been performed throughout the United States and Canada, as well as in Europe. And in 1995, DePreist recorded it with the Oregon Symphony Orchestra and Portland Symphonic Choir, with Raymond Bazemore as soloist. If audiences have responded enthusiastically to the work, critical reaction has been mixed. Commenting on the Washington, D.C., premiere, Paul Hume wrote, "Everything about Flagello's 'Passion' is well put together and effective in sound. The large orchestra, augmented at the end by the organ, sounds sumptuous, the choral writing is solid. In musical values, the work is entirely conservative, conventional, a compendium of ideas ranging from Strauss to the Respighi of 'The Pines of Rome.'"[42] Reviewing a performance in Quebec, Marc Samson found it to be "filled with action and an accommodating dramaticism," calling it "an eminently 'public' work. This was proven by the standing ovation that greeted the conclusion of the performance—quite exceptional for the first hearing of a contemporary work. However, as contemporary as it is, this 'Passion' adopts a conventional and simple language that speaks directly to the listener. . . . With its easily accessible melodic substance, the work makes a singularly striking impact."[43] Reviewing the recording, Tim Smith felt that the oratorio "may go too far in making a connection between King and Christ, and the music is hardly stamped with originality. But much of the romantic score is affecting; the choral writing is assured, and King's eloquent words lose none of their effectiveness when sung to Flagello's straightforward melodies."[44] Reporting on a performance by the Philadelphia Orchestra, Daniel Webster wrote, "The music often uses strong harmonic outlines, ostinatos and rhythmic elements to suggest the march of history and, in the choral writing, creates big events that evoke the outcry of the oppressed. Dr. King's speeches are full of compelling music, and singing those rolling words multiplies their impact," adding, "In other hands, some of the orchestral devices might have seemed derivative."[45] English critic Andrew Achenbach found "Flagello's chosen idiom . . . recognizably 'American' in its open-hearted honesty and bustling vigour,"[46] while Francis Brancaleone described Flagello's musical language as "quite personal and distinctive," adding that it "rests on the use of chromaticism and vocal lines inspired by Romantic ideals inflected by 20th-century techniques. Flagello achieves impressive emotional impact, builds vivid musical climaxes and leaves a strong musical imprint."[47]

After 1968, a number of subtle changes began to appear in Flagello's music. In some works the sense of tonality—though unmistakably present—is suggested more remotely, while the level of harmonic dissonance becomes more complex, sometimes approaching polytonality. Titles seem increasingly enigmatic, at times suggesting cryptic meanings known only to the composer. Some works seem to reflect a greater depth of inner exploration, as motifs seem to take on personal meanings, their recurrence in several works suggesting implicit relationships. However, though he was only in his early forties, Flagello's productivity began to diminish. Between 1969 and 1974, only nine new compositions appeared, all but three of less than ten minutes duration.

The first pieces in which this change can be felt are the *Nocturne* for violin and piano and *Philos* for brass quintet, both miniature masterpieces of intense, concentrated expression, composed in 1969. The six-minute *Nocturne*, though clearly situated in B minor, follows an oblique, angular tonal course that never truly settles into a comfortable cadential resolution. The expressive impact is haunting and unsettling, subtly but vividly portraying a disturbing inner mindscape. The eight-minute *Philos* falls into two parts: a slow, gravely searching contemplation in G minor, followed by a sprightly fugue in D minor based on motivic material introduced in the first part. The first section introduces a motif—a descending half step followed by a descending fifth—that appears in several pieces from this period, almost like a coded "motto"-theme, indicative of some bitter remorse. The title refers to the Greek word for "love," but any such connection to the character of the piece is difficult to adduce. In 1972, *Philos* was recorded by the American Brass Quintet (with Gerard Schwarz as first trumpet); there is no record of its first public performance. The *Nocturne* had to wait until 1996 for its first performance, by Setsuko Nagata and Peter Vinograde, who also recorded it the following year.

Later in 1969, following the completion of these short pieces, Flagello was drawn into a major project whose elements extended the stylistic parameters of his more personal, abstract compositions of the time. Approached by the Preparatory (precollege) Division of the Manhattan School with an invitation to compose an opera that could be performed, as well as enjoyed, by children, he found himself attracted to the medieval morality tale "The Pied Piper of Hamelin." Working quickly, he fashioned the libretto himself, reshaping the story to eliminate its original vengeful ending, which he replaced with a denouement of redemption in which the Piper is revealed as an almost Christ-like "Spirit of Music." Flagello completed the music in January 1970, and the premiere took place in May of that year, under the direction of Cynthia Auerbach.

The Piper of Hamelin was designed to be appreciated on many levels. Not only was it tailored for ease of execution, but it also reflects a certain simplification of the composer's musical style, as well as an uncharacteristically lighthearted approach, with musical "in-jokes" and some rather clumsy attempts at humor. The music is direct and tuneful, while structural unity is maintained throughout, as two simple motifs presented during the lugubrious orchestral introduction generate all the thematic material of the opera. The leading roles require mature, well-trained voices, while the lesser roles may be played by children. Similarly, much of the principal orchestral material is quite advanced technically, though many of the individual instrumental parts are simple enough to be played by young students. The story itself is entertaining at face value, yet there are serious messages about the fulfilling of promises, about forgiveness, and even about taking the work of an artist for granted. But instead of emphasizing themes like betrayal and vengeance, Flagello focused on the transformational and redemptive powers of music. Choosing a rather orthodox structural concept for the opera, he framed its three short acts with spoken excerpts from the famous 1849 poem by Robert Browning. In between these readings, the story is enacted through recitatives and choral numbers, with only a couple of arias toward the end of Act III.

Several aspects of Act III warrant additional comment. An extended orchestral Intermezzo heard at the beginning suggests the loneliness and despair of the townspeople, now bereft of their children. Toward the middle of the Intermezzo, a solo clarinet introduces a tender motif that later emerges as the melody of redemption. (This Intermezzo may be performed as an orchestral extract.) Later, when the Piper reappears and agrees to return the children upon being paid the agreed-upon fee, the townspeople demand to know the Piper's true identity. At this point, in the opera's most fully elaborated aria, he reveals himself as the ubiquitous "Spirit of Music." Then, as bells chime in the distance, the children gradually reappear, singing a simple chant (based on the Piper's aria) in *solfège* syllables. As the chant is repeated over and over, additional musical elements are added to the contrapuntal fabric in an ingenious cumulative *ostinato*, which builds in volume and intensity to an exultant hymn of praise and gratitude, bringing the opera to an ecstatic apotheosis.

Although Flagello's "softening" of the story may at times verge on sentimentality, the opera reveals a fundamental sincerity and authenticity of feeling, not to mention superb craftsmanship in shaping a work of considerable musical substance. The solidity of its structure, and the sheer expressiveness of its music, fueled by a fervent sense of spirituality, combine to create a convincing, and very moving experience.

The Piper has enjoyed a number of successful productions since its premiere. The most auspicious took place in March 1999, when it was revived by the Preparatory Division of the Manhattan School of Music in a production conducted by Jonathan Strasser to mark the retirement of Dianne Flagello, after twenty-five years as the division's director. *New York Times* critic Anthony Tommasini acknowledged that the opera "succeeded wildly with its intended audience," but his begrudging description of the work as "effectively conceived, but not especially distinguished musically," and hackneyed comments like his description of the Act III Intermezzo as "an overly long passage of mood music for orchestra" which "sounded like a melodramatic film score in search of a film" all recalled the contemptuous Modernist critical clichés commonly encountered during the 1960s.[48] Nevertheless, the Manhattan School production was recorded and released commercially on compact disc within a few months.

One of the most significant works of Flagello's later maturity is the Symphony no. 2, completed in Minori, Italy, during the summer of 1970. Bearing the peculiarly worded subtitle, *Symphony of the Winds*, the piece is scored for a small ensemble of twenty-two winds and brass, plus percussion—that is, a standard symphony orchestra minus strings. This complement, omitting saxophones, baritone horns, and other standard components of the concert band instrumentation, distinguishes it from that aggregation to whose repertoire so many mid-twentieth-century American composers contributed so prolifically. When asked by a program annotator about the significance of the work's subtitle, the composer responded by providing movement rubrics that indicate a metaphorical as well as literal use of the word "winds": I—*Moderato com-*

odo, "The torrid winds of veiled portents"; II—*Aria*, "Dark winds of lonely contemplation"; III—*Fuga*, "The winds of re-birth and vitality." These cryptic inscriptions are matched by music of similarly enigmatic character.

The form of the first movement is a clear *sonata allegro*. The opening measures introduce two motifs that direct the course of the entire symphony. The first of these is built around the interval of a third, which governs not only the shape of all subsequent themes but also the key relations within and between the movements. The second idea refers back to the motif identified in *Philos*—a descending second followed by a descending larger interval of varying size, but usually a perfect fifth. Both motifs are contained within the exposition of the restless first theme. The second theme is presented first with an eerie calm, but then is reiterated with a demonic vehemence. This leads to a much fuller restatement of the first theme, concluding the exposition. The development treats the material through a series of brief, erratic, and rhythmically turbulent episodes, continuing the movement's tone of nightmarish grotesquerie. An abbreviated recapitulation is followed by a coda that reduces the rhythmic energy without providing any resolution of the foregoing upheavals.

The second movement is built around a gentle melody, pastoral and almost improvisatory in character, which alternates with a more somber, soulful passage that ends in a cadential figure of strange, unearthly gravity. The movement culminates in an explosive, brooding climax highlighting the "*Philos* motif," before ending with the grave cadential figure.

The final movement is a full-length fugue, whose subject contains within it the symphony's two main motifs. By far the most conventional portion of the work, the movement pursues its course with a dark vigor, although during the development a ray of optimism intrudes, the first of the entire piece. After a triadic harmonization of the main motif in augmentation, followed by a *stretto*, the work comes to an assertive close.

There is no question but that the finale of the symphony—effective and pleasant as it may be within itself—is weakened by the gratuitousness of its emotional resolution and by the reuse of devices—for example, triadic harmonization of motif in augmentation, *stretto*—already employed to similar purpose in the Symphony no. 1, and detracts from the impact of the work as a whole.

Nevertheless, the *Symphony of the Winds* clearly represents an attempt to explore a more extreme expressive domain, and the first two movements are as remarkable for their unusual and disturbing psychoemotional states as for the clarity with which they are shaped and articulated formally.

Shortly after its completion, the *Symphony of the Winds* was recorded by a wind ensemble in Rome, but the release of this recording was delayed for many years. The work's first public performance did not take place until March 1979, when it was played in Ithaca, New York, by the Cornell University Wind Ensemble, conducted by Marice Stith. Stith managed a recording series that documented his group's performances, and Flagello's symphony was released in this series a few months after the premiere. The recording served to introduce the work to the band world, resulting in several subsequent presentations, but its unusual scoring and the availability of performance materials only by rental discouraged wider exposure. The Italian recording was finally released on compact disc in 1995. Paul Cook wrote, ''Flagello's sense of balance saves this work from the amateurism found in a lot of similar music written specifically for symphonic 'bands.' ''[49] Rob Barnett described the symphony as ''an importunate, angst-ridden and gloomy carousel charged with aggressive vitality and framing a central movement which does not travel hopefully.''[50]

Flagello completed his next composition early in 1971: a short *Ricercare* scored for the unlikely ensemble of nineteen brass plus percussion. The work is similar to its predecessor in its unusual and somewhat impractical scoring, in its rather cryptic choice of title, as well as in the impression it suggests of reaching for a deeper, more symbolic mode of expression, an enigmatic sort of ''hidden meaning.'' The term *ricercare* is ambiguous in itself, having held a multiplicity of meanings throughout musical history. Perhaps the most familiar is its usage during the early Baroque period to refer to instrumental compositions in a ''learned,'' contrapuntal style. However, Flagello himself indicated a more remote implication, pointing to the term's etymological connection to the word meaning ''to seek,'' explaining that this composition was about ''the foolishness of humanity, always seeking, but never finding, the answer.''[51]

The main motif of the *Ricercare* comprises a rising half step followed by a rising major-seventh. (This motif bears some resemblance to the ''*Philos* motif''—a relationship confirmed as the work unfolds.) Of secondary importance is a figure comprising an ominously repeated pair of minor-quality chords, strongly reminiscent of "Siegfried's Funeral Music" from Wagner's *Götterdämmerung*. The piece—a mere seven minutes in duration—falls into five short sections. A gravely portentous introduction presents and elaborates the two main motifs. This is followed by an animated section that provides a fuller, more conventionally articulated thematic statement, rather grim in character, based on the first motif, and eventually culminates in a plangent presentation of the *"Philos* motif." With a muted trumpet solo accompanied by suspended-cymbal offbeats, this passage almost suggests the dark, full-bodied sound of progressive jazz associated during the 1950s with Stan Kenton. A slow, subdued interlude follows, before the eruption of a stentorian *tutti* statement of an A minor triad, echoed softly by three horns playing an F minor triad. Another A minor eruption is echoed this time by an F-sharp minor triad in the horns; then a third time, by an E-flat minor echo. (Flagello referred to this section as "the voice of God."[52]) The section culminates in a shattering explosion of dissonance, as the trumpets blare out a climactic phrase built from the first motif, which finally resolves in hard-bitten iterations of the second motif. A rather banal *Allegro* leads to a full return of the animated thematic statement heard earlier. A coda of remarkable triteness brings this strange work to an end.

The initial performance of the *Ricercare* took place several weeks after its completion, by a brass choir at the Manhattan School of Music, under the composer's direction. The work is of particular interest because it reveals both the strangely enigmatic expressive concerns that preoccupied Flagello during the early 1970s and the beginning of what appears to be a loss of creative energy or concentration, as one short-breathed idea follows another almost arbitrarily. Although several fully realized works were still to come, the *Ricercare* seems to foreshadow the creative decline that was to occur.

Flagello completed one other work in 1971, a setting of *Remembrance*, by Emily Brontë, author of *Wuthering Heights*. The poem's theme—the premature death of a "Sweet Love of Youth" recollected with resigned acceptance years later—appealed to the composer, who shaped a touching setting for mezzo-soprano and string quartet (or string orchestra), with flute *obbligato*. The flute suggests an eerie night-wind evocative of a mood of Gothic romance. The chromatic melodic line only occasionally defines a tonal anchor, while the sparsely textured accompaniment is often surprisingly acrid in its dissonance. However, this context only highlights the poignant Straussian lushness of the music that sets the verse beginning, "No other Sun has lighted up my heaven; No other Star has ever shone for me." As a whole the setting demonstrates Flagello's mature mastery of the gradients of tonality and harmonic dissonance. A recording of the string-orchestra version of *Remembrance* made in 1979, with mezzo-soprano Maya Randolph, was not released until 1992.

Flagello completed nothing more than a few short songs in 1972. However, he began work on a one-movement piece for violin and orchestra, which he initially planned to title *Testament*. The violin-and-piano score was not finished until the end of the following year, by which time the title had been changed to *Credendum*, that is, a statement of belief, with a dedication to the memory of the composer's father, who had died earlier in the year. *Credendum* remained in this form, unperformed until 1985, when Semyon Bychkov programmed the work with the Buffalo Philharmonic. By this time Flagello's cognitive ability had begun to deteriorate, but he managed to complete the orchestration in time for the premiere in September.

The statement of belief indicated by the title refers to the underlying theme of nearly all Flagello's music: a belief—almost equated with religious faith—in music as a vehicle for profoundly felt emotions, asserted defiantly in a world both jaded and cynical toward such ideals. *Credendum* is based on three short motifs introduced by the violin during the impassioned soliloquy that opens the work and an additional motif that appears later on. The first is what has been identified here as the "*Philos* motif"; the second is a turning-note figure; the third, based on a falling major-seventh, resembles the main motif of the *Ricercare* in its treatment. The motif that appears later is built around a falling minor-third in a cretic metrical pattern—a "death motif" found also in Giannini's *Medead* and the primary thematic idea of the latter's similarly haunted Symphony no. 5. These motifs are developed by the violin through a rhapsodic succession of brief episodes evoking intensely contrasting emotional states, ranging from passages of mystery and contemplation to moments of jarring nervous agitation that erupt in tumultuous *tutti* explosions. Toward the work's conclusion these restless shifts of affect seem to resolve into a warmly heartfelt hymn whose lyricism is made all the more touching (as just described regarding a comparable passage in *Remembrance*) by its juxtaposition within a context of such turbulence. However, even this emotional oasis culminates in an anguished climax, followed by an epilogue of sad resignation. Within Flagello's output *Credendum* is most closely linked to the 1962 *Capriccio* for cello and orchestra, a work of similar scope, form, and character. However, while the later work contains many evocative and eloquent passages—most notably the hymn-like melody toward the end, which is one of the composer's most characteristic and personal lyrical effusions—the episodes, though linked motivically, fail to convey the sense of an inevitable and meaningful progression of psychoemotional insights found in the *Capriccio*. This episodic quality, already noted in the *Ricercare*, again suggests Flagello's gradual creative decline and eventual cognitive deterioration.

The premiere of *Credendum* took place in Buffalo, New York, in September 1985. Ansgarius Aylward was the soloist with the Buffalo Philharmonic. The response of the local critic was noncommittal. The work was not played again until 1995, when the celebrated violinist Elmar Oliveira, who had played under Flagello twenty-five years earlier as a student, agreed to record *Credendum* with the Slovak Philharmonic of Kosice, under the direction of David Amos. With Oliveira's committed advocacy, the work was received with considerable enthusiasm. On the syndicated radio program *First Hearing*, violinist Cho-Liang Lin, unaware of the identity of either soloist or composer, described *Credendum* as "a very beautiful piece, . . . so romantic and lush."[53] Mark Lehman found it "an elegiac and at times mysterious piece whose rhapsodic fervency achieves solace in a coda of transfiguring beauty and serenity."[54] Paul Snook called it "a deeply pondered personal statement of aesthetic values which eschews the ready melodic appeal of the earlier works by utilizing a more complex harmonic language to more ambiguous ends: but the hallmarks of expressive intensity and total emotional conviction and authenticity remain markedly and consistently Flagellan."[55] The work reminded Steven Schwartz of "Barber's Second Essay in the depths it stirs. . . . The violin sounds more like 'the voice in the desert . . . dry from weeping.' This piece strikes me as a great work indeed."[56]

With one or two notable exceptions, most of the music composed by Flagello after 1973 indicates a continuing decline in creative energy, lacking the concentration and focus of the works from the 1960s and early 1970s. During the next twelve years, he completed only four works of substance and scope, along with a few short pieces of little consequence. The tone and character of this music display the same bold assertions of metaphysical defiance and despair found in his earlier work. And, indeed, in their opening moments and other isolated passages, these pieces speak with undiminished eloquence. But in many cases their elaboration fails to fulfill the promise suggested by their opening measures, as they seem to strain vainly to generate musical content that will support their expressive aims. The result is often a predictable succession of short musical paragraphs that begin either boldly or dolefully, build promptly to shattering climaxes, and then subside, as the next passage is prepared. These works often culminate in radiant epiphanies achieved on a major triad in second inversion—a device that proved highly effective in earlier works (e.g., "Ben doverrieno" from the *Contemplazioni di Michelangelo)*, but eventually became a facile contrivance. Also found in the late works is a return to musical ideas that are more clearly tonal and melodic. However, the cryptic treatment of motifs noted in the music of the early 1970s continues to be found in these works.

After completing the short score of *Credendum* in 1973, Flagello composed nothing else during the 1970s, aside from a few songs and other trifles. However, Marice Stith's 1979 performance of the *Symphony of the Winds* led him to offer Flagello a commission in 1980 to compose a new work expressly for symphonic band, a medium that the composer had almost perversely avoided, despite the welcome exposure it had afforded to so many other American composers, Giannini notable among them. Now, with the promise of a performance and a recording, Flagello eagerly accepted the commission and began work on what was to be called *Odyssey*.

Finished early in 1981, *Odyssey* is an abstract symphonic fantasy of barely ten minutes duration. A slow, funereal introduction exposes the principal motif, a descending minor-second. This motif is further explored during the agitated section that follows, during which a subsidiary motif is introduced by the piccolo and English horn. The subsidiary idea, of Middle Eastern cast, also highlights the minor-second. After further elaboration of the subsidiary motif, a multisectional development follows. Beginning like a sinister march, this section is swept along by driving triplet figures whose momentum is interrupted several times by references to the brooding introduction. After further elaboration of the two motifs, the energy subsides, leading to a mournful melody introduced by the clarinet. This melody, which embraces both motifs, builds to a large, climactic statement, in which a suggestion of hope sweetens the prevailing tone of grief. However, the tone quickly becomes strident, casting a shadow over the work's final chords.

The first performance of *Odyssey* took place in Ithaca, New York, in March 1981. The composer conducted the Cornell University Wind Ensemble, and an LP was issued soon afterward, as part of the Cornell recording project. The work is a revealing example of the creative decline described above. Although the introductory section is as eloquent as any passage Flagello ever composed, the developmental section that follows seems repeatedly to pump up bursts of energy that become rapidly depleted, rather like air pumped into a leaky tire. The concluding melody begins poignantly, but the climax it achieves seems trite and hollow.

Between 1980 and 1983, Flagello was immersed in the composition of his final opera, *Beyond the Horizon*. But during this period he also produced a cycle of four songs to his own texts for mezzo-soprano Barbara Martin. Not surprisingly, these songs share a number of musical ideas in common with the opera-in-progress. He entitled the cycle *Quattro Amori*, as each song deals with an aspect of love: the first, "The Nazarene," concerns spiritual love; "At Night" deals with romantic love; "Pulcinella and Colombina" with sexual love; and "The Bowl and the Throne" with lost love. Again, except for the third, which, when performed with appropriate theatricality, is quite funny, each song opens with a lofty introduction, pregnant with portent, then begins to spin out a promising melodic line, which soon stumbles into a banal, overwrought climax. Covering the first performance of *Quattro Amori*, given by Barbara Martin at the Carnegie Recital Hall in April 1983, critic Tim Page described the songs as "sweaty."[57]

Certainly the major achievement of Flagello's last years was his operatic adaptation of Eugene O'Neill's early (1920) tragedy *Beyond the Horizon*. The play concerns a farmer's two sons: Rob, a dreamer and lover of poetry, who longs to discover the world "beyond the horizon," and Andrew, a practical man who loves working on the farm. Andrew has a girlfriend, Ruth. The play begins shortly before Rob is to leave on a voyage with his uncle, a sea captain. That evening Rob confides to Ruth that one of his reasons for leaving the farm is his love for her, a feeling he can contain no longer. At this Ruth admits that she has been suppressing her own love for him as well. Rob presents this revelation that evening at dinner, announcing that he has decided against going to sea. Hiding his own hurt, Andrew graciously offers to go in his place. This last-minute decision, in which each brother betrays his own destiny, proves to be the undoing of both. During the years that follow Rob proves hopelessly inept as a farmer and as a husband, and Ruth grows to hate him, while Andrew becomes involved in questionable business dealings and loses most of the money he has made. The play ends as Rob, dying of tuberculosis, crawls out of his room to watch the sun rise over the horizon one last time.

Flagello's artistic temperament, so strongly attracted to both emotional idealism and dramatic intensity—not to mention his own impulses toward self-destruction—revealed a marked affinity with that of the great Irish American dramatist, so adapting one of O'Neill's plays into an opera was natural if not inevitable. Although as a play *Beyond the Horizon* is weakened by an excessive number of hyperemotional outbursts and confrontations, and by the obvious contrivance of the brothers' temperamental polarization, these very factors enhanced its suitability for operatic treatment—especially by a composer like Flagello. His own debilitated mental and physical state made a commitment to such an ambitious task extremely difficult, but once under way the process of composition went smoothly and spontaneously. He prepared the libretto himself, drastically paring down the play's verbiage. Though far more fluent and mature, the musical language he adopted for the work bears a curious similarity to that used in *The Sisters*, composed some twenty-five years earlier. (Coincidentally and probably of no significance, the two works share a New England setting.)

Flagello completed the short score of *Beyond the Horizon* in April 1983. Unfortunately, it remained in this form at the time of his death; there is no orchestration, nor has the work ever been heard in any form. However, the project galvanized his creative energy to such an extent that the resulting score seems free of the defects that weakened others of his last works. The opera is organized and unified by motifs associated with the main characters and symbols of the play. Among the work's musical and dramatic highpoints are the aria in which Rob expresses to Andrew his longing to leave the farm, the duet in which Rob and Ruth confess their secret love for each other (both in Act I, Scene 1); a dramatic *passacaglia* (Act I, Scene 2) in which Andrew announces that he will go out to sea in Rob's place, to their father's consternation and rage, culminating in the father's banishment of Andrew from the farm forever; the explosive confrontation three years later (Act II, Scene 1) in which Ruth hurls at Rob the revelation that she still loves Andrew—a revelation interrupted by his arrival home; the opening of Act III, Scene 1, which holds perhaps the bleakest music Flagello ever composed; into this scene Flagello interpolated "Rejection," a song he had set in 1973 to his own text, which aptly conveys Ruth's mood and state of mind, now bitter beyond despair after the death of her child and the ruin of the farm, as Rob lies in his room near death; and, finally (Act III, Scene 2), Rob's death scene. *Beyond the Horizon* promises to be a compelling music drama awaiting only a suitable orchestration for theatrical viability.

Shortly after completing the short score of *Beyond the Horizon* in 1983, Flagello turned his attention to the orchestration of *Credendum*, as well as undertaking a commissioned work for saxophone quartet and orchestra. By this time his cognitive deterioration had reached the point where it interfered with his ability to execute the administrative and technical tasks required in carrying out these projects. Those friends and colleagues to whom he turned in desperation for assistance were impressed by his determination and by the concentration he was able to muster and apply in the face of such evident impairment.

Flagello worked on what was to be his final composition from May 1984 until June 1985. He decided to call it *Concerto Sinfonico*, to indicate his conception of a symphonic work with the saxophone quartet as a composite protagonist, rather than simply a virtuoso vehicle. The first movement, *Allegro non troppo*, begins with the same driving dotted-note rhythm that figures prominently in the Third Piano Concerto and the *Te Deum*. A dominant pedal, augmented by a gradual piling on of dissonances that seem to culminate in a hysterical shriek, launches the first theme in A minor, whose chief motif is a descending fourth, followed by an ascending minor-second. This three-note motif serves as the basis of the entire work. The second theme—a lonely, plaintive melody derived from the first theme—is introduced by the alto saxophone. After this theme reaches a climax, a furious development of the first theme follows, beginning with a *fugato* played over an irregular rhythmic *ostinato*. This is followed by an introspective reflection on both themes, which even admits a blossoming of faith and love, before leading with grim resolution to the driving recapitulation and coda, bringing the movement to a defiant conclusion.

The second movement, *Lento movendo*, is another one of Flagello's dark, mournful barcarolles, this one based on the material from the first movement, primarily as heard in the second theme. The barcarolle gradually reaches a climax, ushering in a turbulent central section that builds to a chilling explosion, of a kind Flagello came increasingly to identify as "the voice of God." The central section ends in sad resignation. The opening barcarolle returns briefly, then concludes with a reminder of the three-note motif from the first movement.

The third movement, *Allegro giusto*, opens with a variant of the three-note motif, played by the timpani, cellos, and basses. The character of the movement suggests a grim, sardonic *scherzo*, with newly fashioned themes derived from the first-movement material. The *scherzo* is followed by a grotesque "trio" section. Then the *scherzo* material is subjected to a thorough development, which eventually builds to another stark proclamation from "the voice of God," followed by a shattering cataclysm. After the tumult subsides, slow harp *arpeggios* accompany a hopeful return of the work's main motif. But the mood darkens, as the second theme answers solemnly over ominous tremolos and timpani strokes. All hope seems dashed, as the driving rhythm that opened the work now hammers it into defeat.

Although inferences about a composer's personal life drawn from the character of a musical work are unreliable, and although the tone of Flagello's music is often dark and tempestuous, it is difficult to experience the *Concerto Sinfonico* without hearing in its consistent tone of anguish, agitation, and dread a sense of what the composer experienced while confronting the physical and mental disintegration that his illness had already begun to wreak. On the other hand, it seems miraculous that a work composed under such circumstances might stand as a fully autonomous, thematically unified musical structure that requires no extrinsic knowledge or awareness in order to understand and appreciate. The premiere of the *Concerto Sinfonico* took place in Buffalo, New York, in November 1985. The Amherst Saxophone Quartet was accompanied by the Buffalo Philharmonic, conducted by Semyon Bychkov. As cited earlier, the work was received by the local press with considerable favor.

After the premiere, many errors, inconsistencies, and discrepanc-

ies were discovered in the score and parts, due to Flagello's deteriorated condition and the haste with which the materials were
prepared. A great deal of editorial work was necessary in order to
prepare an accurate, practical performing edition. An alternate version of the work was later arranged for symphonic band, and the
Concerto Sinfonico has since been performed a number of times in
both versions.

CONCLUSION

By the time Flagello died in 1994, his music had already begun to
win favorable attention, much of which has been cited here.
Although public performances have continued to be scarce, the
explosion of repertoire that has occurred since the advent of the
compact disc has resulted in a rich representation of Flagello's
music on recording. A compact disc devoted entirely to the piano
music appeared in 1991; another devoted largely to reissues of material originally released on LP appeared in 1992; a third all-Flagello
disc appeared in 1995; a fourth, featuring orchestral music not previously recorded, was issued in 1996; and another, devoted to chamber music, in 1997. An additional disc devoted to previously
unrecorded orchestral music was released in 2003. Other individual
works appeared on recording during this period as well. However,
awareness and recognition of Flagello's music is still in the earliest
stages. Although, as indicated, recordings of his music have been
enthusiastically received, those critics who have commented on
them have tended to be specialists in unfamiliar twentieth-century
repertoire; for the most part, generalist critics of the mainstream
media have yet to encounter this music. Reviews of individual
works have been cited throughout this chapter. Comments of a more
conclusive, summary nature are also worth noting for the common
themes that emerge.

> Flagello never forsook his ideals about late-Romantic style and strong
> sense of melody. Until his death two years ago, he continued to advo-
> cate those principles in vocal and instrumental works that only now
> are reaching a wider audience. . . . Flagello worked within the same
> tonal framework as some of his contemporaries like Samuel Barber.

They prevailed in their belief despite what was going on around them and . . . their aesthetic is finding a strong base of new adherents.[58]

What Flagello brings to his art is, first of all, an absolute conviction in the primacy of emotion: the music throbs with vitality. It can be exciting or turbulent, sweetly melancholy or tragic—but it is always openly and fiercely passionate. Flagello was also a fine craftsman, devoted to the principles of motive economy and classic balance, and his intense emotional expression is achieved with discipline and rigor. Moreover he could and did write old-fashioned tunes—surging, expansive melodic arches, sparkling or pounding dances, sinuous or restlessly winding melodies that lodge in the memory. The resulting music is vehement and powerful, free of the posing or irony that often deface so-called "new romanticism."[59]

Flagello used the tonal resources and rhetoric of 19th Century romanticism in his own very personal way. His music has less perfumed sensuousness and seems more direct, heartfelt—almost brusque—compared to the refinement and supple fluidity of, say, Barber. Its biting harmonic clashes and vehement rhythms that quickly accumulate torrential force have a brawny, masculine toughness. This is not to say that Flagello's music doesn't have sensual allure. There are harmonic riches and indeed gorgeous melodies aplenty in the music on this disc, but they are almost never offered hedonically—as ends in themselves, to be luxuriated in—but rather as the expression of the composer's troubled, passionate spirit.[60]

[Flagello's music typically displays] a volubly anxious or ecstatically effusive lyricism cresting an omnipresent undertow of violence. This may grab you by the lapels . . . or draw you in seductively with a subtlety suggestive of late Fauré, . . . but the argument is always dynamic, even at its most relaxed, volatile, and often turbulent. . . . In sum, for all that Flagello owes to late-Romantic models, there is an abundance and compression of utterance in these works that is reminiscent of Schoenberg or Pettersson at their most tortured and densely wrought, though spared the former's complications or the latter's grandiose sprawl by Flagello's deftly pointed mastery of form.[61]

Flagello was perhaps the most effective exponent of the American lyrical post-romantic ideal in the generation that followed Barber. His profound belief in the expressive power of music is manifest in every piece. . . . His finest works date from the '60s, when the style he espoused was at its most unfashionable. . . . One of America's most neglected modern romantics has at last (albeit posthumously) gained real time in the record catalog and his music is worth exploring.[62]

The works of Nicolas Flagello utilize a familiar language and embody the aesthetic ideals represented by much of the beloved music in the repertoire. Yet despite his adherence to a conventional language, he expressed himself in a voice unmistakably his own, created by his personal use of these materials, while revealing a consistent metaphysical vision that is reflected, in one way or another, throughout his work. Furthermore, the standards of craftsmanship that he brought to bear on his materials in realizing this vision, and the seriousness of his dedication, resulted in a consistency of quality that is rare—even among the acknowledged masters. These are all characteristics generally associated with "greatness." One can only hope that the western art-music tradition remains sufficiently viable and fluid to embrace new creative voices and allows them to take their natural places in its pantheon.

NOTES

1. William Flanagan, Review, *New York Herald Tribune* (27 November 1957).

2. Arthur Cohn, "The Music of Nicolas Flagello," *American Record Guide* (July 1965): 1054.

3. Enos Shupp Jr., Review, *New Records* (January 1966).

4. John Gruen, Review, *New York Herald Tribune* (23 February 1961).

5. Richard Freed, Review, *New York Times* (17 May 1965).

6. Allen Hughes, Review, *New York Times* (19 March 1966).

7. Winthrop Sargeant, Review, *New Yorker* (26 March 1966): 178.

8. Interview with Walter Simmons, 8 December 1971, broadcast on WKCR-FM (New York).

9. Walter Simmons, Review, *High Fidelity/Musical America* (November 1982): MA40.

10. Herman Trotter, Review, *Buffalo News* (2 November 1985).

11. Anonymous Obituary, *New York Times* (17 March 1994).

12. Bill Zakariasen, Review, *Westsider* (23–29 June 1994): 13.

13. Cohn, "Flagello," 1054–1055.

14. Paul A. Snook, Review, *Fanfare* (July–August 1996): 166–167.

15. Bret Johnson, Review, *Tempo* (January 1997): 59.

16. Cohn, "Flagello," 1054.

17. Herman Trotter, Review, *Buffalo News* (24 April 1983).

18. Mark Lehman, Review, *American Record Guide* (July–August 1995): 113.

19. Conversation with Walter Simmons, 26 July 1982.

20. Cohn, "Flagello," 1054.

21. Rob Barnett, "A Trio of CDs: The Music of Nicolas Flagello, the Unregarded American Romantic," *Classical Music on the Web* January 2001, http://www.musicweb.uk.net/classrev/2001/Jan01.

22. Mark Lehman, Review, *American Record Guide* (July–August 1996): 112.

23. Snook, Review, 1996.

24. Adrian Corleonis, "Want List 1999," *Fanfare* (November–December 1999): 165.

25. Dwight Pounds, Review, *Owensboro Messenger-Inquirer* (21 February 2000).

26. Cohn, "Flagello," 1054.

27. Adrian Corleonis, Review, *Fanfare* (September–October 1999): 218.

28. Steven Schwartz, Review, *Classical Net* 2001, http://www.classical.net/music/recs/reviews/p/phx00143b.html.

29. Mark Lehman, Review, *American Record Guide* (September–October 1997): 130.

30. Edwin Safford, Review, *Providence Sunday Journal* (27 July 1980).

31. Lehman, Review, 1997.

32. Shupp, Review, 1966.

33. Anonymous Review [Lima, Peru] *El Comercio* (15 July 1981).

34. Robert Cummings, Review, *Classical Net* 1998, http://www.classical.net/music/recs/reviews/p/phx00107a.html.

35. Michael Mark, Review, *Music Journal* (Summer 1971): 62.

36. Roger Hecht, Review, *American Record Guide* (July–August 2003): 95.

37. Arnold Rosner, Review, *Classical Net* 2003, http://www.classical.net/music/recs/reviews/n/nxs59148a.html.

38. William Zagorski, Review, *Fanfare* (September–October 2003): 121.

39. Adrian Corleonis, Review, *Fanfare* (September–October 2003): 120.

40. Johnson, Review, 1997: 64.

41. James Reel, "An Interview with James DePreist," *Fanfare* (November–December 1995): 113.

42. Paul Hume, Review, *Washington Post* (20 February 1974).

43. Marc Samson, Review [Quebec] *Le Soleil* (12 April 1979).

44. Tim Smith, Review [South Florida] *Sun-Sentinel* (15 January 1995).

45. Daniel Webster, Review, *Philadelphia Inquirer* (16 January 1997).

46. Andrew Achenbach, Review, *Gramophone* (April 1997): 54.

47. Francis Brancaleone, Review [Suburban New York] *Journal News* (January 2001).

48. Anthony Tommasini, Review, *New York Times* (16 March 1999).

49. Paul Cook, Review, *American Record Guide* (May–June 1996): 114.

50. Barnett, "A Trio of CDs," *Classical Music on the Web* January 2001, http://www.musicweb.uk.net/classrev/2001/Jan01.

51. Conversation with Walter Simmons (21 March 1975).

52. Conversation with Walter Simmons (21 March 1975).

53. *First Hearing*, produced by WQXR (New York), April 1996.

54. Lehman, Review, 1996.

55. Snook, Review, 1996.

56. Steven Schwartz, Review, *Classical Net* 1997, http://www.classical.net/music/recs/reviews/v/vmg07521a.html.

57. Tim Page, Review, *New York Times* (10 April 1983).

58. Anonymous Review, *Scranton* [PA] *Sunday Times* (28 April 1996).

59. Lehman, Review, 1996.

60. Lehman, Review, 1997.

61. Adrian Corleonis, Review, *Fanfare* (September–October 1997): 183.

62. Alexander J. Morin, ed., *Classical Music: The Listener's Companion* (San Francisco: Backbeat Books, 2002), 319–320.

SELECTED BIBLIOGRAPHY

Barnett, Rob. "A Trio of CDs: The Music of Nicolas Flagello, the Unregarded American Romantic." *Classical Music on the Web* January 2001, http://www.musicweb.uk.net/classrev/2001/Jan01.

Cohn, Arthur and Philip L. Miller. "The Music of Nicolas Flagello." *American Record Guide* (July 1965): 1054–1055.

Corleonis, Adrian. Review of Albany CD. *Fanfare* (September–October 1997): 183–84.

Corleonis, Adrian. Review of Naxos CD. *Fanfare* (September–October 2003): 120.

Johnson, Bret. Review of three CDs. *Tempo* (January 1997): 59, 64.

Lehman, Mark. Review of Artek CD. *American Record Guide* (July–August 1996): 112–113.

Lehman, Mark. Review of Albany CD. *American Record Guide* (September–October 1997): 129–130.

Morin, Alexander J., ed. *Classical Music: The Listener's Companion*. San Francisco: Backbeat Books, 2002, 319–320.

"Nicolas Flagello, 66, American Composer [obituary]." *New York Times* (17 March 1994).

"*Odyssey*: Birth of a New Work [sound filmstrip]." Pleasantville, N.Y.: Educational Audio Visual, 1982.

Rosner, Arnold. Review of Naxos CD. *Classical Net* 2003, http://www.classical.net/music/recs/reviews/n/nxs59148a.html.

Schwartz, Steven. Review of Artek, Albany CDs. *Classical Net* 1997, http://www.classical.net/music/recs/reviews/v/vmg07521a.html.
Tawa, Nicholas. *A Most Wondrous Babble.* Westport, Conn.: Greenwood Press, 192–193.
Zagorski, William. Review of Naxos CD. *Fanfare* (September–October 2003): 121

ESSENTIAL DISCOGRAPHY

Albany TROY-234: *Prelude, Ostinato, and Fugue;* Piano Sonata; Violin Sonata; Suite for Harp and String Trio; *Declamation; Nocturne* (Setsuko Nagata, violin; Peter Vinograde, piano); www.albanyrecords.com.
Artek AR-0002-2: *Overture Burlesca;* Piano Concerto No. 2 (Tatjana Rankovich, piano); Piano Concerto No. 3 (Rankovich); *A Goldoni Overture; Credendum* (Elmar Oliveira, violin); (Slovak Phil. Orch., Kosice, David Amos, cond.); www.artekrecordings.com.
Citadel CTD-88115: *The Land* (Ezio Flagello, bass-baritone); *Symphonic Waltzes* (Tatjana Rankovich, piano); *Serenata;* Symphony No. 2, "Symphony of the Winds" (I Musici di Firenze, Orchestra da Camera di Roma, Nicolas Flagello, cond.); www.home.earthlink.net/~citadel/index.htm.
Naxos 8.559148: *Theme, Variations, and Fugue; Sea Cliffs;* Symphony No. 1; *Piper of Hamelin*—Intermezzo (Slovak Radio Orch., Bratislava, David Amos, cond.); www.naxos.com.
Phoenix PHCD-125: *She Walks in Beauty* (JoAnn Grillo, soprano); *Capriccio* (George Koutzen, cello); *Contemplazioni di Michelangelo* (Nancy Tatum, soprano); *Lautrec*—Ballet Suite; *Remembrance* (Maya Randolph, soprano); (Orchestra Sinfonica di Roma, Nicolas Flagello, cond.); www.phoenixcd.com.
Premier PRCD-1014: *Etude; Two Waltzes; Three Episodes; Prelude, Ostinato, and Fugue; Divertimento* (w/Paul Price Perc. Ens.); Piano Sonata; *Electra* (w/ Paul Price Perc. Ens.); (Joshua Pierce, piano).

Index

About the Author

Walter Simmons is a musicologist and critic who has been intensely interested in 20th-century music since his early teens. Holding a master's degree in theory and musicology from the Manhattan School of Music, he has contributed to the *New Grove Dictionary of American Music, American National Biography*, and scores of other publications, including *Fanfare, American Record Guide,* and *Musical America*. In addition, he has been active as a radio host and producer, a program annotator, lecturer, and teacher, and as a producer of recordings and educational materials about music. He is a recipient of the ASCAP/Deems Taylor Award for music criticism and the National Educational Film Festival Award. Hundreds of his writings can be found on his Web site at http://www.walter-simmons.com.